D1453308

THE ASSAULT ON ASSIMILATION

The ASSAULT on ASSIMILATION

John Collier and the
Origins of Indian Policy Reform

Lawrence C. Kelly
Foreword by John Collier, Jr.

University of New Mexico Press   •   Albuquerque

© 1983 by University of New Mexico Press.
All rights reserved. Manufactured in the United States of America.
Library of Congress Catalog Card Number 83-1288.
International Standard Book Number 0-8263-0657-8.
First Edition

Design: Barbara Jellow

Library of Congress Cataloging in Publication Data

Kelly, Lawrence C.
  The assault on assimilation.

  Includes bibliographical references and index.
  1. Collier, John, 1884–1968.   2. Indians of North America—Gov-
ernment relations—1869–1934.   3. United States. Bureau of Indian
Affairs—Officials and employees—Biography.   I. Title.
E93.C7K44   1983   973.91′092′4 [B]   83-1288
ISBN 0-8263-0657-8

For Pecky
Friend, Companion, Lover, Wife
My Pearl of Great Value

Contents

Illustrations

Foreword
An Introduction to John Collier

Lawrence Kelly, as a scientific historian, has tracked and narrated an overwhelmingly detailed saga of my father's struggles to give Native Americans a legal and ceremonial future. This is a journal of civil rights strategy, documenting how a private citizen, with time and persistence, can bring change within our constitutional government. When my father began to lobby for the Native Americans, and for the Pueblo people of the Southwest in particular, Indian lands were dwindling under the allotment system and by forced sales and encroachments, ceremonial life was threatened, and Indian children were appallingly educated. At the terminus of my father's commissionership in 1945, tribalism was secure; cooperative Indian enterprise and ceremonialism had become legally constituted rights. In the years since then Indians have moved to direct their own education, and Red Power has become formidable. No single acts brought about these changes; rather it was the public current of Indian determinism and the result of thousands of strategies working together. Lawrence Kelly's analytic approach offers a historical account of this fermenting energy.

As a scholar Kelly has drawn heavily from the various files containing documentation on my father's activity. His book represents a volume of material on John Collier's enterprise that can be found in no other source. But there is also an emotional and personal content, not represented in the documents, that could only be seen through the eyes and memory of his family.

This introduction is my child's-eye view of John Collier as my father, enriched later by living beside him for much of the last fifteen years of his life. I have drawn this life portrait not as a scientist but as my father's youngest son.

What kind of man emerges from Kelly's vast and reliable accumulation of data? My father appears as a driving man of one purpose, using every stratagem to raise funds and influence important people. We see a brilliant charismatic man, relentlessly pursuing his humanistic goals. We see a man who will not accept defeat, and in the end usually turns the tables on his adversaries in the struggle for power.

Indeed, all these qualities were there, and more than have been described. Much of my father's activity took place at a crisis pace which required instant decision making. Characteristically, under stress and danger my father would become a man of calculated action. But this clarity of decision was about the welfare of others, not about himself. Kelly depicts an extroverted highly polarized personality, and this, I believe, was my father's outer and professional nature. But in the eyes of his wife, Lucy, and in the vision of his youngest son, an inner man was visible, wracked by the indecision of a creative struggle he never mastered. This is the discrepancy in Kelly's description—between the driving public leader, the outer man, and the man who raised a family of mice in his desk drawer at the Bureau of Indian Affairs.

Why did my father devote his life to the ethnic welfare of the American Indian? We, his intimate family, knew some of the motives. If he was devoted to the tribal Indian, he was as vehemently opposed to civilized modernity. I believe my father saw civilization in destruction through one historical default after another. He saw modernity as a disaster that was defeating man's perfectability. He saw the Indian as the last remnant of natural perfection, a model that must be preserved for human rejuvenation.

It is important to recognize that his admiration of the Indians, and other people close to nature, had been shared by American idealists before his day. The motivation that sent George Catlin forth to paint the last wild Indians was not unlike my father's zeal. In the nineteenth century, in Catlin's Philadelphia and elsewhere, American intellectuals such as Ralph Waldo Emerson, Henry David Thoreau, and Margaret Fuller were extolling an ideal philosophy of "primitivism," conceiving of "natural man" as untainted by the vices of civilization, while James Fenimore Cooper and Henry Wadsworth Longfellow were composing eulogies about wild Indians they had never seen. Catlin's mission was to bring back the evidence of the unspoiled natural Indian.

My father's background had something to do with his involving himself in minority ethnicity. He came from a prestigious and aristocratic southern family. I believe he saw himself as a renegade from his caste—a family of slave holders and leaders in the Confederacy, with a family decoration for driving the Cherokees out on the Trail of Tears. Yet my father expressed pride in his aristocratic background: "On our honeymoon in England we were riding lower class on a train to Scotland, dressed in our roughest clothes, when a country man leaned forward and exclaimed, 'Oh, you are a gentleman, aren't you!'" Was it class anxiety that drove him into settlement work with immigrants in New York City? Was it for social idealism or redemption that he befriended and brought north a black woman to companion and assist my mother? There were strong expressions that Alice was an equal member of our family, and Alice in turn adored my mother and "Big John." Alice was a Fundamentalist who worried about our souls. On one occasion to assuage her anxieties my mother told Alice that Big John would be talking in church that night. But Alice shook her head sadly and responded, "John is not going to talk about salvation but only about the woes of the world!"

But my father *did* try to redeem the world. In the spirit of James Agee's and Walker Evans's *Let Us Now Praise Famous Men*, he was continually praising great men unknown and "with no memorial." He eulogized the dignity of mountaineers in the Great Smokies, the wisdom of ancient black men, the statesmanlike bearing of Pueblo men like Pablo Abeyta of Isleta, Martin Vigil of Tesuque, and Antonio Mirabal of Taos.

Lawrence Kelly's image of my father as a dedicated political reformer does not show my father as he appeared in the wilderness. His intensity in wild ecology was equal to his intensity in national politics. But no stranger meeting him on the trail, dressed in his rustic mismatched garments, followed by his faithful dogs, would imagine that this character could be a skilled legal opponent in Washington. For in the wilderness in the 1920s this rustic man was a poet feeding his family on stale bread begged from the Fallen Leaf Lodge. His pack contained pre-Christian Celtic classics and the *Oxford Book of Verse*. His language in the field with us boys was about natural science, or tales of wonder and fright that matched the writings of Lord Dunsany, Edgar Allen Poe, Conan Doyle, and Joseph Conrad.

There were periods in the twenties when my family was bankrupt, camping in the Sonoma Mountains or on a wild beach in Southern California. In my child's-eye view, these were the richest memories I have of my family and my father. For my father this enforced poverty brought times of freedom and adventure, camping under a sea cliff where each week a friend left us five gallons of water and a sack of potatoes, living by ingenuity, wholly absorbed in winds and tides. These were the most fulfilled periods for my father also. Each night we peered into the magic of our driftwood fire as my father sucked on his pipe or began whistling, calling up a story, waiting for the magic that seemed to usher from the glowing coals, piracy still lingering in the Okefenoke Swamps of Georgia, mummies awakening in the British Museum. My father's inner self came forth and mastered in these wild encampments.

What the archives do not reveal is that this man I have described was the center of John Collier, that he carried with him through all his political career. This was the man who finally dominated my father in his final years of withdrawal.

A powerful influence on all my father's activities was his visual and conceptual view that only focused sharply on distant circumstances. It was as if he could not comprehend or involve himself with life directly before him. In Washington he would write my mother five times a day, but when home in California in brief periods he would often withdraw into himself, sucking on his corncob pipe, lost in time and space. This gave him an aloof role, as if he could not actually see circumstances at hand, which at times left his family separated from him. One example of his lack of awareness took place on a journey east. We stopped for lunch in a midwest tavern where the radio was blaring. My father got up on a chair and turned the radio off, saying, "I don't suppose any of you are listening to this racket." It was the World Series!

If this was a flaw in my father's relations with others, it was also a cause of default in carrying through his programming as Indian Commissioner. His long view created sound visionary and even revolutionary schemes for developing modern Indian self-determination. His design for reeducating Indians after years of negative white schooling was one of his most brilliant reforms—the elimination of off-reservation boarding schools in favor of reservation-wide day schools that would strengthen the community and tribal base of Indian societies. On the Navajo Reservation day schools were to be part of the soil conservation program to "save your soil and save your culture." Schools were to be bilingual, assisted by community aides. Texts were in both the tribal language and English, based on the cultural content of each tribe. Red sandstone schools were built largely with Indian labor all over the Navajo Reservation. But implementation failed at that time because my father's philoso-

phies were forty years in the future and in direct opposition
to the historical efforts of civil service white teachers who
were to carry out the program. Personnel directly in his
Washington office and staff in the field helped scuttle this
program, tragically, because my father could not, or would
not, communicate his ideals to individual agents and teachers. His rapid field trips to the reservation largely ignored
the people whose cooperation was essential to making the
community self-determined education a success. Even under the best of circumstances, the culture of the Bureau of
Indian Affairs would have been a very difficult thing to
change. Yet there was at least one functioning community
school, the one at Navajo Mountain, one of the most isolated spots on the reservation. The school was administered
by Lizbeth Eubanks, a Navajo-speaking white teacher who
genuinely integrated white education into Navajo culture.
Thirty years after the New Deal and the disaster of stock
reduction, a Navajo corporation, D.I.N.E., founded the
Rough Rock Demonstration School, which followed closely
the design and purpose of community-determined education
envisioned by my father.

My father first approached the Indians in the role of phi-
losopher and poet when he was in his thirties. His commu-
nications then appeared to me essentially the same as his
friendship with the mountaineers of the Great Smokies. He
met the Indians in the same place and time that D. H. Lawrence did, in Taos, New Mexico, in the early 1920s. Both
men found in the Indians a human perfection they had been
seeking: pure men (and for Lawrence also pure women) ma-
tured outside of our modern civilization. But my father
clashed with Lawrence over sensuality. When the first edition of *Lady Chatterley's Lover* was smuggled out of Italy
into my father's hands, he condemned the writing as trash. I
do not believe this rejection was of the explicit treatment of
sex; rather, the direct sensual intimacy may have threatened him, challenging his own emotional vacillation. Lawrence in turn had little patience with my father's political
concerns, as Kelly reveals.

My father came to Taos to write verse, but he quickly saw political and legal threats against Indian lands and the ceremonial freedom of these Pueblo Indians. In good faith he wrote Washington about the abuses he had observed. He received a curt letter back from the commissioner of Indian affairs advising him to mind his own business or face removal from Indian lands. This was the turning point of my father's life. He became a lobbyist for the American Indian.

Lawrence Kelly admirably tracks my father's career from this point forward to gain recognition and legal rights for the Native Americans. This began more than a decade of ceaseless activity in an office on Capitol Hill, years in which he developed into a political lawyer and activist who brilliantly drew senators to his side, wrote their speeches, and guided their strategies.

Financing a full-time lobbyist is costly, especially when the lobbyist's family must be supported too. My father was remarkably adroit in gathering donations, and he approached his own upper class with a demanding confidence. His most loyal patrons included a circle of wealthy Jewish lawyers and civic leaders in San Francisco and elsewhere. Jewish intellectuals were among the most responsive to the plight of Indian ethnicity. Was this empathy based on their own minority survival? I believe that as an ancient people with thousands of years of unbroken lineage, the Jewish people in turn responded to the ancient life and heritage of the Southwest Indians. Through the years of private lobbying our family was completely supported by this group, who also volunteered their legal skills in fighting the early legal battles.

In these years we lived in California on a wooded mountainside in a rustic three-story shingled house. In these years, when my father returned to my mother after long winters in Washington, it was usually to leave at once for camping in the High Sierras. My father, again the nature man in run-down office shoes and baggy pants, ragged sweater and slouched business hat. The lobbyist, at home at last in the wilderness, a skilled collaborator with nature and mountain! Or—the lobbyist at home with his family, pounding his office typewriter all night. At home with his family, while the phone rang and rang with telegrams, faraway voices wanting guidance. Summertime at home, meeting crises.

Then came the crises of political history. Roosevelt was elected president. "If you can't fight 'em, join 'em!" And Roosevelt appointed my father Indian Commissioner, the very power role he had fought through his years as a lobbyist. My father's closest supporters raged, "Don't take it! You're a propagandist, not a politician or administrator!"

Twelve years of political power, spending millions on the welfare of the Native Americans. I saw my father change. He emerged in razor-creased suits, but still lugged his bursting brief case, which held, along with legal papers, books with titles like *The Water of the Wondrous Isles* by William Morris and *Green Fire* by Fiona Macleod.

My father's success as a political administrator surprised his closest friends. Again there was the conflict of personality between a dreaming absent-minded rustic who appeared unable to meet the routine responsibilities of society and an actionist with precision processes and a legalist's logic, a man of daring and master of circumstance. The commissionership was a peak challenge my father could not draw back from. In Washington he was under constant attack for his collectivist activities with the immigrants of New York City and his close bond with many radicals, including John Reed. His documented background reveals his open alliance with revolutionary causes. It is my understanding that he fought his own legal battles with legalistic skills that made him invulnerable.

Behind his barricade of informality was his *noblesse oblige*, his formal "good breeding" which disarmed his opponents. He appeared so vulnerable that he threw his opponents off balance when he fought back, beating Washington lawyers at their own skills. His success was his conceptual genius, his precision in strategic decisions. In another dimension, success was also his gift for drawing brilliant people to him. His failure, as I have described, was his far-sighted perception. Those most loyal to him became blurred by proximity, so that too often he rewarded small achievements of his enemies and ignored the men and women crucial to the success of his programming. This blurred foreground allowed him to make some disastrous appointments and blinded him to the saboteurs in his own administration.

Can any man control his internal oppositional forces? We see my father achieving brilliantly in political battle and envisioning a modern future for the American Indians—a future vision he held for all tribal groups. Does such vision and achievement allow my father to return to his beloved dogs and Lucy, his wife, in Alexandria with fulfillment? As if only the dogs would comprehend, after taking these creature friends on a loud barking ride in the family car, he would retreat to his solitude and his own inner sense of failure. What plane of abstraction was my father seeking, all night writing verse that was destroyed each morning, leaving him physically drained, sometimes unable to drive in to his Department of the Interior office? Verse after verse, poetry of classical content, verse about the history of his classical mysticism, but rarely, or never, about his own passion. An isolated man who could reach the gods in their temples but never arrive at the simple fulfillment of self.

Yes, he did arrive at fulfillment when walking upward over Rocky Mountain earth. He reached his plateau of fulfillment without a line of verse. Why did my father return? What did my father fear he might find in himself? Or was it the demands of his aristocracy that he must descend into society's abyss, as it were, to slay the dragon? Would we have forgiven him, had he stayed in the mountain mists to win his own obscure perfection? Would he have forgiven himself if he had rejected his reforming social role?

My father's times claimed him as a great man. Red Power Indians honor him for establishing a legal base for Native American posterity. Anthropologists honor him for establishing a working premise for a future of native ethnicity. Generally he is admired for being a great humanitarian. But what if we must recognize that all these achievements are abstractions or the casualties of my father's inner battle that he never won? Are we praising him for his outer shape, as a great man, and ignoring the inner goals he struggled so artistically to achieve? History also acclaimed Albert Schweitzer for his humanitarianism in Africa. Schweitzer boldly wrote in *Out of My Life and Thought* that his promise was atonement for his guilt before God, which for fifty years in Lambaréné he proceeded to do—without the collaboration of any black friendship. Should we hold this against Schweitzer's medical achievement? Should we honor my father less because the figments of his zeal were symbolic images—humble black people, mountaineers, striving European immigrants, the American Indians and later the Micronesians? If this abstraction of achievement belittles his life work, so we must cast down the work of all great artists and the whole nonobjectivity of human salvation.

Thirty-five years after discovering the Indians my father returned to Taos. Washington, City College in New York, Knox College in Illinois—where else could he go but return to Taos? I, his youngest son, was living there with my wife, Mary, and three sons. The return was not for us, but maybe to complete a circle, to Taos where the struggle began.

The Indians knew he was coming, mysteriously, and the caciques planned his return, with a ceremonial program to give my father all the fulfillment his life of political struggle had made impossible for him to possess. Forty years in Indian memory or forty months, they knew in time he would return. But it soon was clear that my father had returned not to the Indians but into his own solitude. He settled in the farther environs of the valley, away from the Indian center. He would not see Indians or accept the love and honor they held for him. It appeared he was returning to his own unfulfillment, for despite a remarriage he returned unhappily. First he read the *New York Times*, dropped it, read the *Christian Science Monitor*, and discontinued this also—for despite its dedication to human welfare, its pages also reported a world in destruction in my father's eyes.

Outside deep blue storm clouds gathered in the mountains, lightning flashed in silver sheets of rain, but still my father would not come out from within and embrace the violence and beauty of nature that has never changed. The Indians, ten miles away under their sacred mountain, appeared not to exist. "Papa, they are still there! Tomorrow they dance the Red Deer Dance. You must go and see for yourself!" He went with us. We seated him on an adobe rooftop above the circle of ceremonial deer kneeling before the Deer Mothers. Singing dropped to a low hum as the Mothers blessed each dancer clothed in a fresh deerskin, and then the Koshare clowns rushed in and "killed" the deer with turkey-feather bows and straw arrows, saving the village from starvation.

My father was there. But his eyes were focused inward. Is this the ritual of dying, to draw within? Or was my father obsessed with what he saw as his creative failure, at the abyss?

My father lived on some fifteen years in Taos. During this time he wrote two books, *On the Gleaming Way* and his autobiographical memoirs, *From Every Zenith*. Most of the time I left him alone, respecting his withdrawal. Though our adobe houses were a hundred and fifty feet apart, we were simply not in his focus. When my two brothers and I were very young, my father would conjure up magical stories, but not once in his last years in Taos did he project himself to his grandsons.

A few Indians came to see him, including political activists from the Pueblo, and a few times he drove to the Indian village and called on his one remaining friend and collaborator from the 1920s, Antonio Mirabal.

What if he could have returned to the Pueblo and participated in the ceremonious fulfillments of the caciques? Death is rarely mentioned among these Indians; one day they are just no longer there! Would the caciques have also spirited my father away, into the folds of their sacred mountain?

My father had a White death in the Holy Cross Hospital

in Taos. My brother, Donald Collier, and his wife, Malcolm, flew out from Chicago and joined in a moment of silent prayer at a funeral parlor. My father's third wife, Grace, myself, the Reverend Romero of the Ranchos Presbyterian Church, and one Indian completed this last gathering. No Indians had been invited, but Eliseo Concha, son of John Concha, one of my father's earliest Indian friends, intuitively knew of my father's death and found his way to this farewell.

John Collier, Jr.
Professor of Anthropology and Education
San Francisco State University
January 1982

Preface

I met John Collier only once, in August 1960. I had just completed the research for my dissertation at the University of New Mexico when someone asked me if I had made an effort to talk with him. I confess that it had never occurred to me that someone about whom I had been reading in the files of National Archives might still be alive. After some inquiry, I was astonished to learn that Collier was living in Talpa, New Mexico, a few miles south of Taos, only a hundred miles distant. I wrote, told him that I was working on Navajos in the 1920s and early 1930s, and asked if he would be available to answer some questions. After a delay occasioned by his confinement in the Taos hospital, he replied and invited me to come.

I remember feeling some trepidation about quizzing "the great man" on his career, but Collier quickly put me at ease. He met me at the door of his small adobe home in an oversized, baggy sweater, which made him appear small and shrunken. After exchanging a few pleasantries, we went

through the house and out the back door where the Sangre
de Cristo Mountains dominated the landscape and Wheeler
Peak seemed only yards away. Waving his arm in the direction of the mountains and the Pueblo, he launched into a
sermon on the role of nature in Pueblo lifeways and on the
importance of returning Blue Lake to the Taos Indians.
Without knowing it, I had been introduced to John Collier,
mystic, and to the poetic rhetoric with which I would become familiar in later years.

I had come prepared to talk about concrete events, about
the formation of the All Pueblo Council in 1923, about Navajo stock reduction, the creation of the Navajo tribal council, and about his quarrels with Herbert J. Hagerman, a
special government agent to the Navajos and Pueblos in
the 1920s and 1930s. As we talked about these subjects, I
witnessed another Collier, the zealous defender of Indian
rights, the powerful propagandist, the noncompromiser
who viewed all his opponents as villains. The formation of
the All Pueblo Council had been strictly the work of the Indians, Collier told me; his only role had been to help publicize it and to assist the delegates in formulating the English
version of their resolutions. Navajo stock reduction, however drastic, was a necessary measure to ensure conservation of the Navajo rangeland and it had been approved by
representatives of the Navajo people. The Navajo tribal
council of the early 1920s was a "yes-man's council," created by Albert B. Fall and tightly controlled by the Interior
Department through the machinations of Herbert Hagerman. As for Hagerman, he was a "Santa Fe snob," allied
with the reactionary elements of that city who had consistently opposed Collier and his reforms throughout the
1920s. At the end of our conversation, I asked him if there
was anything he would do differently if he could relive the
past. The only thing he mentioned was his approval of the
Navajo tribal council's resolution banning the use of peyote
on the reservation. That, he said, had been a mistake and a
violation of the constitutional right to freedom of worship.

Reviewing the fading notes of twenty years ago, I am

struck not so much by what Collier said as by the impression of the man that I took away from the brief interview. I remember being puzzled at the time by the contrast between his mildness and his persuasiveness when he was describing Pueblo culture and values and the vehemence with which he denounced his enemies. Over the years I have ceased attempting to resolve the contrast between the two John Colliers I saw that day, and have simply come to accept them both. John Collier was a gifted and persuasive spokesman for the rights of American Indians and he was at his best when expounding their cause and demanding protection of their rights. He was also a ruthless and hyperbolic propagandist who consistently maligned the motives of his opponents and who left behind him a trail of broken friendships and bitter estrangements.

In 1950 Arthur M. Schlesinger was invited to deliver a series of lectures on the topic of *The American as Reformer.* The lectures were sponsored by a foundation endowed by one of Collier's earliest supporters, John Randolph Haynes. There is nothing to indicate that Schlesinger had ever heard of John Collier or that he knew of the relationship between Haynes and Collier, but in his description of the reformer he penned a characterization that I early found particularly suited to Collier: "The reformer is apt to be self-righteous, untidy in dress, truculent, humorless, with a single-track mind and an almost ostentatious liking for the hair shirt and martyrdom: he makes virtue repulsive. . . . The reformer, in other words, is a disturber of the peace. He trespasses on forbidden ground and commits assault and battery on human complacency." However distasteful and disagreeable Collier's methods were, I have come reluctantly to believe that in the climate of public opinion in his generation, they were necessary in order to obtain a hearing for the rights of American Indians.

It is perhaps necessary to say something about why John Collier deserves a two-volume biography, or at least to explain why it will take me two volumes to assess his career. One reason is that Collier actually had two careers, one among immigrant workers in New York and California, and another among American Indians; the goals, methods, and personalities of the latter are not fully comprehensible without a description of the former. A second is that this study is both a Collier biography and an analysis of American Indian policy between the years 1920 and 1945, either of which could have been a book in itself. A third is that in addition to describing the reform of federal Indian policy during the second quarter of this century, it has been constantly necessary to correct and to modify already existing interpretations, most of which have been grounded in Collier's perspective of the events of this period. I have attempted to keep this aspect of the book confined to the footnotes as much as possible in order not to tax the patience of readers who are interested only in the narrative. Last, in an attempt to re-create the atmosphere of the era and the passion of the conflicting arguments that divided the protagonists in the struggle for reform, I have deliberately sought to quote the participants extensively wherever possible. All of this has led to a manuscript that is oversized. Whether the final product is worthy of the effort or its subject, each reader will judge for himself; but I would like to express my thanks to the two editors, Elizabeth Gard Salimbeni and Elizabeth C. Hadas, who had faith in me and in John Collier, and thus made possible the publication of this study in a two-volume format.

This first volume takes Collier's career to the year 1928. It is concerned mainly with an examination of the development of his ideas about the nature of American society in the crucible of the urban immigrant ghettos of New York before 1920, and in his transfer of these ideas to the rural ghettos of the American Indians prior to the New Deal. Volume 2 will be concerned mainly with Collier's implementation of the Indian New Deal, its successes and its failures, or what I choose to call, The Dream and the Reality.

Acknowledgments

During the years in which I have been researching the career of John Collier, it has been my privilege to meet many persons who knew him or who knew of records relating to his career. At the risk of omitting some of those individuals and institutions, I would like to acknowledge my debt to the following:

Members of the Collier family: Mrs. Eleanor Collier Keenan and Mrs. Louise Collier Stanton Whiteley, Collier's younger sisters, who made available the family manuscript written by their sister, Julia Collier Harris; Mrs. Charles A. Collier, Collier's sister-in-law; Charles, Donald, and John Collier, Jr., sons of John Collier, all of whom granted me interviews; and Mrs. Grace Collier, widow of John Collier.

Libraries and librarians: Isabel Erlich of the Atlantic Public Library, who supplied material on the career of Collier's father, Charles A. Collier, and Joyce Schober of the San Francisco State University Library, who provided me with material on Collier's teaching career at that institution.

xxvii

Individuals associated with Collier or his associates: Mrs. Grace King, who supplied me with a family manuscript describing the early career of Stella Atwood; Winifred Pomeroy, Collier's personal secretary from 1926 to 1943, who granted me several interviews and later gave me her personal papers relating to Collier; the late Pearl Chase, who opened her extensive files to me before donating them to the University of California at Santa Barbara; the late Charles de Young Elkus, Jr., who made his father's papers available to me; the late John W. Young, who corresponded with me about his association with Collier; and Bonnie Evans and Harrison Smith, grandchildren of Mabel Dodge Luhan, who gave permission to quote from Mabel Dodge Luhan's published works.

My greatest debt is to the institutions that house the papers upon which this volume is based, and to the members of their staffs who guided me through those papers and granted permission to quote liberally from them: Robert V. Kvasnicka, Jane F. Smith, and Renée Jaussaud of the Legislative and Natural Resources Division, National Archives; Donald Gallup and David E. Schoonover, curators of the Collection of American Literature, Beinecke Rare Book and Manuscript Library, Yale University; Judith A. Schiff and the late Herman Kahn, Manuscripts Division, Yale University Library; William D. Eppes and other members of the staff of the Cooper Union Library; members of the staff of the Manuscripts and Archives Division of the New York Public Library; Christian F. Brun and Diane E. Nassir of the Department of Special Collections, University of California at Santa Barbara Library; members of the staff of the Ohio Historical Society, Inc.; members of the staff of the Historical Society of Pennsylvania; Mrs. Virginia Rust of the Huntington Library; the Department of Industrial Relations, State of California; members of the staff of the Special Collections Division, University of New Mexico Library; Dorothy Wells, librarian of the Government and Public Affairs Reading Room, and Anne Caiger, Historical Manuscripts librarian, both of the University Library, University of California at Los Angeles; and members of the staff of the Bancroft Library, University of California, Berkeley.

Research support for this book was provided by the Indiana University Foundation and the Faculty Research Committee of North Texas State University. I am particularly indebted to the American Philosophical Society for support early in my research and to the National Endowment for the Humanities for a fellowship during which much of the writing took place.

So many different persons have worked on the various drafts of this book that it is impractical to acknowledge them all by name. I do wish, however, to thank Mrs. Eloise Green, the departmental secretary, who patiently presided over the typing and retyping process. My daughter Sheila Ann Kelly prepared the index, thereby contributing to the increased longevity of her father.

Part I

Formative
Years

1

Childhood and Adolescence (1884–1906)

John Collier was born in Atlanta, Georgia, on May 4, 1884. His paternal grandfather, one of Atlanta's earliest residents, was also born on May 4 and it was after him that young John was named. In later years, Collier's eldest sister, Julia Collier Harris, could recall that "he was a very handsome child and grew to look like a miniature edition of his grandfather."

The family into which Collier was born was both wealthy and socially prominent. His mother, Susie Rawson, was the only child of a Vermont immigrant who walked to southern Georgia in 1832, took up farming, and by the time of the Civil War had become the owner of more than a hundred slaves. In a day when few women attended college, Susie Rawson enrolled in the Wesleyan College for Women at Macon, Georgia; following her graduation she toured England and the continent. After the Civil War, his livelihood destroyed, her father moved to Atlanta, where he built the large two-story brick home in which all his grandchildren were reared and then invested his remaining capital in downtown Atlanta real estate. The income from his estate, "a handsome one" initially, was to support his daughter and her family during the years when Collier's father was deeply involved in civic affairs.

Collier's father, Charles A. Collier, was the son of a prominent Georgia jurist who moved from Milledgeville, then the state capital, to Atlanta in the 1850s, at a time when the city was beginning to boom as a major railway center. He attended the University of Georgia, graduating in 1869, then studied law with his father, and was admitted to the bar in 1871. The law, however, failed to hold his interest, and he soon turned to banking and commerce. By 1890 he had risen to the post of vice-president and head of the Capitol City Bank in Atlanta, and he also served as a director of the Bank of Georgia and as president of the Gate City Gas Light Company and the Refrigerating Construction Company. As his business stature grew, his involvement in civic affairs and local politics also increased.

Collier's parents were married in 1875 when his mother was twenty-two and his father twenty-seven. Their marriage "must have appeared most favorable," he wrote in later years, for his mother was a beautiful woman, and his father was charming, gifted, and well on his way toward a position of prominence in Atlanta business circles.

Collier was the middle child in a family of seven children, three boys and four girls. His oldest sister, Julia, married Julian Harris, the son of Joel Chandler Harris, and she later published a biography of her famous father-in-law. His older brother, Rawson, whom Collier idolized as a child, "was extremely pugnacious," and was finally sent away to a military academy. Of another older sister, Henrietta, Collier wrote that he could remember very little "except that she was a lovely girl, kind and deeply human." A younger brother, Charles, and two younger sisters, Eleanor and Louise, from whom he was separated soon after his father's death in 1900, were better known to him later in life than in childhood.

Collier remembered his childhood as an essentially happy

one until his thirteenth year, when his mother died at the age of forty-four. "I grew up in a family with strong feelings but with a tradition of undemonstrativeness," he wrote, "and with a constant atmosphere of 'public work.'" The family was "of vigorous Methodist tradition," but the children attended private Catholic schools and Collier himself became a brief convert to Catholicism following his mother's death. When he was still a baby, a severe case of pneumonia raised doubts about his survival. At four he was bedridden for almost a year after a fall from a bannister in the family home in which his left arm was severely fractured. The arm was not properly set by the family physician; when complications developed, it had to be rebroken and set a second time. Years later, when the anxiety of this ordeal was only a memory, Julia Collier Harris could laughingly recall that the attention young John received during his illness aroused mild jealousy in his brothers and sisters. "John became so spoiled," she wrote, "that he had to be paid anywhere from a nickle [*sic*] to a quarter to blow his nose." Although the arm healed, it remained "permanently shortened and fragile." Aside from these childhood illnesses, Collier's health was generally excellent the remainder of his life, though his slight, short frame almost inevitably evoked the adjective "fragile" in descriptions by contemporaries.

His mother's death in 1897 ended the happy days of childhood. In his memoirs, Collier wrote that he sensed as early as 1893 that his mother, "the person I was nearest to, was undergoing some devastating experience." What that experience was he declined to say, hinting only that it had tragic overtones that eventually led to her death. In all probability, Susie Collier suffered a nervous breakdown. In reporting her illness, the *Atlanta Constitution* noted that she had been "in delicate health" for several months before a trip to New York where she was treated for "nervous prostration." After a tooth extraction in mid-March, she became "critically ill with a high fever," and was "completely prostrated." She was then removed to a hospital where, after a week of futile effort on the part of several physicians, she died on March 24. Julia Harris, in her history of the family, wrote that her mother's health declined as the result of several factors. "Repeated child-bearing, heavy social obligations, the invasion of her privacy and the realization that her father's estate, built up through the years with so much care and such ardent hopes, was in grave danger because of my father's complete absorption in other matters—all this made deep inroads on my mother's health and happiness."

Following his mother's death, Collier and his younger brother Charles were sent to a Roman Catholic convent in rural Sharon, Georgia; his younger sisters went to live with Julia Harris. For Charles the experience was a "misery," but for John it was "a time of precious quietude," and, as indicated earlier, he became a brief convert to Catholicism. His passage out of Catholicism came two years later at fifteen, when he experienced a conflict between Catholic theology and the theory of organic evolution. This discovery of evolution was the single most important intellectual experience in his early life. Although it was several years before he would seek to deepen his understanding of the theory and its method formally, his commitment to its general concepts was immediate and absolute. It freed him, he later wrote, "from the absolutist God of any creed, and philosophy," and it launched him on a search for his own role in the "on-going work of creation."[1]

Collier's father, whose absorption in civic affairs had been a contributing factor in his mother's fatal decline, was one of Atlanta's leading citizens by the early 1890s. His son remembered him as a man of "strong personal magnetism," a man of "terrific will and a great pride . . . completely a man of the world." A close friend of both Henry Grady and Hoke Smith, two of Georgia's leading spokesmen, Collier spearheaded important efforts to invigorate and publicize the concept of the "New South," and as the mayor of one of the region's largest cities, he became an ardent champion of gas and water socialism and public ownership of the city's transit system.

In 1887, the same year as his election to the office of alderman, Charles Collier was named president of the Piedmont Exposition, to be held in Atlanta in the fall. The old city fairgrounds had been sold some time before and the work had to begin with the clearing of a new site in a heavily wooded area on the city's outskirts. In the short space of one hundred days, Collier supervised the erection of pavilions and exhibition buildings. To the amazement of everyone, the exposition opened on time. Grover Cleveland, the first Democratic president since 1860, and his new bride were the guests of honor. When they arrived in Atlanta on October 18, they were escorted by Collier and Henry Grady from the railroad depot to the exposition grounds where, despite a pouring rain, they were greeted by the largest crowd ever assembled in the city. In his speech opening the exposition, Collier stressed the role of the fair in bringing together "the people of a once divided city" in a common task of advancing Atlanta as the commercial gateway to the South.

The results of the Piedmont Exposition were more than satisfactory. Two hundred thousand visitors clogged the city, bringing "a rich harvest . . . in money receipts," and in their wake came a steady stream of new inhabitants from other parts of the nation. Collier's success in organizing the exposition was rewarded by increasingly responsible positions in city and local government. In 1888 he was reelected alderman; in 1889 he served as mayor pro tem and was named chairman of the county Democratic executive committee. In the early 1890s he shifted his interests to county government, winning election to the board of county commissioners; and in 1894, on the eve of his most important civic contribution, he became chairman of the board of county commissioners.

When the Chicago World Fair was held in 1893, the South was unrepresented. William Hemphill, the business manager of the *Atlanta Constitution* and a former mayor, concluded in 1895 that a great opportunity to publicize the "New South" had been lost at Chicago. Together with other progressive businessmen, he began to formulate plans for a gigantic exposition in Atlanta that would emphasize the re-

sources and opportunities available in the South. As enthusiasm grew, the exposition took on an international flavor.
By inviting exhibits from Central and South America, Cuba,
and Mexico, the promoters hoped to stimulate trade between
those regions and the South, with headquarters in Atlanta.
For the job of organizing what finally became known as the
Cotton States and International Exposition of 1895, they
turned to Charles Collier.

Under Collier's supervision and with the financial support
of the business community, the city, and the county, the Cotton States and International Exposition became the symbol
of a resurgent South. More than two million dollars was invested in 6,000 exhibits, which sprawled over a hundred-
and-ninety-acre tract. During the days of the exposition, an
estimated 800,000 persons flocked to Atlanta, then a still
relatively small metropolis of 75,000. Victor Herbert and
John Philip Sousa were commissioned to provide the music
for the opening, and Booker T. Washington delivered his
famous "Atlanta Compromise" at the dedication ceremonies. Special buildings devoted to the progress of the Negro
since the Civil War and to the accomplishments of American women (the buildings were designed by a Negro and a
woman architect) punctuated the theme of southern progress to which the fair was dedicated. When the exposition
closed its gates in January 1896, national and international
publicity had brought Atlanta fame and prosperity. According to one local historian, the city had been pulled from the
depression of the past three years and had been transformed
from "a provincial capital to a lusty young metropolis."

The year following this triumph, Charles Collier was
elected mayor of Atlanta. During his two-year term, from
1897 to 1899, he became identified with issues and causes
that were soon to be labeled "progressive." During his first
year in office he secured a reduction of the city property tax
through efficiencies that he ordered in city government.
When he left office on the first day of the new century, he
could proudly point to the fact that Atlanta's standing in the
bond market was "unequalled by any other city in the

South," and he could also claim that for the first time in the city's history, an outgoing administration was passing on a comfortable cash surplus instead of a deficit to its successor.

After noting in his first annual report the "enormous costs" of services provided by the Georgia Electric Light Company, Collier launched a drive for a municipally owned electric generating plant. He also called for expansion of the existing municipal water department. The voters approved city-owned electricity, but in a separate referendum defeated the expansion of the water department. Collier blamed the defeat on "the idiotic requirements" of the state constitution (a majority of the citizens who voted in the special referendum approved the expansion, but the turnout was light and a majority of the eligible voters, required by the constitution, was not attained), and on the machinations of "the officers and agents of an unscrupulous corporation" that wished to further its "grasp on the public patronage."

In his farewell speech to the city council in 1900, Collier denounced the street railway franchise, which had placed the city's transportation in the hands of the Atlanta Consolidated Street Railway Company. Its services, he charged, were "unsatisfactory," and he accused it of having "attempted to throttle competition," and having "insolently trampled upon the rights of the people." He urged his successor to bring the traction system under city ownership. Like his father, John Collier would be a vigorous champion of municipal ownership of basic utilities. The strong rhetoric that characterized his father's public statements would also be a characteristic of his speech.

On one issue Mayor Collier admitted that his administration had failed. This was the matter of adequate schools for the city's Negro population. Like all the southern states, Georgia began to construct a public school system only after the Civil War; the process was both slow and costly. There had been improvements in the city's white schools, the mayor noted, but he termed the existing Negro schools "utterly inadequate." More than 700 Negro children were not attending school, he announced, because no schools existed for them. The others were attending classes whose size had doubled in the past few years; dual sessions were the rule in all Negro schools. The mayor's comments on the situation appear muted alongside denunciation of the private utility corporations, but such a stance was not unusual in the ˚South in 1900. Even to have voiced the criticism in his annual report required some degree of courage in a state where Tom Watson's Negro-baiting tactics were soon to make him the dominant political power. Like his father, John Collier would always be sympathetic to the plight of the Negro, but his southern upbringing apparently never permitted him to view the Negro minority in the same way that he would the immigrant masses of the North or the American Indian.[2]

In 1900 former Mayor Collier was appointed United States representative to the Paris Exposition Commission, which was charged with preparation for another World's Fair to be held in that city in 1901. He spent much of his time abroad. One day in late September 1900, he returned home and, after spending a long evening with his children, he retired to his room at the rear of the house. In the early morning hours of September 27, residents of the neighborhood were awakened by the sound of a shot. Rawson and John Collier, who had been asleep upstairs, hurried to the rear of the house, where they found their father mortally wounded by a pistol shot in his left side.

The newspapers reported that Charles Collier had accidentally wounded himself when he fell from the porch while trying to frighten away a burglar. Charles Collier himself gave the story of the burglar before he died. At the coroner's inquest, a neighbor testified that she had heard voices, "as of a conversation or of someone trying to drive a dog away," before the shot, and another witness said that she heard the wounded man cry out "I have killed myself." The coroner ruled death from accidental causes.

John Collier, however, never accepted the verdict of accidental death. It was his belief that his father had taken his own life, and this tragedy, coming so closely upon his mother's death only two and a half years earlier, filled him with a despondency that lasted for many months. It was as if, he wrote, "the doom of the house of Usher had descended on the family." Standing beside the graves of his parents in October 1900, he resolved in the slightly esoteric, partly poetic phrasing that marked all his writings, "to live in behalf of the world's hope. I saw my life, short or long, as one among the countless billions wherein the striving of the cosmic purpose moves, in joy that contains regret and pain, toward ends which are multitudinous, yet are one, on the road which is the goal."[3]

In his memoir, Collier later described the two years between his father's death and his departure for Columbia University in 1902 as though they were one. He remembered finishing high school, where he "learned nothing, practically," and he recalled that he spent the summers tramping through the southern Appalachian Mountains, the only place where he found solace for his grief. But of external events there was little to recall. It was the internal change that he remembered most vividly, particularly the growing sense of what he later called "cosmic consciousness," the sense of being a part of a great plan for the betterment of mankind. On one of his camping trips, he had a vision of a bird that issued this summons to him: "Onward, into the struggles not lost and not won, and the immortal effort toward creation in which I, the bird, need you." In later years he would learn to describe this vague sense of purpose that was developing within him in the words of Friedrich Nietzsche, but at the time the influences were primarily Wordsworth, Whitman, and the forces of nature.

In 1902 Collier left Atlanta for New York City to enroll at Columbia University. Joel Chandler Harris secured an introduction to drama critic and well-known professor of dramatic literature Brander James Matthews, who sponsored Collier's enrollment in graduate, noncredit courses in literature and showered him with free passes to the theater. For a year Collier immersed himself in the study of literature and drama, both of which became lifelong interests, and then he abruptly shifted his interest to biology. The decision was not his own, but rather that of a magnetic woman whose acquaintance he had made earlier in Atlanta, Lucy Graham Crozier.

Lucy Crozier was small, dark, and crippled since childhood by a hip disease. A native of Knoxville, she made her living in New York, tutoring "particularly to the very rich." Her influence on Collier's intellectual formation was enormous, for it was she who introduced him to Nietzsche, to Lester Ward, and to the symbolist movement in literature. Collier acknowledged his debt to her, "the individual who was to have a deciding influence on my whole later life," when he dedicated his *Indians of the Americas* to her in 1947.

Philosophy, literature, and sociology were the focus of Miss Crozier's interest. All the authors to whom she introduced Collier had two things in common: an emphasis on man's ability to grow, to will, and to shape his future; and a conviction that emotion and intuition were more important than intellect in attaining the goals to be sought. Confident that her own tutelage in literature was superior to the university's, she steered Collier into biology so that he could master the methodology of the natural sciences through laboratory training. "By chance," he was to study under Edmund Beecher Wilson, an eminent zoologist whose studies of the role of the cell in human development and heredity were later to earn him international recognition.

Collier did not find the laboratory work easy. It was a year that he remembered as one long "torment" before everything at last fell into place. This sudden insight into the scientific method occurred during the summer of 1904 when he was working on a special project at the Woods Hole Marine Laboratory in Maine. At the end of the summer he was offered an assistantship at the University of Chicago, but again Miss Crozier intervened. The purpose of his study, mastery of the scientific method, had been attained, she explained; it was now time for him to begin work in a new field, "public enterprise."

The scheme Miss Crozier proposed for Collier's entry into the field of public affairs was nothing less than the transformation of the South through a "cross-fertilization of biological stocks." Unemployed immigrants from the North would be transported to the mountain areas of the Carolinas, Georgia, and Alabama, where they would be dispersed among the native inhabitants. In time, the injection of this new blood and these different cultures would bring about a modification of the "character of the old-new South" and revitalize the entire region. Collier's job was to sell the idea to the heads of southern railroads, who would provide the transportation, and to obtain the goodwill of local chambers of commerce, who would find farms or jobs for the immigrants. His valuable family contacts, Miss Crozier argued, would open the door to acceptance of the project.

Collier first took the idea to Washington, to Lester Frank Ward, for his approval. He recalled walking down the dimly lighted halls of the Smithsonian Institution until he came to a door with a sign that read: "If you want to see me, drop 10¢ in the slot." When he did, the door swung open and Ward received him. Apparently without commenting upon the practicality of the plan, Ward gave his "unconditional endorsement" to the scheme. Collier then proceeded southward.

For six months he attempted to peddle the plan to any businessman who would listen, but at last Lucy Crozier agreed that the project was a failure and it was abandoned. The lesson he learned was that he "was naive, wild, and ignorant and had better grow up and then begin again."[4]

Instead of returning north, Collier next accepted an invitation to become the executive director of the newly organized Associated Charities of Atlanta. Coming from a young man of only twenty-one, his proposal for a new approach to charity work was impressive. It was that no cash or goods handouts be made; instead, the organization would be dedicated to making work opportunities available. "Obviously the achievement of that idea . . . , even today, would be all but impossible," he wrote later of this experience. It took the directors only four months to arrive at the same conclusion. They dismissed Collier in a raucous session of the board and turned to more conventional methods of dispensing charity. As for Collier, his reaction to this second failure in the field of public service was to retreat from public life. As he had done following his father's death, and as he would do on several later occasions when failure seemed to overwhelm his efforts, he packed a few necessary items and headed for the mountains of northern Georgia and western North Carolina. This time his wanderings lasted for almost six months.

In November 1905, Collier ended his retreat and took a job as a reporter with the *Macon Telegraph*. During the six months he pursued this journalistic career, he rose to acting city editor as alcohol took its toll among the other members of the staff. Then, in June 1906, because "the experience was complete," and because he had concluded that his formal education was not yet finished, he abruptly resigned and set sail for Europe. His intention was to study abnormal psychology at the College de France in Paris.

Nowhere in Collier's writings is there an explanation for his choice of abnormal psychology. Pierre M. F. Janet, the man under whom he elected to study, was a pioneer in the psychology of the unconscious, though his contributions were largely overshadowed in this country by the better known works of Sigmund Freud. It may have been that he was seeking insight into the premature and tragic deaths of his parents or the recent instances of insanity he had observed in the aunt and uncle with whom he lived during his camping and hiking expeditions in the mountains.

Collier's European trip, as well as the years of study in New York, were made possible by a small inheritance from his parents. An income from his mother's depleted estate made possible the two years of study in New York and paid his expenses during the year of his exploratory venture into the field of public service. This income, together with an insurance policy left by his father, financed the year and a half in Europe. This income from these sources was not large, but together with frugal habits, which during one period included a strict vegetarian diet, it freed him from "a feeling of parsimony or of anxiety."

The study of abnormal psychology was initially sidetracked for a period of six months as a result of a chance meeting with Lucy Wood, a junior at Smith College, whom he met on the voyage to Europe. Lucy, her two sisters, and a friend, all from Philadelphia, were bound for Paris for the summer. Collier intended first to go to Germany to visit a friend and fellow disciple of Lucy Crozier, Natalie Braine. Instead, after learning that Natalie had just broken off a "hopeless and genuinely tragical" affair with an "older, married man," Collier took her to Paris where they joined the Wood sisters for a tour of Brittany. When Lucy returned to America in the late summer, Collier and Natalie Braine continued their travels in England and Wales, where they visited the mother of yet another of Miss Crozier's students, Herman de Fremery. In the fall, Natalie resumed her education in Paris, but Collier, smitten by Lucy Wood, took passage back to America on an immigrant ship and then traveled to Northhampton, Massachusetts, where he conducted what must have been one of the strangest courtships Smith College had ever seen.

Joined by his friend, Herman de Fremery, Collier invited Lucy and a friend for a camping trip in the nearby woods. Admitting that his "naivete" must have "appeared incredible to the College president," who summoned Collier to his office upon their return, he at first attempted to explain that there had been nothing wrong in his conduct, and then, as if realizing for the first time the true nature of his feelings, he proposed to Lucy. She accepted and the two went immediately to Philadelphia to secure her parents' approval. Colonel and Mrs. Wood, for whom Collier formed a "profound attachment," accepted him into the family "unreservedly." They gave their approval to the marriage and to the return to Europe for the delayed year of study. In a gesture stemming either from his southern sense of chivalry or perhaps from the manners of the heroes in the romantic lit-

erature in which he had been immersed for years, Collier
made out a legal transfer of his share in the family estate to
his new wife and the couple was married in Philadelphia on
October 22, 1906. Immediately thereafter, they returned to
Europe for what Collier later recalled was an "indescribably
wonderful" year of study and further travel.[5]

In 1943 Collier divorced Lucy Wood, but whatever their
later differences, she served as his emotional anchor
throughout the early years of his stormy public career and
she was the only one of his three wives whom he mentioned
in his autobiography. According to a close family friend,
Hutchins Hapgood, Lucy Collier was "John's exact opposite." Whereas Collier was primarily interested in things
"abstract and impersonal," Lucy's interests were "exclusively in the human and in the sensuous values of life."
Three children were born to the marriage: Charles in 1909,
Donald in 1911, and John, Jr., in 1913. "Her warmth and
physical nature, physical in the largely temperamental and
human ways," Hapgood wrote, "gave his roving spirit a tangible home."[6]

Upon his return to Europe, Collier at last plunged into his
work in psychology at the College de France. But, as had
been true throughout his largely informal academic career,
the most important influences he experienced again came
from outside the classroom. Although he attended Janet's
lectures and was stimulated by what he learned, "the most
important discovery" he made that year came during a tour
of northern Europe and England, which the Colliers made
in the company of James Ford, a Harvard professor of social ethics whom they met in Ireland. Under Ford's direction, Collier was introduced to the labor, cooperative, and
syndicalist movements, which were just beginning to stir
throughout Europe, and he began to read the works of Robert Owen, Sidney and Beatrice Webb, and other utopian socialists. The examples of economic cooperation he observed
had such a profound effect upon him that upon his return to
America he resolved to introduce them among the urban
masses of New York City.

Some time during the summer of 1907, the Colliers returned to the United States. They landed at Boston, which Collier found in contrast to New York, "overgrown, unplanned, and inhuman." Before setting out on a new career, he took his bride to the Great Smoky Mountains for three months of camping. When the winter came on, they returned to New York, took an apartment in one of the city's "model tenements," and supported themselves by freelance writing until Collier found permanent employment in the field of community organization. The years of preparation and academic education had ended.[7]

2

The People's Institute (1906–14)

In his memoirs, John Collier wrote that the years between 1907 and 1920, the years of his involvement in community development work in New York City, "were controlled by a belief which died hard in me: the belief that what I may call the Occidental ethos and genius were the hope of the world. . . ." Haunted by a fear that western, industrial society "might also become the world's doom," he resolved to dedicate his life to making changes in the system that would preserve its essential virtues. "My unwearying task," he wrote, "was to make some difference in that Occidental ethos and genius."[1]

The New York to which Collier returned in 1907 was filled with opportunities for a young man imbued with a sense of mission and a determination to improve the society in which he lived. The phenomenal increase in immigration, particularly from southern and eastern Europe, which began in 1905 and lasted until the outbreak of World War I, was filling the city's tenement districts and enlarging the boundaries of its ghettos. Prompted by this increased immigration, native resentment, which had been temporarily diverted by the jingoism of the 1890s, was again on the rise. In the working-class and immigrant districts that Collier had explored during his student days at Columbia, the terrible fruits of a virtually unregulated capitalism were all too apparent. The need for change was everywhere evident. The problem was how best to bring it about.

Many young people Collier's age found the answer to that question in settlement-house work. Beginning in New York City in 1886, when Stanton Coit founded the Neighborhood Guild, later renamed the University Settlement, the settlement-house movement expanded in 1889 to embrace Vida Scudder's College Settlement and Jane Addams's Hull House. After 1893 these early experiments in settlement work were widely imitated throughout the nation as increased urbanization and the severe industrial depression of 1893 combined to sharpen the plight of the urban poor.

The goal of the settlement houses was to bring about assimilation of immigrants with the least amount of cultural shock, and to ameliorate the worst aspects of the urban environment. The houses sought to provide practical help and instruction as the new arrivals adapted to a sometimes frightening, always confusing, urban, industrialized society, and they sought to create a sense of community among the frequently disparate segments of the neighborhood. They taught young mothers the proper methods of child care; they dispensed advice on sanitation, nutrition, homemaking, and personal hygiene; they provided midwives, nurses, and medical care. They conducted classes in sewing, cooking, civics, English, and they prepared adults for their naturalization examinations. They attempted to provide recreational outlets for children and juveniles, and they formed social and cultural clubs for the adults. They were, as Eric Goldman has noted, the leaders in "the first systematic 'Americanization work,'" and as he has also observed, "the Americanization they advocated was no one-way street."[2] Recognizing that the acceptance of new ideas

Figure 1.   The young John Collier, circa 1910. From the John Collier Papers, Yale University Library.

and customs from abroad would enrich American culture by increasing its diversity, the settlement workers invariably encouraged the immigrants to preserve those parts of their heritage that did not conflict with their adjustment to American life.

The young Collier was in perfect accord with the goals and the ideals of the settlement houses, but he found their geographical and ideological boundaries too narrow for his purpose. His interest lay in some larger organization, one that would embrace the entire city, or at least a significant portion of it. A "radical" program of economic and social change to be achieved through education and political action, not simply amelioration, was his goal. The path to this goal led first, briefly, to the League for Political Education

Figure 2.   Collier's sons, from left to right, Charles, John, Jr.,
and Donald, circa 1916. Courtesy John Collier, Jr.

and then to the People's Institute, where he remained for
the next ten years.

The League for Political Education was the creation of
Robert Erskine Ely, an ordained Congregational minister
who, upon graduation from Union Theological Seminary in
1888, sought first in Boston and then in New York City, to
organize the "intelligentsia of the upper classes" into a political force for economic and social reform. Ely's work consisted primarily of identifying problems in city life, locating
speakers who could effectively describe these problems, and
then arranging for a series of luncheons, dinners, and sym-
posia at which league members were briefed on the need for
reform. Armed with the information they received and with
the moral indignation that undoubtedly accompanied the

presentations, the wealthy patrons of the league were expected to effect social change through the financial and political pressure they could exert through their parties and at the polls. The league, however, did not work directly with the common man, and for this reason Collier, whose natural sympathies lay with the poor and the disadvantaged, soon resigned. He and Ely remained lifelong friends and in 1923 when Collier needed someone with wealthy and influential friends to head his American Indian Defense Association, he chose Ely.[3]

The "luminous, impassioned spirit" of the founder-director of the People's Institute, Charles Sprague-Smith, was an additional incentive for Collier to change jobs. In him, Collier found the embodiment of the link he sought between the world of ideas and the world of action. The son of a Congregational minister, Sprague-Smith attended Amherst, where he obtained a master's degree in 1875; he then traveled and studied in Europe for five years, mastering twelve languages and receiving from Oxford a certificate stating that "no one of his years has accomplished as much as he in the field of languages." In 1881 he was appointed Gebhardt professor of German language at Columbia, a position he held until 1891, when his growing interest in Scandinavian and Icelandic literature caused him to resign. For the next few years, he taught comparative literature at a number of Ivy League schools as a visiting professor. By 1896, his interest in languages had broadened to embrace entire cultures. In that year he founded the Comparative Literature Society in New York, with the goal of "conserving and making mutually comprehensible the city's many ethnic cultures." It was but a step from this organization to the People's Institute.[4]

The People's Institute, created in 1897, was the product of two complementary forces. One was the necessity to find an acceptable outlet for the mounting restlessness in that city's immigrant and working-class districts, a restlessness that had become particularly noticeable since the severe depression which began in 1893. The second was the need of the Cooper Institute, founded in 1859 by the manufacturer

Figure 3.   Lucy Wood Collier with Charles Collier, and Sparkill, New York, home in the background, circa 1910. Courtesy
John Collier, Jr.

and philanthropist, Peter Cooper, to fulfill the terms of its
charter which provided that "courses of instruction on social and political science should have preference over all
other subjects of expenditure." The physical proximity of
the Cooper Institute to the city's Lower East Side, where the
poorest and most radical of the city's inhabitants lived, suggested to Sprague-Smith that both problems could be solved
by a common program, a series of nightly lectures and forums that would "bring together the world of culture and
labor to cope with the problems of social unrest and assist
in the peaceful, democratic evolution of our society." On a
winter's evening in 1897, Abram S. Hewitt, Cooper's son-
in-law and the chairman of the Cooper Union board of
trustees, invited a few of the city's notables to his study to

Figure 4. The Collier children and classmates in the "Home School," Sparkill, New York, circa 1917. From the John Collier Papers, Yale University Library.

hear Sprague-Smith's proposal. When the presentation was concluded, Felix Adler, Samuel Gompers, R. Fulton Cutting, and Grace H. Dodge agreed with Hewitt that the plan was sound, and the People's Institute was born.[5]

Between the time of its founding and the time Collier joined as a "civic worker," at forty dollars a month, in February 1908, the institute had greatly enlarged its program. The evening lectures conducted by Sprague-Smith and an increasingly large number of guest speakers of national prominence (Booker T. Washington, Jacob Riis, President William Howard Taft, Samuel "Golden Rule" Jones, to mention a few) remained the heart of the program. Friday nights, however, were now reserved for the heads of municipal bureaus to report on the activities of their departments and to respond to questions posed by members of the audience. On Sunday evenings, the People's Church, "creedless and professionless," offered instruction and discussion on ethical topics for those whose allegiance to traditional religion had lapsed. Patterned after Sprague-Smith's own strong belief in the "brotherhood of man and the existence of a force that makes for righteousness," it required only the test of "sincerity" for membership. Two spokesmen for liberal religion and social reform, Lyman Abbott, the aging editor of the *Outlook Magazine,* and Rabbi Stephen S. Wise, the leader of Reform Judaism, were, after Sprague-Smith, the most frequent speakers at these Sunday night forums.

By 1908 the institute had also branched out into action-oriented programs. A Civic Club composed of newly naturalized citizens was formed to instruct new voters in the issues, responsibilities, and techniques of voting. A People's Lobby was formed to mobilize support for municipal ownership of utilities and transportation, for the construction of public parks, and for tenement-house regulation. The institute showed a marked interest in cultural programs, presenting dramas, symphonies, and concerts at prices the people could afford. These programs were so successful that commercial theaters soon entered into arrangements with the institute to procure reduced rates for its patrons, and in 1910 an estimated 120,000 workingmen and students availed themselves of these cultural activities. From this arrangement, the institute also emerged as a moral force in the world of commercial entertainment. In 1910 Jacob Riis credited it with the first efforts at stage censorship in New York City, noting that with every ticket sold, the institute gave a guarantee of moral wholesomeness. Indeed, Isadora Duncan, who was to become one of Collier's idols, was once refused approval by the institute on the grounds that she danced with bare knees.[6]

It was the action-oriented programs that claimed Collier's attention during his tenure at the institute. Sprague-

Smith, who preferred the more academic enterprises of the lectures and the forums, recognized his young protégé's interest and appointed Collier to the post of civic secretary, a position that gave him control over the institute's recreational and cultural programs. Collier's experience as a newspaperman was also recognized. He was made editor of the *Civil Journal*, the institute's publicity medium. From these two positions he soon attracted favorable attention to the institute, at the same time expanding his own influence throughout the city.

One of Collier's first assignments as civic secretary was an investigation of the cinema industry. He viewed this new medium with mixed emotions. On the one hand, he deplored the effect of the cinema on older dramatic forms: the Sicilian marionette shows, the Chinese theater, and the Old World festivals and pageants that he admired for the values and cultural traditions they transmitted in the course of providing entertainment. Confronted with the novelty and broader subject matter of the movies, many of these folk-art forms were languishing, and some had ceased to exist, a situation Collier greatly lamented. On the other hand, Collier viewed the cinema as a medium with "great potential for education and for life." It could become, he believed, truly a "people's theatre" which, in responding "to the yearnings of the common people of the world," could awaken each individual to the beauty and harmony in the world and assist him to become alive "to himself and the world and the people around him."[7]

For several months in 1908 Collier toured the city's two hundred and fifty movie houses, observing both the subject matter of the films and the physical conditions of the theaters themselves. What he learned from this investigation was that the cinema industry was "without any kind of restraint," and that no one had seemingly yet formed "any kind of social view of its purpose." A typical showing, he found, consisted of four films, each ten to fifteen minutes long and each designed to appeal to a different segment of a potential audience. The result was that some films were not

suitable for some viewers. Many of the exhibitors to whom
he talked shared his concern about this problem, but they
argued that they were without power to rectify the situation
because they had no control over the films they received
from the distributors and did not know in advance the subject matter of the films. Collier also observed that many of
the theaters, often no more than small rented halls, were
deficient in sanitary facilities and highly susceptible to the
dangers of fire. The more he probed, the more he came to
believe that local control could be exercised effectively only
over matters of health and physical conditions. Some kind
of national controls would have to be created to cope with
the subject matter of the films themselves.[8]

The report Collier submitted to the institute's board of
directors in early 1909 called for a stringent municipal licensing ordinance to eliminate the hazard of fire and to improve ventilation, lighting, and sanitary facilities in the
theaters. It also called for a review board to preview all
films to be shown in the New York City area. The function
of the review board was to make recommendations concerning the desirability or undesirability of all films submitted to it, and it could recommend changes and deletions.
Under no circumstances, however, was it empowered to
prevent the showing of films. In March 1909, Sprague-Smith
created the National Board of Censorship of Motion Pictures under the institute's sponsorship and named Collier
to the position of general secretary. Three months later, at
the request of motion pictures exhibitors and producers,
the board accepted the responsibility for reviewing all films
produced in or imported into the United States. In 1910,
with the cooperation of a friendly mayor, the licenses of
all film operators were revoked until Collier and other
members of the board had rewritten the city's licensing
ordinance.[9]

Despite its title, the National Board of Censorship never
sought or approved legal censorship of the film industry. Indeed, it was partly in reaction to municipal censorship laws
passed in Chicago in 1907 and San Francisco in 1908 that

the board had been created. When the New York City council passed an ordinance for police enforcement of a censorship law in 1913, Collier secured the mayor's veto; and in 1915, when the Supreme Court of the United States upheld the Chicago ordinance, he wrote a lengthy article denouncing this invasion of the "right of free speech" in which he advocated the adoption of a voluntary system of controls such as those imposed by the national board.

Collier's consistent position on the issue of censorship during his five years as general secretary to the national board was that the board's function was to assist producers and directors in gradually improving the quality of films, "educationally, morally, and artistically," through the articulation of acceptable standards and guidelines. He emphasized cooperation between the board and the industry. In these early years he was apparently successful in obtaining the cooperation he sought, for he later wrote, "in no instance, although millions of feet of film were destroyed or remade, were the Board's findings ever rejected by the producers."

To determine acceptable standards and guidelines, the national board relied upon the collective judgment of a thirty-two-member self-perpetuating governing committee, whose members were originally chosen by the People's Institute board of directors. One hundred and twenty volunteers, divided into subject-matter subcommittees, "individuals of intelligence, with leisure to give to the work," daily reviewed the films submitted for distribution within the nation. The decisions of the subcommittees passed across Collier's desk, where he approved, or did not approve them. When there was disagreement between the subcommittees and Collier, or when a producer disagreed with the judgment of either, an appeal was made to the governing committee, which made the final decision. Each month a bulletin containing a description of the films reviewed, together with the board's decision on each, was circulated to 450 exhibitors and "collaborators" throughout the nation.

The national board's work was not, of course, perfect. No

system of national representation on the governing committee, for example, was ever devised during these early years. Most of its members were in some way connected with the operation of the People's Institute, and they could hardly claim to speak with authority for the entire nation. Collier himself admitted that the board's work was sometimes deficient and that some of its judgments were unsound. He particularly lamented the fact that it never found a way to control "where any given film shall or shall not be shown," and he regretted that the board had given its approval to *The Birth of A Nation*, although he believed the standard under which its approval had been obtained— "The Board shall not stand guard on behalf of the pride, or interests of any special faction, section, or race"—to be generally good. Whatever its failings or its mistakes in judgment, Collier argued, they were not occasioned by an allegiance to the "narrow or political" standards that legal censorship would employ. In making its judgments, he wrote, the national board gave weight to those considerations likely to affect the "whole public," not just "the child or a particular sect." The creative genius of a director or a producer was not to be stifled by a system that would prohibit the showing of his work. Rather, by cooperating with the producers in an attempt to work out guidelines, both the producers and the general public would be gradually brought to a common understanding of the medium's role in society. Like many of the reformers of his generation, Collier's ultimate argument for a voluntary rather than a legal system of controls was based on his faith in "the people." The people, if permitted free access to any motion picture, would eventually rectify any mistakes the national board itself might make.[10]

In 1914 Collier resigned his post as general secretary to the national board and severed all his connections with its work. Within a few years, the organization became truly national in scope and representation and was reorganized as the National Board of Motion Pictures. Its function, however, remained the same: "to broaden the social usefulness of the motion picture, recreationally, culturally, and educationally." In 1934, on the occasion of its twenty-fifth anniversary, Collier's contribution to the board was recognized when he was invited to attend its annual luncheon as the guest of honor. His appearance, the invitation said, would be "highly appropriate since you practically organized the Board and acted as its first secretary."[11]

In the fall of 1909, Collier's interest in action-oriented programs brought him into the contest for mayor of New York City. A major issue in the campaign was the ownership of the city's traction franchise. Two candidates, Republican William Randolph Hearst, who had been bested in a similar struggle in 1905, and Democrat William J. Gaynor, whom Hearst had been unsuccessful in persuading to run for the office in 1905, both advocated municipal ownership of the transportation system. Hearst first supported Gaynor, but when Gaynor refused to disavow the support of Tammany Hall, he withdrew his endorsement and entered the campaign himself. The two men became bitter enemies during the campaign, and the animosity lingered on after Gaynor's election.

Collier supported Gaynor in 1909; Sprague-Smith backed Hearst. Their political differences occasioned no problem, but after Sprague-Smith's sudden death in 1910, the institute, under Collier's influence, moved into a close alliance with the Gaynor administration. The appointment of Frederick C. Howe, the urban reformer who had achieved national prominence as Tom Johnson's lieutenant in Cleveland, to Sprague-Smith's vacant position in 1911, and the election of Henry de Forrest Baldwin, a prominent and wealthy lawyer-reformer, to the post of chairman of the board of directors of the People's Institute that same year, furthered the commitment of the institute to programs initiated by Collier during the year in which the institute was without formal leadership.

Mayor Gaynor's administration proved a disappointment to many of his supporters. Once in office, he vacillated on the issue of municipal ownership of transportation, and in the end it remained in the hands of private investors. He did, however, bring a new emphasis on honesty and efficiency to city hall. Through an investigation of graft and corruption in the police department, a reorganization of administrative offices that eliminated much deadwood, and his insistence on strict use of the civil service list in new appointments, he gave needed encouragement to the cause of reform. Gaynor appointed many former social workers to important posts in city government, and he particularly supported programs for public recreation and playgrounds for children. Collier, whose admiration for Gaynor "had been complete since years before he became mayor," blamed his hero's failings on an assassination attempt in 1910, which left Gaynor's health severely impaired during the remainder of his term. He stuck loyally by Gaynor thoughout his four-year term and was rewarded by the city's support for a scheme that he and others at the institute had been evolving since 1910: the use of the city's public schools as neighborhood social centers for recreational and educational purposes.[12]

The origins of the school–social center movement, of which Collier's experiment was but a part, are obscure. Before his work there had been several similar projects in New York City, all of them organized by settlement-house workers. James K. Paulding, one of the first residents of University Settlement and a member of the National Board of Censorship of Motion Pictures, and Mary K. Simkhovitch, the director of Greenwich House, both pioneers in the national playground movement, established recreation centers in the schools of their areas shortly after the turn of the century. In Boston, Mary Follette proposed a wider use of school facilities as early as 1900 and John Dewey established a school–social center in Chicago in 1902, shortly before he left for Columbia University. Both Mrs. Simkhovitch and Dewey advocated the concept of neighborhood social centers housed in the schools before national associations of educators and social workers prior to 1905, but it was the work of Edward J. Ward in Rochester, New York, that brought national attention to the movement.[13]

Ward was a former Presbyterian minister whose interests in athletics and young people led him out of the active ministry into the field of social work. An outstanding athlete who participated in wrestling, football, and track in his college days, Ward converted his manse in Silver Creek, New York, into an athletic and recreation center shortly after his appointment as pastor in 1905. His success in attracting young people was so spectacular that he conceived the idea of "turning his church edifice into a social center and allowing his flock to go to the other clergyman of the town for their preaching." This idea failed to appeal either to the other parsons or to Ward's congregation, but in 1907, a progressive school board in Rochester, New York, learning of Ward's work, invited him to become director of its newly created school–social center system. Ward accepted the challenge, and within three years, with full administrative and financial support from the school board, he had built a flourishing program of social centers.

Under Ward's direction, the social center concept was expanded beyond its original emphasis on recreation and playground facilities. The Rochester social centers gradually evolved into neighborhood libraries, meeting halls for social and cultural clubs, public baths, and community theaters. By 1910, Ward was referring to his centers as "a training center for democracy" and insisting that they be used as forums for open discussion of community problems and programs, in the style of the New England town meetings. A Voters' League was organized to combat political apathy and social disorganization in the neighborhoods and to press for a program of civic betterment. It was this entry of the social center into the field of city politics that brought the program to an end. In 1910, the ward bosses, fearing the potential for reform implicit in the Voters' League, gained control of city hall and discontinued the appropriations.[14]

Despite the brief life of the Rochester experiment, it received national publicity and touched off discussions and

debates in educational and welfare circles. Ward himself accepted a position with the Extension Division of the University of Wisconsin in 1910 and immediately set about
organizing social centers throughout that state. In 1911, the
University of Wisconsin convened in Madison the first, and
apparently the only, National Conference on Civic and Social Center Development. Two hundred delegates from all
parts of the nation gathered to hear papers on the potential
uses of the school—social centers. Governor Woodrow Wilson delivered the principal address in which he hailed the
social centers as experiments in grass-roots democracy. Little agreement on the exact nature of a social center emerged
from the sessions, but at the conclusion of the conference,
the Social Center Association of America was formed and a
second national meeting at the University of Kansas was
scheduled for the following year. Josiah Strong, the Congregational minister who founded and presided over the American Institute for Social Services, was elected president;
Frank P. Walsh, a Kansas City lawyer soon to be appointed
chairman of the federal Commission on Industrial Relations, was elected first vice-president; and Louis Brandeis,
third vice-president. Ward was named executive secretary.
Despite the "almost religious enthusiasm" that accompanied the conference, no record of a second meeting exists,
nor does the Social Center Association of America appear to
have become a reality. The National Education Association
at its annual meeting in 1911, however, resolved to encourage the development of schools as social centers and in
1912 the U.S. Bureau of Education printed and widely distributed a bulletin describing the formation and history of
social and recreational centers. That same year all the major
political parties endorsed the concept in their political plat-
forms. In 1916 Ward left Wisconsin to assume responsibility
for community organization work in the U.S. Bureau of
Education.[15]

Collier was one of the delegates to Ward's conference as a
representative of the National Board of Censorship of Motion Pictures. Afterward he published a glowing appraisal of

the movement in the pages of *Survey* magazine, in which he termed the social center the "keystone in the arch of American life," the one institution that could bridge the growing gap between "science and scholarship" on the one hand and "public action, family and emotional life" on the other. Collier did not, however, attribute the genesis of his New York social centers to Ward's influence; instead, he traced their lineage directly from Sprague-Smith's pioneering work in adult education at the People's Institute. The New York centers, he maintained, had their origins in the public-forum movement, and from the beginning their emphasis was on adult, particularly immigrant, education, and on citizen participation in civic affairs. It was after Sprague-Smith's death in 1910, he wrote, that "the school became available for community use" through the intervention of Mayor Gaynor, and the work "of educating people through forums and civic clubs passed over immediately . . . into the school community centre movement."[16]

Collier's first, experimental, school–social center resulted from a field study of juvenile crime conducted in 1910 by Edward J. Barrows, a fellow staff member of the People's Institute. Although Barrows's findings were not published until 1914, his inquiry revealed a close connection between juvenile crime in the Hell's Kitchen area of New York City and the absence of playground and recreational facilities. After reading Barrows's field notes, Collier and Luther H. Gulick, the former director of the city's public school physical education program, conceived a plan whereby the city's parks and public schools would be used after hours as neighborhood social centers. With the support of the president of the Board of Aldermen, John Purroy Mitchell, they persuaded the Board of Education to permit an experiment at P.S. 63 in the Gramercy Park district beginning in 1912.[17]

Under Collier's direction, the social centers sponsored by the People's Institute grew steadily from the experimental center at P.S. 63 until there were fourteen in 1916. They differed from the Rochester centers in a number of important ways. From the start, the administration of the New York centers was independent of the administration of the schools. Unlike Ward's centers, where the school principal also served the director of the social center, the directors of the New York centers were not subject to the local principal except in matters of housekeeping. Collier also insisted that the New York centers strive for self-determination in the areas of program planning and execution. One representative from each club or interest affiliated with the center was to sit on its governing board. To maintain independence from both city hall and outside philanthropies, he argued, the centers should eventually become self-financing through the levy of a small admission fee for the use of their facilities and for attendance at their public programs. Although the goals of self-government and self-support were imperfectly realized in practice, P.S. 63, the showcase center, achieved a semblance of autonomy. Originally supported by $5,000 from the city recreation department and $3,500 from various philanthropies, by 1916 it had raised a budget of $2,500, sufficient to support most of its varied programs.

As the social centers spread throughout the city, so, too, did Collier's concept of their purpose and importance grow. The American public school system, he argued, because of the necessity to avoid sectarian and religious influences in its work, had sacrificed the "ethical and civic virtues," "the social and emotional development of the child," at a time when the influences of the family and the church were dwindling. The social centers could fill this void by offering classes in "citizenship, ethics, social good will, play and aesthetics." Agreement on values and the proper method of their transmission, he was certain, could be reached by bringing together in a common program all the members of a neighborhood: adults, young people, and children. Collier hoped to make the social center "the institutional center of the neighborhood," a place where common goals could be forged and basic values examined and reinforced. Above all, the social center would be a means of developing a sense of community among peoples of different cultures, religions, and languages.

Collier's interest in preserving immigrant customs and traditions and his concern for wholesome entertainment, originally stimulated by his investigation of the motion picture industry, were reflected in the New York social centers. He successfully advocated the showing of motion pictures at P.S. 63, opened it to public dances, sponsored amateur theatricals, immigrant pageants, and festivals in its auditorium, and encouraged its use as a meeting hall for neighborhood social clubs and labor unions. A small fee was charged for the movies, the dances, and the use of meeting rooms. This income not only served to make the center self-supporting, but also subsidized other activities, like a dancing school, not profitable in itself. Eventually these activities were criticized by the owners of commercial recreational facilities and by saloonkeepers who provided meeting halls to their customers. The social centers, these people claimed, were competing with private business. Collier was at first cautious in his response to this criticism, but by 1913 he was openly defending the social centers as a healthy means of combating the commercial monopolization of entertainment with its "fearful work of disrupting the family." On one occasion he wrote: "Although not a socialist in some other particulars, I am entirely a socialist when it comes to the municipal ownership and operation of amusement places." He particularly defended the presentation of motion pictures at the social centers on the ground that they would provide muscle that independent proprietors could not for improving the quality of movies.[18]

By 1914, as a result of his friendship with Mayor Gaynor and Alderman John P. Mitchell, Collier had emerged as a force in city politics. During budget hearings on the city's recreation program in 1913, he appeared as a critic of the existing order. The city's recreation centers, he declared, were too few, too limited in their programs, and excessive in their emphasis on discipline. The solution to the problem of limited funds and the evident need for increased leisure facilities throughout the city, he testified, was the expansion of the school–social center experiment. With Mitchell's support, he argued that the recreation budget would go further and accomplish more if existing school facilities were used after school hours as neighborhood social centers and if expensive professional recreation directors were replaced by neighborhood volunteers and governing boards. In addition to creating a broader distribution of existing funds, he maintained, the social centers would also be better able to provide "for group activities adjusted to local needs." The present system of building separate schools, playgrounds, parks, and libraries, was not only wasteful, he wrote in 1914, but also divisive in its impact on community life. As old leisure institutions disappeared during the exodus from the farm to the city, from Europe to America, these "specialized institutions" had grown up. Their unintentional, yet harmful, effect was to "separate members of the family, separate individuals from groups, and separate age groups." The result had been the collapse of community life, the destruction of neighborhood cohesion, and the decline of intelligent civic participation on the part of most citizens. Support for the concept of a self-governing and partially self-supporting neighborhood social center was the best means to restore a sense of community at the same time that "the social, the utilitarian and the civic elements of leisure life" were being nourished.[19] In November 1913, Mitchell was elected mayor of New York City. Support for the continuance of the school–social center program was assured.

While Collier was establishing himself as a leader in the national school–social center movement, he was also becoming increasingly involved in a number of other, more radical, activities apart from his official duties at the People's Institute. The moment of this involvement can be determined almost precisely. It began shortly after Mabel Dodge returned from Europe in the early winter of 1912.

Born Mabel Ganson in Buffalo, New York, in 1879, Mabel Dodge had been twice married and twice disappointed when she returned to America after nine years spent abroad, mainly in Italy. Reared in an atmosphere of luxury, indulgence, and splendid isolation from the harsh realities of everyday life, she was educated in Buffalo finishing schools and had made the grand tour of Europe before she married Karl Evans in 1900. Shortly after the birth of her only child, John Evans, her husband was killed in a hunting accident, whereupon the young widow suffered a nervous collapse and was packed off to Europe for her recovery. On the boat she met Edwin Dodge, a wealthy Boston architect, whom she subsequently married in 1903. Most of the years of her self-imposed exile in Europe were spent in Florence, where she amused herself with a constant flow of house guests at her mansion, the Villa Curonia. Twice a year the Dodges visited Paris, where Mabel eventually made the acquaintance of Leo and Gertrude Stein. The Steins taught her about modern art, and Gertrude, during a sojourn at the Villa Curonia, composed a verbal "portrait" of Mabel.

Mabel Dodge returned to America in 1912, ostensibly to place her son in school, but she also admitted to having grown tired of Europe. At the same time, the prospect of returning to America filled her with dread and disgust. "Remember, it is *ugly* in America," she told her son; "It is ugly, ugly, ugly! Never forget that." Yet, if one had to return, she reasoned, there was only one place to live, New York City. And so it was that she established herself at 23 Fifth Avenue, on the edge of Greenwich Village and only a short distance away from the People's Institute.[20]

To assuage her misgivings about having returned to America, Mabel Dodge plunged into the task of redecorating her four-room apartment, painting the walls and the woodwork all in white, installing white curtains in every room, and even placing a white bearskin rug on the living room floor in front of the white marble fireplace. The effect she desired was at last achieved. New York had been "diminished," it had been made to "stay outside in the street," where it could not contaminate the white, sterile cocoon she had created. Once the work was finished, however, she found herself lonely and bored, and she grew increasingly melancholy and dissatisfied.

Edwin Dodge did what he could to cheer his wife, but Mabel had grown tired of him, too; indeed, she wrote, his presence was increasingly standing between "me and real life." Gradually, during the winter of 1912–13, she was drawn out of her depression and into a new life through the efforts of two young, amiable bohemians, Carl Van Vechten and Hutchins Hapgood. Both Van Vechten and Hapgood had a score of friends among the artists and writers of Greenwich Village, and Hapgood, from his days as a journalist, had a particularly wide-ranging acquaintance with most of the city's radicals: the labor leaders, the socialists, the anarchists, and the suffragists. Before long, the two of them had introduced Mabel to the cream of pre–World War I bohemianism and radicalism: Lincoln Steffens, Walter Lippmann, Robert Edmund Jones, Frances Perkins, Mary Heaton Vorse, Mary Austin, Emma Goldman, Alexander Berkman, Edwin Arlington Robinson, Bill Haywood, Margaret Sanger, Marsden Hartley, Andrew Dasburg, Floyd Dell, Max Eastman, and Amos Pinchot. In time, Lincoln Steffens suggested to Mabel that "evenings" be organized at which her guests could advance or expound upon some new idea or cause in which they were involved and then be subjected to cross-examination. In this way, the most famous salon in America was launched.[21]

Mabel Dodge believed that the one gift that had been given to her was the ability to make things happen. She was neither particularly intelligent nor inventive, but she believed that her presence acted as a catalyst upon others who possessed these traits. Most of her contemporaries have agreed with her assessment. Max Eastman, for instance, wrote that "she had neither wit nor beauty, nor is she vivacious or lively minded or entertaining . . . , for the most part she sits like a lump and says nothing." But, he discovered, there is "something going on, or going round, in Mabel's head or bosom, something that creates a magnetic field in which people become polarized and pulled in and made to behave very queerly." There had been many famous salons in history before hers, he added, but "Mabel's was the only one ever established by pure will power."[22]

Mabel Dodge first came to the attention of Americans outside the salon through her participation in the International Exhibition of Modern Art at the Sixty-Ninth Regiment Armory in February 1913. Asked by the exhibition's promoters to write an article on Gertrude Stein, she replied with an essay linking Stein's writings, still unknown in America, to the paintings on exhibit. "Gertrude Stein," she wrote, "is doing with words what Picasso is doing with paint. She is impelling language to induce new states of consciousness." Mrs. Dodge also threw herself into the task of collecting examples of modern art for the exhibit, and she wrote out a check for $500 to support its work. By the time the Armory Show opened, she was convinced that it was her own idea, that it was "her own little Revolution." As thousands flocked to gawk and gape and sneer at the exhibits, they also began to ask, "Who is Mabel Dodge?", for in the pages of the exhibition's magazine there appeared not only Mabel's article on Gertrude Stein, but also Gertrude's "portrait" of Mabel Dodge. Both Gertrude Stein and Mabel Dodge were born at the International Exhibition of Modern Art.[23]

Shortly after the close of the exhibit, Hutchins Hapgood and his wife, Neith, invited Mabel to meet Bill Haywood, the I.W.W. leader who had just been released from jail following his participation in the Paterson, New Jersey, silk-workers' strike. Haywood was bitter about the fact that the New York papers had refused to cover the strike and, as a result, had kept workers in New York City from coming to the aid of the strikers across the bay. Mabel suggested a huge pageant in Madison Square Garden as a way of publicizing the strike and of raising money for the strike fund. The idea took hold and preparations began that same evening for staging in dramatic form a reenactment of the Paterson strike. John Reed, who was covering the strike for *The Masses*, volunteered for the job of organizing the pageant, and soon he and Mabel were working closely together on its production. When the pageant was held in June 1913, Mabel's interest in radicalism had long since been replaced by a consuming passion for Reed. Shortly afterward, she spirited him away to Europe, temporarily abandoning the salon and her New York friends.[24]

Through his acquaintance with Hapgood and Fred Stein, a director of the People's Institute since 1898, John Collier was drawn into Mabel Dodge's circle at the same time that her affair with John Reed began. Stein, a wealthy banker-philanthropist, was a cousin to Leo and Gertrude Stein; Hapgood and Collier had been close friends since shortly after Collier came to the institute, when their mutual interests in immigrant cultures and ghetto life had brought them together. Although he still addressed Mabel as "Mrs. Dodge" at this time, Collier was a frequent dinner guest at her home and he sometimes spoke at these events "on some phase of the problem of community."[25]

The Paterson strike pageant left a vivid and indelible imprint on the young Collier's imagination. Years later he could still remember how that evening had excited and inflamed him. The strikers, several thousand strong, made "Madison Square Garden shake with such roaring as may have attended Caesar's funeral," he recalled. They generated "a collective intensity . . . surpassing anything the writer has yet witnessed. . . . This was the high water mark of spontaneous community drama; it cannot be paralleled often under the normal condition of life, alas!"[26]

The same evening as the Paterson strike pageant, Lillian D. Wald celebrated the twentieth anniversary of the Henry Street Settlement with a somewhat different kind of pageant. In the streets surrounding the settlement, a crowd only slightly smaller than the one assembled in the Garden watched and enthusiastically received the performances of immigrant groups who demonstrated native dances and acted out important events in the history of their native lands.[27] The example of these two dramatic performances was not lost on Collier, who for some time had been seeking a new means to attract public attention to the social center movement.

In the spring of 1914, Collier assembled three thousand immigrants in the production of what was billed as the East Side Pageant of Nations. Supporters of the New York social centers had for some time been "troubled by a certain absence of large movement" at the schools, despite their success in sponsoring a score of neighborhood activities. In addition, Collier wrote later in an unusually candid evaluation, the degree of adult participation in the New York social centers had been largely negligible, the teamwork thus far achieved between different nationalities had been "petty, lacking in horizon," and there had been a nagging disposition among the various groups represented to "quarrel about small issues and not to cooperate on great ones." To break through the barriers of race and to mollify the benefactors of the centers, Collier suggested to the governing board of P.S. 63 the idea of a pageant. The purpose of such a production, he explained, would be to bring about "greater solidification in the neighborhood" and to "make a beginning in the assimilation of what is beautiful and picturesque in the foreigner's national life." The idea was accepted by seventeen different immigrant groups associated with the P.S. 63 social center, and they immediately set about organizing a gigantic folk-festival to be held on June 6, 1914.

The East Side Pageant of Nations was immensely successful in attracting attention to the school–social center movement and to John Collier. A week of festivities preceded the pageant itself when fifteen thousand spectators thronged the streets surrounding the school to view the immigrants celebrating "their national festivities in the dress and manner of their overseas homes." Germans, Bohemians, Austrians, Slovaks, Croatians, Ukranians, Russians, Italians, and "Spanish-Rumanian-Turkish Jews" participated in the events, which lasted until far into the night. At the ball that climaxed the day, Margaret Wilson, the president's daughter, who was deeply involved in settlement-house, charity, and social-center work in New York City, attended as the guest of honor. Also in attendance were Lillian Wald, poet Edwin Markham, Percy Mackaye, one of the nation's foremost directors of civic pageants, Mary Simkhovitch, Mr. and Mrs. Jacob Schiff, Lyman Abbott, Frederick Howe, and Samuel A. Lewisohn. The pageant, Collier told reporters, vividly demonstrated how the public school could be used to "bring about real community life."[28]

At the same time that he was involved in the planning for the East Side Pageant, Collier was also deeply engrossed in a plan to publicize the plight of the working classes through testimony before the newly created federal Commission on Industrial Relations. Since the bombing of the *Los Angeles Times* building in 1910, Paul Kellogg, the editor of *Survey* magazine, and a host of social workers led by Lillian Wald, Jane Addams, Florence Kelley, and Mary Simkhovitch, had been alarmed at growing newspaper publicity devoted to tales of labor violence. To counter this offensive against the labor movement, they urged the federal government to make a full-scale investigation into the cause of labor unrest. In 1912 President Taft responded to their entreaties by recommending to the Congress the creation of the federal Commission on Industrial Relations. Through the sponsorship of Senator William Borah of Idaho, a bill drafted by Kellogg and his associates was passed and signed into law in August 1912. Taft's nominees to the commission, however, were unacceptable to the Senate, which blocked action until after Woodrow Wilson's inauguration in 1913. Not until September 1913 were acceptable appointments to the commission confirmed. Shortly thereafter, the commission chairman, Frank P. Walsh, announced his intention to hold a series of public meetings at industrial centers throughout the nation in an effort to publicize the problem of unemployment and the poor conditions under which many workers labored. In addition to Walsh, one of the foremost proponents of industrial unionism in the nation, three leaders of American industry, three labor leaders, one woman, Mrs. Borden Harriman, and Professor John R. Commons, of the University of Wisconsin, were named to the commission.

The Walsh investigation was clouded by acrimony and dissent from the beginning. At the suggestion of Professor Commons, Walsh appointed a research staff composed of Charles McCarthy of the Wisconsin Legislative Reference Service, a friend of Collier's since the Madison Conference on Civic and Social Center Development held in 1913, Crystal Eastman, and the young Selig Perleman. McCarthy, the director, soon quarreled with Walsh over the nature of the investigation, with the result that he was fired and the research terminated. In the public hearings, Walsh sought to pin the responsibility for labor strife on big business. As violence grew in the Colorado coal mines during the winter of 1913–14, he especially attacked the Rockefeller interests and lashed out at educational and philanthropic foundations, which he accused of being allied with big business in a class war against the workers. When the commission's findings were finally published in 1916, so deep was the division between members of the commission that three separate sets of recommendations were forwarded to the Congress, which refused to adopt any of them.[29]

As the commission prepared for its New York hearings on problems in the garment industry, Collier proposed to Mabel Dodge that she chair a committee that would plan "a program and present evidence" before the commission with the object of using the hearings in such a way as "to attract public opinion and possibly to formulate the industrial revolutionary idea in a somewhat new way." In a letter written to her on December 31, 1914, he outlined a plan whereby "a group of radicals" could be brought together to prepare "a body of testimony with dramatic carrying power." Unless such a plan were formulated, he cautioned, the revolutionaries, whose motives were "largely unorganized, personal," would run down to testify in a manner whose effectiveness would resemble "Chinese fire-crackers [rather] than the fourteen-inch projectiles" he hoped to fire.[30]

Mabel, however, refused to take the job of committee

chairman, pointing out that she was completely inexperi-
enced with and ignorant of industrial problems. She did,
however, circulate Collier's letter among her radical friends,
and she convened two meetings at her home in early 1914.
The minutes of both, reproduced in her memoirs, indicate
that a good deal of talk resulted from Collier's proposal, but
that the actual contribution of the committee to Walsh's
work was negligible.

While Collier was engrossed in planning for the East Side
Pageant and busy with preparing testimony for Walsh's
commission, he was also involved in several lesser projects.
So busy was he during these first few months of 1914 that
Mabel Dodge recalled that he was "always looking wind-
blown [even] on the quietest day."[31]

First he gave literary form to the field notes that his colleague Edward J. Barrows had made on juvenile crime in
1910. This resulted in a report entitled "The City Where
Crime Is Play," published by the People's Institute in early
1914. Through the efforts of his brother-in-law, Julian Harris, then the Sunday editor of the New York Herald Tribune,
the report was published in abridged form in the Sunday
Tribune. In it Collier argued that juvenile crime was often
the result of the city's failure to provide adequate playgrounds for the children of the poor. The only place many
children had to play was in the streets. Street play was forbidden by city ordinance, however, and the police were quick
to arrest offenders. It was "an intolerable situation," Collier
wrote, wherein many ghetto children, having spent many of
their leisure hours in activities technically in violation of
the law, were no longer able to distinguish between crime
and play. Collier concluded the report with an appeal for
greater use of neighborhood schools and parks as social
centers where local groups could "establish and enforce
their own codes, and attempt to compete with commercial
amusement and gang avocations of the area."[32]

Shortly after this successful venture into the world of publication, Collier was briefly caught up in a scheme to take
over and reorganize The International magazine "as an in-

dependent radical organ." *The International*, largely a journal of poetry, was edited by George Sylvester Viereck, who
enlisted Collier's aid in appealing to Mabel Dodge for financial assistance. In February, 1914, Collier called a meeting at
Mabel's apartment to discuss the proposition and to determine its feasibility. Mabel, however, declined to support the
venture. Apparently it collapsed, for Viereck continued to
concentrate on poetry until the magazine's demise in 1918.[33]

Mabel Dodge said that she had been "too preoccupied
with personal problems" to support Collier and Viereck in
their plans to radicalize *The International*. Her interest in
radical causes had waned considerably since the spring of
1913 when she met John Reed; now in early 1914, when the
mercurial Reed had abandoned her temporarily, she was
again involved in the familiar, aimless, search for distrac-
tion that marked the end of her love affairs. One of her more
bizarre experiments involved her in a near brush with the
law, which demonstrated her dependence upon Collier at
the time.

During the late winter of 1913–14, Neith and Hutchins
Hapgood introduced Mabel to Hutchins's cousin Raymond
Harrington, who had just returned from conducting eth-
nological research among a group of Oklahoma Indians who
belonged to a peyote cult. When Mabel learned that Harrington had some peyote with him, she begged him to conduct a ceremonial in her apartment for a group of friends.
Max Eastman and his wife, Ida Rauh, Andrew Dasburg, the
Hapgoods, and a young house guest, Genevieve Onslow,
were invited to attend. In the course of the evening Mabel's
guests underwent differing degrees of hallucinatory experience. Hapgood announced that he had seen "the Soul";
Dasburg saw "what Sex is"; and Genevieve Onslow, who
apparently had a bad trip, fled from the house in terror after
she had a vision of "God." Fearful that the newspapers
might somehow get hold of the story, Hapgood and Mabel
Dodge turned instinctively to Collier, who had "a great
many strings in his hands that we knew he could pull if he
wanted to." Collier hurried over from the institute to coun-

sel against notifying the police, and eventually the missing girl turned up, although Mabel could not remember just how she was finally found.[34]

In the midst of his numerous activities during the spring of 1914, Collier suddenly pulled himself up short and began to review "the gains and losses since 1908." There swept over him "the longing, experienced again and again and again in my life, for wilderness." In March he abruptly resigned from the People's Institute and took his family to the mountains near Andrews, North Carolina, where they remained for the next seven months.

In a letter to Hutchins Hapgood written in April 1914, Collier explained his decision to divorce himself from the pressures of his New York work by saying, "I have been increasingly overstimulated for years past, and have come away in the hope of getting a new sort of mental and physical life." Early in his retreat, he invited both Hapgood and Mabel Dodge to visit, then immediately rescinded the invitation to Mabel because she "draws the mind out of one . . . and challenges the psychic centers and would in general counteract the placidity, dreaminess, and life of the brown-plowed earth which is the thing I need—perhaps critically need—now." In the end neither Mabel, who was recovering from her affair with Reed and desperately wanted to see Collier ("I thought of Collier who understood everything. One could talk to him of anything in the world and he would understand; he seemed to have a boundless grasp of human possibility."), nor Hapgood (whom Mabel wrote "is in danger of acute neurasthenic breakdown. He has used stimulants, wine, women and journalism to excite his *higher centers* too long . . . ,") disturbed his retreat. In other letters he complained of mental and emotional exhaustion, insomnia, irritability, of a sense of haste, which had become "my form of chronic worry," and he belittled his years at the People's Institute, calling them "years of fire-fighting activity" that absorbed his energy without resulting in anything of permanent value.[35]

Although the records from this period in his life are few
and incomplete, it is evident that Collier was undergoing
one of those painful, periodic, self-evaluations that afflict
many people as they enter their middle years. All his work
of the past six years he now found empty and meaningless.
Gradually he groped toward a new career as a writer. He
read a good deal (William James, Henri Bergson, Raymond
Poincaré), he wrote poetry (he had already published privately two books of obscure and highly subjective verse), he
sketched out a book that he titled *The Literature of Personal Destiny* (never completed), and he wrote a lengthy
study of the theater, which was published serially in the
Survey in 1915 and 1916, under the title "The Lantern
Bearers." The theater articles were largely a statement of his
own thoughts on the use of drama for community purposes
and an exposition of the theory of censorship he had worked
out during his tenure on the National Board of Censorship
of Motion Pictures.

It is remarkable that Collier accomplished as much as he
did during this period of retreat, for his work was constantly
interrupted by an almost endless series of family illnesses
and deaths. In May his youngest son, John, Jr., who was less
than a year old, was stricken with bronchial pneumonia and
confined for a period in an Ashville, North Carolina, hospital. Next, Lucy Collier was forced to undergo a "complicated operation." Then, both her parents died suddenly of
cancer. His medical expenses, he wrote Mabel Dodge in October, had risen to over $1,000, and his plans "for study, for
writing" had all been "blocked." Nevertheless, each month
brought a release from the tensions and the worries that
had prompted his resignation, and by November, filled with
"an increased bien-être, a greater joy in life and the world,"
he was ready to resume his public life.[36]

In his memoirs Collier recalled that by the end of 1914 he
felt "the necessity of plunging back into the work at The
People's Institute." His contemporary correspondence, however, does not substantiate this view. In a letter written a
month before his return to New York, he informed Mabel

Dodge that he was "definitely out of practical work" and that while he had not yet decided upon a new career, he was certain that his next job "will not be with the People's Institute." Perhaps he would enter some new kind of public service or engage "in speculative literary undertakings for a number of years." In any event, he was not returning to New York City. Philadelphia, Lucy's home, would be his address in the future.[37]

3

The Community Center Movement (1914–19)

It is not clear what caused John Collier to abandon his plans for a new career unencumbered by attention to "practical matters." Instead, he did return to the People's Institute. Perhaps he decided that supporting a family through free-lance writing was too risky a venture. Perhaps the People's Institute, having lost the services of Frederick Howe, who resigned in August 1914 to become U.S. commissioner of immigration, prevailed upon him to return. Two years elapsed before a new director was named, and during the interim period Collier was again able to exert considerable influence on policy matters from his position as civic secretary.[1]

Whatever the reason, the Colliers returned from the North Carolina wilds to their Sparkill, New York, home some time in November 1914. The home, "a pre-Revolutionary Dutch farmhouse," had been given to them by Lucy's father in 1910. At that time they had it redecorated, adding additional rooms. It now occurred to Collier that the structure was an excellent place for a small private school for his three sons and the children of some of his friends.

Figure 5.   Carpentry class, the "Home School," Sparkill, New York, circa 1917. Persons unidentified, but the woman may be Mattie Bates, and the child in the foreground may be John Collier, Jr. Courtesy of John Collier, Jr.

"The Home School," as the Colliers referred to it, was patterned on the educational theories of John Dewey. Because both John and Lucy were to spend the work week in New York pursuing their own careers, a resident teacher was needed. Their choice fell upon a middle-aged disciple of Dewey, Mattie Bates, who was charged with responsibility for the "teaching and moral life of the children." Miss Bates was enthusiastically recommended to other parents by the Colliers as a person with "experimental and creative interest in the development and nourishment of intellectual interest through responsible, constructive activity."

In keeping with Dewey's dictum, the Home School es-

Figure 6.   "Food Scouts of Public School 40, eating the right
kind of lunch while visitors look on. January 1918." John Collier
appears second from the right in adult group standing at the head
of the table. Lucy Wood Collier is believed to be the woman
standing third from the left. From the People's Institute Records,
Manuscripts and Archives Division, the New York Public Library,
Astor, Lenox, and Tilden Foundations.

chewed discipline for permissiveness. The children, who
were limited to a maximum of twelve between the ages of
seven and nine (except for the Collier children, who were
younger) were taught practical skills along with academic
subjects. "Work, play, and study," Collier wrote, were integrated into a curriculum that kept the child "perpetually
absorbed in varied activities which were joyful." In the summer they went naked, tended the garden, and swam in the
old mill pond. It was an idyllic existence that contrasted

sharply with the conditions in the inner city, where Collier was often so absorbed in his work that, as he once wrote to Mabel Dodge, he had not even "seen Lucy except for one evening in weeks."

The Colliers attempted to charge fifty dollars per month for each child in residence, but the tuition was rarely met. There was "no money object" in soliciting the other children, however, according to Lucy Collier, who wrote that the real purpose was to provide a stimulating "education for the three boys." The Home School continued until 1919, when Mattie Bates became unable to work and the Colliers moved to California.[2]

Collier's interest in the education of children was also evident in another area. Immediately upon his return to New York, he became caught up in a scheme proposed by Mabel Dodge and Walter Lippmann to rehabilitate the aging Isadora Duncan, who had just returned from Europe following the outbreak of World War I. Since first seeing her dance in 1909 (the ban of the People's Institute against her appearance there had not deterred him from viewing her performances elsewhere in the city), Collier had become one of her most devoted and loyal followers. On several occasions in the intervening years, he dedicated poems in her honor, one of which, a rather stilted and sophomoric elegy written at the time her children drowned in 1913, he republished in his memoir. For Collier, Isadora Duncan was "a genius, orphic and dionysian in one," "a Sappho from the Grecian islands," and his idealization of her genius made it impossible for him to recognize the Isadora was past her prime and headed rapidly downhill.

In 1915 Isadora Duncan was a moody, unstable drunk whose dissipation had robbed her of the grace and vitality that had once made her famous. She arrived in New York some time during the winter of 1914–15 with a troupe of young girls, whom her sister, Elizabeth, had collected from various parts of Europe. She rented a large studio in Greenwich Village and soon after announced her intention to found a school where she could teach her art to a new generation of dancers.

Her plea for the school was unveiled in a remarkable performance at Carnegie Hall in 1915, where she appeared before her audience in a flowing robe, posed immobile on a barren stage for half an hour, and then, still without dancing, delivered her appeal for a place in which to teach. Despite her obvious inability to manage such an undertaking, "still the illumination of old times held its own," Collier recalled. Mabel Dodge and Lippmann took up the cause and soon were busily planning a series of performances featuring Isadora and a group of her children to publicize the appeal. There was talk of renting the Harvard stadium and the Yale bowl, but, in Mabel's words, "it fell through somehow, and we tried to think of something else for her."

The something else turned out to be a scheme concocted by Mabel and Juliette Poyntz, the educational director of the International Ladies Garment Workers' Union. It called for obtaining one of the New York City armories free of charge for the instruction of "not fewer than 1,000 girls of the working classes" in the Duncan tradition. Collier believed that the ILGWU could have obtained an armory simply for the asking, but he succumbed to the argument of Mabel and Juliette that this would be, indeed, too simple. Instead, young Mayor John P. Mitchell was to be brought to visit Isadora, "uninformed of the motivation" for his visit. Isadora would demonstrate her method, unfold her plans for a school, and the mayor would accede to her every wish. It was Collier, "who knew how to get things done in the city," who was to arrange for the mayor's appearance.

At four o'clock on the appointed day, Collier delivered the unsuspecting mayor into Isadora's studio, "The Ark." The huge room was illuminated only by a few shaded lamps, which dimly revealed several large, low couches, a piano, a group of Isadora's charges robed in pale blue tunics, and Isadora herself in the flowing Greek costume that was her customary stage attire. In the shadows Mabel Dodge, Walter Lippmann, and several other intimates waited.

Mayor Mitchell, visibly shaken, was introduced to Isadora by Collier, who then wandered away to permit her to make her appeal. Momentarily disappointed by the mayor's physical appearance, Isadora quickly recovered, and grasping the mayor's hand, she pressed it against her body, and drew him "with a strong and a powerful haul" toward the central couch, where she intended to "enthrone him beside her on the orange dais." Still fondling his hand, she sank onto the couch and began to murmur "endearments" into his ear. At the last possible moment, the stunned mayor extricated himself from her grasp and, "looking wildly about him, made a dash for the piano stool," a safe distance away.

After a short pause, Isadora rose from the couch, looked intently at Mitchell and then began to upbraid him for having imprisoned a mother recently convicted of murdering her children. At this point, Collier, who had been reclining on one of the lesser couches, "feet crossed, shoes muddy, ashes dropping from his cigarette onto the silken covers," aroused himself long enough to divert Isadora from her harangue and to steer her into a description of the school.

Sullenly, Isadora launched into a presentation that could scarcely have been better calculated to repel the mayor. Her children, she shouted at the mayor, would "live in beauty." They would be surrounded by "music and art and poetry"; they would not have to go to school "with horrid dirty school books"; they would be spared "church on Sunday" and sermons delivered by "stuffy old men in ugly buildings." As she became more impassioned in her delivery, Isadora leaned toward the mayor. Her gown slipped from her shoulder, baring her breast. Muttering "saccharine, saccharine," Mitchell rose and fled from the studio. With that, Collier reported, the "final New York enterprise to rehabilitate Isadora Duncan" came to an end.

Walter Lippmann later wrote Mabel that it had been "a nasty, absurd mess, and she is obviously the last person who ought to be running a school." He had been a "damned fool" for deluding himself into thinking that somewhere there could be "one spot of freedom and beauty." Such spots, Lippmann wrote, "exist only in the imagination we weave about performers like Miss Duncan." Mabel agreed: "She was a channel for great powers . . . but one couldn't do anything with her or for her, or fit her in."[3]

Many years later, Collier wrote in a similar vein. The debacle with Mayor Mitchell finally forced him to recognize the reality of the situation, he wrote. "Isadora had become a self-abandoned alcoholic, and a psychotic sufferer"; nothing further could be expected from her. His contemporary writings, however, belie this insight. In the series of articles he wrote for the *Survey* in 1915–16, he continued to sing her praises and he blamed the failure of her appeal for a school on the "philistine community of New York," which had rejected her unique talents to their own detriment. He also cited the incident to illustrate his favorite theme. New York had lost a great opportunity to demonstrate "the practicability of enfranchising children and lowly folk into great art expression and of recovering the beauty of social life," he wrote, because there had been "no communal disposition to use her, no communal machinery for using her, and no communal realization of the momentous thing she was— an announcer of something wonderful and true. . . ."

The truth is that Collier was unable to abandon the vision of the dancing school as had the others. Isadora had botched the plan, it was true, but Collier's fascination with the idea led him now to Elizabeth Duncan, Isadora's elder sister, whom Collier had met and befriended when she landed penniless at Ellis Island in late 1914. Elizabeth, he now discovered, was really the brains behind Isadora's school. Much as she had earlier taken away from Elizabeth the troupe of young girls who accompanied her to America, so, too, had Isadora appropriated the idea for an American school from her sister. Elizabeth still retained control over a younger group of girls, aged eight to twelve, the nucleus of a school, and Collier, "the ubiquitous Collier," as Mabel Dodge now referred to him, soon arranged for Elizabeth to meet Mabel Dodge. Impressed by a performance of Elizabeth's students, Mabel agreed to cooperate with Collier in founding an Elizabeth Duncan school under private auspices.

Using money that she had saved to purchase an abandoned life-station across the bay from Provincetown, Massachusetts, Mabel bought a huge, old frame home overlooking the

Hudson River at Croton, New York, for Elizabeth's school. Collier secured financial support from a group of wealthy German-American industrialists, many of whom, ironically enough, were the owners of the same Paterson silk factories he and Mabel had attacked so eagerly two years before. Samuel Lewisohn, the wealthy copper baron and a financial supporter of Collier's enterprises at the People's Institute, offered to help by purchasing the abandoned life-station for Mabel's part-time use and by contributing five hundred dollars to the school. Under constant prodding from Collier, other supporters were gathered together in Mabel's apartment in 1915. Walter Lippmann returned, Norman Hapgood (Hutchins Hapgood's brother), the editor of *Collier's* magazine, Inez Milholland, the feminist leader, and Luther Gulick, Collier's coworker in the social-center movement, were brought into the scheme. By February, Collier was able to inform Mabel gleefully that it "really looks as if we were (*sic*) going to get out of the underbrush in the Duncan school matter, within a few days now."

In early March, an application for incorporation of the Elizabeth Duncan school was officially filed. Collier now cautioned Mabel against permitting people to serve on the school's board of directors simply because "they have given money or may give money, or because they represent influence. . . ." Spelling out a policy that he would employ effectively in organizing the American Indian Defense Association in 1923, he advised her to place the wealthy supporters on advisory or honorary committees; the directors who would exercise real control should be chosen only from among those who had demonstrated "spirit or the particular knowledge or the enthusiasm to make them intrinsically valuable." He would be willing to serve as a director depending upon the final "make-up of the Directorate."[4]

Once the school was organized, as was true of so many enterprises that Collier and Mabel Dodge cooperated in establishing, interest in it subsided. Mabel moved on to a complicated affair with Maurice Sterne, a painter who eventually became her third husband, and Collier became active once again in the advancement of the social-center movement.

No records survive to indicate the nature of Collier's work at the People's Institute from the time of his return to the city in late 1914 until the summer of 1915. In July of the latter year, the institute announced the establishment of the New York Training School for Community Center Workers at 70 Fifth Avenue, a few blocks away from Mabel Dodge's apartment. Collier was named the director of the school.

Some time during his long retreat in the North Carolina mountains, Collier apparently concluded that the reason so much of his pre-1914 work appeared to be mere "fire-fighting activity" was that there had been no method, no unity in the school–social centers he had helped to found. Individuals picked at random and largely dependent upon their own native skills had been assigned to the centers, often without adequate preparation for the work they were undertaking. As a result, the centers had developed unevenly and somewhat chaotically. Aside from the Gramercy Park center at P.S. 63, the other nine centers in existence in 1915 were rarely mentioned in either the press or the institute's own correspondence. Although never quite certain what a training school should do (he preferred instead to talk about the "spirit" of the training school), Collier became confident that he could construct a curriculum and direct a program that would prepare professionally trained directors for what he now called "community centers."

The New York Training School for Community Workers, while nominally under the direction of the People's Institute, was in reality Collier's own personal project. Upon his return to New York, he first sought and received the endorsement of Mayor Mitchell for an expansion of the social centers. Five new centers were established between 1914 and 1916. He then persuaded several of his influential and wealthy friends to incorporate the training school. Luther Gulick, who had joined with him in 1911 to create the first school–social center, was made chairman of the board. Frederick C. Howe, the former director of the People's Institute, Henry de Forrest Baldwin, the institute's board chairman, and Samuel A. Lewisohn, who provided most of the capital for the venture, were the other members of the original board. The teaching staff, composed of unpaid specialists in various aspects of city life, included such notables as A. A. Brill, Mabel's psychiatrist and the first Freudian psychologist in America, Hutchins Hapgood, Frederic Howe, the poet and dramatist Percy Mackaye, Charles Beard, Mary Simkhovitch, and James Ford, the Harvard professor who had introduced Collier to the cooperative movement. John Dewey and William H. Fitzpatrick of Columbia University Teacher's College, served as educational advisors.

The first class was enrolled in October 1915. It was limited to thirty-five students, who were expected to complete the course of instruction in seven months. In keeping with Collier's lifelong personal distaste for formal academic methods and requirements, there were no entrance examinations and no admission requirements beyond "a natural ability to do this kind of work, and basic educational tools." The curriculum, derived from Collier's brief experience as a graduate student and his passion for on-the-job training, consisted of fifteen hours of "practice" weekly in the existing community centers; sixty hours of classroom work in "seminars," which focused on fifteen different aspects of urban life, such as city planning, immigration policy, and social insurance; and periodic meetings with Collier in what he called "practicums" or "experience meetings," at which time theory and experience were to be reconciled through group discussion. No academic credit was awarded, nor were examinations administered. In imitation of Swedish folk schools, the training school would only certify that the graduates had completed the curriculum.

There were no texts for such a program. Instead, Collier later recalled, each instructor informally created his own texts as he went along. The failure to publish these texts, he thought, was probably "a disservice to the cause of urban community studies," but the staff was too busy creating and doing to afford the luxury of writing. There were books, especially the works of William James, William McDougall's *Social Psychology*, Havelock Ellis's *Sex in Relation to Society*, and Lester Ward's *Dynamic Philosophy*. In addition, use was made of all kinds of published material dealing with the cooperative movement, European syndicalism, and the community development movement.[5]

The establishment of the training school as a means of coordinating the development of the New York community centers was but a step toward Collier's larger plan to resurrect the defunct social-center association that Edward J. Ward had attempted to create in 1911. The dual objective of the training school, he wrote in 1918, was first, to recruit and train leaders for community work, and, second, "to conduct propaganda and demonstrations which would popularize and develop the community movement itself." As soon as the training school term was well under way, Collier began to plan for a national convention of community center workers.

In the spring of 1916 the initial organization for the convention was completed. An executive committee composed of Frederick Howe, Percy Mackaye, Fred Stein, Luther Gulick, Collier, and Carol Aronovici, a young Rumanian refugee who had taken a doctorate in architecture at Brown in 1911 and had then proceeded to establish himself as one of the nation's leading authorities on metropolitan and urban planning, drew up an announcement and secured the endorsement of one hundred prominent community leaders. Lillian Wald, John Dewey, Margaret Wilson, Franz Boas, Charles McCarthy, Charles Beard, and Haven Emerson, the New York City health commissioner who would assume the presidency of the American Indian Defense Association in 1924, were listed among the sponsors. Gulick was named the provisional president of the conference, Collier the secretary.

The National Conference on Community Center Problems was held in New York, April 19–22, 1916. Several hundred delegates, representing sixty-eight cities and towns and a variety of kinds of community centers (school centers, playground centers, recreation centers, settlement-house centers, forums, and the Boy Scouts), were greeted by Luther Gulick, who set the theme for the conference in his welcoming address. There were, Gulick informed his audience, two principal characteristics of a true community center: self-government and self-support. Gulick was followed by James Ford, who narrated the history of the movement, lavishly praising the pioneering work of Edward Ward, but suggesting that the American movement could profit from greater ties to the industrial and consumer cooperative movements of Europe. Collier concluded this first session with a description of the New York community centers, which, he stressed, had from the beginning striven toward the twin goals of self-government and self-support enunciated by Gulick. The conference, Collier said, would be devoted to a discussion of the problems encountered by the various kinds of community centers in the hope that a national organization of communication and cooperation between centers could be organized.

The theme of self-government and self-support that Gulick, Ford, and Collier all espoused at the opening session of the conference was undoubtedly calculated to quiet the supporters of Edward J. Ward in the audience. As far back as 1913, when he had reviewed Ward's book, *The Social Center*, Collier had criticized Ward's concepts of community-center organization, all the while praising him for his "thoroughly radical" emphasis upon the use of the social center as the nucleus for political action in the greater urban environment. Instead of accepting the school principal as the social-center director, Collier advocated greater democratization through "a leader salaried by the community." He also opposed what he called the "absolute democracy of individuals," which Ward's policy of admitting individuals to social-center membership entailed. Instead, Collier advocated that membership in the social centers be open only to "cohesive social groups, labor unions, political clubs, dancing societies, and ethnic organizations." Only by using already existent groups, Collier maintained, could the community center bind the neighborhood together. Ward, who was in attendance at the meeting as a representative of the U.S. Bureau of Education, however, was not to be denied. The second day he rose to denounce Collier and his supporters "as a little coterie of New York extremists."

Charging that the group of delegates headed by Collier "represented the ideas and philosophy of Bill Haywood, the I.W.W. leader" and stood for "syndicalism of a pronounced type," Ward appealed to the conference to disavow their attempt to take away control of the social centers from the school principal and to entrust it to members of the neighborhood community. New York, he contended, was already suffering from "far reaching abuse in permitting its school property to be used by irresponsible groups"; to extend the concept would be tantamount to "removing the Stars and Stripes from [our] school buildings." Backed by what one reporter called "the Western group" of delegates, Ward concluded that the "community centers should be directly controlled and supervised by public authorities with the school principal or deputy present at all meetings." As further insurance for public control, he argued, all funds for its work should be secured only from "public taxation."

Charles Beard immediately responded to Ward in a speech in which he charged that Ward's proposal was designed to hinder "the unchecked freedom of discussion" that had been a hallmark of the New York centers. Collier, too, rose to reply. He called Ward "a modern Don Quixote," and pointedly noted that Ward's Rochester experiment had collapsed because it was too closely controlled by the public authorities. He suggested that the degree of public control over the social centers be left to the individual localities, but he recommended as an ideal the New York system where "responsible citizens," rather than public school officers, were chartered by the municipality to supervise the center, and he insisted that the community centers be free to raise income in addition to appropriations from local tax revenues.

An important issue, that of whether the community centers should be autonomous or under public control, was thus squarely joined in the opening days of conference. Collier's position was significantly weakened when Margaret Wilson threw her influential support to Ward. The result was an unsatisfactory compromise engineered by Gulick, which postponed the matter until the following year. At the close of the meeting, the delegates adopted three resolutions: (1) public buildings should generally be available to people as a right, instead of by permission; (2) community centers should be administered through "responsible public officials"; and (3) tax monies should be used to promote and develop the centers. The decision on what kind of public officials should administer the community center and whether tax support should be the exclusive method of financing the centers was thus delayed until the next annual meeting. Harry Lipsky, a member of the Chicago Board of Education was elected president of the organization and Collier was elected secretary. President Woodrow Wilson was named honorary president. An executive committee composed of Ward and three of Collier's supporters, Edward L. Burchard of Chicago, Celeste Parrish of Atlanta, and Mary Follette of Boston, was named to prepare plans for the next meeting to be held in Chicago.

After the delegates returned home, the issue of control was again raised, this time in the pages of the national publication of the National Playground Association, *The Playground*. In June 1916, Howard S. Braucher, the editor, attacked Collier and his autonomous community centers in much the same style as Ward had done at the conference. In two articles Braucher denounced the Collier proposal, charging that it "attacked the fundamental basis of most of the work being done presently in the United States." Viewing the community center primarily as a recreation center, Baucher made two telling arguments against the autonomous centers.

Collier's proposal, which would permit the people to determine the activities of a community center through their financial support in the form of admission charges, he argued, would swiftly result in the centers catering only to the "passive and mass amusements": motion pictures, dramatic productions, and public dances. Individual participation in athletics, music, debate, and other recreational activities would fade away because people would not pay to engage in these desirable activities. "People," Braucher wrote, "will pay to see professional baseball," but they would not pay to play sandlot baseball themselves.

Braucher also made another important point. Conceding that the neighborhood would best be served if its residents were active in the administration of the schools, the parks, the community centers, and other activities, he charged that in reality very few persons would be able to afford the leisure time required for effective participation in these varied activities. "Very soon, there would be time to do nothing else," he wrote. "Life is too short for each individual to give time to every problem, we must specialize, we must delegate, we must work through others if we are to have effective lives."

Braucher's criticism of the Collier plan apparently went unnoticed or was ignored by Collier until 1919 when it was revived in the pages of the *Survey*. Having abandoned the community-center movement by this time, Collier made no effective reply to Braucher's criticisms, but instead confined his rebuttal to the charge that Braucher and Ward were simply interested in protecting their vested professional interests in the recreation centers and were fearful of the loss of philanthropic support if the centers became truly self-supporting.[6]

The inability to reconcile the Ward and Collier positions on the formation of community centers was again apparent at the second annual conference held in Chicago, April 17–19, 1917, just a few days after the United States entered World War I. Although the number of delegates was larger and their geographical representation broader than at the first meeting, the conference was ignored by both the Chicago and the New York newspapers. What little we know about this meeting comes largely from Collier's own necessarily colored account.

The central issue at this second meeting, as Collier remembered it, was the clash between his concept of national organization and that of Ward's. The issues of public control and financial support, so important the year before, were subordinated to the larger debate over whether the national organization should represent all persons involved in community center work in a mass organization of individuals or whether it should, as Collier advocated, represent a confederation of different groups, "each group autonomous but interacting with other groups. . . ." To protect his position, Collier believed, he "had no choice but to accept the presidency of the conference, since otherwise, Ward, representing the mass constituency idea, would have become president."

Collier's victory at Chicago proved to be pyrrhic. While the delegates voted at the close of the meeting to form a permanent organization with Collier as president, and also to hold their next annual meeting at the Cooper Union in New York, this vote was apparently that last act of the new national organization. Collier continued to use the title "President, National Conference of Community Centers" until 1919, but there is no evidence that the organization functioned after the Chicago meeting in 1917. Perhaps it was the war, with its restrictions on civilian travel, that prevented a third national meeting, but a more likely explanation is that Collier's victory drove out Ward and his supporters, thereby preventing the formation of a truly national organization.[7] It is also possible that the near collapse of the New York community centers following the mayoralty election in 1917 placed such a burden on Collier's energy that he was unable to offer effective leadership to the national organization.

Throughout the years 1915–18 Collier's seemingly boundless energies were centered mainly on the community-center movement. Although often engaged in numerous sidelights, he managed to supervise the expansion of the centers throughout New York City from his position as director of the training school and he almost single-handedly provided the drive and determination that resulted in the creation of the National Conference of Community Centers. On the surface these were years of high hope, significant advances, and public approbation, but beneath the public facade that he carefully and successfully labored to create, John Collier was constantly plagued by nagging personal doubts and pressing financial problems, which threatened at any moment to overwhelm all his public enterprises. On occasions of crisis, then as in later life, he had the habit of dashing off long letters and memoranda in which he answered his critics, upbraided himself, or simply attempted to list both sides of a particular argument. These compositions were never mailed, but were instead quietly filed away, the immediate purpose of catharsis having been fulfilled.

One of the first examples of these periodic self-evaluations that has survived is an essay entitled "The Mystery of Lester Ward," apparently written during the late summer of 1916. It was a trying time, "the severest of my life," he wrote on another occasion to Mabel Dodge, who, together with Lucy, the boys, and the Hapgoods, was spending the summer at Provincetown where Susan Glaspell, Jig Cook, and Mary Heaton Vorse were preparing for the first production of Eugene O'Neill's *Bound East for Cardiff*. Collier was immersed in the details of the National Conference of Community Centers and he was also battling for the survival of the training school, which had just completed its first year. "None of our enterprises are yet assured for next year," he complained. In addition, there was no money to pay the salary of the school's staff. To free himself from the details of his daily work, he had briefly plunged into a bout of reading, which filled him with a "sense of great Events, of movement at the foundations of the world." Momentarily inspired by a vision "of great basic forms charged with electric potential [where] energy leaps sparkling from form to form," he had no more than laid down his books when he was overcome with despair at his inability to implement the "Ward synthesis" in his own work. Instead, he knew immediately "that the horizon will shrink to little technical nearness and apparent practicalities, and the distance . . . will be inhabited again with projections of a little personal hour dreaming of immensity and eternity." "I have not the vigor . . . ," he concluded, listing his demerits as "a lack of power to follow in thought the path of greatest resistence," and "immersion in a world of specialization, of attention to parts, of endemic sentimentality."[8]

A similar period of depression swept over him in 1917 when some of the staff members of the training school became openly critical of his administration. In their statement to the director, they charged that the catalog description of the school "gives the impression of a big institution where we have a very small one." They also complained that the "expert advice and instruction" needed to train their students adequately was lacking, that the instruction that was imparted was too heavy on "philosophy and enthusiasm" and too lacking in the techniques and practical knowledge necessary "to equip each student so that he may maintain his foothold wherever placed." Finally, they told Collier, too many programs had been initiated and then dropped, and the practice work had suffered from a lack of attention because "we are without adequate means or personnel for supervision."

At first, Collier attempted a rebuttal to the charges. Though the school was small in numbers, he replied, "it is in fact a big institution," as anyone "who knows how graduate departments of universities are organized," would recognize. The teaching staff, while too small for lecture classes, he admitted, was bolstered by the "best social experts in New York" in its seminars where, for the "conversational" method advocated by the school, they were more than adequate. He was particularly indignant at the charge that the school was deficient in technique and practical knowledge. It was impossible in eight months to teach the students everything they should know. To attempt to do so would result in "classroom cramming and superficial imitative work." The training school "exists to prove that conventional academic methods are not always the right methods," he wrote, and "in certain specialities we repudiate the possibility of formal teaching—notably forum work, dramatics, and hospitality." The virtue of the training school as compared with social-work programs at the surrounding universities, he chided, was that it "does impart the specialities of human conduct and social organization . . . and the experience of experimentally attempting something." The training school simply could not be evaluated by conventional methods; it was to be judged by "results, not methods." Nor was it true that the school had abandoned important programs. The training school had never intended "institutional work"; from the beginning, its goal had been "progressive social experimentation—work organic and therefore adaptable." The truth was that the past two years had seen "much foundation work which is just becoming immediately useful: We have been building our house while we were living in it." That, he said, "is the new conception of education and of social action. What other use would our school have? "

Having answered his critics in the self-righteous manner that was his lifelong custom, Collier then admitted to other shortcomings. He had not sought advice frequently enough; he had been "hasty rather than thorough"; he had not thought out the reasons for certain programs; he had "improvised rather than planned." More serious than any of these failings, however, he admitted, was the fact that he had depended upon his "radicalism to justify itself *qua* radicalism rather than through the delivery of the goods."[9]

The year 1917 was a particularly difficult one. After assuming the presidency of the National Conference of Community Centers in the spring, Collier was often called upon for speaking engagements. In addition, he assumed the chairmanship of the Committee on Public Education, a political lobby seeking the reelection of Mayor Mitchell in the face of vigorous opposition from Tammany Hall. He was also engaged in a new enterprise, the Gramercy Park Community Clearing House, through which he hoped to demon-

strate the need for community centers to coordinate the
welfare programs of the city and those of private philanthropic organizations with the "real needs of the people."
The future of the clearing house, which he hoped to have
municipalized because of his inability to finance its activity
through private sources, and the future of the community
centers were both heavily dependent on Mitchell's reelection, the chances of which, as the summer went on, he
knew to be precariously slim.

Against this background of increasing work and doubt,
he penned a letter to the director of the People's Institute, Charles Sanderson, which because of its candid self-
evaluation, is reproduced below.

August 8, /1917/[10]

My dear Dr. Sanderson:

I will state how the Institute's and my relation looks to
me now . . . without reference to qualifying considerations;
and will put the letter aside.

I. Point of View of the Institute

My Values:

1. I have Sprague-Smith's instincts and philosophy toward life, society, people; natively, by previous education
and by absorption from him. I have carried them forward in
a more many-sided way in relation to modern things. So
the tradition and vital principle of the Institute gains
through me.

2. I am determined the Institute shall concern itself with
social action rather than social friction: that is, with the improvement of social structure; the release of energy rather
than the restriction of non-essential evils; social safety
through social achievement; an intensified and enriched
rather than a merely extended democracy; the encouragement of variety rather than the search for uniformity . . . I
am *determined* exactly as Sprague-Smith was, that where I
work this philosophy and religion shall prevail, that no
other possible advantage could substitute for it; and while I
would not sink the Institute rather than adulterate the principle, I would at once separate myself from the Institute
rather than adulterate it . . . .

3. I am energetic, persistent, ingenious, inventive: being

convinced that to do and not to talk is our mission . . . .
This means that I press constantly away, not merely from
sterile successes but from reliance on the talk method . . .
and as said above, I do this with energy, doggedness and
inventiveness.

I. My demerits:

1. I attempt to do more than I can do. The result is a condition of hastiness on my part, the great enemy of efficiency and wisdom; of a certain lack of *fibre* in the separate
parts of the work, and of coordination . . . . The causes are
(a) a dominance of the idea of vision with (b) a correspond-
ing paling of the sense of responsibility for the things
which the idea or vision have produced, (a) an exaggerated
lack of concern for myself, with (b) an egoism which would
be appropriate to a child at play, (a) a sensitiveness toward
and concern with the personalities of those working with
me which makes for their own self-discovery but makes
against discipline, with (b) an indisposition to concern myself methodically (rather than sporadically) with their actual
deficiences, the difficulties under which they labor, the
complexes into which they gravitate with one another . . . .

2. The very factors mentioned above have caused me to
neglect our trustees and the work of getting and educating
and holding our financial support.

3. Due to a combination of past experience, egotism, im-
patience of forms, hatred of safeguards, red-tape, efficiency
tests based on false values; and due to self-indulgence and a
refusal to intellectually recognize that truth must be efficient in lesser ways as well as in ultimate ways, and that
current modes of measurement must be used until better
modes are devised: due to this and other causes good and
bad I have tended to always travel, as it were, unarmed and
naked in the jungle, not to speak of the town. . . .

What wonder that I have caused bewilderment, exas-
peration, even distrust. And from the standpoint of the organization, the law of diminishing returns must come into
play if it has not already done so, the liability total must
rise faster and be more indisputably correct than the
asset total.

II. Point of View of Myself

The Advantages.

1. Probably no other institution in which I would want

to work, would have had so much use for my values or so much toleration for my demerits . . . . I have been marvelously allowed, expected, and by the situation required, to develop my powers. The Institute did not discover me to myself, did not awaken me to the world, but it has enabled me to work over into social practice enough of nearly everything vital in me, to insure that it will continue to function socially, to function in reality, that is. So that my very nature is indebted to the Institute. Again: in so far as I have been prevented from expressing myself, from doing things, in so far as I have failed, I have been compelled to see that it was not due to religion, capital, the villainy of others or the mental inferiority of others, while at the same time I have been prevented from becoming fatalistic about my own impracticality. Such an advantage does not often come to idealistic and temperamental people.

So I have become habitually sanguine about the social order and about myself, and have acquired (for the benefit of others at least) a philosophy of perpetual adaptation on behalf of essentials.

2. The above relates to the past and its results. Looking forward it is clear that personally I have yet a big forward step to take psychically and as a worker; while if all I have put down here be correct, and some big X quantity hasn't been left out, then it follows that anything I have achieved in the past is but a ghost to what I *could* achieve through changes in my own mechanics or in the mechanics of the organization. In other words, I haven't been graduated yet, and haven't finished my work yet, viewing the Institute as a school of life and a vehicle of action.

II. The Disadvantages.

1. . . . I have overworked, have failed to develop on the scientific side as I might have done (as I must do), have gone for long periods amid states of mind and conditions of work which have abolished all the joy of living other than the mere abiding sense of determined adventure, and that remote life of imagination, astronomy, speculation about life, mysticism. Is there . . . no possibility or little possibility of bridging the gulf, of getting a real integration, of achieving compatibility?

2. There is another phase of my nature which has never

had its "innings." I am happy in quiet and in nature, and am *at last* sure that thought and mood lead me toward reality, not away from it. My youth is passing and yet is not gone. Staying in the Institute, hazarding the continuance of conditions like those of the past, I am jeopardizing my higher and deeper career. Nearly every clearest insight tells me that while the past years of social work have been only a fragment, almost no more than a somnambulism, yet they have been enough when viewed as a period of education for my real work. Nothing tells me that I can succeed in this real work (in general, literature) but I know that my type of work is such that I must succeed greatly in it or else fail completely; and I believe that only a protracted concentration in quiet can bring an answer to the problem. Such a quiet might be had while continuing my social work (i.e., my Institute's work,) but nine years have only brought its opposite; and time is passing and the balance inside of me is trembling.

3. To stay with the Institute merely as one talking and writing and not carrying forward the work of engineering, would be no solution, for the reasons stated on the first page. The Institute's role is action, not talk; experimental sociology is action, with talk only as a means, and those who conceive inventions must, in this field at least, build their own models. The thing that has stirred me in an unpleasant way of late, has been the insistency of, for example, Lewisohn, on the supreme importance of mere executive hustling, with the complementary thought that those who possess ideas must, unless they are the most obviously effective of hustlers, retire to a sort of birdcage for the delectation of community. The Institute can become more efficient while remaining loyal to its aims and to the inevitable methods which go with those aims, but if the point of view just caricatured should prevail the Institute would have to change its very aim or else crumple under the criticism. In an immediate way, the morale of the workers will be destroyed and the creative ones will suffer most of all, as this view bears in on them. It has preyed on Miss Taylor and Miss McDowell already, and it has filled me with ire till I worked across to the point of view of this letter.

Well, for what it is worth——   © Mrs. Grace Collier

Despite his misgivings about continuing in the employment of the People's Institute, Collier did not resign in 1917.
Instead, he intensified his efforts toward converting the public schools to community centers on a national scale. As he
now expressed it, American entrance into the war made the
conversion more necessary than ever before.

The school–community center movement, he wrote in
the *American City*, shortly after becoming president of the
National Conference of Community Centers is the "newest
embodiment of the democratic idea. The proper assembling
place for the energies of the war—especially the civil energies—is the school building." Schools, he maintained,
should "be mobilized every afternoon and evening and Sat-
urday and Sunday for patriotic work." Not only could much
useful war work be coordinated through the community centers, but in addition, by bringing "citizens" together, "bonds
creating Americanism among Americans and immigrants
alike" could be forged. To illustrate the importance of the
community center in the work of integrating immigrants
into the American way of life, he announced in October 1917
that the training school would undertake a new program
to train teachers for americanization work in community-
center night schools.

In Pittsburgh, before the National Conference of Social
Work in June 1917, Collier elaborated on the theme of the
community center as the coordinating point of the civilian
war effort. The war, he told the delegates, had given "the
average man" a new lease on life. It had demonstrated that
an "organized laity" guided by a "social expert" could perform "many tasks undreamed of—can do the equivalent of
offices trained for years." By participating in and organizing
necessary, patriotic tasks like Red Cross work, war-bond
drives, and food-conservation campaigns, the common people were experiencing "the recovery of a sense of dignity
and power." "Today people are pawns and onlookers, not because of designing leaders," but because of "the unconscious
evolutions of social mechanisms," he wrote simultaneously
in the *Journal of Home Economics*. The war was demon-

strating that the community center was a particularly efficient vehicle for coordination in the urban areas.

During the summer of 1917 Collier also launched a bid to
absorb public and private welfare programs into the community-center movement. His experience in New York City,
he told the delegates to the National Conference of Social
Work, had demonstrated that the typical public welfare
bureau in a large city was so "highly centralized, standard-
ized," that it failed to administer adequately to the needs of
the people whom it supposedly served. Private philanthropic
welfare programs were similarly structured. There was a
need, he argued, for bringing these bureaus into a closer relationship with the leaders of already existing groups of the
"plain people" in such a way that the people themselves
could cooperate in improving their lives and their environment. Such a relationship had been successfully created at
the Gramercy Park Community Clearing House where the
poeple had taken over "some measure of their own destiny"
in cooperation with public and private welfare authorities.
He urged social workers to become community-center workers, to abandon the emphasis upon doing things for others,
and instead "to discover and energize the small groups already existing in the neighborhood, define their opportunities, make it financially possible for them to function." The
purpose of the community-center movement, he said, was
"not to do away with technique or with professional leadership, but to fulfill it," to create "a feeling of intimacy, or
interdependence between government and individual . . .
so that the individual will shape himself instead of being
shaped." He delivered a similar message to home econo-
mists a few weeks later, urging them to abandon their narrow and specialized view and to enter into the "community
center environment" where they could "do some good in
the real—the socially and psychologically real—world."[11]

Collier's numerous speeches and articles extolling the
virtues of community centers were based upon the optimistic belief that the war had demonstrated their need,
that the movement had finally come into its own and could

not be denied. Nothing could have been farther from the truth in his own bailiwick, New York City. In January there were rumblings of discontent from school principals in Queens and Brooklyn, who charged that People's Institute–administered community centers there had exhibited "immoral motion pictures" and had condoned "indecent and immoral dancing" at three public high schools. One of the principals attacked the practice of charging admission fees for the movies and the dances, saying that the practice of admitting anyone who could pay the fee had resulted in the attendance of "undesirable elements" who would otherwise have been excluded from the facilities. The *New York Times* did not report the nature of the offensive movies, but it did quote the principals as saying that the "immoral dancing consisted of bodies in close contact and the head of the female pressed against that of her partner."

More serious than the complaints of the professional schoolmen was the defeat of the Mitchell administration in the fall 1917 city elections. As chairman of the Committee on Public Education, Collier had waged a vigorous campaign against the Tammany Hall opposition, publicly issuing a call in October for "volunteers to oppose the election of Tammany Hall candidates" because of the prospect "that the public school will be exploited if they are elected." Following Mitchell's crushing defeat in November, a new and unfriendly Board of Education abruptly closed the public schools to all extracurricular activities except the americanization classes, citing the coal shortage as its reason for doing so.

John Collier's response to Mitchell's defeat and to the closing of the New York community centers was truly remarkable. It was also typical of the determination and ingenuity he would exhibit again and again during the 1920s when his efforts in behalf of the American Indian appeared to be heading toward certain defeat.

A few days after Mitchell's defeat, Collier talked to reporters who asked why he believed that the mayor, who had generally supported the interests of the average man, had been so soundly whipped. Collier responded that the election had demonstrated what the People's Institute had been saying for years: "No set of persons can successfully self-constitute themselves as arbiters of the public weal, to dictate gratuitously what form of government, good or bad, the people shall have." The lesson of the campaign, he said, was that "forcible feeding of good government to the body politic is at an end; the people have started in to reform the reformers and haul down the uplifters." The time had come to quit trying to make citizens of the New York masses; in the future, advocates of good government would have to recognize that their true task was to "help them make good citizens of themselves." We must, he concluded "work from the bottom—from the masses of the people—and not from the so-called top."[12]

Having lost his public support in the city, Collier now turned to the federal government for help. The americanization classes organized by the training school in the fall of 1917 had earlier attracted the attention and support of the Council of National Defense, the nation's chief preparedness agency, which was composed of six cabinet officers and seven civilians under the chairmanship of Secretary of War, Newton D. Baker. Franklin K. Lane, an ex-officio member of the council as secretary of the interior, was particularly interested in the americanization program because of his desire to coordinate all americanization work through a subordinate office in his department, the Bureau of Education.

It was immediately after the mayoralty contest, Collier wrote, that "we realized that community work must be made over into war work if it was to be kept going in New York." Relying upon the goodwill that the training school enjoyed as an early proponent of americanization work, and utilizing the name of the National Conference of Community Centers, Collier urged the Council of National Defense to consider the possibility of "carrying out war work through neighborhood organization." His plan, essentially a combination of the school–community center idea and that of the clearing house, "involved the organization of the people

into autonomous groups and organization of all war work
and social agencies into an advisory body cooperating with
the people in each locality . . . ." In early 1918, the Council
of National Defense officially endorsed his plan and urged
the formation of "community councils of defense" in every
city in the nation.

Under Collier's direction, pressure was now applied to
the New York City Council for adoption of the plan. The
Council of National Defense officially requested the city to
assume leadership of the community-council movement.
President Wilson issued a stirring call in behalf of the councils in February 1918, in which he also advocated the school
as the most appropriate site for the location of the councils.
In March, the president hailed the councils as a force that
would "weld the nation together as no nation of great size
had ever been welded before." Simultaneously, the president's daughter, Margaret Wilson, requested the New York
Board of Education to delegate its authority over community work to a single director who would then assume complete responsibility for the conduct of community councils
located in the public schools. Meanwhile, Collier was lobbying throughout the city "to get the plan adopted officially
in its most radical shape."

In June 1918, the City Council and the mayor gave their
blessing to the use of the public schools as community councils. Shortly thereafter the Board of Education appointed
Dr. Albert Shiels, the former superintendent of the Los Angeles school system and a member of the training school's
advisory council, to the post of community-council director. Within less than six months Collier had revived the defunct community-center movement in the city and had
placed it on a seemingly firmer footing than it had ever before enjoyed.

The training school also prospered. Collier reported in
1918 that its programs had doubled in "volume and variety"
over the previous year. The training school had become
"quasi-official now. Our lectures are held in the public library; our Americanization course is practically a normal

school for the Board of Education and the Committee on Aliens of the Mayor's Committee on Defense; and our practice centers are maintained through the official cooperation of no less than 13 departments of the New York City Government." In the 1918–19 term he planned to convert the training school into "a genuine war work school."[13]

Collier's phenomenal success in promoting the community councils, however, at last resulted in his decision to withdraw from the work of the People's Institute. On June 13, he wrote Dr. Sanderson that it was "at last clear that I must ask the Trustees for a leave of absence, with pay if this can be done, preferably for an indefinite time." His reason was simply that "I have a supreme opportunity in the Community Council work, which furthermore is the largest fulfillment of the Institute's purposes during all the years of its work. Community Councils must have first call on my energies, thought, influence, and time." He had been offered a position on the executive committee of the Greater New York Community Council and the job of secretary at the "demonstration Community Council . . . of the Bellevue-Gramercy area," he told Sanderson. To perform these important tasks it was necessary that he "be politically unhampered"; as matters then stood, many of the people and the institutions to which he would have to appeal for funds and assistance "regard the People's Institute as a competing institution and insist on regarding me as one whose duty it is to look out after my own organization first." The request for a leave of absence was granted, apparently with pay; Collier continued as a lecturer at the training school, but its administration was divided among Lucy Collier and other members of the staff.[14]

Following his decision to devote full time to the community-council movement, Collier again became active as a speaker and a writer. In July 1918, he addressed the National Education Association at its annual meeting in New York. His theme, later expanded into a series of articles appearing in the *Survey* in August and September was "The Community Council—Democracy Every Day." President Wilson, he reminded the delegates, had pledged that "we should not merely win the war but in winning the war we should pledge ourselves to such ends, commit ourselves to such methods, as would restore our spiritual birthright, our destiny, to us." The war, he wrote in the *Survey* articles, had alerted the nation to dangers not "perceived before Germany crossed the Belgian frontier: the subsidence of the spiritual level, the death of adventurousness, the crushing out of human nature by physical nature and corporate machinery—that slow death which accompanies . . . the control of life by methods which take responsibility away from the average man." While the immediate purpose of the community-council movement was to win "a martial victory," it looked "far beyond" the war: "we are seeking for our people the restoration of the life of the spirit, for our children the restoration of great opportunity." He also warned that where people were brought together "to talk and to decide," political and economic topics would eventually come under scrutiny, but he hoped that criticism would not be misunderstood by "the authorities," that the councils would not be charged with "disloyalty"; otherwise "the result will be bad for the nation."

While Collier was attempting to enlist support for the movement in the East, Edward L. Burchard, the secretary of the National Conference of Community Centers, and Carol Aronovici were performing a similar service in the Midwest. Both appeared before the National Conference of Social Work at Kansas City in May. Aronovici's paper advocated the use of the schools as community-council centers; Burchard's traced the evolution of the school–community centers into the community–council movement. Like Collier, Burchard stressed that there was potential danger to established ways in the growth of the community councils. Private philanthrophy, he warned, could conceivably "lose its life in this sea of public social resources." He urged the private agencies, however, not to take a narrow, selfish view of the community-council movement, but instead to "perform a unique service by finding [their] niche in this more democratic community public life."[15] Burchard's speech was the first indication of growing opposition from the private philanthropic organizations to the community councils, an opposition that, together with the signing of the armistice in November 1918, would result in their collapse. During the summer and fall of 1918, however, such a possibility seemed quite remote. Indeed, all indications were that the community-council movement would grow.

When the influenza epidemic swept the nation in the early fall of 1918, Collier, who had become interested in the possibility of using the community councils as neighborhood public-health centers, quickly assumed leadership of a city-wide effort to cope with the disease. In cooperation with the city health department, he turned the training school into an "influenza district headquarters," from which all medical services throughout the city were coordinated. Available doctors, nurses, and practical nurses were mobilized and dispatched in accordance with requests for medical assistance originating in the community councils. An estimated 40,000 persons were provided medical attention or advice through the network of the community councils.

Collier's interest in public-health work was undoubtedly stimulated by his wife, Lucy Collier, who had been active in local child-health programs sponsored by the institute since 1911. During the winter of 1917–18 Lucy Collier and a co-worker at the training school, Sally Lucas Jean, a former school nurse from Baltimore who joined the institute in 1917 to organize a department of health services, became engaged in a study to determine why so many young men called for active service were failing to meet the minimum standards set by the army. Under the direction of Dr. Emmett Holt, a New York specialist in childhood diseases, a team of physicians visited a number of city schools, where they performed extensive physical examinations. Holt's report, issued in the spring of 1918, revealed that malnutrition was widespread among school-age children and was the chief cause of the draftees' inability to pass the army's physical examinations. It estimated that 6 million children were suffering from the debilitating effects of malnutrition throughout the nation, and it indicted the nation's schools for "their tragic failure" to provide adequate health care for students in their custody. Holt's report was forwarded 'to the Council of National Defense, where it was closely studied. Almost immediately, Secretary of the Interior Lane seized the initiative by urging the creation of a national committee to continue the study. He pledged the full support of his Bureau of Education to the venture.

In June 1918, with Dr. Holt as president, the national Child Health Organization was created at the People's Institute. According to Lucy Collier, who became associate director, the purpose of the Child Health Organization was to interest "schools throughout the country in the use of scales [the new height-age-weight standardization scales] as an index of health, and in the daily teaching of health habits." At the request of Secretary Lane, the Child Health Organization created a special division within the federal Bureau of Education to prepare literature "printed on government presses and sent on request, free of charge, to teachers throughout the nation." By 1919 there were an estimated 10 million students enrolled in its school health program.

The leadership of the Child Health Organization was provided almost solely by persons associated with the People's Institute. In addition to Holt, Lucy Collier, and Sally Lucas Jean, who was named director of fieldwork, the board of directors included Collier, Mrs. Charles Beard, John Dewey, Father John A. Ryan, Mrs. Willard D. Straight, one of the institute's primary financial benefactors, and Ray Lyman Wilbur, the physician-president of Stanford University.

During the four years of its existence, the Child Health Organization met with a "phenomenal response from mothers across the country." Monthly health reports on each student and the teaching of health rules through games and jingles became commonplace in many schools. The Child Health Organization pioneered the modern hot lunch program and it enlisted the support of the General Federation of Women's Clubs, a potentially powerful lobby as the women's suffrage movement neared its goal; in 1918, Mrs. P. V. Pennybacker, the outgoing president of the federation was added to the board of directors. In 1922, several years after the Colliers had moved to California, the Child Health Organization merged with the American Child Hygiene Association to form the American Child Health Organization. Secretary of Commerce Herbert Hoover, whose wartime activities as director of the American Relief Administration had earned him a reputation as a leading humanitarian and organizer, was named president of the new organization, much to Collier's later disgust. Hoover, whose "philosophy, viewpoint, and administrative approach" were "utterly at odds" with those of the Child Health Organization, "thrust himself into the management" of the American Child Health Organization through the offer of financial support, according to Collier, and within two years he had "killed out the genius" of the former organization. Collier never forgave Hoover for his part in dismantling the Child Health Organization. His resentment was to surface frequently after 1929 as the two men publicly debated the direction of federal Indian policy.[16]

By October 1918, the community-council movement in New York was on the threshold of rapid expansion. Seven experimental councils had been created throughout the city, and a carefully prepared publicity campaign was now beginning in the pages of the city's newspaper. In language reminiscent of Collier's speeches in 1917, these articles proclaimed the neighborhood council as the best "means of direct communication between the government and the people" and characterized them as "neighborhood democracy made effective by organization. . . ." The war, they said, "pointed up the disorganized social condition of the nation" and revealed the need "to centralize the capacities, resources and liabilities of neighborhoods." Moreover, the coordination of energy that the councils would make possible was "not alone a war-time measure, it is a peace time necessity." The principle upon which the councils were founded, "to help unfortunates to help themselves," would, if continued after the war, ensure that there would not be a return to "Government from above." Instead, the continuance of community councils after the war would ensure that "it will be the will of the people creating the Government for the people." Having once learned how to work together, "the people will learn to give and take and in this democratic way the class barriers that have caused so much social and industrial unrest will be broken." A campaign for raising $170 million to build "a war chest" to obtain unity of effort among public and private war activities organizations was planned for November.

With the signing of the armistice on November 11, 1918, the community-council movement momentarily floundered. Despite the publicity campaign stressing the need for postwar community organization, the sense of urgency was lost once the national defense had been assured. The war chest campaign was cancelled. It was Secretary Franklin Lane who infused new life into the movement when, on November 17, he sent telegrams to all state community-council directors, urging them to proceed "at once" with the organization of what he now called "community councils of reconstruction." The end of war had indeed removed the need to organize for national defense, he explained, but pressing problems of demobilization, reconversion, and relief remained. In January 1919, echoing Lane, the director of the Council of National Defense called for a comprehensive program of community councils to cope with the problems of "returned servicemen, children, health, and Americanization." The necessity for "assimilating all foreign-born citizens into true American citizenship" remained one of the nation's chief tasks in the postwar period, he said. Under constant prodding, the community councils of New York were merged with the General Committee of the Council of Organizations, thereby uniting four hundred men's and women's organizations in the city. By May 1919, eighty-four community councils were in existence throughout the city.

The rapid growth of the community councils in New York, however, was matched by a correspondingly swift decline in Collier's influence in the movement, and in civic affairs generally. At its October 1918 board meeting, the directors of the People's Institute voted to "make every effort to transfer the work of the training school to some existing educational institution in the city before February 1, 1919, unless sufficient funds can be raised before then." The impetus for this decision apparently came from two different sources. Valentine Everett Macy, the wealthy philanthropist-financier who served as board chairman of the city's Teacher's College, had dedicated a considerable portion of his life to affiliating Teacher's College with Columbia University. He was also the treasurer of the training school. In the fall of 1918 he approached Collier with a proposal that the training school, leaderless since Collier's resignation in June, be incorporated into Teacher's College. Collier was adamantly opposed to the idea because of his deep-seated belief that teacher's colleges did nothing for their students except "stereotype their minds." After Collier's refusal, Macy withdrew his financial support from the training school, placing its future in jeopardy. Sam Lewisohn and Manny Strauss, the two other major supporters, now expressed doubt about its continuance. Strauss agreed to raise money to carry on the school if Collier's salary as director, which had run about $5,000 annually before his resignation, was not included.[17] On November 14, 1918, Collier addressed the following letter to the trustees of the training school and the trustees of the People's Institute, in which he summarized the work of the school and begged for a reprieve from the board's October decision. Because this letter also contains Collier's summary of the activities and philosophy of the training school, it is reproduced below.

November 14, 1918[18]

To the Trustees of the Training School for Community Workers and of the People's Institute:

We must meet in the near future to decide upon one of various alternative possibilities which lie ahead of the

Training School. A report on the work immediately behind
the school and some references to its history further back,
may assist in visualizing the future.

. . . (1) In three and a half years the school has given
whole time training to about 85 pupils and part time training, theoretical and practical, to about 235 more.

It is hard to measure educational results. More than 90%
of our regular students have been graduated into professional community work, and they have "made good." We
believe that all of them have carried away a method and
point of view which they owe to our school.

(2) The school's propaganda and demonstration work has
fused with the work of so many other organizations that it
cannot in every instance be sharply defined. The following
are among the achievements of the school:

1. The creation and development of the National Community Center Association.

2. The establishment of the National Community Center
Magazine.

3. The operation of four demonstration community centers which have served not merely as laboratories of
method for New York but as demonstration centers of national influence, inasmuch as they have been written about
and visited.

4. The reorganization of the William McKinley Community Center (P.S. 63) in which the new methods of group
government and of the regulation of community activities
through charter and contract were first put into operation.

5. The institution of community night schools for immigrants; the policy which we established has now been
adopted for all elementary night schools.

6. The bringing in of organized labor to the use of school
buildings. (This work began at P.S. 40 and has now been
extended to eight schools.)

7. We conducted a demonstration summer play school
three years ago, whose results are today as significant as
ever, though they have not been reproduced.

8. We conducted a demonstration summer health school
in P.S. 40 last summer. Food and health education, organized play, and symbolic dancing were used; many agencies
cooperated.

9. Through the alumni of P.S. 40 we have set in motion a work of vocational guidance to be extended over a two or three year period. It is experimental work, designed to carry further the experience gained by the Henry Street group and others.

10. We have kept to the fore our conception of Americanizing the immigrant through bringing his group into a vital relation with the community. We have not merely preached and written this idea but have continuously demonstrated it at the Wingate Center.

11. We set in motion the work which has resulted in the municipalization of school lunches. We were active in the campaign throughout.

12. We were responsible for the beginnings of the Child Health Organization and have been active in all its work. We shared the responsibility for arousing the interest of Secretary Lane in the problem of child health—from which it has come about that child health publicity is being carried out through the Bureau of Education at the expense of the government, the government's expenditure being some $12,000 a year.

13. We have been the leading continuous influence in the development of communal policy within the Department of Education, especially with reference to all phases of the use of school buildings after day school hours.

14. We shared in the creation and operation of the Community Clearing House, which joined 13 municipal departments in a cooperative activity within the Gramercy area and which forced out the methods of joint action between officials and citizens which are now one half of the National Community Council plan.

15. All of these results mentioned above, prepared the way for the Community Council of National Defense (now the Community Council of Reconstruction) whose origin dates back to the week after the mayoralty election in New York, 1917. The Community Council includes the community center but goes indefinitely beyond that conception which we had three years ago. It is really a synthesis of the community center as developed under our Training School leadership with the Community Clearing House mentioned above. Our real work has therefore become first of all the

work of training for the varied activities of Community
Councils. Our responsibility for the creation and development of Community Councils has been as follows:

After the election we realized that community work
must be made over into war work if it was to be kept going
in New York. We presented to various departments at
Washington a plan for carrying out war work through
neighborhood organizations. The plan involved the organization of the people into autonomous groups and the
organization of all war work and social agencies into an advisory body cooperating with the people in each locality;
this was the purely local phase of the plan, which in New
York City has been developed into an organization by bor-
oughs with a city clearing house, touching every phase of
the municipal life as well as of war work.

At Washington, the machinery of the National Community Center Association was devoted to getting this plan
adopted, and after the plan had been adopted by the Council of National Defense the National Community Center
Association lent itself to the task of focalizing through the
Community Council plan the various war programs of the
government and of quasi-government agencies.

Meantime, the Training School and the Community
Clearing House were struggling to get the plan in its most
radical shape adopted officially by New York. After four
months of effort, we succeeded.

At this time I secured permission from the trustees of
the People's Institute to give my whole time if necessary to
the development of Community Councils of National Defense. Except for the work of the Training School, I have
done nothing else since June 1st but Community Council
work; our effort was at its most intense and difficult stage
through the summer and there were no holidays.

We brought Dr. Shiels to New York, who was succeeded
by Dr. John Willis Slaughter, an ideal director for the Community Councils . . . .

In brief, we can point to the Community Council of National Defense both in its national and in its local aspects,
as an achievement which would not have been brought
about, so far as human knowledge can claim, save through
the activity of the Training School and its associated
organizations.

Meantime, the Training School is this year going forward with a curriculum more thorough and many-sided than that of any preceding year and with a student enrollment larger and more promising than the enrollment of any other year save the first.

Our Problem for the Future

It seems clear that the Training School cannot be financed as a wholly independent institution, and it is doubtful whether its best usefulness could be realized were it to remain wholly independent.

There are two kinds of affiliation which we might consider. The first is an affiliation, which would involve subordination, with one of the large universities or with the School of Philanthropy. The second is an affiliation, which would *not* involve subordination, with certain organizations which are doing public work—primarily the Community Councils of National Defense but likewise the Cooperative League of America, the U.S. Employment Service, and possibly the Red Cross.

If there is any financial help to be obtained, it probably lies in the direction of the second group of affiliations.

Looked at from the standpoint merely of public advantage, the following are some of the arguments for going under the wing of a large permanent educational institution.

(1) Students who took our course would receive academic credits in a more regular way than is now possible.

(2) Our methods of training through practice might become, within narrow limits, contagious; in other words, the universities might learn from us something about training for public service.

(3) Larger numbers of students would be brought within our influence if we were part of a university or even if we were an extension branch of a university. (We have obtained this same advantage through offering part-time courses, as when last year we enrolled 104 Americanization students for part-time work, or as when this year we have brought the employees of the U.S. Employment Service, as well as some special students, into our course on Public Employment Problems which is proving altogether successful.)

Disadvantages of Becoming Subordinate to a University

Our methods are thoroughly unconventional. They are not loose or unmethodical, but unconventional they certainly are. Their virtue lies in their unconventionality— which is another way of saying that we have found out how to get a point of view into a student and how to turn him into a producer rapidly, and that neither our point of view nor our pedagogical method are of the kind that universities like or are accustomed to.

Any of the universities would judge not our output but our method, and going under their control would mean accommodating to their habitual methods. It would mean not only a shrinkage of horizon for our students; more specifically it would unnecessarily protract their training and would insulate them from the realities into which we are seeking to plunge them.

We are not famous or wealthy or powerful enough to demand special privileges in any of these larger permanent institutions, and we would be compelled to adopt the protective coloration with which those who know universities are so familiar.

Advantages of Affiliating with Organizations doing Practical Work

The advantages of affiliating with organizations doing practical work, are primarily as follows:

(1) Our students become producers from the first day. Their output day by day is subjected to the test of effectiveness rather than of form.

(2) The practical organizations mentioned above, have now drawn to their support much of the best business brains and a good deal of the best academic brains of the community. All of these organizations appreciate the need for training, and a training school affiliated with them can draw on the best talent of each of these organizations without paying for it. This is precisely what we are now doing, with remarkable success, through our connection with the Public Employment Service.

(3) By having a regular affiliation with these public orga-

nizations, our Training School will be in a position more or less to shape the policy and forge out new methods for these organizations.

(4) There is a growing conscious need for specialized training, felt by those at the head of all of the organizations above mentioned. They ought to be willing to pay for this education just as employers pay for the education of their employees. The time has come when we should ask them to support the Training School and abandon the Training School if they will not support it at least in substantial part.

(5) As for our possible influence in pioneering on behalf of the universities in this field of training for public service: the prestige that we would get through being the official Training School for, for example, the Community Councils of New York, would do more to make Columbia University hospitable to our point of view and method, than anything we might demonstrate within Columbia University itself.

(6) Finally, the Training School is an outgrowth of the People's Institute, and the People's Institute exists to promote public movements. The original intention of the People's Institute will be best fulfilled if the Training School, retaining a certain measure of academic freedom for itself, and continuing to be an organic part of the Institute, can at the same time become an organic part at least of the Community Councils and possibly of the other movements mentioned above.

Recommendations

The staff of the Training School appears to be a unit in believing that the important connection for the school lies in the direction of practical movements, that any tie-up, closer than now exists, with academic institutions, should be postponed until after an attempt has been made to get into a stronger relation with for example, the Community Council movement.

It is not necessary that those who are financing Community Councils should incorporate the Training School budget in the Community Council budget. If the Community Councils are in the next month to raise a large sum of money, those who give this money would probably be willing, if so requested by the Executive Committee on Community Councils, to give the relatively small additional sum needed for the Training School.

In order to discuss these possibilities, we are arranging for a meeting of the Trustees both of the Training School and of the People's Institute, and to this meeting we are inviting Dr. John Willis Slaughter, Director of Community Councils.

> Respectfully,
> John Collier
> © Mrs. Grace Collier

Collier's attempt to forestall the dissolution of the training school was not successful. As a result of the cancellation of its winter fund drive, the New York Community Council was unable to offer economic assistance. On January 6, 1919, bowing to the inevitable, Collier submitted his resignation to both the training school and the People's Institute. In his letter to Director Sanderson he stated that he had talked recently with Samuel Lewisohn about his continued association with the institute and had informed Lewisohn on that occasion that it was his understanding that the institute's resources "were insufficient to retain me even if the Training School were given up." He also told Lewisohn that "no proposition had been made to me to remain under any conditions." Lewisohn assured him that "it was not his idea that I should be separated from the Institute" when his leave of absence expired, and he offered to take up the subject with other members of the board. Collier then stated that he would have to have a salary increase and "the subject was left indefinite."

Since his conversation with Lewisohn, Collier continued, he had not heard anything from anyone. In the meantime, he had "been asked to become organizing secretary for the National League for Constructive Immigration Legislation. While it goes exceedingly hard for me to draw out from the Institute or Training School or Community Council work, I apparently have no option. I have therefore accepted this offer and am resigning from the Institute and the Training

School, to take effect February first." Wistfully, he concluded: "I hope so to work things out that, although giving
whole time to the Immigration League, I can have a good
deal to do with local New York developments and with the
community movement nationally."[19]

The National League for Constructive Immigration Legislation was the brainchild of the Reverend Sidney Gulick,
a former missionary to Japan and the brother of Luther Gulick, Collier's coworker in the school–social center movement. In 1914, Gulick first advanced a nondiscriminatory
quota scheme "to eliminate discrimination against the Jap-
anese by applying a uniform principle to all nationalities."
Gulick's quota proposal, which was incorporated into law
in 1921, was, in the judgment of one authority, "the one real
effort on the part of liberals to define a clear-cut alternative
to the main drift of post-war restriction" on immigration.
Its basic thrust was a limitation on wholesale immigration
to the United States through the imposition of national
quotas proportionate to the number of naturalized citizens
and their American-born children already residing in the
United States.

In addition to Collier, Gulick was successful in winning a
number of prominent liberals and settlement-house workers to his cause: Norman Hapgood, Frederick Howe, James
Harvey Robinson, Vida Scudder, Oswald Garrison Villard,
George Kennan, and Lillian D. Wald, to mention a few. In
their appeal for national support, they wrote that the "regulation, distribution, [and] treatment of immigrants and
the education of resident aliens for citizenship are matters
of paramount importance." The nation, their literature
stated, was suffering from "an indigestion of unamerican-
ized foreigners" who had unwisely been allowed to "settle
in congested masses and become voters without becoming
properly qualified. They menace our democracy and lower
our standards of living." The language of this appeal was obviously a departure from the descriptions of the immigrants
that Collier had penned for the previous ten years, and in
the fall of 1919 he withdrew from the league.[20]

With his resignation from the League for Constructive Immigration, Collier's New York career came to an end. Just as he had earlier been cut off from the People's Institute, so, too, had he been gradually supplanted in the hierarchy of the New York community-council movement. In April 1916, Dorothy Whitney Straight, one of the institute's principal benefactors, collected a group of her wealthy friends to discuss a new experiment in the field of community organization. The National Social Unit Organization (NSUO), which resulted from this meeting, had as its goal essentially the same purpose as the community councils: the promotion of democratic community organization "through which the citizenship as a whole can participate directly in the control of community affairs." But the NSUO departed from the means that Collier had long advocated to achieve this goal. The NSUO was an essentially philanthropic organization that sought to organize neighborhoods through the work of highly skilled and well-paid specialists whose salaries were paid jointly by the NSUO and local communities willing to participate in the program. It was obviously an experiment in community organization that was to be organized from the top down, rather than from the bottom up, as Collier had advocated. Nor were communities organized by the NSUO to have any control over the finances of the venture. In 1917, the NSUO launched a liberally financed, three-year experiment in Cincinnati.

Two years later, at the height of the "red scare," the NSUO announced the creation of a national planning and research staff to prepare for expansion of the experiment. Simultaneously, Secretary of Interior Franklin K. Lane, who had just failed in his efforts to obtain federal appropriations for the continuance of the community-council movement, was successfully persuaded to accept the national chairmanship of the NSUO. Daniel Guggenheim came forward to assist in raising the expansion fund; Charles Edison, the board chairman of Commonwealth Edison, accepted the office of treasurer; Mrs. Daniel Guggenheim and Mrs. Charles Tiffany joined the board of directors. At a dinner held at the

Women's University Club in New York on October 14, 1919, the decision to expand was made following a speech in which the point was made that "a new social order is looming on the horizon." That new order, the speaker warned, "would come inevitably." The only choice that lay before the distinguished assembly was whether the change would come by "revolution or in a sane, normal way, in a constructive idea of democracy or in a destructive idea."

Two months after the decision to expand the experiment, the New York community councils and the National Social Unit Organization were merged in such a way as to ensure the dominance of the NSUO philosophy. In exchange for placing the director of the New York community council on the board of the NSUO, it in turn received six seats on the board of the community council. Dorothy Straight and Mr. Daniel Guggenheim were chosen as two of the new directors. Elaborate plans for the inauguration of a "unit" in New York were announced late in December 1919. Then in early 1920, the NSUO suddenly dissolved. The "red scare" was now waning and the mayor of Cincinnati had refused to renew the NSUO contract there.

Throughout the summer and fall of 1919, Collier watched helplessly as the community-council movement collapsed. In June he and James Ford journeyed to Atlantic City to deliver papers before the National Conference of Social Work. Both men cautioned against the substitution of philanthropy for "independent, self-operating neighborhood community councils," and Collier punctuated his speech with the statement that "the prestige of the good, of the rich, of the upper class reformer is nearly ended." In July he gave reporters a guarded endorsement of the NSUO, but he carefully distinguished between the self-supporting aspects of the community councils and the reliance of the "units" on philanthropic assistance. By September he found it necessary to defend the concept of self-government against the charge of anarchism, but he could not resist a veiled denouncement of the NSUO for its reliance upon "the distant philanthropist," the "non-resident, irresponsible philanthropist" whose financial control would eventually bring "control over the people's thinking, the people's sentiments, the people's leisure life, the people's cooperative action . . . ." Although he was invited to speak at the October dinner at which the decision was made to expand the NSUO nationally, both his ideas and his services were pointedly ignored. In November, in a kind of valedictory address to the New York community-center movement, he vigorously championed its original aim—"to bring every citizen and every group into daily contact with the serious problems of the community"—and he characterized the NSUO experiment, by contrast, as "just an improvement society." It was his last statement in behalf of the school–community center movement. In October 1919, turning his back on ten years of urban community development work in New York, he left for California to begin a new career.[21]

In later years, writing without the benefit of the contemporary records used here, Collier described the years from 1908 to 1919 as "the hardest years of my life to relate." They were, he said, largely "blotted out from my memory by the later events of my life." He referred to the defeat of the Mitchell administration, the withdrawal of financial support from the training school, and the collapse of the national community-center movement following the armistice as only "circumstantial details" in the "perishing of the great New York endeavors." The real cause of his failure in New York, he concluded in retrospect, was the triumph of the "gesellschaft mode of life." The People's Institute, he wrote, was "formed expressly to counteract this isolating of the self within the crowd," but its efforts "to bring to the common folk of New York . . . the gemeinschaft mode of life (the sufficing brotherhood, within innumerable local communities which are moved by shared purposes) . . . faded before the scorching onset of the gesellschaft mode of life— before the shattering, aggressive drive toward competitive utility."[22]

Perhaps Collier was right. Perhaps the impersonal and

relentless "pressures of the non-constructive outer (western) world" were too strong for any individual to overcome. But such an explanation, a comforting and popular one among intellectuals in the postwar decade, does not tell the complete story. By 1920 John Collier had developed certain character traits that made it difficult for him to work cooperatively with other people. Since these characteristics were to become even more pronounced after he turned his attention to the reform of federal Indian policy, it is well to pause briefly here to examine them.

During his years at the People's Institute, Collier's efforts to revive civic pride and citizen participation in the affairs of urban government revealed his lifelong dedication to the democratic process, to the involvement of every individual in all matters that affected the quality of his life. Underlying his support of first the school–social center movement and later the community-council movement was a strong belief in both the capability of the common man to participate in matters of public concern and his desire to do so. These early years also revealed Collier's tendency to assume that the goals and the values of the common man were identical with his own.

In practice, however, Collier came to realize that the common man had to be aroused to participation in civic affairs; it was not sufficient just to make the opportunity available. He also learned that the average man had to be guided toward activity in behalf of the right causes. This was the lesson he first learned in 1914 when, having observed a lack of adult participation in the social centers and an absence of cooperation between different ethnic groups, he successfully solved both problems by organizing and directing the Pageant of Nations.

After his return to New York from the wilderness in the fall of 1914, Collier immediately resolved to create a sense of direction and a unity of purpose within the social-center movement. It was for this reason that he organized the training school for community workers. The training school, however, represented a subtle shift in his thinking. The concept of an elite now entered into his theory about the democratic process. A "social expert" was now necessary to direct the actions of "the organized laity." It was also necessary to impart certain techniques to this elite that would enable them to evoke "the spirit of individual spontaneity and also of sustained group thinking" from the residents of the neighborhoods in which they worked. The disparity between his earlier faith in the ability of the common man and his new insistence upon an elite was possible only because Collier was certain that the ideas and values of the two were identical. It would have been inconceivable to him that substantive differences might arise between him and his constituents or between him and other men of goodwill.

So convinced was Collier of the righteousness of his cause and the purity of his motivation that he found it impossible to accept compromise or to tolerate opposition. Anyone who dared to challenge his authority or question his methods was written off as corrupt, the representative of vested interests, or, at best, misguided. This black-and-white approach to the solution of complex problems, first observable in his fight with Edward J. Ward and later in his refusal to permit any other institution to share in the training of community-center directors, turned all his battles into crusades of right against wrong, of justice against injustice. It won him the undying loyalty of his supporters and it made him an implacable foe to his opponents. But it also limited his effectiveness as a reformer for, as both these instances also revealed, there was a strong tendency in Collier's nature to destroy a program or abandon an idea rather than share it with others.

Collier's use of liberal rhetoric should not cause us to overlook the dogmatism that pervaded most of his actions. In those areas where he formed a passionate attachment to certain means, there was only one way to accomplish the desired reform: his way. Because he was so often right in his analysis of the best way to correct injustice, this character defect was usually shrugged off by his supporters. But in a number of instances, John Collier was wrong, and in these instances his intolerance to criticism and his jealous resentment of competition were to cloud his judgment and weaken his cause.

Collier also exhibited difficulty in matching means with ends. Although he was usually quite clear in describing means, he often found it difficult to articulate ends or goals with the same precision. This difficulty was particularly apparent in his efforts in behalf of the social center–community council movement. Here the goal was a vague replacement of government for the people with government by the people. Had the goal of the community-council movement been realized, it is obvious that the ground rules for political activity in urban America would not just have been changed, they would have been revolutionized. But Collier never looked that far ahead. Most of the time he was preoccupied with the survival of a few experimental centers or councils. Profiting from the experience of Ward in Rochester, he was able to see that political and financial autonomy were necessary means toward the survival of the movment. Yet, despite his public statements extolling autonomy, it is obvious that the New York experiment was, from its inception, heavily dependent upon forces outside the neighborhood. First, it was dependent upon support from the Gaynor and Mitchell administrations; later, it relied upon support from the federal government. Collier never acknowledged this dependence in his descriptions of the movement. He tended instead to describe the community-council movement in glowing abstractions, all the while keeping it alive by means which made it impossible to attain the desired goal. When the inevitable collapse came, he placed the blame upon selfish philanthropists and politicians, not upon the movement's financial dependence upon the philanthropists and politicians.

A similar conflict between means and ends was to become apparent in Collier's struggle for the reform of federal Indian policy. During the 1920s, when he became the leading critic of an outmoded and archaic system, the means that he advanced for the reform of federal Indian policy won ever-increasing respect. The vagueness that enveloped his statements about the goal of federal Indian policy was a distinct advantage. Sometimes he seemed to envision the isolation of the Indians from a corrupting white society, a proposal that brought him support from intellectuals who saw virtue in the primitive life. At other times he appeared to call for interaction between the two cultures, a position that won him friends among the supporters of the traditional forces of assimilation. It was only after he became commissioner of Indian affairs in 1933, when it became necessary to define goals, that the conflict between means and ends became apparent. Some of his supporters who approved the idea of financial autonomy for Indian communities were opposed to the concept of cultural independence. Others who favored the goal of cultural autonomy could not accept the idea of political autonomy, the idea of Indians governing themselves apart from their white neighbors. Still others, while favoring political autonomy, found it impossible to accept either financial or cultural independence. Thus, just as there were strengths and weaknesses in Collier's passionate dogmatism, so, too, were there disadvantages as well as advantages in his vague description of goals.

It is necessary then to distinguish carefully between what Collier said and what he did, between what he advocated and what he accomplished. It is also necessary to distinguish between his interpretation of events and that of his opponents. These distinctions are perhaps so obvious that one might question the necessity to mention them. The reason is that John Collier was such a gifted polemist that it is his side of the story that has survived. Wherever he went during the 1920s and 1930s, he always carried with him a portable typewriter. Whenever there was an idle moment, he dashed off a newspaper or a magazine article, a press release, or a newsletter. An incredible volume of words, which told only his side of the story, poured forth from the tiny machine. When the United States Senate undertook to investigate the condition of the Indians in 1927, it was Collier who planned the hearings and provided most of the witnesses. When he became Indian commissioner, he created the only magazine in the bureau's history in order to broadcast his version of the story. His *Indians of the Americas*, first published in 1947 and now in its fifteenth printing, has sold more than 300,000 copies. It remains a standard source for the history of federal Indian policy in the twentieth century.

In general, the history of federal Indian policy between the years 1921 and 1945 has been told only from Collier's point of view.[23] In the following pages, an attempt will be made to provide greater perspective against which to evaluate the substantive changes proposed during this exciting and significant period.

Discovering the American Indian (1919–21)

After delivering his parting blast at the philanthropists, Collier left New York for California. His sights were still fixed on community development work. His knowledge of American Indians remained slight and superficial, and his concern for their cultural survival, controlled as it was by what he called the "prevailing anthropological view of these years that all primitive and ancient cultures were doomed to be swallowed up by the white world," was all but non-existent.[1] Yet within the year he would discover among the Pueblo Indians in New Mexico the kind of community life he had unsuccessfully labored to create for the past eleven years. A new and more important career was in the making, one that would have been impossible without the support and encouragement of numerous Californians whom he was to meet during a nine-month stint with the California State Housing and Immigration Commission.

The California State Housing and Immigration Commission (CSHIC), created in 1914, a year after a riot of hop field workers at Wheatland, had achieved an enviable record as a progressive force in the assimilation of recent immigrants in the years before Collier became a member of its staff. Under the direction of its able president, Simon J. Lubin, a Sacramento businessman who during his college days at Harvard had spent "extended periods of residence in New York City's lower east side and at [Boston's] South End house," it had from the beginning adopted the doctrine of "immigrant gifts": the concept that had permeated the settlement and community-center movements and that said the immigrants had something to offer America. Lubin drafted the bill that created the CSHIC, and, following its passage, Governor Hiram Johnson named him the commission's first president. Starting with a belief that "before a man should be asked to become a good American by being worthy of his surroundings, those surroundings should be made worthy of a good American," Lubin launched an investigation of labor-camp facilities in 1914. So successful were his efforts to publicize the horrendous living conditions he found there, that the legislature brought the camps under public regulation in 1915 and charged the CSHIC with enforcement of the new law. Lubin subsequently inaugurated investigations into other phases of migratory worker life, unemployment, and unemployment relief, and he initiated an educational program for the children of migrant workers through the use of "home teachers," whose loyalties were to the CSHIC and the workers rather than to local school boards.[2] After the United States entered World War I, the commission embarked upon an ambitious americanization program in conjunction with the California State Council of National Defense and the General Federation of Women's Clubs (GFWC).

The moving force behind the americanization campaign was Mary (Mrs. Frank A.) Gibson, a Los Angeles resident who was both a member of the CSHIC and the chairwoman of the state Committee on Americanization of the GFWC. In 1917 Mrs. Gibson successfully appealed to the California Council of National Defense for financial assistance to

launch her americanization program. This work was encouraged by the CSHIC, which authorized her to take personal charge of the new experiment in its name.

One of Mrs. Gibson's first programs was the training of
fifty teachers in the techniques of "home teaching and general immigrant educational work." To supervise the training of these teachers she chose Ethel Richardson, a pioneer
in adult education in California and a former employee of
the state board of education. In another phase of the work
she assigned specific tasks associated with the americanization program to various women's organizations affiliated
with the state Council of National Defense. The Association of Collegiate Alumnae was given the task of surveying
immigrant working conditions in large factories; the Wom-
en's Christian Temperance Union was given responsibility
for a housing and recreation survey in immigrant communities; the Daughters of the American Revolution were
charged with arrangements for patriotic meetings among
immigrants; and the Native Daughters of the Golden West
were requested to arrange for foreign-language speakers at
these rallies and meetings.

In 1918 Mrs. Gibson proposed to her fellow members on
the CSHIC that the commission urge the federal government to create a cabinet-level Department of Americanization to coordinate and supervise the bewildering variety of
state and local programs that had sprung up since American
entrance into the war. Her suggestion was approved by the
commission, but when President Lubin broached the idea
before a national Americanization Conference in Washington, D.C., in April 1918, he failed to receive its endorsement. The CSHIC, however, voted to assume the task on a
state level that same spring. With the backing of the state
board of education, Ethel Richardson was appointed assistant superintendent of public instruction in charge of americanization. Under her direction, special courses to train
teachers to work with immigrants were organized through
the extension division of the University of California.
Mrs. Gibson attempted to further the work by calling upon

each of the five hundred women's clubs in California to institute seminars for the training of americanization workers. The idea, she later wrote, seemed "quite simple" at the time, but she was soon forced to recognize that it was impractical: there were "few or no persons of competence to lead [the seminars]." Miss Richardson also arrived at a similar conclusion by the fall of 1918. Not only were there not enough competent instructors to staff the extension classes, she reported, but her experience had taught her that "Americanization is not a problem for the schools alone; it requires all the force . . . of the community."

Despite the fact that the americanization program was obviously floundering in a sea of inexperience, in the spring of 1919 the California legislature passed a bill making part-time citizenship classes compulsory for all persons under the age of twenty-one whose mastery of the English language was below a sixth-grade level. As the only agencies in the state with any experience in the field, the CSHIC, the state board of education, and the extension division of the university were charged with responsibility for implementing the program. In June 1919, besieged by requests for advice and leadership from local school boards, the CSHIC voted to create the office of Director of Americanization and to "secure the services of some immigrationist of national reputation" to direct the work. It was at this stage that Collier came upon the scene.

At its July 1919 board meeting, the CSHIC hired Carol Aronovici as director of housing. Shortly after assuming his duties in September, Aronovici suggested Collier as a candidate for the americanization position. At the same time, the governor made funds available for a series of americanization institutes to be held throughout the state. In early November 1919, Collier was brought to Los Angeles by Mrs. Gibson to conduct the first of these experimental institutes. Within the next six weeks he traveled to Fresno, Sacramento, Oakland, and San Francisco, lecturing to more than a thousand teachers who were subsequently certified by the state board of education as "Teachers of Americanization."

Collier's institutes were anything but orthodox, but he apparently satisfied Mrs. Gibson and others who were behind the americanization work. The CSHIC, which had discovered that "Americanization was not flag raising and patriotic howling; that it was not suppression of speech and honest opinion; that it was more than teaching English to foreigners," gave him a free hand and he soon turned the classes into forums that "were much like those of the People's Institute." He discussed the European cooperative movement, the Russian revolution, St. Francis of Assisi, and Havelock Ellis's theory of sexuality. According to his own account, he was well received. At the CSHIC board meeting on December 12, 1919, Mrs. Gibson recommended that Collier be officially retained by the commission as its director of community organization. After listening to Collier outline plans "he thought would be useful in California," the commission unanimously voted to employ him in cooperation with the University of California extension division. A salary of $3,000, to be divided equally between the two agencies, was agreed upon. At its January 1920 meeting the commission created a committee composed of two university professors, Lubin, and Mrs. Gibson to supervise Collier's work. This committee subsequently charged Collier with three specific duties: the development of a system of adult education in English and citizenship, the training of americanization and community workers, and the organization of "community centers built up around the schools" throughout the state. The goal was to be the teaching of citizenship through participation in the affairs of the local community.[3]

Collier plunged into his new job with his accustomed zeal. In February 1920, he persuaded the commission that a publicity agent was absolutely necessary for the success of his work. In March, Mrs. Gibson successfully convinced her associates that Collier needed an assistant. In May, on the motion of Mrs. Gibson, the commission voted to retain Collier for an additional year at $6,000 plus expenses. Mrs. Gibson requested that no mention of the increased salary be made to the State Board of Control because she hoped to raise the additional sum by "contributions from outside sources." When this proved impossible, the commission approved a motion in July requesting the state to appropriate the salary increase.

By May, Collier and the public relations man were blanketing the state with press releases describing the community-organization program. During one three-week period more than 350 news stories were released. Wherever Collier traveled, copies of his speeches were furnished to the local newspapers and the Associated Press was always given a summary of his statements.

By July, the CSHIC was ready to embark upon an ambitious publication program to acquaint Californians with its work in the americanization and community-development fields. Although the commission refused to make a public declaration of policy concerning these programs, agreement was "tentatively" reached upon two basic principles that were to guide Mrs. Gibson and Collier in the preparation of this literature. First, the community–development program was not to be a substitute for the work of existing groups, but rather was to be the means by which these groups and the "mass of unorganized people" could be brought into better relations with one another. Second, the conservation of the immigrant heritage was to be a prime goal of the program. After agreement on these principles, it was decided that Collier and Mrs. Gibson were to prepare a manual "of about seventy five pages" on the topic of community organization; 5,000 copies were to be run in the first printing. The board of education was authorized to prepare a manual on *English and Citizenship Teaching for Immigrants.* In preparation for the presentation of an enlarged CSHIC budget for fiscal 1921–23, Mrs. Gibson urged the publication of a twenty-five-page report on "The Fiscal Support of Immigration Education, Public Education and Community Organization in the State of California," and she suggested that a monthly newsletter be created entitled "A Report on Community and Immigrant Education Development in California."[4] Approval for all these projects was granted by the commission.

In the midst of all this activity, Collier and the community-development program suddenly came under attack by a conservative businessmen's organization that called itself the Better America Federation. Backed by Harry Chandler of the *Los Angeles Times*, the Better America Federation was a front for antiunion businessmen who were advocating the adoption of an open-shop statute in the legislature. In July, the Better America Federation circulated a secret letter throughout the state attacking Paul Scharrenberg, one of the CSHIC commissioners. Scharrenberg, whom Collier and his friends considered "a conservative labor leader" was accused of lobbying for "radical labor measures." On September 13, the federation openly attacked the CSHIC in the pages of the *Sacramento Star* through a public letter charging Chairman Lubin with supporting the "I.W.W. and other Reds." Specifically, the letter charged that Lubin, through "pull with the War Department and Secretary of War [Newton D.] Baker," had been given access to records of the Justice Department investigation of Wobbly activity in northern California. Lubin, the letter charged, had warned "these I.W.W. criminals" of the investigation and some of the evidence against them had been suppressed. Although Lubin denied the charges, the California legislature launched a probe of CSHIC activities, which eventually resulted in a discovery that it had overspent its previous appropriation by $2,000. Subsequently, CSHIC appropriations for fiscal 1921–23 were cut by the amount of its community-development budget and the increase in Collier's salary.

At its October 18, 1920, board meeting, the CSHIC commissioners received a report from their chief executive officer that recommended, in view of the reduced appropriation, a substantial reduction in the staff of the CSHIC and the curtailment of the publicity and community-organization programs. With the exception of Mrs. Gibson, the board members apparently agreed with the argument that Commissioner Scharrenberg later offered: to save the other pro-

Figure 7.   Dr. John Randolph Haynes. From the Department
of Special Collections, University Research Library, University of
California, Los Angeles.

grams of the CSHIC, the community-development program
would have to be sacrificed. Six days later at a special meeting held to discuss "the matter of the adjustment of the
Commission's budget," Collier submitted his resignation,
to take effect November 1. It was unanimously accepted by
the board, with Mrs. Gibson abstaining. At this same meeting, the board abolished the positions of publicity agent
and director of teacher training and ordered the discon-
tinuation of all publications. At a later meeting, the board
advised all staff members that in the future the community-
organization work of the CSHIC would be strictly limited
"to the giving of advice as to what may be done" in the field.
No information on community development was to be dispensed except upon "application for advice."

Figure 8.   The Taos Society of Artists in Couse's Yard, 1932.
Standing (left to right): Walter Ufer, W. Herbert Dunton, Victor
Higgins, Kenneth Adams. Seated (left to right): E. Martin Hen-
nings, Bert G. Phillips, E. Irving Couse, Oscar E. Berninghaus.
Front: Joseph H. Sharp, Ernest L. Blumenschein.

In his memoirs, John Collier wrote that he had been the
victim "of the [U.S. Attorney General A. Mitchell] Palmer
red witch hunt hysteria." He had been warned that he was
being watched by operatives from the Department of Justice, but he "proceeded without regard to these warn-
ings . . . ." This assessment was no doubt a correct one, but
it was also true that Commissioner Lubin had concluded
that Collier's zeal had outrun his usefulness to the total
work of the CSHIC. In October 1920, in response to a request for guidance from the CSHIC executive officer, Lubin
wrote that in the past some commissioners had exceeded

their authority in attempting to direct departments personally. Unauthorized publicity, particularly, "has been a thorn." Some employees had placed their specialities ahead of the entire commission and "some employees or commissioners may have shown special loyalty to each other." These problems had been solved by recent resignations, he advised, and he now anticipated no problems in returning to the main concern of the CSHIC.[5]

Collier's CSHIC experience was not, however, without its rewards. Through Mrs. Gibson, Collier was introduced to Dr. John Randolph Haynes, one of southern California's wealthiest and most influential philanthropists. A physician who had made his fortune in Philadelphia, Haynes retired to Los Angeles in 1887. There he invested his money in real estate and then proceeded to devote his time to a host of political and social reforms. In 1895 he was instrumental in forming the Direct Legislation League, which in 1899 succeeded in broadening the base of city government in San Francisco and in 1903 won the adoption of initiative, referendum, and recall amendments to the Los Angeles city charter. Together with Rudolph Spreckles and E. T. Earl, Haynes formed and liberally financed the People's Lobby, a muckraking organization that publicized the misdeeds of state legislators. When Hiram Johnson became governor in 1903, he called upon Haynes to draft amendments to the state constitution that made possible the adoption of the initiative, referendum, recall, and direct primary.

Haynes was also interested in municipally owned power and water and public ownership of national resources. Through his efforts, the largest municipally owned light and power company in the nation, the Los Angeles Water and Power Board, was created in 1920. Throughout the 1920s he served as a vice-president of the National Popular Government League, which he and Nebraska Senator George Norris had created in 1913 to lobby for federal development of the nation's water-power resources. During the war he served as a member of the California Council of Defense,

Figure 9.   The Collier family camping in the Arroyo Seco,
New Mexico, summer 1921. From left to right: John, Jr., Donald,
Lucy Wood, Charles. In the foreground the Airedale, Rags,
whose puppies are being carried by Donald and Charles. Courtesy John Collier, Jr.

where he became interested in adult education and community organization. Haynes was a fervent advocate of national
prohibition and a pioneer in the movement for "negative eu-
genics": the sterilization of the unfit and use of contracep-
tives to control "undesirable" population growth.

Haynes took a paternal interest in Collier, and Collier re-
ciprocated with an admiration that knew no bounds. He
was first attracted by Haynes's "absorption in and complete
acceptance of scientific empiricism applied to the whole
field of human problems." Haynes, he wrote, accepted the
theory of evolution "without limit and with its most radical
agnostic postulates," and he belonged "completely to the

philosophical schools of John Stuart Mill, Huxley, and Lester F. Ward." But what he most admired was Haynes's "passion for liberty and social justice," his "revolutionary" social
philosophy, which sought "radical ends through available
instruments and mechanisms." Once Collier discovered the
American Indian, Haynes was to supply much of the money
and many of the contacts to keep him going. Haynes's Los
Angeles home would become Collier's "own home and office in Southern California," and there the two men would
discuss politics and philosophy "far into many nights."[6]

When Collier resigned from the CSHIC, his sponsors,
Mrs. Gibson and Dr. Haynes, "were ready to take up the
fight." This would have meant "a prolonged political struggle," however, for which he had no stomach at the time.
"All the disillusionment of my last year in New York, when
all our endeavors had failed, surged over me again," he
wrote, and he decided to do "what I had always done before
when failure struck." With Lucy, the three boys, and two
dogs he set out for Sonora, Mexico, with the intention of
seeking solace in the wilderness. But before long, his past
caught up with him in the person of Mabel Dodge.

In 1915, following the establishment of the Elizabeth
Duncan school, Mabel Dodge leased a farm adjoining the
school and encouraged a young Russian painter named
Maurice Sterne to move in with her. Though neither of
them was particularly enthusiastic about the affair, and
Mabel was to effect a brief reconciliation with John Reed in
the spring of 1915 before breaking off the affair permanently,
there was enough in common to hold them together for
a while: Mabel wished to make a sculptor out of Sterne;
he was in need of financial support. In 1917, lacking anything better to do, Mabel proposed that they get married
and Sterne consented. Shortly afterward, Mabel became so
bored with her third husband that she sent him off to the
West on a solo honeymoon trip. First he traveled to Wyoming and then, at the invitation of a friend, he went to
Santa Fe, New Mexico.

By 1917, New Mexico had become something of a mecca

for American artists. Frederick Remington was probably the first to recognize its potential on a visit he made in 1882. Then came Joseph Henry Sharp, who, after a short visit to Taos in the early 1890s, continued on to Paris, where his description of New Mexico appealed particularly to two of his fellow painters, Ernest Blumenschein and Bert Phillips. In 1897, Blumenschein and Phillips accepted a commission for illustrations in *McClure's Magazine* and, after spending the summer in Colorado, they settled in Taos for the winter. Blumenschein thereupon decided to spend half of each year in Taos and he subsequently persuaded Irving Couse and Herbert Dunton to leave New York. In time, Sharp returned and by 1914 the fledgling artist's colony at Taos had expanded to include Walter Ufer and Victor Higgins, both of whom came from Chicago, and Oscar Berninghaus, who came from St. Louis. During and after World War I, other painters, writers, sculptors, and poets flocked to the state. Some came in search of the bold, clear, colors that they said could be found nowhere else on earth; some sought refuge from civilization and an escape into the "primitive." They all found the cost of living low and the environment enchanting. Most of them took up residence in either Taos or Santa Fe, with most of the painters preferring Taos, and the writers, Santa Fe.

The natives were bewildered by this influx of foreigners. In each of the two towns where the invaders settled, there was a handful of Anglos or the descendants of old Spanish families who controlled affairs and owned most of the property. At Taos, there was a community of Indians settled in a pueblo that quickly became famous for its symmetrically tiered apartments separated by a sparkling mountain stream. In Santa Fe, there was a populous Mexican community that performed all the necessary menial tasks at very low wages. A native New Mexican has recorded her impression of these events.[7]

New Mexico had been discovered by a hitherto unknown race who used unfamiliar words with accents very strange.

They spoke of Amerindian culture, of colonial arts, of racial rhythms, and of such color that even a native began to see red, white, and blue in a muddy ditch. Some painted pictures, some wrote books, and poems, and they all went nuts about something: ruins or Indian dances, old Mexican plays, or tin sconces. Their women appeared in men's pants and cowboy hats; their men wore velvet blouses and Navajo jewelry. They took over adobe huts and filled them with battered furniture, noseless wooden *santos*, torn Navajo blankets, copper kettles with holes in them, and Indian ceremonial garments acquired by all sorts of trickery.

As roads and plumbing reached Taos, the camp followers of the artistic shock troops moved in. Bankers co-operated in the foreclosing of mortgages, and whole villages were made over. Mabel Dodge came west with Maurice Sterne . . . .

And Mabel did indeed come west in December 1917. But she did not come to join the artists, of whom she had grown tired. Instead, she came to get away from the "world of escapists I had lived among, this crowd of reformers, artists, writers, labor leaders, philosophers, and scientists . . . ." She came seeking time and leisure "to be" and to escape the "competition, self-assertion, the feeling of personal influence [which] was probably the greatest enhancement my generation knew." And she came because of her curiosity about the Indians, whom Sterne had asked her to "save." In the letter that prompted her journey to New Mexico, he had written:[8]

> November 30 [1917]
> Do you want an object in life? Save the Indians, their art-culture—reveal it to the world! I hear astonishing things here about the insensitiveness of our Indian office—through ignorance, solely, for they mean well—the stupidity and the pathetic crimes committed by its agents through a sense of superiority of the white color and white civilization (including, I suppose, the "Great White Way" . . . .) That which Emilie Hapgood and others are doing for the Negroes, you could, if you wanted to, do for the Indians . . . .

Figure 10.   Mabel Dodge and Tony Luhan, 1934. From the Pearl Chase Papers. The Community Development and Conservation Collection, Department of Special Collections, University Library, University of California at Santa Barbara.

As usual, Mabel found her desire for peace and her desire to control events at odds. She did, however, spend the remainder of a long life at Taos, where she built a splendid adobe home adjoining Taos Pueblo. To it she invited all her former friends and a host of new ones. Her interest in saving the Indians was an off-again, on-again thing, but in 1918, when she and Sterne agreed their marriage was finished, she attached herself to a Taos Indian named Tony Luhan, with whom she remained until her death. Tony moved in with her in 1918, and was thereby ostracized from Taos Pueblo life; the two were not married until 1923.

One of her former friends whom Mabel sought to interest in the Indian cause was John Collier. Shortly after learning that he had moved to California, she invited him to visit her in her new surroundings. Collier replied that he wanted "desperately to come to Taos," because he was gradually "entering a new life . . . and I believe much consciousness might unfold if I could be at Taos." He simply could not find the time, however. He had only a year, he wrote in the summer of 1920, "to get under way a complex of new things all over California: community organization, a new sort of teaching and a new literature dealing with all this subject."

Mabel did not give up. She continued to press her invitation. When Collier resigned from the CSHIC, she was one of the first to whom he confided his new plans. "At last we are . . . free," he wrote some time in late October, 1920. He had decided "definitely" to get out of "social and public work for an indefinite time. It was as far back as 1914 that we first tried to take this step." His immediate plans were to go to the desert of southern California and northern Mexico "to live, all of us: and for myself, I hope to write." If he were financially able, he would come to Taos instead, but this would have to wait "until we have accumulated enough savings to move into your neighborhood."[9]

Recognizing that only his pride was keeping him from coming to New Mexico, Mabel now bombarded Collier with new invitations by letter and by telegram. A great deal of money was not necessary, she implied, since she had just completed the construction of several new apartments adjoining her villa, where the Colliers and other guests were expected to stay free of charge. Her insistence and the offer of a loan prevailed. On December 11, 1920, Collier and his family arrived from Los Angeles after an arduous journey by rail and stagecoach. Their emergence onto the Taos plateau in a "blinding snowstorm" at sundown, "strangely and profoundly" excited Collier, as it has many other travelers when they suddenly emerge from the canyon of the Rio Grande on the road north from Santa Fe.

The Christmas ceremonials were under way at the pueblo when Collier arrived. A combination of Christianity and ancient Indian traditions unfolded before him as the Indians bore the statue of the Virgin from the church on Christmas eve, chanting and dancing a ritual "a thousand or three thousand years old." Three days later he witnessed the Red Deer dance, and although he found it impossible to describe the dance in words, he felt it enter "into myself and each one of my family as a new direction of life—a new, even wildly new, hope for the Race of Man."

Before his Taos visit, Collier's only acquaintance with the American Indian had been a brief, romantic experience during his New York days. In 1910–11, when he and Luther Gulick were forming the first school–social centers, he had spent "hundreds of hours with the Gulicks in their home" where preparations were under way for the founding of a girl's organization similar to the Boy Scouts. Gulick and his wife, Charlotte, both of whom were active in outdoor recreation projects, particularly summer camps, worked closely with Daniel Beard and Ernest Thompson Seton in the creation of the Boy Scouts of America. In 1912, the Gulicks created the Camp Fire Girls. At Gulick's request, Collier served as one of the first directors and in 1912 he composed the "Fire Makers Delight," a pledge used in the ritual. Still, he had never met an Indian and the Taos experience was to give him a totally new perspective on this "new" ethnic minority.

During the five months he remained at Taos, Collier began gradually to shed the pessimism that he had previously held about the possibility of the survival of primitive peo-

ples. In his memoirs, he later wrote that during this period
he discovered among the Indians the functioning communal society he had sought vainly to construct in New York
and California. The Indians, he found, "possessed the fundamental secret of human life—the secret of building great
personality through the instrumentality of social institutions." By the time he left, he had persuaded himself that
their society must be preserved at any cost and he said to
himself "with absolute finality . . . . *This* effort toward
community must not fail; there can be no excuse or pardon
if it fails."[10]

The sense of resolution and personal dedication to the
preservation of Indian culture that Collier recalled in his
memoirs is, however, strangely lacking in the fragments
of his surviving contemporary correspondence. In a letter
to Dr. Haynes written in January 1921, his only concern
was with the need for a broadly based program of community development in California, a project that he estimated
would take five years to organize. In March, when he left
Taos to investigate a teaching position at San Francisco
State Teacher's College, he did evince a concern about the
Indians, but his concern was with their health, not with
their cultural survival. In a letter to a Dr. Lucas, whom he
wrote for help in obtaining a full-time physician to treat the
Indians, he explained that a Turkish physiologist who was
also visiting Mabel, Dr. Eshref Shevky, had recently discovered the existence of syphilis among the Taos Indians. With
the cooperation of the county health officer and the Indian
superintendent, Shevky had administered Wassermann tests
to a group of Indians and concluded that probably twelve
percent of Taos pueblo had contracted the disease. On the
basis of Shevky's findings, "a project for emergency health
work for all the 20 pueblos had been laid before the Red
Cross," he wrote, adding: "the sociological as well as the
medical interest in the enterprise is great; it is likely to lead
to very much bigger things very soon . . . ." In July, he wrote
directly to Commissioner of Indian Affairs, Charles Burke,

informing him of the need for medical care at Taos. This time his concern was for two Indian women suffering from trachoma and for one who was insane.[11]

Aside from these few instances of concern for better medical care among the Indians, however, Collier's attention in 1921 was focused mainly on his new career as a teacher of sociology. So convinced was he that this was to be his new life's work, he purchased a home in Mill Valley, north of San Francisco, during his March interview. In mid-May, against the wishes of Mabel Dodge, the Colliers left Taos for several leisurely months of camping before they returned to California. Their visit ended on a sour note. At Española, New Mexico, only shortly after they had made their departure, a telegram from Mabel arrived charging that the Colliers had broken "some valuable old objects" in the apartment where they had lived and that the boys had put several holes in the roof of the structure. Collier replied that Mabel should have expected some wear and tear from a family with "three irrepressible boys," and he offered to pay for refurnishing the apartment. He dismissed her argument that they were responsible for all the defects of the apartment, however, saying that the broken furniture had been broken before, the roof had leaked every time it rained even before the boys began to play on it, and all the linen had fallen apart during the first washing. He had made a mistake in accepting her offer to visit, he wrote. Despite the free lodging, Mabel had made them "hire a servant," and this plus other unforeseen expenses had cost him more than $400 at a time when his only income was $100 a month. "The nature of our mistake becomes evident: having so little money we should not have come to live near one who is wealthy, who has never experienced poverty—still less, to live in her house." But Mabel, too, had made a mistake. She had "assumed that because we took benefits from you, you could tell us what to do." He enclosed a check for $150 to repay the loan that had enabled them to make the trip from southern California.[12]

Despite the apparent hostility in this exchange of letters, Collier and Mabel Dodge remained basically good friends.

The telegram was only Mabel's way of expressing displeasure that Collier had not remained to champion the Indian cause. He knew, as her friends always did, that the mood would pass with time. Within a year he would find a practical reason for undertaking the Indian defense and he would also find the financial backing that would make his involvement possible. Meanwhile, he turned his attention to directing the new program in social science at San Francisco State Teacher's College.

Because he was both the director and the only instructor in the department of sociology, Collier was free to fashion the curriculum as he saw fit. In typical fashion, he attempted to cover every possible topic of current interest in the twelve-hour sequence that he created. In Sociology 12, the introductory course, he dealt with the "methods through which current sociological and anthropological data may be employed in the teaching of civics and social science." The topics discussed were population, industry, agriculture, the role of chemistry and physics in modern life, the distribution and use of natural resources, immigrant backgrounds and problems, conflicts and adjustments between races and national groups, and the status of such primitive groups as the Polynesians and the American Indian. Sociology 13 was "a study of contemporary civilization," which enabled him to lecture on the historic migrations of people, war, the conservation of natural resources, the currency problem in Europe, labor problems and industrial management in the United States, the rural-life movement, community organization, and contemporary life in "Russia, China; and the nationalist movements in Ireland, Eastern Europe, and India." Sociology 14 dealt with problems in "education, criminology, medicine, the organization of the arts, politics and industrial relationship, considered exclusively in their relation to the principles of psychology." It was designed to be a "history of the development of psychology during the past fifty years, and will seek to give a clear if elementary understanding of the main concepts and methods and data of genetic, analytical, and social psychology." During the 1922

Figure 11.   Indian Commissioner Charles H. Burke at his desk
in the Indian Office, 1920s. Courtesy of Josephine L. Burke.

summer session, Collier offered in addition to these basic
courses a seminar in "Special Sociology," patterned after the
seminars of the New York Training School for Community
Workers. The course was open to students without previous
training in sociology. Its topics were "practical, present-day
social questions to be chosen by those who attend"; its purpose was "directed to the discovery of the elements of uni-
versal and human importance in the questions treated, and
to the principles and human importance with which these
questions can be related."

   Although this record of what Collier taught has survived,
there is nothing to tell us how well he succeeded, what
problems he encountered, or how he viewed his brief career

Figure 12.   Stella Atwood. From the John Collier Papers, Yale
University Library.

as a college teacher. The only fragment dealing with this period of his career is a brief statement to Dr. Haynes in the
summer of 1922 in which he expressed wonderment at the
size of his three classes: he was teaching more than six
hundred students in three classes. He told Haynes: "there
seems a great felt want for sociology teaching."[13]

   While he prepared his lectures, Collier found his thoughts
frequently returning to the Indians. Gradually he was drawn
into greater and greater involvement in the field of Indian
affairs. Upon his return to California, he suggested to his
good friend, Mrs. Gibson, that she interest the California
women's clubs in the Indian health problem at Taos. Instead, she introduced him to a Riverside acquaintance, Mrs.

Stella Atwood, who had only recently succeeded in persuading the national council of the GFWC to create a national committee on Indian welfare. At the same time, Mrs. Gibson set out to find a way to enable Collier to devote all his time to this new work of the GFWC.

Since 1916, when she succeeded in creating a committee on Indian welfare in the southern district of the California GFWC, Stella Atwood had been interested in the plight of the California Indians. Unable to bear children as the result of treatment for malaria when she was a child, and troubled by a tubercular hip disease, which gave her a pronounced limp, she had concluded as a young woman that her poor health ruled out the possibility of marriage. Harry Atwood, a young medical student from an adjoining farm in rural Minnesota, did not agree, however, and he proposed to Stella when she was twenty-two. For five years she put him off, but in 1893, persuaded at last that he knew what he was getting into, she agreed. The following year the young couple moved to California and settled at Moreno, a few miles outside of Riverside. Under her husband's care, Stella Atwood soon overcame most of her disabilities. Within a few years the frail girl who weighed only 85 pounds at the time of her marriage grew two inches and increased her weight to a more normal 118 pounds. This sudden transformation in her health produced an equally sudden transformation in her activity. Stella Atwood became a dynamo for improvement and reform in the Riverside community.

For ten years, until her husband's practice was established, she taught school, first at Moreno, where she conducted a one-room school for fifty children, and later in Riverside, after a shortage of water forced them to leave Moreno in 1900. In 1904, the first year after she quit teaching, she was elected to the Riverside school board. As a result of her efforts, manual-training instruction was soon introduced into the high-school curriculum, and a junior college district, only the second in the state, was created. In 1913, she organized the women of Riverside block by block in support of a bond issue that enabled the city to municipalize its limited

water supply. She was also one of the organizers of a settlement house in Riverside, serving briefly as its director, a
member of the Riverside draft board during World War I,
and a vice-president of the local Red Cross. In 1916 she became the Riverside representative to the southern district
convention of the California GFWC.

In 1917, Stella Atwood became chairman of the Indian
Welfare Committee for the southern district of California.
At the 1918 state convention she secured the adoption of a
resolution creating an Indian Welfare Committee for the entire state, to which her good friend Mrs. C. C. Arnold of
Riverside was appointed chairman. During the next two
years the two women undertook a survey of conditions
among California Indians in conjunction with the United
States Board of Indian Commissioners. In addition to com-
piling information for the use of the board, Mrs. Arnold
expressed the hope that the survey would "instill a new attitude of mind on the part of whites toward Indians." In
1920, as the result of this work, legislation was introduced
into Congress to permit the Indians of California to file suit
in the Court of Claims for lands they had lost during the
gold rush of 1849. When a fact-finding subcommittee of the
House Committee on Indian Affairs held hearings in California in the spring of 1920, Mrs. Atwood presented the results of the survey and called upon the congressmen for
additional legislation to improve the conditions of California Indians.

In 1920 Mrs. Atwood was elected chairman of the southern district of the California GFWC. In this capacity, she
served as a delegate to the biennial national council meeting of the GFWC held at Salt Lake City in 1921. There she
and Gertrude Bonnin, a college-educated Sioux affiliated
with the Indian Rights Association of Philadelphia, together lobbied for the creation of a national committee on
Indian Welfare. Again Mrs. Atwood was successful. In recognition of her work in behalf of the California Indians, the
directors of the GFWC appointed her the first chairman of
the new committee. Shortly after her return from Salt Lake

City, Mrs. Gibson arranged for her introduction to John Collier.[14]

Before her association with Collier, Mrs. Atwood had already established contact with Commissioner of Indian Affairs, Charles Burke. Within a few days after President Harding appointed Burke in the spring of 1921, she wrote the new commissioner to acquaint him with the problems of the California Indians. She also told him of her plan to create a national Indian welfare committee in the GFWC and she invited Burke to address the delegates at the Salt Lake City meeting. In this way there began a correspondence that Commissioner Burke once wearily described to a friend as "not only frequent but voluminous." Mrs. Atwood's prominence in the GFWC made it impossible for Burke to ignore her, despite the fact that replies to her correspondence consumed a disproportionate amount of his time. As a result of Mrs. Atwood's persistence and Burke's decision to segregate her correspondence into a special "Atwood file," it is possible to trace the origins of the assault on the Indian Office with some precision.[15]

Even before her appointment to national office, Mrs. Atwood had undertaken the removal of several objectionable Indian agents in California. She was encouraged in this work by the Indian Rights Association of Philadelphia, the oldest Indian protection society in existence at the time. S. M. Brosius, the IRA's legal council and field representative was in contact with Mrs. Atwood as early as May 1921, offering encouragement to her efforts to oust Charles T. Coggeshall, the superintendent of the Northern Mission Agency at Banning, California. After being rebuffed by the Indian Office, Mrs. Atwood appealed to President Harding's sister, a Mrs. Remsberg who resided in Santa Ana. Within a few days after Mrs. Remsberg wrote her brother, Coggeshall was transferred and he was subsequently dismissed from the Indian service. The IRA, which had unsuccessfully attempted to drive Coggeshall from the Indian service for years, was impressed. By September, Brosius was advising the Philadelphia office that Mrs. Atwood's success in orga-

nizing Indian welfare committees in many states was "the
most promising aid for Indian betterment I have known for
a long time. TWO MILLIONS OF WOMEN are already back of
the movement." In another letter the IRA secretary, Matthew K. Sniffen, advised that Mrs. Atwood "will prove to be
a very strong ally to our cause."[16]

In September 1921, at about the time she met Collier,
Mrs. Atwood wrote Commissioner Burke calling for the removal of three more agents, two of them in California, and
a third, Horace J. Johnson, the superintendent of the Northern Pueblo Agency in Española, New Mexico. In this same
letter she set forth clearly her goals in the field of Indian
affairs:

> . . . I think I have expressed to you in previous letters my
> conviction that you have in your hands a wonderful oppor-
> tunity to make an administration that may be historical. A
> square, straight policy for the benefit and protection of the
> Indians, an undeviating and uncompromising attitude to-
> ward the officials who exploit and abuse the Indians will
> bring you the backing of our great organization and of all
> others who stand for right and justice. In my mind you
> have assumed the office at the psychological moment when
> these things can and must be accomplished.
>
> Since I have been in this work, I am amazed at the inter-
> est that is being displayed in so many different quarters on
> the Indian question. Organizations are springing up on
> every hand, and I am asking our women to cooperate with
> all accredited organizations. If we all work together, there
> is a support that will help you to accomplish anything you
> wish along constructive lines and toward administering
> justice to these defenseless people.
>
> I think my policy may be summarized in two sentences.
> I will work *for* the Indians but not with them. I want to
> work *with* the Indian Office but not for it. The Indians are
> a primitive people. If you work with them and go over their
> wrongs with them (and they have plenty of them) their pas-
> sions are aroused, and like all primitive men they get
> violent and unruly, they brood over their troubles and get
> morose until they are ready for almost any deed of vio-

lence. The only way to do, as I said above, is to work *for*
them and not with them. I hope to work with your office in
perfect harmony.

You must feel assured by now that I have undertaken
this task earnestly and sincerely and that I shall spare no
effort to accomplish what I consider right. I want your full
confidence. I want access to all the authentic information
necessary to a proper understanding and adjustment of the
situations that present themselves.[17]

It was only after her introduction to Collier that Mrs. Atwood's concern shifted from the relatively simple policy of
removing undesirable Indian agents to the more fundamental issue of institutional and legislative reform. This transformation was associated with a growing interest in the
Pueblo Indians of New Mexico, whose existence had been
unknown to her previously. In October 1921, she wrote
Commissioner Burke about a bill pending in Congress to resolve a dispute over land titles between the Pueblos and
their white neighbors. Burke replied that she need have no
concern about "the so-called Bursum Bill," which was being
personally attended to by Secretary of the Interior Albert B.
Fall and several special assistants in the Justice Department. She persisted, however, and Burke at last put her in
touch with both Fall and Ralph E. Twitchell, the chief Justice Department investigator. In November, Twitchell advised Mrs. Atwood that he was preparing to recommend
against Senator Bursum's bill. In December, both Twitchell
and Fall journeyed to San Diego to participate in the program of the League of the Southwest and to talk to Mrs. Atwood in detail about her criticisms of the Indian Office.

While she was preparing for the visit of Secretary Fall and
Colonel Twitchell, Mrs. Atwood revived Collier's charges
that the health situation at Taos was serious. The cases
of trachoma and insanity about which Collier had written Burke the previous summer remained unattended, she
chided in early December. Commissioner Burke quickly replied that she and Collier were misinformed. Andrea Lujan,
one of Collier's alleged trachoma victims, had been exam-

ined by a physician who reported that she was not suffering from the disease. Pasqualita Concha, the second trachoma case Collier had reported, had been taken to Laguna for treatment, but she had fled from the hospital there and no one knew her present location. Francesca Espinoza, whom Collier maintained was in need of psychiatric treatment had so improved that plans to send her to an asylum had been abandoned. In addition, the commissioner testily noted, Andrea Lujan had complained to the Indian Office because she had been subjected to so much inquiry.

In mid-December, Mrs. Atwood advised Commissioner Burke that her meeting with Secretary Fall had been more than satisfactory. Fall had addressed the League of the Southwest, and at the conclusion of his speech "the whole audience sprang to their [sic] feet with cheers and it was one of the thrilling moments of my life." She talked with the secretary privately, at which time she outlined new demands calling for immediate citizenship for all Indians, the consolidation of the California Indian agencies, increased pay for Indian agents, and restrictions on the powers of Indian agents. Fall, she said, was favorable to these suggestions and he "agreed with me in my general policy, which pleased me greatly." She was not so pleased with Colonel Twitchell, who twice failed to keep appointments with her. By January, however, Twitchell had succeeded in convincing her that he had been unavoidably detained in Los Angeles, and he had also convinced her that the Pueblo situation was being closely watched.[18]

Meanwhile, Collier's influence was apparent in another area. In December Mrs. Atwood wrote to Stephen Mather, the director of the National Park Service, about the possibility of making Taos a national monument. Although she had not seen the pueblo herself, she advised Mather, it was her "understanding" that it was "one of the finest examples of Pueblo civilization . . . a unique and ancient type of civilization . . . the finest type of communal living that has ever been conceived." In order for the Indians to "continue in the beauty and purity of this civilization" it would be necessary to protect them both "from the encroachments and absorption of [their] white neighbors" and from restrictions imposed on them by the Indian Service. By February Collier was attempting to enlist the support of Mabel Dodge for this scheme, which was now enlarged to include Zuñi. A "big pow-wow" was scheduled for May in Los Angeles, he informed Mabel, at which time he and Mrs. Atwood hoped to launch a national campaign for the designation of the two pueblos as national monuments and also to form a cooperative marketing association for Pueblo craft goods.[19]

By May the impractical national-monument scheme had fizzled. Instead of the big "pow-wow" that Collier had envisioned in Los Angeles, a much smaller, though potentially far more important, meeting took place in May at Azusa, at the ranch of Mrs. Kate Vosburg, the wealthy daughter of Azusa's founder, Jonathan Sayre Slosson. A prominent member of the California GFWC, Mrs. Vosburg had become interested in the Indian work of Mrs. Atwood and Collier through the efforts of Mary Gibson. On May 6 she invited the pair to her ranch to hear their proposal for an independent investigation of Indian affairs under the sponsorship of the GFWC. At the close of the presentation, Mrs. Vosburg offered to finance Collier's activities for two years ($5,000 per year plus expenses) if he would sever his teaching connections and devote full time to field investigations under Mrs. Atwood's direction. Collier subsequently secured a release from his teaching contract, effective September 1, 1922, and shortly thereafter left for Taos.

In a letter to Dr. Haynes written a week after the meeting at Azusa, Collier described the changes in federal Indian policy that he hoped to attain within the next two years. "As a very minimum," he wrote, "we can be very sure of rectifying a number of wrongs and contributing to a new public opinion." He hoped first to change the federal government's attitude toward "aborigines and subject people." Next, he intended to educate the public to the "cultural and human values of folk different from ourselves." He also hoped to make a contribution to "rural life economics" and to the "education of the adolescent, regarding which the Indians have everything to teach us." He thought it would also be possible to persuade the churches doing missionary work among the Indians "to accord their practices more with the realities of Indian life" and he hoped to "force the archeologists and anthropologists to acknowledge that they have a duty . . . to help keep the Indian cultures alive if that is possible." If these results could be attained, he continued, it would "amount to a good deal at a time like the present when so few worthwhile objects are surely attainable."

Beyond these immediate goals, however, Collier also listed what he termed "the *larger results*" he hoped to attain "if we [can] bring enough ingenuity, industry and passion to bear." Because these "larger results" were an embryonic formulation of the reforms he would seek to effect in the next twenty years they are quoted below:[20]

> 1. (Condition precedent to the rest) Forcing a modernization of the Indian Service and a correlation of this service with other government and state services, especially public health, education and agricultural and rural credit aid. Forcing a system of accounting for funds in the Indian Service.
> 2. Conferring citizenship on the Indians, or at least on many groups of them, while at the same time enabling them to hold their lands communally, which means maintaining a continued guardianship over their reservations.
> 3. Trying out, with the help of the Department of Agriculture especially, whether the Indians cannot be helped to exploit [in] an all-round way the natural resources on their own lands. The present system of exploitation through contracts and leases has the result first of robbing and then of pauperizing the Indians through doles. What negroes and cast-bound [sic] Hindus have proved capable of, certainly the Indians, who are trained cooperators and born artizans [sic], will be capable of, if we give them a chance. This suggestion implies much with regard to rural life education and the conservation of natural resources through community effort.
> 4. Remaking the school system both primary and secondary; basing it more largely on esthetics and on arts-and-crafts, on rural industry, etc., and carrying it out so as to

strengthen rather than mutilate the tribal relationships. We have a wonderful chance here to develop "socialized schools" which would have an influence on the whole school system of the country.

5. The *greatest* hope: to keep alive the Pueblo civilization with its cultural elements and its romantic point of view. To make possible for these archaic communities to live on, and to modernize themselves economically (on a cooperative, communal basis) while yet going forward with their spiritual life . . . .

On this last point: it is no more a forlorn hope or a mere dream than the revival of the Irish national soul appeared to be when Douglass Hyde . . . started the Gaelic revival in 1893.   © Mrs. Grace Collier

Although Collier displayed a remarkable understanding of the weaknesses of federal Indian policy in his letter to Dr. Haynes, his education and Mrs. Atwood's were just beginning. A few days after the Azusa decision, Mrs. Atwood received a letter from an unknown Altadena resident, Frank Wills, a Bell Telephone executive. "I understand that there is trouble in Taos," he wrote, "go out and see about it." The note was accompanied by a check for $300. Immediately Collier arranged for an invitation from Mabel Dodge, and within a week Mrs. Atwood and Mabel Chilberg, another prominent GFWC member and Mrs. Vosburg's companion, were in Taos. From New Mexico they continued eastward to the biennial meeting of the GFWC at Chautauqua, New York, where the announcement of Mrs. Vosburg's gift was received with enthusiasm. Following the convention, they proceeded to Washington. There Mrs. Atwood engaged Commissioner Burke in several long conversations and was entertained at his home. Although they discussed the Pueblo situation, Burke did not inform her that Senator Bursum was preparing to submit a second bill, drafted by Secretary Fall and his associates, on the topic of the tangled Pueblo land question. In late July, exhausted from her long journey, she returned to Riverside, congratulating herself on a summer well spent in the Indian cause.

In early August, Mrs. Atwood's sense of well-being was

suddenly dissipated. From Senator Carl Hayden of Arizona she received a copy of the second Bursum bill. Immediately she wrote to Burke, angrily charging him with having deliberately deceived her about the Pueblo situation when she was in Washington. Citing a number of decisions that had to have been made before the bill's submission, she concluded: "all of [this] means that you must have had a conference on this subject, and I want to know at the earliest possible moment how you feel about it . . . My feeling is that it is decidedly against the best interests of the Indians and just as soon as I get authentic information on the status of the bill I shall make up my mind how to proceed."[21]

On August 9 Burke replied to her questions about the Bursum bill. It had, he assured her, been carefully considered by the Indian Office, the Land Office, the departmental solicitor, and by Secretary Fall himself. In his opinion, the bill would "ultimately and reasonably promptly adjudicate the differences that have long existed between the Pueblo Indians and the Mexican and other landowners." It was an extremely complex piece of legislation, he cautioned, but he reposed full faith in Colonel Twitchell, who had drafted most of the provisions, and Secretary Fall, himself "an able lawyer." He was sure that when she had had an opportunity to read the bill more carefully, she would agree "that we can safely accept it."

In this instance, as on several later occasions, Commissioner Burke seriously underestimated Mrs. Atwood's determination. Already convinced that he had not been aboveboard with her in their discussions earlier in the summer, she replied on August 18 with a stinging denunciation of the secrecy that surrounded the submission of Bursum's second Pueblo bill. "The more I ruminate on that Pueblo bill the more I see the far-reaching results to the detriment of the Pueblo Indians that will attend its passage." The "eminent counsel" Burke mentioned in his letter should have been able to create a bill "without flaw; but I do not agree that it is. Apparently the interests involved are so tremendous that it is impossible to get away from their influence."

According to her reading and that of "three different men from three different parts of the country," the bill was "bad" in that it ruled in favor of the non-Indian claimants to the land and failed to offer adequate compensation to the Indians. It was her intention to challenge the bill, she implied.

Burke replied immediately. The tone of his letter, which was to become familiar to critics of federal policy in the years ahead, was one of aggrieved disbelief that Mrs. Atwood could suspect him of not having adequately protected the Indians' interests. In politics, he lectured her, it was necessary to make concessions to the opposition, in this case to the non-Indians who claimed title to the disputed lands. One had to be practical, seek compromise, and accept "half-a-loaf" if anything were to be done. He presumed that she could "bring to bear enough influence to prevent [the bill's] passage," but the result would only be that no action would be taken by the Congress and "the poor Indian will go for another indefinite period hoping against hope." He urged her to reconsider her stance and to work together with his office to effect a compromise bill that the Congress would accept.[22]

While Commissioner Burke and Mrs. Atwood were busy exchanging correspondence over the Bursum bill, John Collier was preparing himself for the fieldwork among the Pueblos, which he would begin September 1. In the midst of his heavy summer teaching schedule, he somehow found time to undertake a study of federal Indian policy by reading through the annual reports of the commissioner of Indian Affairs. In June, apparently as a follow-up to the letter to Dr. Haynes in which he described the changes in federal policy he hoped to effect in the next two years, he wrote an article for *Survey Graphic* entitled "The Red Atlantis." Denouncing federal policy as "autocratic and lawless," Collier repeated here the prescription for reform that he had earlier given Haynes: recognition of the Indians' civil rights, conservation of remaining reservations through cooperative enterprise, preservation of the communal and tribal way of life, agricultural and industrial assistance. The article ap-

peared in the October 1922 issue, and was accompanied by a
companion piece by Stella Atwood and illustrations "arranged by Mabel Stern." Although the timing was entirely
fortuitous, the article's appearance at the height of the
storm over the Bursum bill was to mark Collier as a leading
figure in the growing chorus of the Indian Bureau's critics.

In mid-summer Collier completed his study of federal Indian policy and he again wrote Dr. Haynes to inform him
of his conclusions. His reading had convinced him, he informed Haynes, "that the Indian was doomed from the beginning by our national policy of giving land and water
rights to individuals and corporations as a 'sacred right.'"
Nevertheless, Collier was optimistic about the future: "Practically it appears that there is enough still remaining of the
best Indian life in connection with unused natural resources
belonging to Indian groups by all acknowledged law and
right, so that we can yet do what we didn't do earlier."
There were "fascinating" opportunities among the Indians
to "prove out" the feasibility of cooperative and communal
use of natural resources, the superiority of socialized education, and the need for community-development experiments. "I have come to believe," he concluded, "that the
present is a *good* time to make this effort, from the standpoint of interesting the public; and (as it goes without saying) a difficult time from the standpoint of the Government
(the political) situation. But changes may be nearer than we
think, and the right use of the Indian question can help in
political change. It will be supremely difficult all 'round,
that's clear."[23]

Thus, by the summer of 1922 the groundwork for a con-
certed investigation of federal Indian policy had been prepared. Through Mrs. Atwood, the support of the GFWC,
whose political clout had yet to be adequately measured
but whose potential was considered sizable, could be relied upon. Through the generosity of Mrs. Vosburg, Collier
was assured of adequate financial support for at least two
years. As a result of his New York experience, he was prepared for the political infighting that would be necessary to

achieve the reforms he desired. His numerous influential friends in both the East and the West, and his own experience in dealing with the news media, would make available easy access to the machinery for molding public opinion. Only one ingredient was lacking, an issue of major importance to demonstrate the bankruptcy of federal Indian policy. Luckily for Collier, Secretary of the Interior Albert Fall was to provide that very issue in legislation that he introduced and supported during the summer of 1922.

Part II

Questioning
Tradition

5

Federal Indian Policy to 1922

In 1922 federal Indian policy was not a topic likely to arouse a strong response from many Americans. If they thought about it at all, they probably concluded that there was no longer any need for a policy toward the Indians. After all, the once-proud warriors were no longer a threat to whites, even in the West, and for many years there had been reports that their numbers were declining, through assimilation and through the dying off of the full bloods. Ever since the coming of the first white man to the North American continent, it had been assumed that in instances of conflict between Indians and whites, it was the Indians who must make the concessions. In the face of a virtually insatiable land hunger on the part of the Americans, the Indians were forced to retreat westward onto ever smaller reservations of land. Except for an occasional Indian agent, a romantic writer like Helen Hunt Jackson, or some obscure missionary, there were few to question the justice of this policy. It had become part of conventional wisdom.

In the early days of the republic, the federal government, following the example of its European predecessors, recognized the Indian tribes as independent sovereign nations and sought to pacify them through the negotiation of treaties. By these treaties, the Indians were often persuaded to part with a portion of the lands that the government agreed was theirs, in return for a cash settlement or guaranteed annuities, or both. The government also provided aid in the form of teachers and licensed traders. In the main, both sides considered the exchange a good one. There was still plenty of land for everyone.

Occasionally, however, the Indians resisted the white advance and refused to negotiate further land cessions. As white frontiersmen, defying both the Indians and their own government, continued their westward course, the Indians frequently resorted to violence. At this stage, the federal government would be summoned to restore peace, usually with the result that the uprisings were crushed and the vanquished Indians coerced into signing new treaties, which resulted in new losses of land. The fiction of sovereignty and negotiation was thus preserved.

It was President Thomas Jefferson who first envisioned a solution to this constant conflict between Indians and frontiersmen and to the hypocrisy that surrounded the treaty-making process. After the purchase of Louisiana in 1803, Jefferson several times suggested to the Indians that they escape from the ever increasing white pressure on their landed estates through removal to an area west of the Mississippi River. In 1809, a few Cherokees accepted his offer and moved to the Arkansas Territory. Most of the Indians, however, refused to move, and because Jefferson was unwilling to use force, little came of his idea until after the War of 1812.

The second war with Great Britain coincided with the rise of a remarkable Shawnee Indian by the name of Tecumseh. Together with his brother, the Prophet, Tecumseh expounded the thesis that the Indians were being overrun by the whites because they had abandoned the old ways and had become corrupted by the white man's civilization. He urged Indians on both the northern and the southern frontiers to unite in a common program calling for a revival of the primitive way of life and a refusal to sell any more of their land. Before he was able to construct an alliance of the frontier tribes, fighting broke out between some of the northern Indians and the United States and between the United States and Great Britain. Sensing that the war might be the Indian's salvation, Tecumseh urged his followers to join with the British against the United States. In the fall of 1813, the northern tribes were defeated by General William Henry Harrison at the Battle of the Thames. The following spring, the southern members of the ill-fated confederation were annihilated by General Andrew Jackson at the Battle of Horseshoe Bend. At the conclusion of the war in 1815, many of the tribes were forced to negotiate new land-cession treaties as the price for having chosen the wrong side in the war. These cessions were immediately followed by a new rush of whites into the frontier areas east of the Mississippi River. By 1820 states had been organized in the entire area east of the river except for what was known as the Michigan Territory, and pressure to remove the remaining Indians was building.

The removal of the Indians west of the Mississippi River was accomplished during the administration of Andrew Jackson, the first president to be chosen from a frontier state. For many years before becoming president, Jackson had been convinced that treating the Indians as independent nations and negotiating treaties with them was a farce. This idea, he believed, had resulted from historical circumstances (the example of the European states, the weakness of the United States during and immediately after the revolution), rather than from any well thought out theory of sovereignty or law. In his view, the Indians should be treated like any other group of people inhabiting the United States and the Congress should legislate for them as it did for white Americans.

As F. P. Prucha has pointed out, "Jackson derived two important corollaries" from his view "of the limited political status of the Indians within the territorial United States." He did not accept the idea that the Indians held domain over western land until their title was extinguished by treaty and he was equally opposed to their establishment of independent enclaves within the territory of the individual states.[1] Consequently, when he was faced with a serious conflict between the rights of the Cherokee Indians in Georgia and the demands of the citizens of Georgia that the Cherokee Nation be brought under the laws of that state, he sided with the Georgians. Stating that the Indians could either choose to disband their tribal societies, take up allotments on individually owned parcels of land, and submit to the laws of the state in which they resided, or else remove to a new location west of the Mississippi River, he called upon the Congress in 1829 to enact legislation providing for their removal. Under duress, most of the Indians chose to move; within a decade most of them had been transported to the Indian Territory, what is now Nebraska, Kansas, and Oklahoma, which had been created by legislation in 1834. Here their tribal integrity and way of life were to be guaranteed by the federal government against further white encroachment.

Alone among the tribes, the Cherokees of Georgia attempted to overturn the removal edict. They appealed to the Supreme Court for a vindication of their prior treaty rights. Much has been written about how the Court upheld the rights of the Cherokees against the state of Georgia and about how President Jackson callously refused to exercise his executive powers to uphold the Court's decision and the Cherokee's rights. The really important issue, that of whether the Indians' rights were coequal with those of the federal government, however, has been glossed over. When Chief Justice Marshall declared in the majority decision of the *Cherokee Nation* v. *Georgia* that the Cherokees were not really an independent nation, but rather a "domestic dependent nation" whose relation to the United States resembled that of a "ward to his guardian," he in effect weakened the Indian claim to sovereignty and gave credence to Jackson's interpretation that Indian rights were inferior to those of the citizens of the United States. When Jackson refused to interpose the power of the federal government against the laws of the state of Georgia, it became immediately apparent that rights supposedly guaranteed by treaties were indeed a "farce" when they conflicted with the desires of the majority of Americans. Although the fiction of negotiating treaties was maintained until 1871, it was now clear to everyone but the Indians that the treaties could easily be broken.

For twenty years after the imposition of the removal policy, relations with the Indians were relatively quiet. The acquisition of the Pacific Northwest in 1846 and the vast region of the Southwest in 1848, however, added new territories and new Indian tribes to the United States. During the 1850s treaties were signed with many of the Indians of the Northwest and the upper plains in which vast quantities of land were ceded. In addition, the federal government attempted to confine these Indians to prescribed hunting grounds, a practice that led eventually to the reservation system. The Indians of California were practically annihilated by the gold seekers who poured into that state after 1849 and, although some treaties were negotiated, they were never ratified by the United States Senate. There were so few Americans in the other areas of the Southwest that no attempt was made to force the Indians there upon reservations, although numerous treaties limiting Indian activity were signed.

It was the coming of the railroad and the outbreak of the Civil War that signaled the next major transformation of federal Indian policy. In 1854 the Kansas-Nebraska Act destroyed the Jefferson-Jackson concept of an Indian Territory protected from white encroachment. To build a railroad binding California to the rest of the nation, Stephen A. Douglas proposed the creation of new territories in the Louisiana Purchase area, leaving only the area of present-day Oklahoma as an unorganized Indian territory. Congress authorized the negotiation of new treaties with the Indians in this region through which they agreed either to accept relatively small tracts of communally owned land designated "reservations," or to take up individually owned "allotments" within the newly created territories. Seven of the tribes chose allotment, but they were quickly dispossessed by the onrushing whites.[2] The question of slavery in the territories far outweighed the Indian question at this time, and, as a result, there was no outcry as there had been in 1832.

The passage of the Kansas-Nebraska Act also destroyed the tenuous compromise between North and South that had been made in 1850. Within the next seven years, crisis followed upon crisis until, in April 1861, the South seceded from the Union and the Civil War began. As military units stationed along the frontier were withdrawn, Indian unrest in the Southwest and on the plains erupted into raids against the whites who had steadily infiltrated these areas during the past decade. Portions of the Five Civilized Tribes in the Indian Territory were persuaded to join the Confederacy, thereby precipitating a demoralizing civil war, which further undermined their tribal cohesiveness. When the Civil War ended in the spring of 1865, the decision was reached immediately to form a new Indian policy that would bring the Indian-white conflict on the Great Plains to an end.

In 1866, the Five Civilized Tribes were forced to negotiate new treaties in which they ceded the western half of the Indian Territory, thus creating a vast area in which to relocate some of the southern Plains Indians. The following year, after two years of investigation, a joint congressional committee reported that peace could be achieved only by the application of the reservation policy begun in the 1850s to all the Indians. The poverty and cultural disorientation of the Indians demanded better security and some degree of economic support, the committee reported. This could only be guaranteed if they were confined to fixed locations. It was also important that they be restricted if the transcontinental railroads were to be built.

Accordingly, new treaties were negotiated in 1867 and

1868. At Medicine Lodge Creek in southern Kansas, the Comanche, Kiowa, Plains Apache, Arapaho, and southern Cheyenne Indians signed treaties that assigned them to reservations in the western half of the Indian Territory. In 1868 the various Sioux groups assembled at Fort Laramie in Wyoming Territory. There, a large preserve embracing the western half of present South Dakota and a portion of North Dakota was created for them. In later years, smaller reservations were assigned to the Ute, Shoshone, Bannock, Navajo, and Apache Indians. The reservation policy was not, however, successful. The Indians could not be persuaded to confine their activities to the relatively small areas assigned them in 1867 and 1868. Nor could the whites be persuaded not to trespass on these newly created reserves. Fighting between the Indians and the U.S. Army flared throughout the West from the summer of 1868 until 1874, only to be revived in 1875 when gold seekers poured into the heart of the great Sioux reservation in South Dakota. Not until 1890, when the battle of Wounded Knee ended the conflict, did the Indians at last cease to resist.

Despite the sporadic and bloody fighting that occurred after the adoption of the reservation system in 1867, the concept of autonomous Indian enclaves remained fixed in federal policy for the next twenty years. In 1871, as previously noted, the government at last abandoned the fiction of negotiating treaties with the Indians. Thereafter, relations with the tribes were determined by federal statute and presidential executive order. Although Congress subsequently assumed the right to withdraw or modify tribal rights previously guaranteed by treaty, much as Jackson had urged in 1829, the executive branch of the government frequently extended the boundaries of Indian reservations in the far West through the issuance of executive orders withdrawing public lands from white entry and reserving their usage to the tribes. The nature of the Indian title to these executive-order reservations was unclear, but because of the sparseness of the white population, the question was not debated until the 1920s.

With the adoption of the reservation system and the abolition of the treaty system, the internal affairs of the tribes
came under increasing scrutiny by the federal government.
A conscious effort was begun to civilize the Indians. Government farmers were employed to teach them the agricultural arts. Missionary societies were subsidized to bring
them the benefits of Christianity and formal education.
Tribal autonomy and the authority of native leaders were
deliberately weakened by enlarging the powers of Indian
agents and by congressional restrictions on tribal gather-
ings. Great emphasis was placed on the twin virtues of individual ownership of property and personal responsibility. By
the mid-1880s, however, most of the people who worked
with the Indians in the civilizing process ruefully conceded
that their work had had little effect. The Indian emphasis
on hunting, the aversion of many tribal groups to agricultural pursuits, and the strength of communal ties had all
proven superior to the blandishments of civilization. Individual responsibility and agriculture would not be accepted
until the Indian was forced to fend for himself on individually owned plots of land, they concluded. In 1887, well-
meaning reformers joined with the proponents of statehood
in the remaining territories of the West to enact the Dawes
Severalty Act.

The Dawes Act gave formal approval to a policy of assimilation. Assimilation of Indians into the mainstream of
white American life had always been the goal of federal policy, but before 1887 the government was reluctant to force
the process. No matter how cruel or unfair the removal policy of the 1830s may have been, it did envision allowing the
Indian to accommodate himself to white society at his own
pace. Until he was prepared to merge with his white neighbors, he was to be protected in the exercise of his traditional
way of life. The reservation policy adopted after the Civil
War also upheld the rights of Indians to determine their
own affairs, although a greater attempt was made to persuade them to change. Now all this was to be changed.
Henceforth, the Indian would be forced to pursue his for-

tune as an individual, shorn of the emotional and economic supports of his tribal society. Furthermore, he would be forced to seek his fortune as a farmer or perhaps as a stockman, because these were the accepted means of livelihood among whites in the West. Recognizing that Indians would not be able to make the transformation overnight, the Dawes Act provided that the reservation be divided into individual allotments, with the allotments to be held in trust by the government for twenty-five years, or one generation. During this period an Indian could not alienate his title, nor could he be taxed by local or state governmental bodies. After reservation lands had been allotted to individual Indians, any surplus lands were to be purchased by the federal government and subsequently opened to white entry. The proceeds from the purchase of the surplus lands were to be held in trust by the government, subject to appropriation by Congress for the education and well-being of the Indians. Each Indian would become a citizen of the United States and the state in which he resided, and, at the expiration of the trust period, he would be given a fee simple patent to his allotment. Only the Five Civilized Tribes, the Osage, and several small bands of Indians in the Indian Territory were exempted from the provisions of the Dawes Act.

Between 1887 and 1904, the Dawes Act was applied with a vengeance throughout the Indian country. The Osage were eventually persuaded to accept allotment, and in 1893 special legislation was approved extending the philosophy of the Dawes Act to the Five Civilized Tribes. When they resisted, the Curtis Act was passed in 1898 dictating their submission. By 1907, when Oklahoma became a state, tribal lands had disappeared, leaving only individual Indian allotments. Although allotment continued as late as 1931, it slackened after 1904 when Francis Leupp became commissioner of Indian Affairs in the Roosevelt administration. Leupp concluded that the policy had been disastrous for many Indians and he forbade its application in the Territories of New Mexico and Arizona.

Altogether, it has been estimated that Indian landholdings declined from 113 million acres in 1887 to 47 million acres in 1932. More important was the demoralization that accompanied the breakup of the reservations. Many Indians refused to accept the agricultural way of life, preferring to lease their allotments to whites. Many Sioux who managed to survive through cooperative livestock enterprises were persuaded to sell their herds at high prices during World War I. Then they lapsed into penury and idleness. The discovery of oil and other minerals on Indian allotments after 1900, particularly in Oklahoma, resulted in looting and fraud, which rivaled the exploits of the late nineteenth-century robber barons. In 1906 the Burke Act, framed by the same Charles Burke with whom Mrs. Atwood had conducted her lengthy correspondence, made it possible for the secretary of the interior to terminate the wardship status of any Indian adjudged competent to handle his own affairs, before the expiration of the twenty-five–year trial period envisioned in the Dawes Act.

In 1917 Commissioner of Indian Affairs Cato Sells, impatient at the time it was taking to assimilate the Indians "into the body politic of the Nation" under the wardship provision of the Dawes Act, announced what he called his "New Policy," a policy that he said meant reduced appropriations by the government and more independence for the Indians. In short, he proposed to apply the Burke Act to all adult Indians of more than one-half white blood and to a large number of others of less than one-half white blood whom his "competency" commissioners adjudged capable of managing their own affairs. Within the short space of four years, Sells and Interior Secretary Franklin K. Lane issued more than 20,000 patents-in-fee to Indians judged competent, in many cases over their protestations of incompetency.[3] Sells called his New Policy the "beginning of the end of the Indian problem." To a small but growing number of persons who saw these "competent" Indians quickly losing their lands, it looked more like the beginning of the end of the Indian himself.

By 1921 a small number of persons in the nation were beginning to question the wisdom of the allotment policy. There were others, particularly those from New Mexico and Arizona, who chafed at the remaining restrictions on Indian lands and the reluctance of the federal goverment to apply the provisions of the Dawes Act to the Indians in those states. The most outspoken of this latter group was undoubtedly Albert B. Fall, former senator from New Mexico and now, in the Harding administration, the secretary of the interior.

Born in Frankfort, Kentucky, in 1861, Albert Bacon Fall was a product of the western frontier. Driven first by poor health and later by personal ambition, he drifted west as a young man of twenty, first to the Indian Territory, then to Texas, Mexico, and finally in 1887 to Las Cruces, New Mexico. In the course of his wandering, he was alternately a schoolteacher, a cowboy, a clerk, a miner, and a prospector. His formal education was slight, but through the kindly interest of William Lindsey, a Kentucky jurist and later United States senator, he read enough law to pass the bar examination in New Mexico Territory. During his prospecting days, he met influential men like Edward L. Doheny, with whom he was to be later associated in the Teapot Dome scandal, and he mastered Spanish.

Shortly after opening his law practice in Las Cruces, Fall entered territorial politics as a Democrat. In the early 1890s he served one term in the lower house and one in the upper house. Then in 1893, by appointment of President Grover Cleveland, he became a justice of the territorial supreme court, thereby earning the monicker "judge," which accompanied him the rest of his life. In 1897, and again in 1907, he served briefly as attorney general of New Mexico Territory. During the war with Spain, he joined a territorial regiment, but did not see active service. Afterward, and until 1902 when he reentered the political arena, he devoted himself exclusively to his steadily growing private law practice.

From his Las Cruces law office, Fall was active in numerous civil and criminal cases, which steadily contributed to his political stature in southern New Mexico. He also opened a law office in El Paso, in partnership with W. A. Hawkins, one of the Southwest's most successful corporation lawyers. Through his association with Hawkins, Fall was introduced to the world of big business. He became interested in mining, timber, and railroad promotion, particularly in Mexico, and he soon became a specialist in Mexican law. Some time during this period he also concluded that his political future was limited if he remained a Democrat in a Republican-controlled territory. In 1904, just after his return to the upper house of the territorial legislature, he openly proclaimed his allegiance to the Republican party. Republicans were not pleased by his decision, but Fall's political strength in the southern half of the territory could not be ignored. In 1910 he was elected a delegate to the constitutional convention, which prepared the way for statehood, and he was an important force in the drafting of the constitution. In March 1912, along with the Republican boss of the north, Thomas B. Catron, Fall was chosen by the New Mexico Senate to represent the state in the Senate of the United States.[4]

Almost from the first day of his entrance into the Senate, Fall began a campaign against the nascent conservation movement Theodore Roosevelt had launched in 1901. During Roosevelt's administration, some 230 million acres of land in the West were withdrawn from entry in order to protect mineral, timber, petroleum, and water-power sites from private exploitation. According to conservation philosophy, these lands represented a great national heritage that should be developed for the benefit of all the people of the United States and not for the personal enrichment of a few individuals or corporations. But to westerners like Albert Fall, conservation was simply a euphemism for a sinister conspiracy, concocted in the East, to deprive citizens of the West from exploiting natural resources for their own benefit. When Fall went to Washington in 1912, more than one-third of the land in New Mexico was controlled by the federal government in the form of forest reserves, Indian reservations, and mineral lands withdrawn from entry. As a territory, New Mexico had been forced to accept conservation, but Fall was determined that as a state its citizens would have the same chance to amass wealth through the exploitation of natural resources as had others before them.

During his eight years as a United States Senator, Fall inveighed against conservation without notable success. Early in his first term he introduced several bills that would have returned all federal lands to the states, but none of these passed. In one of his earliest speeches, he ridiculed the philosophy of conservation, saying that in New Mexico conservation meant "a restriction upon the individual." It meant that upon "forest reserves and Indian reserves, the gentle bear, the mountain lion, and the timber wolf are conserved, so that they may attack [the citizen's] herds, his cattle, his sheep." In another speech he drew laughter from his colleagues when he proposed that New Mexico "be included within an Indian reservation or a national park" because so much of its land was exempt from local and state taxes desperately needed for road development, schools, and other public services.[5] Despite the amusement that his caustically witty remarks provoked, Fall was deadly serious, if ineffective, in his attempts to remove federal restrictions on the development of the public domain in New Mexico.

In one area, Indian affairs, Fall did achieve limited success. In the years before statehood, Indian reservations in Arizona and New Mexico, particularly the Navajo reservation, were frequently expanded by presidential executive order. Less than a month after his election to the Senate, Fall met with President Taft, the secretary of the interior, and the commissioner of Indian Affairs, to discuss a halt to the expansion of the Jicarilla Apache reservation in northwestern New Mexico. In a report to one of his constituents, Fall stated that he hoped to follow this conversation with a bill to open "such portions of [Indian] reservations as are being used to the detriment of our people." In 1913, with the support of the Arizona representatives, he succeeded in prohibiting the allotment of public-domain lands to any Indians within the two states. Thus, while he was not suc-

cessful in securing the abolition of the reservations, as the
legislature of New Mexico had petitioned the Congress in
1912, he was successful in putting a halt to new Indian
encroachments on the remaining public domain. When the
Indian office found a loophole in this legislation and continued to patent public domain lands to Indians, Fall joined
with Senators Marcus A. Smith and Henry F. Ashurst of Arizona in 1918 to secure legislation prohibiting the creation
of new Indian reservations or their enlargement "except by
act of Congress."[6] Thereafter, landless Indians, who for forty
years had relied upon the executive branch of the federal
government for assistance, found themselves at the mercy
of a Congress determined not to permit them one additional
inch of land.

By 1918 Fall's inability to effect any significant change in
the federal goverment's attitude toward the development of
western lands so depressed him that he seriously considered not running for reelection. In a letter to a friend he
wrote:[7]

> I came into the Senate hoping that I might be able to do
> something for the life and development of the state of New
> Mexico . . . . I flattered myself that . . . I was as well quali-
> fied as anyone to act intelligently upon the needs of New
> Mexico with reference to mining, railroads, stockraising,
> agricultural [sic], irrigation and practically every other pos-
> sible development.
>
> I found here under the last year of the Taft administra-
> tion, a condition existing in the Interior Department which
> offered little or no encouragement to any practical plans for
> working along the line which I have indicated.
>
> I very much hoped that the Democratic administration
> might see things in a different light, particularly in view of
> the plank in their platform which, while not entirely re-
> pudiating the conservation of Pinchotism, yet promised
> development and assistance in opening up our natural
> resources.
>
> Any such expectation or hope has failed to receive confir-
> mation to the present date. Much to my disappointment,
> Mr. Lane as Secretary of the Interior, has displayed a woe-

ful lack of understanding the needs of the West and, even when grasping any part of such needs, has then been hampered with interference from some other member of the Cabinet.

I found that there had developed under this Administration that spirit of bureaucratism which had been developing for so many years under previous administrations; and I found the Democratic Congress absolutely determined, apparently, not only to obey every command, but to yield to every indication of desire communicated to them, either directly or indirectly, from any department of government. I have found this to be particularly so with reference to the Committee on Public Lands and to the general membership of the lower House, which is guided entirely in its conferences and in its conclusions by advice from the Interior Department.

All this has been exceedingly disappointing, and, in fact, my experience here in inability to get action, has been very wearing upon one who had been accustomed to dealing with businessmen in a business way and achieving results.

Of course, all these conditions, while yet existing and influencing me and, in fact, confirming me in my personal desire and determination not to come back to the Senate, have, to some extent, been changed by the different conditions and problems created by the war.

Fall concluded this letter with the hope that the war "may result in materially altering, if not entirely changing, the form of government as we have known it . . . ." This hope, as well as pressure from the state and national Republican organizations, caused him to reconsider, and he ran successfully for reelection.

The changes that Fall hoped the war would bring did not materialize. For a while he and other opponents of conservation thought they might convince the Congress that conservation would have to be abandoned in order to win the war. In 1919, using the war argument, Fall and several other western senators successfully opened executive-order Indian reservations to the mining of "metalliferous minerals," but they lost the main fight in 1920 when, after five years of

debate and delay, their opponents succeeded in enacting the
General Leasing Act. Instead of permitting private ownership and development of the public-domain lands that
Roosevelt and Taft had withdrawn from entry, as many
westerners like Fall advocated, this act permanently reserved title to the federal government and permitted only
the leasing of the land under federal regulation and supervision. Although the General Leasing Act was obviously
unsatisfactory to men like Fall, it did at least break the
deadlock over the development of these lands. Geologists
and mining engineers now began to fan out over the West in
search of minerals and oil.

Despite the many defeats he had suffered during his eight
years in the Senate, Albert Fall's pessimism about the development of New Mexico vanished during the summer of
1920 when his colleague and good friend Warren G. Harding
was nominated as the Republican candidate for president.
"With Harding as President," he wrote exultantly to the
governor of New Mexico shortly after the convention,
"New Mexico will have the opportunity to realize during
the four years commencing March next some of her ambitions with regard to control of her public lands and other
matters which we believe are essential to our general welfare and prosperity."

Fall's new optimism grew during the summer and fall of
1920. In June his private secretary, C. V. Safford, confided
that it was Fall's hope during the Harding administration
"to secure for New Mexico all the unreserved and unap-
propriated lands in the State . . . ." After Harding's victory
in November there was much speculation about Fall's possible appointment as secretary of state, but after being
closeted with the president-elect in his Florida retreat in
mid-January 1921, Fall emerged as Harding's choice for secretary of the interior. The nomination was not well received
in conservationist circles, and for a brief period the Indian
Rights Association of Philadelphia attempted to block the
appointment on the grounds that Fall had previously attempted to improve his Three Rivers Ranch property at the
expense of the nearby Mescalero Apache Indians. In Febru-

ary 1921, Herbert Welsh, the president of the IRA, wrote to Henry Cabot Lodge warning him "how unfortunate a second Ballinger would be for the Harding administration." Lodge's reply, "He is a thoroughly upright and high-minded man and no more capable of using his office for his own financial interest than you are or any other honest man," was to haunt him throughout the remainder of the 1920s.

More important figures than Welsh were involved in a plan to defeat Fall's nomination. Led by Gifford Pinchot and Harry A. Slattery, conservationists and progressive Republicans banded together behind Senator Robert La Follette of Wisconsin in an effort to challenge Fall's credentials during Senate hearings on his nomination. Harding, however, foiled this plan when he went to the Senate chambers immediately after his inauguration and personally submitted his cabinet choices to his former colleagues. Caught off guard by this maneuver, the opposition failed to develop, and Fall, along with the other nominees, was unanimously confirmed by the Senate without formal hearings. Despite this reversal, the conservationists kept a close watch on all of Fall's activities and within a few months they were convinced that their initial suspicions had been correct. Fall was attempting to open Alaska to private development, he was actively seeking to transfer the Forestry Service from the Department of Agriculture to Interior, and there was a distinct odor of corruption surrounding his secret leasing of several federally owned oil reserves to Harry Sinclair and Edward Doheny.[8]

Fall's negotiation of the leases on the Teapot Dome and Elk Hills naval oil reserves is now well known. While on his way to Los Angeles to speak with Mrs. Atwood, Fall received Harry Sinclair at his Three Rivers Ranch in eastern New Mexico. In return for $233,000 in Liberty bonds and $85,000 in cash, which Fall later said represented a one-third interest in his ranching enterprises, arrangements were made to lease the Teapot Dome oil reserve in Wyoming to Sinclair's wholly owned Mammoth Oil Co. A month earlier Fall had accepted a loan of $100,000 from his old friend Edward Doheny, at the same time that he promised Doheny a

highly favorable leasing arrangement on the Elk Hills and
Buena Vista naval oil reserves in Kern County, California.
In early April 1922, the leases were signed by Fall without
competitive bidding and without publicity. Shortly after
Fall was forced to make them public later that same month,
Senator Robert La Follette introduced a resolution into the
Senate calling for an investigation of the leases. The resolution was adopted by a vote of 58 to 0, but the chairman of
the Senate Public Lands Committee, Reed Smoot of Utah,
was an old friend of Fall's, and for over a year the investigation languished.

Then, in 1923, Senator Thomas Walsh of Montana, himself an opponent of conservation who had once voted to
lease the naval reserves, became suspicious. In October, he
reopened the investigation. Fall, who had resigned from the
Interior post in April 1923, after serving only two years,
contemptuously sent Walsh a truckload of documents when
he was summoned to appear before Walsh's committee.
After patiently sifting through these papers, Walsh forced
from Doheny and Sinclair in early 1924 the admission that
they had made loans to Fall at approximately the time that
the leases had been signed by the former secretary. Criminal proceedings were then undertaken against the trio.

In 1926 Fall and Doheny went on trial for conspiracy, but
the jury determined they were not guilty. The following
year federal courts ordered Doheny's Pan American Company to pay the federal government for the oil taken from
the Elk Hills lease and declared the Teapot Dome lease invalid. That same year Sinclair and Fall were tried in criminal court. Sinclair was found not guilty, although he was
given a brief sentence for jury tampering. Fall was found
guilty of accepting a bribe, sentenced to one year in the penitentiary, and fined $100,000. In July 1931, broken in health
and almost penniless (he lost control of the ranch in 1929),
Fall entered the federal prison at Santa Fe, New Mexico.
The fine was never paid. Fall's last years were spent in
obscurity and near poverty in El Paso, where he died in
1944.[9]

Whether as a result of being overshadowed by the more spectacular nature of the Teapot Dome scandal or because of a lack of interest, Fall's role in reshaping federal Indian policy during his two-year stint in Washington was almost totally ignored in the contemporary press. The same has been true of subsequent historical studies of this period in American history. And yet, Fall's efforts to open the remaining Indian estates to exploitation were an integral part of his philosophy for the mineral development of the West. Foiled in his efforts to develop the public domain for private gain, Fall sought new areas of exploitation for miners and oilmen. He found these in the Indian reservations, particularly those in New Mexico and Arizona, most of which had been created by presidential executive order in the later nineteenth century. Not only would the opening of these vast preserves provide added profits for their developers, but, according to Fall's plan, they would also provide much needed tax revenues for the states in which they were located. Because Fall's attitude toward the Indians who occupied these lands so closely corresponded to the conventional wisdom, he almost succeeded in this endeavor. Only the fortuitous decision of Collier and Mrs. Atwood to launch an independent investigation of Indian affairs in the summer of 1922, and the furious assault they mounted against Fall in 1923, prevented him from carrying out his intentions in this field. And only because of his success in stopping Fall was it possible for John Collier to organize the sustained drive for Indian policy reform that he led throughout the 1920s.

Thus, just as Teapot Dome served as a catalyst to resolve the struggle over the use of the nation's natural resources in favor of the forces of conservation, so, too, did the actions of Secretary Fall toward his Indian wards provide the impetus that made possible the reversal of the assimilationist philosophy during the New Deal era.

Albert Fall had no love for Indians, and in all his dealings with them he always sought a solution that benefited white propertied interests rather than the Indians. For this reason, in his contemporary writings, as well as in his influential *Indians of the Americas*, John Collier painted a picture of Fall as the evil mastermind behind every anti-Indian piece of legislation that surfaced during the years 1921–23. Collier specifically charged Fall with the three anti-Indian activities that prompted the rise of the reform movement. First, there was the "notorious Bursum bill," through which Fall allegedly sought to deprive the Pueblo Indians of land and water rights along the Rio Grande. Second, Fall ruled that Indians did not hold title to executive-order reservations, an action that threatened their claim to ownership of some 22 million acres of land. Third, Fall attempted to push through Congress the "Omnibus bill," which would have destroyed the remaining Indian landed estates by individualizing tribal property and removing Indians from federal custody.[10]

Collier's successful attempt to symbolize in Albert Fall all that was wrong with traditional Indian policy was a useful tool in his campaign to reform the system, particularly after Fall was indicted for his part in the Teapot Dome scandal. At the same time, however, this tendency to personalize the evils of the system often did violence to the facts themselves. For instance, Fall's denial of Indian title to executive-order reservations was designed to open these lands to oil and gas exploitation, not to deprive Indians of their rights to surface ownership. Fall had little to do with the Omnibus bill of 1923, which stemmed directly from a congressional investigation conducted in 1919–20 and which was the handiwork of Representative Homer P. Snyder of New York, chairman of the House Indian Affairs Committee. The Bursum bill was a classic product of New Mexico politics and tradition and in its original form, as we have seen, was actually defeated in committee by Fall in 1921. Significantly, the one bill in which Fall had a direct and personal interest, the All Year National Park on the Mescalero Apache reservation, was never mentioned by Collier because he found its publicity value already preempted by the Indian Rights Association.

Because of the complexity of the legislation proposed during the years 1921–23 and in order to place the events of these years in their true prespective, the following chapter is devoted to an examination of that legislation, before September 1922, when Collier entered upon the scene.

Figure 13.   Albert B. Fall. From the National Archives, Still
Pictures Branch.

Albert B. Fall and the Genesis of Reform
(1921–22)

When Albert Fall became secretary of the interior on March 5, 1921, he had definite ideas about only one group of Indians, the Mescalero Apaches, whose reservation in south-central New Mexico bordered his Three Rivers Ranch to the east. Created in 1873 by executive-order withdrawal from the public domain, the Mescalero reservation contained 474,000 acres, most of them mountainous and timbered. In 1921 the reservation was inhabited by only 628 Indians.

Fall's interests in the Mescaleros dated back to 1906 when, by shrewd purchases and eventual foreclosure upon the former owner, Patrick Coghlan, he acquired title to the 103,000-acre Three Rivers Ranch. In the years that followed, Fall slowly expanded his holdings in the area. In 1913, Three Rivers became the center of a vast cattle-raising empire when Fall merged his holdings with those of one of his sons-in-law, Mahlon T. Everhart, and a group of bankers from Pueblo, Colorado. Although the combine actually owned

Figure 14.   Holm O. Bursum. From Twitchell, *Leading Facts of New Mexican History.*

only strategically located water holes, it controlled state and federal lands in an area 50 miles long and 25 to 35 miles wide between Tularosa and Oscuro, New Mexico. In all, the range dominated by Fall and his partners contained more than a million acres.[1]

In addition to his cattle interests, Albert Fall had other, more grandiose ideas for the development of the Three Rivers area. These ideas were dependent upon the exploitation of resources controlled by the Mescalero Apaches and upon the success of the El Paso and Northeastern Railroad, which passed through the heart of his empire.

In 1897 the railroad began construction north from El Paso to Santa Rosa, New Mexico. In its path sprang up the towns of Tularosa and Carrizozo. By 1905, however, the

Figure 15.   Ralph Twitchell. From Twitchell, *Leading Facts of New Mexican History.*

road had fallen on bad times. Water obtained from wells along its right-of-way proved high in gypsum and alkali, with the result that locomotive boilers frequently malfunctioned and schedule delays were commonplace. Shortly before Fall obtained control of Three Rivers, his old friend William H. Hawkins, who served as legal counsel to the railroad, suggested that a pure and dependable water supply could be obtained from mountain streams to the east of the roadbed. Hawkins's suggestion was investigated by the Phelps Dodge Corporation, found feasible, and in 1905, under Hawkins's supervision, the railroad was reorganized under Phelps Dodge ownership. The search for mountain water began immediately.

In 1908 the ownership of waters in Tularosa Creek, just to

the south of Three Rivers, was apportioned by court order. Because the creek originated in the Sierra Blanca Mountains on the Mescalero Apache reservation, the court awarded the Indians priority rights to its water during the summer irrigation season, from April to September. During the remainder of the year, white settlers farther downstream were granted priority. The railroad purchased its water supply from the whites.

Two years after the Tularosa Creek decision, Albert Fall and Mescalero Agent James A. Carrol negotiated an agreement for the division of water in the Three Rivers Creek, which also had its origins in the Mescalero reservation. Following the Tularosa precedent, the Indians living along the creek's banks, only three families, were guaranteed adequate water during the irrigation season. Fall obtained title to any surplus during the irrigation season and to all the water in the creek during the remainder of the year. The contract, duly approved by the Interior Department, obligated Fall to construct a concrete dam and pipeline at the headwaters of the creek in order to reduce water loss from absorption and to prevent erosion of the mountainside. Fall was also obliged to provide lateral conduits from the pipeline to the areas where the Indians practiced irrigated farming. It was Fall's intent not only to sell the water to the railroad, but also to develop a small town at the Three Rivers water station. If the railroad could be made to prosper, he explained to his son-in-law, Clarence C. Chase, the "Three Rivers Townsite" project "will see lots of profit."

Fall's plan to build a pipeline to the railroad was stalled for four years because of a proposal by the Indian Bureau for the construction of an Indian tuberculosis sanitarium on the Mescalero reservation. Had the sanitarium been approved, the Indian need for water would have been greatly increased. At last, in 1914, the plan was abandoned and Fall immediately began construction. At the same time, to ensure adequate water for the locomotives during the summer months, he attempted to negotiate a modification to the original agreement that would assure him the usage of

Figure 16.   John Collier with the painter Gerald Cassidy and an unidentified group of Pueblo Indians at the All-Pueblo Council meeting at Santo Domingo May 5, 1924. Courtesy of the National Archives.

"night water" in the creek during the irrigation season. Although Indian Commissioner Cato Sells agreed that Fall could use whatever water was not needed by the Indians, he adamantly refused to recognize any legal right of Fall to ownership of the night water. A gentleman's agreement between the Apache leader in the area, Shanta Boy, and Fall was finally worked out by the Mescalero agent. For ten dollars a month, Shanta Boy would be employed by Fall to close the Indians' ditches at night when the Indians did not need the water.

The dam and pipeline that Fall constructed in 1914 were paid for by a loan of $17,400 from the El Paso and Northeastern Railroad. Under the terms of the loan, the railroad was guaranteed 75,000 gallons of water daily for its locomotives until 1920. During this period, Fall was to receive $2,700 annually, and in 1920 his debt would be forgiven. The railroad also took an option on the future delivery of 250,000 gallons daily. If the option were exercised, the railroad agreed to pay all expenses involved in enlarging the pipeline, all maintenance expenses on the enlarged water delivery system, and to pay Fall $9,125 annually for the water.[2]

In 1917, when he first began to experience difficulty in keeping his varied enterprises solvent, Fall attempted to sell his water rights in Three Rivers Creek to the railroad for $170,000 cash. As he explained to W. A. Hawkins in May 1917: "I am moved to make the proposition because I have lost so heavily during my term in the Senate, that I am compelled to have money from some source at the very earliest possible moment." To pay off his debts and to reorganize his "cattle and other business interests at Tres Rios," Fall estimated that he needed between $60,000 and $100,000. In similar letters to his sons-in-law, Fall complained that he was "very much in need of money." He was certain, however, that the railroad would either purchase his interest or exercise its option to the additional water before it expired on September 1, 1917.[3]

For reasons not clearly indicated in Fall's papers, the railroad did not accept his offer to sell, nor did it exercise its option to additional water. His plans for the development of the Three Rivers townsite collapsed and his financial problems increased. In addition, Fall now began to encounter difficulties with Shanta Boy and other Mescaleros along the creek who challenged his use of the night water. Perhaps it was this uncertainty over the title to the creek's water that ruined his plans for the sale. In any event, Fall's relations with the hitherto passive Mescaleros deteriorated as the years progressed.

In 1914, Clarence R. Jeffries, the Mescalero agent, proposed that the Indians be permitted to sell a portion of their timber, the proceeds to be used to stock a 10,000-head tribal cattle herd. Fall, who along with other ranchers was leasing portions of the Mescalero range, was opposed to the idea because, as he said, "the range won't hold that many." In 1915, Jeffries was transferred and the idea lay dormant until 1920, when a new superintendent, Ernest Stecker, resurrected it. In August 1920, Stecker successfully persuaded outgoing Indian Commissioner Cato Sells to negotiate a contract for the sale of $500,000 worth of Mescalero timber over a ten-year period. The contract was contingent upon congressional approval of a bill appropriating $500,000 for the Mescaleros from the federal treasury, to be reimbursed over the years from the timber sale.

In his correspondence with both Commissioner Sells and Senator Fall, Stecker enthusiastically outlined the proposal, which he said would "mean a new life" for the Mescaleros. Half of the $500,000, he said, should be used to purchase a tribal herd, which, at current prices, could be expected to net $180,000 annually from the sale of yearlings. From this profit, Stecker proposed to pay each Indian twenty dollars monthly, thus ensuring a steady income. The other $250,000 would be used to construct permanent homes and other farm buildings and to buy out two white landowners who lived within the reservation. With a regular income and permanent homes, Stecker predicted, the Mescaleros would quickly become prosperous, self-supporting Indians who would no longer require federal appropriations for their sustenance.

Although he was no more inclined to favor Stecker's plan than he had Agent Jeffries's earlier proposal, Fall told Stecker in June 1920 that he would gladly assist him in securing congressional approval for the plan. Fall's willingness to back Stecker appears to have been caused by his need for Stecker's support in other matters. In 1920 the Mescaleros opposed the signing of a new lease with Fall's son-in-law, Mahlon Everhart, for grazing rights on the western portion of the reservation. The three Indian families along the Three Rivers watercourse even leased their fields to one of Fall's major competitors, the Harris-Brownfield outfit. Counseling the Mescaleros that Fall's support of the timber contract was necessary to their future well-being, Stecker at last succeeded in renewing the lease, but only for three years rather than the customary five. Stecker also decided at this time to hold Fall to the letter of the 1910 agreement over the division of water in the Three Rivers Creek. He refused to permit Fall to use the night water during the irrigation season, despite Fall's protests that Agents Jeffries and Carrol had permitted this interpretation.[4]

Stecker's bill to sell the Mescalero timber failed to pass in 1920. In early 1921, Senator Charles Curtis, the chairman of the Senate Indian Affairs Committee, informed Fall that the bill would be resubmitted in the new session of Congress, but that he had modified it to eliminate the $250,000 for a tribal herd. Curtis was opposed to the concept of a tribal herd and said it was his intention to individualize the small existing herd "as rapidly as possible." Fall apparently did not comment on the new bill since he would soon be in a position to rule on it administratively as secretary of the interior.

Agent Stecker, who was unaware of Curtis's action, was doing his best at the time to maintain Fall's support for the original bill. At the same time that Curtis was writing to Fall, Stecker replied to several complaints he had received from Fall and Mrs. Fall about the way in which the Indians along the creek were diverting its flow from Fall's storage tanks. He had learned, Stecker reported, that the Indians were diverting the water to the cattle of the Harris-Brownfield outfit, to which they had leased their grazing land. Stecker told the Indians that the Harris-Brownfield cattle would have to be removed from the reservation and that they had no right to give the water to Fall's rival. He also cautioned them that his plan "to better the conditions of all the Mescaleros" depended upon Fall's assistance and "our cooperation with each other."

Immediately upon assuming the office of secretary of the interior, Fall moved to achieve long deferred goals relating to the Mescalero Apache reservation. In April 1921 he ordered an Indian Office engineer to the area to investigate the conflict over water rights. In his report, engineer William Reed advised that there was considerable evidence to indicate that the Indians had been illegally diverting water from Fall's conduit. He urged the office to put a stop to the practice and concluded that the Indians had been led to make "complaint of unjust treatment in the irrigation matters through influence from the outside . . . ." In October, Fall personally directed the transfer of Agent Stecker, who continued to insist upon following the letter of the 1910 agreement. In December, with money he received from Edward Doheny, Fall bought the Harris-Brownfield outfit for $91,500, thus eliminating the only competition to his land and water rights on the western side of the reservation.[5]

Intimately bound up with Fall's desire to control the range to the west of the Mescalero reservation and his claim to the waters of the Three Rivers Creek, were two bills for the creation of National Parks in New Mexico. One of the proposed parks was to be located on a portion of the western Mescalero reservation, the other on the Rio Grande at Elephant Butte, 65 miles west of Fall's ranch, where the federal government was constructing a dam. The Elephant Butte Park was apparently Fall's own idea; the Mescalero Park had its origins in the days before statehood when W. H. Andrews, the territorial delegate, lobbied unsuccessfully for its creation. When Andrews was defeated for the U.S. Senate in 1912, he brought the idea to Fall's attention.

On May 2, 1912, less than six weeks after his election to the United States Senate, Fall introduced bills to create the two parks. He requested that they both be referred to the Senate Committee on Public Lands, but after a challenge by Senator Weldon B. Heyburn of Idaho, the Mescalero Park bill was sent to the Indian Affairs Committee. It was Fall's understanding that the Interior Department would support the Mescalero bill and he thought it likely that the department would also support the Elephant Butte proposal.

The expected support was not, however, forthcoming. On

June 19, 1912, Commissioner of Indian Affairs Robert C. Valentine reported adversely on the Mescalero bill, expressing doubt about the advisability of establishing "recreation parks within reservations." The Reclamation Service, which wanted to develop a reservoir at the Elephant Butte site, also recommended against that bill. Fall was furious. "The present Commissioner of Indian Affairs is an impossible man from every standpoint," he wrote a constituent. "We cannot expect to do anything with [him] . . . everyone here hopes [he] will be succeeded by someone familiar with the West and Western people, possibly at an early date."[6]

When the Democrats took control of the federal government in 1913, Fall revived his scheme. During the summer he called upon the new Commissioner of Indian Affairs, Cato Sells, to enlist his support for the Mescalero Park bill. Sell's assistant, F. B. Abbot, who was familiar with Fall's earlier defeat, was certain that a park could be created "which will actually help the Indians," but other members of the commissioner's staff were doubtful. Fall was told that he would receive the backing of the Indian Office "if at all possible" and in 1914, believing he had smoothed the way for acceptance, he reintroduced the park bill.

Although copies of these early park bills have not been found, it is possible to discern their outlines from protests filed against the 1914 bill, S. 4187. In effect, it called for the allotment in severalty of the reservation, the withdrawal of the Mescalero title to an estimated three million dollars' worth of timber, the opening of the area to mining with no payment to the Indians, and the lease of lots to whites for "summer homes or cottages." Immediately, S. M. Brosius, the Indian Rights Association's (IRA) legal counsel, wrote to protest that Fall's bill "fails to fully recognize the rights of the Indians to the land." Brosius was opposed to opening the reservation to the mining laws of the United States, but he insisted that if it were opened, the Indians must be given all royalties that might accrue from mineral discoveries. Brosius's protest was seconded by the Reverend Richard H. Harper, a missionary of the Reformed Church in America, stationed at Mescalero, New Mexico. Both men were quick to point out that Fall would benefit personally from the bill's passage. On February 25, 1914, Sells replied to both Brosius and Harper, saying that he was aware that "the present bill does not protect the interests of the Indians" and he subsequently submitted an adverse report that killed it.

Still not defeated, Fall tried again in January 1916. This time, in addition to the IRA, the Board of Indian Commissioners and the newly formed United States National Park Service joined in the protest. Again, Sells recommended against the park. After this third defeat, Fall at last abandoned hope of securing the bills' passage so long as Sells remained in office.

Fall's efforts to open the Mescalero reservation were partly rewarded in 1919 when Congress approved the amendment to the Indian appropriation bill, which opened executive-order reservations to the mining of metalliferous minerals. Although Fall himself did not file for a lease, his daughter-in-law, Mrs. Jack M. Fall, his son-in-law, Clarence C. Chase, and his ranch manager, J. T. Johnson, secured ten of the seventy-three leases issued before December 1922. The IRA, which by now was monitoring Fall's every move, charged that these leases were secured after Fall became secretary of the interior and that upon their execution, Fall withdrew the reservation from the provisions of the act.[7]

Soon after becoming secretary of the interior, Fall revived the National Park bills, which he had been forced to abandon in 1916. Suspecting perhaps that his motives might be questioned, he arranged for a display of public support for the parks through two old friends, Richard F. Burgess and W. A. Hawkins. After arranging for a meeting of delegates from the Las Cruces, Alamagordo, and El Paso chambers of commerce in October 1921, at which time their support for the park was pledged, Burgess and Hawkins then began preparations for a larger convention designed to attract support from across the state. By November they were working on a draft bill, which they intended to submit to the convention the following month. Although Fall's advice was sought, Hawkins assured him that his name would not be linked to the bill: "Of course, I understand that you do not want to be known as sponsor of, or as drawing this bill, etc., and of course, you can depend absolutely on no word of that kind being given to the public or even getting beyond me if you make that condition." Under their guidance, the state-wide convention was held in Las Cruces in early December and the draft bill approved. Hawkins was named chairman of the convention and Ralph Twitchell, whom Fall had appointed to investigate Pueblo matters, was named to head a delegation from Santa Fe, where northern sectional jealousy to the park was known to exist. To pacify the IRA, Fall met with Herbert Welsh on November 1. The result, Welsh notified the IRA board, was "the pleasantest, frankest sort of conversation." Although Fall made no promises, he told Welsh that he desired the support of the IRA and welcomed its suggestions at any time.[8]

In April 1922, the Mescalero Park bill was forwarded to Senator Holm O. Bursum, Fall's successor in the Senate, for submission. It was a peculiar measure. No longer just a Mescalero Park, the proposal now called for the creation of an "All Year National Park" comprising 2,000 acres of the Mescalero reservation, 640 acres of the White Sands (35 miles southwest of Fall's ranch), 640 acres of the Malpais lava bed (40 miles northwest of the ranch), and an undisclosed amount of land on the Elephant Butte reservoir. From the viewpoint of the conservationists who had succeeded in creating the U.S. National Park Service in 1916, Fall's bill, ignoring as it did the concept of "natural wilderness areas," was an abomination. From Albert Fall's viewpoint, however, the bill served a very good purpose.

Almost a year before the introduction of the All Year National Park bill, Fall had prepared a companion bill, which represented a refinement of his avowed plans to have the federal government restore the public domain to the states. This bill proposed that the secretary of the interior be empowered to dispose of 10 percent of the total public domain within each state at public auction. All mineral rights would remain with the government; timber and agricultural lands were not to be included in the sale. The proceeds of these sales were to be used to construct roads in the remainder of the public domain as directed by the secretary of the interior. In June 1921, Fall advised one of his friends "confidentially" that the Harding administration, although opposed to "large appropriations for the construction of roads," had agreed to back him in this plan to build roads in undeveloped portions of the West. One item, specifically provided for in the bill that Fall drafted, authorized a road connecting the Mescalero reservation and the Elephant Butte reservoir. Such a road, Fall explained to a member of the Albuquerque Chamber of Commerce, would "open up a vast body of public land and more than 100,000 acres of state land and would give assistance to miners and prospectors in southern New Mexico." Coupled with the extensive road system necessary to unite the various protions of the All Year National Park, Fall might have noted, the region surrounding his Three Rivers Ranch property would become one of the best developed and most easily accessible in all the state.[9]

Despite the precautions he took to enlist support for the bill, Fall did encounter difficulties, particularly within his own department. Before the bill was formally submitted by Bursum, Commissioner of Indian Affairs Charles Burke registered his opposition. In December 1921, Burke informed Senator Charles Curtis that he could not support the measure unless the Indians were reimbursed for their lands and their other interests were fully protected. Stephen Mather, the director of the National Parks Service, attempted to stall a report on the bill, but in May 1922 he was called to Three Rivers. Returning to Washington, he "scribbled out an adverse report in pencil, talked [again] with Fall, and disappeared." Mather did not return to Washington until the end of the year. According to his biographer, his report was "not officially filed and has never been seen since." A minister on the reservation wrote to Burgess to protest that the

Indians had not received a copy of the bill, nor had they been consulted on the matter. Mescalero Agent Fred C. Morgan, who told Commissioner Burke that he had learned about the bill "only through local newspaper reports," also doubted that it was sound.

As a result of the growing chorus of opposition, Fall took steps to bypass Burke, Morgan, and Mather. While making these preparations, he withheld the issuance of a formal report on the bill, much to Senator Bursum's chagrin. At last on June 14, in a surprise move, he informed the Senate that he could not approve Bursum's bill. Instead, he submitted his own draft of a park bill, which, he explained, would be "more for the interests of the Mescaleros than any other legislation of recent years concerning other reservation Indians and their properties."[10]

Capitalizing on the opposition to the Burgess-Hawkins-Bursum bill, Fall now apparently hoped to appear as the Indians' protector. Keeping intact all the major provisions of their bill with respect to park areas, Fall's draft sought to meet the opposition that had arisen. Although he still did not propose to compensate the Indians for their land, his draft did provide that privately owned lands within the Mescalero reservation should be purchased by the secretary of the interior for Indian use, homes should be provided for the Mescaleros, and most important, after removal of the 2,000 acres for park use, the remainder should be set aside exclusively for Indian use, thus removing the reservation from the developing controversy over Indian title to executive-order reservations. This provision apparently won over Commissioner Burke and the IRA legal counsel, S. M. Brosius, who told a member of the Board of Indian Commissioners that he thought "on the whole" Fall's draft was a good measure since it would "solve the problem of the executive order status of the reservation and put a stop to any further attempt to steal it." To pacify Agent Morgan and the missionary who had protested that the Indians had not been consulted, Fall now instructed Morgan to call a council of the Indians in order to explain both Bursum's bill and his own draft.[11]

In Fall's revision there was another provision that bears scrutiny. It would have opened the reservation to oil development by applying to it the General Leasing Act of 1920. That act, however, was amended by Fall to provide that any royalties accruing from the discovery of oil on the reservation were to be divided evenly among the reclamation fund, the state of New Mexico, and the Indians. In other words, although Fall was now willing to guarantee the Indians' title to the surface of the reservation and to abandon the idea of allotting the entire reservation, both significant concessions from his earlier stand, he continued to insist that the Indian title to the subsurface mineral rights was less than absolute. His reasoning, that executive-order Indian reservations were similar in nature to public-domain lands and thus not wholly the property of the Indians, is best illustrated by a ruling he made simultaneously on Navajo lands, a ruling that will be discussed later.

To secure approval for his revision of the Burgess-Hawkins-Bursum bill, Fall resorted to the kind of duplicity that his Teapot Dome activities made infamous. One week after he advised the Senate Indian Affairs Committee that he could not approve Bursum's bill, Fall notified Senator Selden P. Spencer, the new chairman of the Senate Indian Affairs Committee, that he was recommending against the long pending bill authorizing the appropriation of $250,000 to the Mescaleros to be reimbursed from the sale of their timber. He had always been opposed to the cutting of Mescalero timber, Fall informed Spencer, and he regretted the "unwise decision" of the former administration authorizing this contract. Since it was from the sale of this timber that the Mescalero homes were to be built and the white lands within the reservation were to be purchased, it is evident that those provisions in Fall's draft of the All Year Park bill were mere windowdressing to obtain congressional approval for the park.

Even more despicable were Fall's successful efforts to rig the Mescalero council meeting. On June 23, 1922, he wrote to former Agent James A. Carrol, now the land commissioner of the Prairie Oil and Gas Company, asking him to

attend the Mescalero council as "a personal favor to me
. . . ." Fall specified that Carrol should "advise the Indians
either for or against the bill," but it is obvious that Carrol's
function was to allay any suspicions that the Indians might
have. Fall also ordered L. A. Dorrington, an inspector in the
Indian Office, whom he had recommended for the post
of Indian commissioner and whom he had personally appointed to supervise Indian affairs in New Mexico after he
took office, to the Mescalero reservation with orders to assist Morgan in conducting the meeting.

The first Mescalero council was held on June 24. Agent
Morgan read both Bursum's bill and Fall's revision to the assembled Indians and then adjourned the meeting for a week
to permit the Mescaleros to consider the matter. On July 1
a second council was called. Inspector Dorrington presided
at this meeting and former Superintendent Carrol, whom
Dorrington told the Indians "is here by accident," was invited to attend. Dorrington, Carrol, and Morgan, who had
been in conference "all afternoon and evening" the day before, each testified that Bursum's draft was insufficient to
protect the Indian interest. Dorrington and Carrol repeatedly advised the Mescaleros to accept the loss of the 2,000
acres for the park in return for a guaranteed title to the remainder. Dorrington warned the Mescaleros that their title
to the executive-order reservation was shaky at best; they
were, he said, "only camping here." Carrol also emphasized
their precarious position, advising them to accept the protection that Fall's guarantee to the remainder of the reservation offered. Someday, he warned, another secretary of the
interior, "who won't be so nice," might decide to restore the
reservation to the public domain.

Following the arguments by Dorrington and Carrol, several Indians spoke. All of them exhibited considerable con-
fusion about the provisions of the two bills. One Mescalero,
Pigaganzi, said he was in favor of the new homes, but he
wanted to keep all the land of the reservation. When others
spoke to the same effect, Dorrington broke in, saying that
he felt certain the reservation would someday be allotted
and the surplus sold to whites. Now, he stressed, was the

time to prevent this from happening by supporting Fall's bill. He then called for a vote and "everyone in the room approved." On July 3, Fall wrote again to Senator Spencer to report that 90 percent of the adult Mescaleros had attended a council and had given "unanimous support" to his draft of the park bill. It was now possible for him to "respectfully urge the immediate adoption of the bill under discussion."

Fall's unscrupulous method of conducting Indian business and his persistent effort to isolate the Indian Affairs Office from these dealings are further revealed in his handling of the minutes of the Mescalero council. At his request, the transcript of the council, which Dorrington forwarded to Commissioner Burke, omitted all references to the participation of former Agent Carrol. In his own report to Fall on the council, Carrol wrote that he had asked both Dorrington and Morgan "to make no mention of my presence; the reason will be obvious to you." He also congratulated Fall on the manner in which Dorrington had conducted the meeting: "He would be a valuable acquisition to some big oil concern. I have no doubt that Harry Sinclair would gladly take him into his organization."[12]

On July 7, 1922, without committee hearing, the Senate considered the revised All Year National Park bill. Bursum, in response to questions from several senators, exhibited an appalling degree of ignorance about the bill's contents. He assured his colleagues, however, that the revised bill "is unanimously agreed upon by the Indians, recommended by the Interior Department, and very much desired by the people of that section." It had been prepared by the National Park Service, he falsely stated, and was unanimously recommended by the Senate Indian Affairs Committee. Without opposition, the bill was passed and sent to the House.[13]

In July 1922, John Collier was still teaching at San Francisco State Teacher's College. The All Year National Park bill passed without his notice, but it was prevented from becoming law by the opposition of the National Parks Association and its director, Robert Sterling Yard, a former publicity agent for the National Parks Service and a long time friend of NPS Director Stephen Mather. On July 14, a week after the Senate passed the bill, Yard stated his opposition to one of Harding's administrative assistants after failing to gain access to Fall. Yard left a copy of a highly critical article that he said he intended to publish in a future edition of the association magazine. Alarmed at the tenor of Yard's article ("It seems likely that the National Parks Association is apt to make Secretary Fall the subject of a critical publicity campaign, indirectly affecting the administration"), Harding's aide immediately informed Fall of Yard's intent.

On July 17, Fall wrote Yard in his characteristically imperious style. Yard's article, he said, displayed "ignorance" about the proposed All Year National Park. He suggested that Yard consult with him if he wished to be truly informed on the subject. Yard accepted the offer and, according to Fall's account, after several hours of conversation, he "enthusiastically endorsed" the bill, but asked Fall not to attempt to incorporate the All Year National Park in the National Park system. When Fall refused to accept Yard's suggestion, Yard published the article on July 26, 1923. His objections to the proposed park were based not on any consideration for the Mescalero Indians, but rather on his objection to the extensive road and telephone construction necessary to integrate the sprawling park. The roads particularly disturbed him because they would change "the traditional concept of National Parks" as wilderness areas.

Albert Fall, however, was not disturbed by Yard's opposition. In mid-August, seeking to quiet the fears of his friend Burgess, Fall dismissed Yard and the National Parks Association as "ignorant and no hindrance." "I have no patience, nor do I think the House will have any patience with any such opposition to a popular measure," he wrote. But Albert Fall was wrong. The House failed to act on the All Year National Park bill during the summer of 1922, and when the measure was again considered in early 1923, Yard and John Collier had joined forces to oppose the secretary's plans.[14]

The provision in the All Year National Park bill that would have opened the Mescalero reservation to oil development under the provisions of the General Leasing Act of 1920 was intimately related to developments on the Navajo reservation in northwestern New Mexico.

In 1891, in response to requests to open Indian reservations in Oklahoma to oil exploration, Congress approved an act (26 Stat., 795) for the leasing of lands "bought and paid for by Indians." In the early years of the twentieth century an attempt was made to apply this act to Indian reservations created by presidential executive order. After some hesitation, Interior Secretary Richard Ballinger ruled in 1909 that since these executive-order reservations had not been "bought and paid for" by Indians, the 1891 act was not applicable. As a result of Ballinger's decision, executive-order reservations were closed to any kind of mineral development until the passage of the Metalliferous Minerals Act in 1919; even then there was no provision for oil or gas development on the extensive executive-order reservations of the Southwest.

The difficulty created by Ballinger's decision was first brought to Fall's attention in 1914 when he and Senator Thomas B. Catron were approached by an oil producer from Gallup, New Mexico. Their correspondent requested that they amend the 1891 act to make it applicable to executive-order reservations, and he also suggested that they eliminate a provision in that act which required Indian consent to all leases. That authority, the oilman advised, would be better vested in the secretary of the interior: "We can then deal directly with the Secretary without having to get the consent of the Indians, who know nothing about matters of such kind, or any obstreperous Indian agent who for the time being might be in charge of the reservation." There is no evidence that Fall or Catron attempted to accommodate the producer's request at that time, but the plan that Fall implemented in 1922 closely approximated his suggestions.[15]

Shortly before Fall was appointed secretary of the interior, natural gas was discovered in southeastern Utah, within the boundaries of the Navajo reservation. Despite reports from the U.S. Geological Survey that the area was not a promising one for oil development, geologists from the major oil companies began swarming into the area. Because the initial discovery site was near that portion of the Navajo reservation created by treaty in 1868, the companies soon requested permission to discuss leasing terms with the Navajo tribal council.

These requests posed a special problem for the Indian Office because the Navajos did not, at this time, have a tribal council. Since the early years of the twentieth century their huge reservation had been divided into five subagencies, each with its own agent and each operating independently of the others. The agent in charge of the San Juan Agency, where the oil interest centered, advised Commissioner Burke in 1921 that no council of the Indians in his jurisdiction had been assembled for at least twenty years, and he theorized that it had probably been much longer than that. After many delays, Burke at last decided that the Indians of the San Juan Agency should be called into council on May 7, 1921, to hear the proposals of the oil companies. At this first meeting, the Indians refused to grant leases to any of the companies represented.

Following this initial rebuff, the oil companies were permitted to meet with the Indians a second time, in August 1921. This time the San Juan council granted a single exploratory lease to the Midwest Oil Company, a Standard Oil subsidiary. The companies whose bids were denied insisted upon yet a third meeting, but Commissioner Burke, sensing the need for some type of permanent Indian council and desirous of including the other four Navajo agencies in its deliberations, stalled. At last, in March 1922, he reluctantly sanctioned a third meeting with the San Juan Navajos, but the Indians stood firm in their refusal to grant more than one exploratory lease.

The anger and frustration of the oil men, evident in their correspondence with Burke, was approaching a critical point when Albert Fall intervened in the Navajo situation. Seizing upon an ingenious argument put forth by one of the prospectors in 1921, Fall ruled in June 1922 that executive-order Indian reservations could be developed under the terms of the General Leasing Act of 1920. Although this ruling did not solve the immediate impasse on the treaty portion of the reservation, it did have the advantage of opening the lands surrounding the treaty area, in which there was also great interest. From Fall's viewpoint, it also had the additional virtue of eliminating the need to obtain Indian consent to leases and it permitted the state and the reclamation fund to share equally with the Indians in any royalties.

Fall's ruling was based on the argument accompanying a request for a prospecting permit submitted by one E. M. Harrison in the fall of 1921. Recognizing the difficulty of obtaining Navajo consent, Harrison applied for a permit to explore a portion of the reservation withdrawn from the public domain by executive order in 1884. Arguing that the area was still properly a part of the public domain and thus eligible for development under the General Leasing Act of 1920, Harrison submitted his request not to the Indian Office, but to the General Land Office. On January 12, 1922, the commissioner of the General Land Office rejected his petition, stating that the area was Indian land and that there was no law providing for its development except in the case of metalliferous minerals. Harrison, however, was not daunted. He immediately appealed the ruling directly to Secretary Fall.[16]

Throughout the spring of 1922, Fall considered Harrison's appeal. Although he was aware that the departmental solicitor, Edwin Booth, had ruled in January that Indians on executive-order reservations "have the same rights and are governed by the same conditions and considerations" as those on treaty reservations, Fall choose to ignore both the solicitor's opinion as well as the decision of his land commissioner. On March 9, 1922, he instructed Commissioner Burke to draw up a memorandum indicating the amount of land held by Indians under treaty, congressional grant, and executive-order withdrawals from the public domain. The figures on executive-order lands, he emphasized, were to be supplied "quickly and immediately." When he subsequently learned that 22 million acres of land, located mainly in Arizona and New Mexico, had been created by executive order, Fall determined to open them through application of the General Leasing Act of 1920.[17]

Fall first sought congressional approval for his scheme. On May 17, 1922, Congressman Homer P. Snyder introduced a bill that would have authorized oil and gas leases "on unallotted lands on the Navajo Indian reservation." Under the bill's provisions, the secretary of the interior was to be empowered to make leases of "such areas, upon such terms and conditions as he may prescribe." Royalties resulting from the discovery of oil or gas would be evenly divided among the Indians, the state, and the reclamation fund.

Twelve days before his decision to submit the substitute bill on the All Year National Park (which contained an identical statement on oil development on the Apache reservation), Fall wrote Snyder concerning the Navajo bill. He had arrived at the opinion, he said, "that the provisions of the general leasing law of February 25, 1920 are applicable to deposits of oil and gas within Executive Order Indian reservations, because of the fact that such reservations are merely public lands temporarily withdrawn by Executive Order . . . ." Since Snyder's bill in effect accomplished the same result, and at the same time assured the Indians a share in any royalties that might accrue, Fall gave it his blessing. On June 5, Fall appeared as the only witness at the committee hearings. Again, he repeated his argument for considering the executive-order portion of the Navajo reservation as public domain for the purpose of developing its oil and gas resources, and he defended the royalty division among the Indians, the state, and the reclamation fund.

Then suddenly, on June 9, 1922, without waiting for congressional action on Snyder's bill, Fall issued an administrative decision opening all executive-order Indian reservations under the provisions of the General Leasing Act. By this action, he cut the Gordian knot that had previously hampered exploitation of these areas. At the same time, he raised serious questions about Indian ownership of these lands, questions that were not resolved until 1927 when Congress at last overturned Fall's ruling and awarded the Indians full ownership of the executive-order reservations.[18]

Coming upon the scene only shortly after Fall had made his ruling, John Collier concluded that the Harrison decision was a deliberate attempt to destroy Indian title to 22 million acres of land. All the evidence, however, indicates that Fall was trying only to force the immediate opening of the Navajo reservation to oil development and to ensure that the state of New Mexico would receive a share of the oil royalties. Bills to apply the General Leasing Act to executive-order reservations were submitted repeatedly after 1920 without any suggestion that the Indian title was being challenged. Indeed, by assigning all royalties to the Indians, these early bills implied Indian ownership, and it was probably to force a division of the oil royalties that Fall had acted in such a precipitate manner. Furthermore, although the Harrison decision was theoretically applicable to all executive-order reservations, the only prospecting permits ever authorized by Fall applied exclusively to the Navajo reservation. Finally, there is the evidence of the All Year National Park bill. There, while providing that the Mescalero reservation would also be developed according to the terms of the General Leasing Act, Fall expressly vested title to the reservation lands in the Indians. The Harrison decision was certainly a threat to full Indian ownership of oil and gas deposits on executive-order reservations, but it was never a serious challenge to the validity of Indian land titles.

Although Fall's decision in the Harrison case was rendered in June 1922, John Collier did not become aware of it until January 1923. Because by then he was also embroiled in a struggle with Fall over the Pueblo lands and a bill known as the "Omnibus bill," Collier lumped all three measures together as a "land grab" against the Indians and castigated Fall as the villain responsible for their creation.

The Omnibus bill actually had its origins in the New Policy, which Commissioner Sells launched in 1917, and in a wave of postwar demands to liberate the Indians from federal controls. In 1919, Congress authorized an investigation of the Indian Office with a view toward bringing its activities to an end after almost seventy years. Following an arduous tour of nearly every reservation in the nation, a House investigating committee recommended in 1920 that federal responsibility for Indians be sharply curtailed. Specifically, the committee recommended that all Indians who had received an education "to the standards of the seventh grade" and who were twenty-one be made citizens of the United States, and at age twenty-three be certified "competent" to handle their own affairs, have turned over to them "anything due them from the government, and then be required to work out their own salvation." Where there were still Indian lands not being used by the Indians, the committee further recommended that these lands be leased or sold "for the benefit and in the interest of all the people of the country."

Nothing came of the House report, but the sentiments expressed in it continued into the early years of the 1920s, despite mounting evidence that the New Policy had proved a disaster for many Indians. In 1921, Commissioner Burke placed a halt to the practice of issuing competency certificates wholesale to Indians, but the House Indian Affairs Committee continued to press for the program. That same year it recommended again that all Indians over twenty-one who had received a seventh-grade education be made citizens and "liberated" from federal control. In addition, the committee recommended that all allotted Indians of less than one-half Indian blood and all those of more Indian blood who were twenty-one and "competent" be issued fee patents to their land and have all restrictions on their property removed immediately. It also recommended the extension of the General Leasing Act to all unallotted lands within Indian reservations, with the stipulation that "all proceeds be paid to the Indians." Had these recommendations been implemented, there would have been relatively little for the Indian Office to do and, accordingly, the committee also recommended that the Indian health, irrigation, and forestry services be abolished and their functions turned over to the U.S. Public Health Service, the Bureau of Reclamation, and the Forestry Service, respectively.

These and similar bills failed to pass because they were too abrupt in their severance of federal responsibility, but the sentiment behind them was strong. To advocates of rugged individualism, the continued existence of the Indian reservations was an embarrassing and unnecessary carry-over from a past age. As Representative Melville C. Kelly of Pennsylvania put it:

> The reservation system may have served a good purpose in compelling the Indians of other days to forsake their wild, nomadic ways. But its day is long passed. It is today a breeding place of idlers, beggars, gamblers and paupers. It is a prison pen where human beings are doomed to live amid sad memories of their ancestors and among the ghosts of the dead. The sooner the whole tribal system and reservation policy is abandoned, the sooner we write "finis" to one of the blackest pages in American history.

Those who might have disagreed with the harshness of Kelly's judgment nevertheless saw the wisdom of the argument that the Indian Office was duplicating many services provided by other government agencies. In the Harding-Coolidge era, when spiraling government budgets and increasing federal power were under strong attack, this argument had an especially strong appeal.[19]

By 1922 a compromise of sorts was concluded between those who believed the federal government ought to get out of the Indian business immediately and those who believed that many Indians were still in need of supervision and protection. The compromise took two forms. One sought to extend both the benefits and the burdens of citizenship to all Indians, allotted or not, without reference to competency, in the hope that the responsibilities of citizenship would result in an increase of Indian self-reliance and self-support. A second sought to divorce competent Indians from their remaining tribal ties by making it possible for them to receive their share of tribal wealth in return for a quitclaim from any further government services. In 1924 the proponents of Indian citizenship secured the passage of an act granting full citizenship to all Indians (43 Stat., 1255), but attempts to couple taxation and separation from federal guardianship with the privilege of citizenship were beaten back. The supporters of the second approach pushed a bill in 1922–23 that would have permitted the secretary of the interior to appraise all Indian tribal properties and then make a pro rata cash payment to any competent Indian who would agree to remove himself from the tribal rolls and future federal responsibility. This second bill, sponsored by Commissioner Burke and New York Congressman Homer P. Snyder, chairman of the House Indian Affairs Committee, was one of several measures incorporated into what became known as the Omnibus bill of 1923.

Representative Snyder's interest in the bill stemmed from his discovery that each year there were more, rather than fewer, Indians who were "wards of the government." The purpose of the Dawes Act, to make Indians self-reliant, he argued, was being subverted, and the chief cause of this development was the refusal of many otherwise competent Indians to sever their tribal ties for fear they would thereby lose any claim they might have to tribal wealth in oil, timber, minerals, or money on deposit with the federal treasury. Commissioner Burke concurred. In addition, he emphasized the debilitating effect that small, periodic, per-capita payments from the sale or lease of tribal properties were having on Indians. To overcome these liabilities, both men argued that Indians who had been allotted and were certified competent to handle their own affairs should be permitted to take their share of tribal wealth in a lump sum and use it to improve themselves immediately. Both men stressed that the bill would not, as had Commissioner Sells's New Policy, force individual Indians to accept competency; it would simply permit them to apply voluntarily for competency and an immediate pro rata share of tribal wealth, and authorize the secretary of the interior to accede to their request.

In committee hearings on the Omnibus bill three questions were raised. Where would the money come from to pay competent Indians their share of tribal wealth? What guarantees were there that the secretary of the interior would exercise caution in certifying competency? Why should it be expected that Indians who were given this new wealth would be any less prone to squander it than others had done in the past? Commissioner Burke testified that the payments would be made from any tribal funds the tribe had on deposit with the federal government. If the wasteful per capita payments were curtailed, these funds would grow, and an incentive would be created to cause competent Indians to apply for payment and severance from future federal responsibility. Both Snyder and Burke argued that while no ironclad guarantees could be made that the secretary of the interior would exercise good judgment in the matter of competency awards, both believed his decision would be superior to that of the Congress, which in years past had periodically directed the wholesale removal of restrictions on Indians to their subsequent detriment. Both men also argued convincingly that the Indian Office would be better able to care for the needs of incompetent Indians, and at less cost, if it did not also have to supervise the affairs to those who were able to conduct their own affairs.

The real problem, of course, was how to determine competency. It was a problem as old as the Indian Office itself, and despite the failures of the past, Commissioner Burke took a remarkably sanguine view of the problem. Pressed to defend the practice of individualizing the tribal estates, a practice that he agreed had resulted in "ninety percent" of the Indians losing their land and dissipating the proceeds, Burke replied:

A white man sometimes does the same thing and it takes a little adversity to teach him the value of money and how to

get along, and the best Indians we have today are those
whose restrictions were removed and who squandered everything they had and were finally thrown upon their own
resources; many of them are making good.

The very fact that Burke could make such a statement
demonstrated clearly the hold that rugged individualism
still had on the minds of most Americans in the early
1920s. The only acceptable solution to the Indian problem
was a division of the tribal estates and the abolition of tribal
ties. Only when Indians were forced to stand on their own
feet would the Indian problem ever be solved. It was the primacy of this kind of thinking, not the machinations of Albert Fall, that propelled the Omnibus bill through Congress
in the spring of 1923.[20]

It was not the Omnibus bill, however, or the Harrison decision, or the All Year National Park bill that brought John
Collier into the debate over federal Indian policy. Rather, it
was a bill sponsored by Senator Holm O. Bursum of New
Mexico that sought to settle the long-standing dispute over
land and water rights between the Pueblo Indians and their
white neighbors along the Rio Grande.

Under both Spain and Mexico, the Pueblo Indians had
been recognized as the owners of certain lands along the Rio
Grande. When the United States took control of the Southwest following the Mexican war, these property rights were
assured to the Indians in the Treaty of Guadalupe Hidalgo.
In 1856, the U.S. Court of Claims confirmed the Indian titles and ordered that patents be issued to the Pueblos. The
court did not, however, rule on the validity of rival claims
made by Spanish and Mexican land-grant holders to some of
these same lands.

In 1851 the federal government extended to the Indians of
New Mexico the provisions of the Indian Intercourse Act of
1834, which, among other things, prohibited the settlement
of non-Indians within the boundaries of Indian reservations.
Attempts to force rival claimants off the Pueblo lands were

resisted, and in the early 1870s one Antonio Joseph of Taos took his claim to the New Mexico Territorial Supreme Court, which ruled in his favor. Federal attorneys thereupon appealed the decision to the federal courts. In 1876 the Supreme Court of the United States upheld the decision of the Territorial Supreme Court, ruling that the Pueblos were not Indians within the meaning of the Intercourse Act. Instead, the decision read, the Pueblos were perfectly capable of conducting their own affairs and of alienating their lands without federal consent because, while "they are Indians in feature, complexion, and a few of their habits; in all other respects [they are] superior to all but a few of the civilized Indian tribes of the country and the equal of the most civilized thereof."

The effect of the *Joseph* decision was to encourage further alienation of Pueblo lands and to subject the determination of title to the territorial courts, which nearly always upheld the claims of non-Indians. Some lands were taken under claim of purchase from Pueblo officials or individual Indians; others were lost to squatters. It was not until 1910, in the enabling act for New Mexico statehood, that the federal government attempted to establish its sole authority over the Pueblos. In admitting New Mexico to statehood, Congress insisted that "all lands acquired by the Indians through or from the United States or any prior sovereignty, shall be and remain subject to the disposition and control of Congress." As a result of this demand, New Mexico entered the union in January 1912, with the grudging admission in its constitution that the Pueblos and their lands would henceforth be controlled by the federal government.

The nature and extent of federal jurisdiction, however, were almost immediately challenged by the new state. Maintaining that the Pueblos were citizens, the New Mexico legislature talked of taxing their lands. An attempt was likewise made to establish the authority of the state courts over them. The authority of the resident Indian agent, whose position had been created by the Indian Bureau, not by the Congress, was questioned. In order to establish clearly the jurisdiction of the federal government, the Pueblo special attorney, Francis C. Wilson of Santa Fe, drafted a bill in 1912 whereby the Pueblos would cede their land in trust to the federal government for twenty-five years. According to Wilson, this bill would ensure the Indians protection against further land alienation and would also protect them from state taxes. In addition, it would clearly set forth the authority of the federal government in the area of liquor control and it would establish the authority of the Indian agent. At the insistence of Senators Fall and Thomas B. Catron and Representative George Curry, Wilson's bill was permitted to die in committee.[21]

Despite the failure of Wilson's bill, an incident concerning the sale of intoxicants on Pueblo lands enabled the federal government to win its struggle with New Mexico. Shortly after New Mexico statehood, the Indian Office ordered its chief prohibition officer, W. E. ("Pussyfoot") Johnson, into New Mexico to enforce a federal statute prohibiting the introduction of intoxicants into Indian country. Before long, Johnson apprehended one Felipe Sandoval at Santa Clara Pueblo. Sandoval's attorney, a Santa Fe resident named A. B. Renehan, based his case on the *Joseph* decision and the contention that the enabling act and the clause in the New Mexico constitution that ceded jurisdiction to the federal government had both usurped the police powers of the state. Renehan won an acquittal in the federal district court. When the federal district attorney declined to appeal the case, special counsel Wilson prepared a brief that ultimately went before the Supreme Court of the United States.

In 1913 the Supreme Court overruled the district court and reversed the *Joseph* decision. Although the language of the decision was derogatory in its description of Pueblo culture ("The people of the Pueblos . . . adhering to primitive modes of life, largely influenced by superstition and fetichism and chiefly governed according to the crude customs inherited from their ancestors . . . are essentially a simple, uninformed, and inferior people"), it did firmly state that the Pueblos were "Indians in race, customs, and domestic government," and thereby entitled to the protection of the federal government. In addition, the Court ruled that the Indians had been under federal guardianship ever since 1848, thereby raising the question of whether previous land decisions based on the *Joseph* decision were valid. Immediately, some 3,000 claimants to Pueblo lands found their titles in question.

While the *Sandoval* decision was ultimately to provide a defense of the Pueblo lands, the New Mexicans fought against such an interpretation for the next eleven years. They first vented their anger on the Pueblo attorney, Francis Wilson, whom they succeeded in driving from office in 1914. Then, when a surveyor named Joy was ordered to conduct a survey of the disputed lands, the claimants attempted to use his work to establish the validity of their claims. Joy was instructed to catalog the number and extent of all claims within Pueblo boundaries in preparation for a yet undefined settlement. Accordingly, he entered on his charts all the settlers' claims, without requirement of deed or other evidence of title. When he completed his work in 1916, the claimants, arguing that Joy had conducted a holding claims survey, insisted that their inclusion on his charts conveyed ownership. Defiantly, they began to fence their claims and just as defiantly the Indians replied by tearing down the fences and driving off their rivals' livestock. The situation became increasingly tense.

The man who found himself in the middle of these conflicts between the Indians and the New Mexicans was Philip T. Lonergan, a former superintendent of the Albuquerque Indian School who, following the *Sandoval* decision, had been elevated to the post of Pueblo agent. In addition to his problems associated with land, Lonergan also found himself embroiled in a series of conflicts with the Pueblo authorities, who vigorously resisted his efforts to enforce Indian Office regulations within their self-governing communities. Recognizing that a weak Indian agent would be less able to defend the Pueblo land claims, the non-Indian claimants joined with the Indians in their defense of self-rule.

One of Lonergan's first problems dealt with the establishment of a Court of Indian Offenses to try petty crimes and misdemeanors. Although these courts were commonplace on other reservations, the Pueblos, who had traditionally dealt with offenders in their own way and through their own governmental structures, strenuously resisted the innovation. Protesting that the agent's power to appoint Indian judges seriously impaired the authority of their own governing officials, the Pueblos filed numerous protests against the court in 1915–16.

In 1917 Lonergan also became involved in a dispute over the election of a governor at San Juan Pueblo. Refusing to recognize the man whom the Indians had elected, he took possession of the governor's symbols of office, a staff dating back to Mexican rule and a cane presented by President Lincoln, and entrusted them to his own choice. The unsuccessful candidate thereupon appealed to the state court for a writ of replevin, which Lonergan promptly refused, saying the state lacked jurisdiction in the matter. When Lonergan was subsequently held in contempt of court and sentenced to six months in jail, he appealed to the federal district court, which in 1919 upheld his contention that the state had no jurisdiction on Indian lands. While stating that only the federal government had jurisdiction over the Pueblos, the judge also ruled that the Indian governors should be permitted to manage the internal affairs of the Pueblo so long as their rule was "just and in the best interests of the people."

At the same time that Lonergan was involved in these controversies, he found his efforts to protect the Indians against white encroachments diminished by a Department of the Interior ruling that instructed the Pueblo agent not to bring suit against trespassers on Pueblo lands. According to Leo Crane, Lonergan's successor, this order was signed by Andrieus Aristieus Jones, an unsuccessful Democratic candidate for the Senate from New Mexico, who in 1913 was appointed assistant secretary of the interior.

Complaining that the Indian challenges to his authority and the refusal of the Pueblo attorney to investigate the

complaints of white encroachment were making his "situation . . . unbearable," Lonergan filed suit against a group of
New Mexican claimants in 1916, but was forced to withdraw the suit before it went to trial.[22]

In response to complaints from both the Pueblos and the
New Mexicans and in recognition of the need for increased
attention to Pueblo needs, Commissioner Sells transferred
Lonergan in 1918 and on September 1, 1919, divided the
Pueblos into two jurisdictions, each with a resident agent.
To the Southern Pueblo Agency at Albuquerque he assigned
Leo Crane, a former Hopi agent; Horace J. Johnson, a former
Oklahoma agent, was authorized to establish a new agency
for the Northern Pueblos at Española.

The appointments of Crane and Johnson, coupled with
the appointment of Richard H. Hanna as Pueblo attorney in
1918, resulted in a more vigorous defense of the Indians'
rights. In 1919 Hanna prepared ejectment suits, which he
filed in the federal court, against the New Mexican claimants. Crane ignored the Interior Department ruling prohibiting the filing of suits against trespassers, and in 1919 he
successfully won a decision against one offender who had
regularly grazed 3,000 sheep on land claimed by the Indians
of Laguna Pueblo. The result of these actions was a plank in
the state Republican party platform in 1920, which protested Indian Office attempts to "cancel title to lands which
have been occupied by our people for generations," and
which called upon the state's representatives in Congress to
secure legislation that would "do justice to the rightful
claimants of these lands."

Johnson and Crane were also quick to warn against the
effects of the several Indian citizenship bills that were before Congress in 1919–20. Warning that these bills would
have the effect of making the Indians subject to the jurisdiction of the state courts and freeing them from federal protection, both men requested the Indian Office to oppose the
bills. When the House Indian Affairs Committee, on its investigation tour in the spring of 1920, came to New Mexico,
both Crane and Johnson made appearances along with rep-

resentative groups of Indians to protest the citizenship bills.

But, while Crane and Johnson proved to be more vigorous defenders of the Pueblos' land and legal rights, Crane also proved to be more insistent upon establishing the authority of the resident agent over the Indians. One of his first actions after arriving in Albuquerque was to issue a warning to the Pueblo governors not to interpret the federal court ruling in the Lonergan case too broadly. Admitting that the judge had ruled that the Pueblo officials should be permitted to manage the internal affairs of their people, Crane nevertheless warned that this did not mean they could ignore the necessary regulations of the Indian Office. Specifically, he stated that if they continued to harrass the Indian judges, or prevented children from attending the government schools, or neglected the necessary farm or stock work for ceremonials, or if sufficient evidence were presented "concerning immoral practices," he would take "prompt steps to punish those responsible." Agent Johnson was less inclined to interfere with the Pueblo leaders in his jurisdiction, but he noted in 1920 that his willingness to cooperate depended upon their willingness to "work in conjunction with us. I think it is wise to continue this system so long as we can do it to the advantage of the Indian, and I believe that this can be done at the present time."

Crane was particularly outspoken in his criticism of the control that the caciques or religious rulers of the Pueblos exerted over the Indians. He referred to them as "old barbarians" to whom everyone deferred, "even the most intelligent," and he was particularly outraged that their religious authority gave them the right to choose the governors whom he believed should have been elevated by popular vote. His scorn of the governors, whom he blamed for the failure of the Pueblos to protect their lands, was especially severe:

> The mock-serious recognition of the Indian Governors and their petty little courts has operated to hold the agent powerless and to permit the Indians to thoroughly defraud themselves. Today, but one of the ten governors under this agency has enough sense to come in out of the rain. The

nine others are superstition-ridden savages, with no conception of government, law, or efficient control of their own people.

Thus, by 1921, despite the *Sandoval* and *Lonergan* decisions, the dimensions of federal jurisdiction in the New Mexico Pueblos were still far from clear. Agents Lonergan and Crane had repeatedly called upon their superiors in Washington to push for legislation establishing the sole jurisdiction of the federal courts and the Indian Bureau over Pueblo affairs. The Pueblo governors just as insistently demanded freedom from bureau meddling in their internal affairs, and the citizens, whose land titles had become clouded, were equally vociferous in their demands that legislation be secured to guarantee their claims.[23]

On January 6, 1921, in a letter to Senator Charles Curtis, the chairman of the Senate Indian Affairs Committee, Secretary of the Interior John Barton Payne, at last initiated legislation to resolve the Pueblo problem. Closely following the arguments of Lonergan and Crane, he claimed that "the Pueblo government of today is a paternal despotism," dominated by the religious priests or caciques. It was, he continued, inherently undemocratic and "ill adapted to meet the needs which the encroaching civilization of the past years has presented." The *Sandoval* decision and the enabling act for New Mexico statehood had clearly established federal jurisdiction over the Pueblos and made them "wards of the government," but legislation "defining and outlining how that jurisdiction should be exercised," had never been enacted by Congress. In order to remove "many of the difficulties and obstacles now confronting the proper administration of their affairs," Payne enclosed a draft bill that contained three specific proposals. The secretary of the interior was to be given sole jurisdiction over the Pueblos and their lands and be empowered to make "rules and regulations" for their governance. The U.S. District Court for New Mexico was to be given jurisdiction over all civil cases involving the rights of Indians. The alienation or leasing of Pueblo lands was to be prohibited absolutely unless ap-

proved by the secretary of the interior. In routine fashion,
Curtis, who approved the bill, forwarded it to Albert Fall
with the suggestion that he introduce it. If he did not wish
to, Curtis added, he would do so himself, "by request."

At the same time that Payne's bill was being submitted to
the Senate, a bill of a much different nature was introduced
in the House by retiring New Mexico Congressman, Be-
nigno C. Hernández. Hernández's bill, while also granting
the federal courts exclusive jurisdiction in all civil and
criminal cases involving Pueblo Indians, was designed primarily to guarantee the land titles of whites who had taken
up residence within the Pueblo land grants. It called for the
creation of a three-man commission, which would be empowered to issue fee patent titles to all non-Indians who
could demonstrate possession of their lands at least ten
years before New Mexico statehood. The Indians were to be
compensated by money awards that represented "the fair
price of each tract at the date of original occupancy." Outgoing Indian Commissioner Cato Sells declined to approve the
Hernández bill, informing its sponsor that the Interior Department preferred "to have the problem of land titles determined by the federal courts."[24]

Neither the Payne nor the Hernández bill was acted upon
in the waning days of the sixty-sixth Congress. When the
sixty-seventh Congress convened on March 4, 1921, Albert
Fall had become secretary of the interior and Holm O. Bursum had replaced him as senator from New Mexico. Pueblo
affairs took on a new dimension as they now became en-
twined in a political feud between Fall and Bursum.

Before his appointment to fill the vacancy created by
Fall's resignation from the Senate, Holm O. Bursum had
been the workhorse of the Republican party in New Mexico
and a two-time loser in contests for the governorship of
New Mexico. Bursum's principal liability in the elective
arena was an old charge, extending back to territorial days,
that he had embezzled state funds while he was superintendent of the New Mexico penitentiary. Those charges were

brought in 1906 by territorial Governor Herbert J. Hagerman, a "progressive" Republican whom Theodore Roosevelt had appointed to clean up the Republican party in New Mexico before its admission as a state. Since Bursum was also chairman of the territorial Republican committee at the time, his feud with Hagerman touched off an intraparty struggle that divided the Republicans until well into the 1920s. Although Hagerman was subsequently removed by Roosevelt and Bursum was eventually exonerated in the courts, the corruption issue surfaced in each of Bursum's unsuccessful bids for the governor's office in 1911 and 1916.

Despite his failures at the polls, Bursum continued to play an important role within the ranks of the Republican party. In 1912 he gave his support to Fall's successful bid for the Senate, and in 1918, when Fall considered retirement, Bursum played a leading role in persuading him to seek reelection. Largely as a result of Bursum's tireless campaigning, Fall was returned to office that year in a very close race. In return for this support, Fall backed Bursum in his unsuccessful race for the governorship in 1916.

By 1919 Bursum was the National Republican committeeman from New Mexico. In the state convention the following year, he and Fall parted company. Bursum supported the candidacy of General Leonard Wood for the Republican nomination for the presidency, while Fall gave his support to his Senate colleague Warren G. Harding. Fall, who had promised Harding the support of the New Mexico delegation, was embarrassed at his party's defection and he became livid when Bursum persisted in holding the New Mexico delegation for Wood even after it was clear the opposition had secured enough votes to ensure Harding's nomination. The gulf between the two men widened quickly after the election when Fall discovered that the newly elected governor, Merritt C. Mechem, intended to appoint Bursum to his Senate seat if he resigned to become secretary of the interior.

During the 1920 campaign in New Mexico, the *Santa Fe New Mexican*, which was owned by maverick Republican

Bronson Cutting, charged that the Republicans were con-
cocting a "deal" whereby, if the state were carried for Harding, Fall would be given a cabinet position and the new
Republican governor would appoint Bursum to his Senate
seat. Immediately after the election, Fall called upon Mechem to determine if, indeed, the rumor were true. Arguing
that as a result of the *New Mexican*'s charge, Bursum's appointment "would be a very serious error," Fall found the
governor evasive. At last, an angry Fall bluntly told Mechem that if he intended to appoint Bursum, "there would
be no vacancy under any circumstances." Confronted with
this ultimatum, Mechem at last agreed not to appoint Bursum, or so Fall thought. Both men then agreed upon a compromise: if Fall accepted the interior post, Mechem would
name someone other than Bursum to an interim appointment. The governor would then persuade the legislature to
call a special election in the fall of 1921 to determine the
person to complete Fall's Senate term. Fall, who was confident that Bursum could not secure the nomination for an
elective office, agreed not to oppose Bursum if he chose to
seek the office.

When Fall decided in late January 1921 to accept Harding's offer of a cabinet post, he was astonished to find that
Governor Mechem had gone back on his word. The governor, Fall learned, found himself under tremendous pressure
to appoint Bursum immediately as a reward for his many
years of service and to give him an edge in the special fall
election. Hoping to pacify both Fall and Bursum, Mechem
announced that he would accept the recommendation of
the Republican central committee in determining whom to
appoint as Fall's successor. Since Bursum's supporters dominated the central committee, Mechem's decision was tantamount to Bursum's appointment.

Fall was predictably furious at Mechem's defection. Denouncing Bursum as "bull-headed; opiniated; ignorant upon
general subjects; . . . unable to secure his election before
the people under the most favorable circumstances," Fall
complained that Mechem was endangering Harding's al-

ready tenuous control of the Senate. Mechem, he complained, owed him the opportunity to recommend a "safe and satisfactory Republican to fill my seat," and he ominously predicted that the decision would not only "engender strife" in the already faction-ridden Republican party, but it would result in a Democratic victory in the fall election if the Democrats nominated "a good man." Mechem, however, refused to budge, and efforts by Fall's supporters to persuade Bursum to withdraw were unsuccessful. Bursum, they reported, "refused absolutely to back down" on the appointment, apparently in the belief that "if he loses the appointment, he is through politically." On March 11, 1921, after considerable infighting and ill-will, Mechem appointed Bursum to Fall's vacant scat and announced a special election in September to determine its permanent occupant.

Throughout the summer of 1921 Fall flirted with the idea of backing a rival candidate, Henry B. Holt of Las Cruces. He refused to communicate with Bursum, who was then in Washington, and he successfully blocked several patronage appointments that Bursum was endeavoring to secure. Fall also delayed action on two bills Bursum had submitted to resolve the disputed Pueblo land titles. At last in July, convinced by reports from New Mexico that Holt stood no chance to defeat Bursum for the party nomination, Fall capitulated. After a meeting with Harding, at which the president smoothed Fall's ruffled ego by absolving him of all responsibility for the defeat Fall predicted Bursum would suffer in the fall election, he withdrew his opposition.

Bursum's opponent in the 1921 election was Richard H. Hanna, the former Pueblo attorney who had filed the suits in 1919 for ejectment of white trespassers on Pueblo land. Hanna had unsuccessfully opposed Mechem in the 1920 governor's race and he was once again defeated. By a decisive plurality of 8,000 votes, Bursum trounced Hanna in what Fall's biographer has called "a stinging repudiation for the Fall forces." Like it or not, Fall was thereafter forced to work with Bursum on legislation affecting New Mexico.[25]

Pueblo affairs, as they had in the 1920 election, played a major role in Bursum's successful 1921 campaign. At the August convention that renominated Bursum, the keynote speaker was A. B. Renehan, the Santa Fe attorney who had lost the *Sandoval* decision and who had since become the chief spokesman for the non-Indian claimants. In his speech, Renehan denounced the support that earlier administrations had given to Hanna's ejectment suits and drew loud applause. In his acceptance speech, Bursum reminded the audience that he had already introduced legislation to secure the settler's land titles and he promised to persist. In the fall election, Bursum, whose home was in southern New Mexico, was defeated there; the margin of his victory came from the northern counties, where sentiment against the Indians was strongest.[26]

The legislation to which Bursum referred in his acceptance speech was actually two bills that he had introduced in the Senate shortly after assuming office. The first, S. 1938, had been submitted on June 1, 1921. It was a simple measure that confirmed the land titles of all non-Indians who could demonstrate "actual, continuous, and adverse possession of lands not exceeding 160 acres within the boundaries of an Indian pueblo" for ten years prior to the passage of the act. To ensure non-Indian ownership, it specifically forbade any legal action by the federal government or the Pueblos to recover possession of such lands. Neither did it mention any compensation to the Pueblos for their loss. This bill was immediately denounced by everyone, including Commissioner Burke, Secretary Fall, Agent Crane, and the Indian Rights Association, which privately referred to it as "simply a steal."

Six weeks later, with the assistance of A. B. Renehan, Bursum tried a different course. On July 19, 1921, at the height of his bid for renomination, S. 2274 was introduced and, at Bursum's request, was referred not to the Indian Affairs Committee, but to the Committee on Public Lands and Survey, of which Bursum was a member. This bill, like the Hernández bill introduced in the previous session of

Congress, would have created a three-man commission to adjudicate the disputed land titles. Like Hernández's bill, it would have validated the claims of all non-Indians who could demonstrate occupation of their lands for ten years prior to statehood. Unlike Hernández's bill, however, no provision was made for extending federal court protection over the Pueblos, nor was there a provision for any kind of compensation.

As it had in the case of Bursum's earlier bill, the Interior Department recommended against the enactment of S. 2274. Part of the reason for disapproval may have been Fall's general opposition to Bursum at this time; or, it may have reflected a recognition of the bill's inequities. The official reason given, however, was that the department was conducting its own investigation of the Pueblo problem and wished to await a report that Fall had commissioned in the spring of 1921. Fall, who as a senator had evidenced interest only in issues involving southern New Mexico, now found himself in the midst of a controversy whose ramifications he did not fully understand. It was clear, however, that Bursum's two bills, plus the reintroduction of former Secretary Payne's bill by Congressman Homer Snyder in April 1921, were signs that the long-simmering dispute over the Pueblo lands was at last coming to a boil. To advise him on the proper course of action, Fall had appointed Santa Fe attorney and historian Ralph Emerson Twitchell as his advisor on Pueblo affairs shortly after taking office.

"Will you accept appointment Attorney Bureau of Mines with assignment under my direction for special work New Mexico in examining and reporting upon Pueblo Indian titles and disputes," Fall wired Twitchell on April 29, 1921. Twitchell, who had previously written Fall about the possibility of becoming the Pueblo attorney, immediately responded in the affirmative. The seriousness of the problem and Fall's faith in his ability to handle it, he wrote, made him "feel that, after all, life is really worth living." Shortly thereafter, Twitchell advised Fall that the Hanna ejectment suits were soon scheduled to come before the federal court and he urged that the secretary seek a continuation until after he had completed his investigation. During the summer, Twitchell's position was regularized by his appointment as a special assistant to the attorney general, under Fall's direction.

Soon after Twitchell's appointment, the conflict between Agent Leo Crane and the Pueblo governors also heated up. In June 1921, four of the governors traveled to Washington where they presented complaints against Crane's "autocratic rule" and his alleged attempts to destroy the Pueblos' "democratic tribal government" through his use of the Indian judges. Crane hotly denied the charges, denouncing the four governors as the "most reactionary" members of the Pueblos. In September he flatly announced to Commissioner Burke that the Indian service would have to make a choice between the Indian agent and the Indian governors: "There cannot be two methods of control." It was as a result of the governors' visit that Fall appointed his friend Colonel L. A. Dorrington as inspector-at-large for New Mexico, with orders to "take over the general control and superintendence of the affairs of all the Indians in that state." By the spring of 1922 both Crane and northern Pueblo Agent Horace Johnson were to be transferred to other posts.

In September 1921, Twitchell notified Fall that he was ready with a preliminary report on the Pueblo situation, which he called "very complex and in a way, critical." Neither of Bursum's bills were acceptable, he hinted, and a conference with Fall in Washington would be necessary before he drafted a final report. Once again he requested authority to postpone the ejectment suits. Almost immediately, instructions authorizing a delay in the suits were dispatched and Twitchell was ordered to Washington. By late December, the final report was on Fall's desk.

Twitchell's brief contained a lengthy examination of New Mexico land titles, which reached back into the Spanish period. The Pueblo titles granted by the King of Spain in 1745, he reported, were even then in conflict with other land grants the King had granted his Spanish subjects in the New World. During the Mexican period, still other grants, which overlapped those of the Pueblos, were confirmed by the Mexican authorities. In most cases, the present occupants of these lands, whose titles were not being actively challenged by the Indians, would be unable to offer documentary proof of ownership because records had not survived. Other claims to Pueblo lands, many of which rested upon good-faith purchases from individual Indians, were technically illegal since both the Spanish and Mexican governments had held that the original Pueblo grants were communal, not individual. Following American occupation in 1846, the situation had become even more complicated since, before 1913, the federal courts had "universally recognized the right of the Pueblos to alienate lands." It was Twitchell's conclusion that, as a result of the *Sandoval* decision, none of the non-Indian claims could be sustained in court. The situation was, therefore, an "intolerable" one wherein a simple recourse to the courts would result in a grave injustice to many of the non-Indian claimants.

At the same time, Twitchell noted that there had been extensive encroachments on Pueblo lands, without any pretext of purchase or other prior claim, ever since American sovereignty was established. Whenever the Indians had attempted to halt these aggressions by resorting to the territorial or state courts, they had always lost. In his judgment, "the local courts or juries have yet . . . to show where the Indian has ever received justice." In addition, irrigation and water rights along the Rio Grande, without which the contested lands were worthless, were hopelessly tangled and in Twitchell's view, "as the law now stands, I see no one forum having jurisdiction to settle the controversies." The only solution, he concluded, was the creation of some forum not bound by the strict confines of the law that would entertain the arguments of all interested parties. In any event, he wrote in a covering letter, "I cannot harmonize my ideas with the text of the Bursum bill." S. 1938 was "unconscionable in the extreme," and S. 2274, while less obnoxious, was "clearly antiIndian." Both measures were "quite beneath the dignity of a great government."[27]

While Fall was considering Twitchell's report, trouble between the Indians and whites erupted at Tesuque Pueblo. On February 9, 1922, a band of Tesuque Indians dismantled almost 2 miles of fence recently erected by E. D. Newman, a new resident of the area. After appealing to both Twitchell and Agent Horace Johnson, neither of whom gave him any support, Newman appealed to Commissioner Burke, Fall, and Governor Mechem. In his letter to Burke, Newman complained that Agent Johnson was responsible for the trouble because he had incited the Indians to violence by telling them that the land Newman was enclosing was theirs. "The white men here," he warned, "who are a representative bunch of red-blooded, true Americans, are up in arms. They armed themselves the other day and I learned that there is some talk of giving Mr. Johnson a coat of tar and feathers." Despite Johnson's assurances that there was no danger of bloodshed and an investigation by Inspector Dorrington, which exonerated Johnson and concluded that "the Indian claim to the land is probably right," both Fall and Burke concluded that Johnson would have to be replaced. On May 4, 1922, Fall authorized his transfer to the Walker River reservation in Nevada and a month later he also transferred Crane from the southern agency. Johnson's transfer in particular led to a storm of opposition from the Indians and their supporters. No criticism of either agent was implied by the transfers, Burke and Fall advised the complainants. Both were loyal and capable men, but the removal of all parties to old disputes was part of a program to formulate "a definite policy which will result in settling for all time the disputes which are constantly arising concerning Indian rights."[28]

By the time the furor over the transfers was subsiding, Fall had decided upon his course of action. Whether at his order or at Twitchell's discretion (the record says nothing on this point), Twitchell drew up a bill in April that placed the resolution of the disputed land titles in the hands of the federal court of New Mexico. To protect the rights of those non-Indian claimants whose claims dated back into the Spanish and Mexican periods, Twitchell's draft provided that the court should issue a decree in favor of all those who held their lands "adversely, under color of title" since before the signing of the Treaty of Guadalupe Hidalgo. Such a provision, Twitchell argued, would "cover a large percentage of the cases," and since the Indians were not actively opposing these long-standing claims, no compensation need be awarded them. If there was sentiment for compensation for these lands, Twitchell urged, "let the government do so, but *not* upon the ground that the Indian has been unlawfully dispossessed of things that were his at some time or other in the history of the country."

Twitchell's draft also protected the rights of a second group of claimants. All persons who could produce "a valid grant from the government of Spain, or Mexico, or the United States," and all persons and corporations who, "with or without color of title" had maintained continuous possession of their lands since ten years before the passage of the enabling act for New Mexico statehood (June 20, 1910), were also to receive a decree in their favor. The Pueblos, however, were to be compensated for all losses in this category by new lands from the public domain, equal in size and in value to those they lost, or by a cash payment from the federal treasury. Fall immediately endorsed Twitchell's draft and in May began to circulate copies among interested parties.

Several things are worth noting about this Twitchell-Fall bill. First, the idea of a special forum or commission, which Twitchell had seemed to favor in his December report, was now dropped in favor of a decision by the federal district court. Second, that court was now directed to issue decrees to all persons whose claims antedated the year 1900. These were certainly strange recommendations coming from a man who had only a few months earlier denounced Bursum's bill as "unconscionable" and "quite beneath the dignity" of the federal government. There is nothing to indicate Twitchell's motive in making these recommendations, but it is known that he had met with Renehan before drafting the bill and that he was plainly worried about the political impact any bill would have on the fortunes of the Republican party in New Mexico. Unless something was done at this session of the Congress "to bring justice to both sides," he had written to Fall's secretary in February, "the effect it will have on us politically will be very bad." Failure to appease the citizens would result in the loss of a thousand votes "permanently." In this light, it appears that what Twitchell found "unconscionable" in the Bursum bills was not that they deprived the Indians of their land, but that they failed to provide compensation for those losses, something his bill insisted upon for all losses incurred since 1848. Thus, although in some respects Twitchell's draft was an improvement over Bursum's, both clearly reflected the conventional wisdom about the Indian and his land that Collier was about to challenge. However much Twitchell and Fall may have prided themselves on being more enlightened than Bursum, it never entered their minds that the Indians should be awarded the land and the non-Indians awarded either selections from the public domain or a cash settlement.

Despite these deficiencies in Twitchell's bill, which are so evident in retrospect, the bill itself was considered too generous to the Indians by most northern New Mexicans in 1922. Shortly after Fall began to circulate copies among the interested parties, opposition began to mount from Bursum's camp. In early June, Bursum himself, while professing general satisfaction with the draft, advised Twitchell that he was concerned about a clause dealing with water rights, which he believed might be interpreted to give the Indians waters that the non-Indians needed to irrigate their lands. At the same time, Commissioner Burke, who was traveling in the West and had not yet had an opportunity to read the bill, met in Santa Fe with the Indian leaders and the attorney for the non-Indian claimants, A. B. Renehan. From Renehan, Burke learned that the non-Indians intended to send a delegation to Washington later in the month to confer with Bursum and to appear before the Senate committee during its hearings on the Twitchell draft. Burke immediately notified Fall of the possible opposition and advised him that he, Dorrington, and Twitchell all "believed a plan can be worked out that will solve all the problems." In order to effect a compromise with the Bursum forces, Burke recommended that Twitchell be authorized to visit Washington at the same time that Renehan's party appeared.

Thus it was that on July 11, 1922, when Collier was preparing to return to New Mexico and Mrs. Atwood, assured by Burke that all was well with the Pueblos, was resting from her strenuous eastern trip, Albert Fall, Ralph Twitchell, and A. B. Renehan, representing Senator Bursum, assembled in the secretary's Washington office to concoct what soon became known as "the infamous Bursum bill." There are no documents linking Fall's capitulation at this meeting with Bursum's bumbling efforts in behalf of Fall's All Year National Park bill, which had cleared the Senate just four days before, but to overlook the probability of such a trade-off would be naïve. In both cases the pattern was the same. The All Year National Park bill, at Fall's request, was referred to the Senate Indian Affairs Committee, which knew nothing about national parks. The Pueblo bill, under Bursum's guidance, was to be referred to the Public Lands and Surveys Committee, which knew nothing about Indians. With both Fall and Bursum assuring the committees that "all parties" to the legislation were in agreement, both bills were able to avoid public hearings. On the floor of the Senate, Bursum defended both bills and filled the *Congressional Record* with falsehoods and distortions. Commissioner Burke, who evinced some objections to early drafts of both bills, was carefully excluded from the final stages of drafting, and in each case his suggestions for revision were pointedly ignored.

At the July 11 meeting, it was clear that Bursum, who had been ignored and humiliated by Fall before his election, now held the upper hand. Since that victory, Fall had become dependent upon him for all the legislation through which he hoped to change the rules governing the development of New Mexico's natural resources. Now it was Fall's turn to oblige Bursum, and in the discussions that afternoon, Bursum, through Renehan, won everything that he demanded.

The first six sections of the final bill were not in contention. According to Twitchell's later testimony before a Senate subcommittee, he prepared these sections himself with the advice of the leaders of the bar association of Santa Fe. They were concerned with legal details governing the jurisdiction of the court in determining the disputed land titles and in defining, at last, the powers of the court over Pueblo life. Generally speaking, these powers were broad and sweeping and they clearly represented a victory for the Indian agents and a decided defeat for the Pueblo governors.

Sections seven, eight, and nine were essentially Twitchell's original proposals. They provided that all non-Indian claimants who could demonstrate possession of their lands since before June 10, 1900, should be entitled to a decree from the court in their favor and that compensation in the form of land or money should be made to the Indians for all losses subsequent to the establishment of American sovereignty over New Mexico. Although Commissioner Burke had previously objected to a clause in section seven that permitted the boundaries of the non-Indian claims to be determined by "secondary evidence," that clause was permitted to remain.

Section ten dealt with Indian water rights and, as Bursum had earlier indicated to Twitchell, he was not satisfied with Twitchell's draft on this point. Twitchell's draft would have guaranteed to the Indians all the water in the Rio Grande they needed for irrigation on those lands remaining to them after the land titles had been determined. Bursum, on the other hand, insisted that the Indians be awarded only as much water as they were using at the time the decrees were handed down. In order to irrigate more acres, according to Bursum's plan, they would have to appeal to the state courts of New Mexico. In 1922 some of the northern Pueblos, particularly San Ildefonso and Tesuque, where white encroachments were most severe, were not able to cultivate enough acres to feed their people because the whites had seized most of the irrigable land. If Bursum had his way, even if these Pueblos were awarded title to some of the disputed lands, they would not be assured of the water necessary to cultivate them. On this point, Fall overruled Twitchell and the Bursum-Renehan draft of section ten was placed in the final bill.

A revision of section ten, however, was the least of the Bursum-Renehan demands. To ensure that the tracts awarded to the non-Indians would embrace the largest possible acreage, they insisted upon the addition of section fifteen, which provided that all previous surveys of non-Indian lands within the Pueblo grants, made under the supervision of the surveyor general of New Mexico, be accepted by the court as "prima facie evidence of the boundaries therein described." In this way they were able to resurrect the settler's claim from the 1916 Joy survey.

Renehan also insisted upon a final clause, section sixteen, the most outrageous of all. All non-Indian claimants who were unable to comply with the requirements for possession set forth in sections eight and nine, but who could prove they had purchased and occupied their land in good faith *since* 1900, were entitled to request that the federal court determine the boundaries of their claims and fix the value of the same. Thereupon, they might appeal to the secretary of the interior, who could permit them to obtain title by payment to the Pueblos of the sum fixed by the court.[29]

Nine days after the meeting in Fall's office, Bursum introduced the measure as S. 3855. On July 31, Fall advised the Public Lands Committee that the bill met with his approval and that the attorneys representing the various claimants had met with him and were in agreement on its provisions. Within a few days, Stella Atwood received a copy from Congressman Carl Hayden of Arizona, and the fight was on.

The Bursum Bill (1922–23)

Stella Atwood was chagrined and angry at the way Commissioner Burke had deliberately kept her in the dark about Bursum's new bill. Throughout August 1922 she bombarded his office with increasingly sharp letters in which she vowed to fight the bill to its death. At the suggestion of IRA counsel S. M. Brosius, she attempted to enlist the support of Herbert Welsh in the controversy, but Welsh, in the deferential tradition of the IRA, temporized and wanted to consult with Commissioner Burke before committing his organization. When he finally became alarmed in November 1922, he was to learn that it was too late to work with Mrs. Atwood and the General Federation of Women's Clubs. As she coolly informed him at that time: "When I did not receive any reply from you I arranged for other counsel and help; and, as you know by this time, I have been able to carry the matter through to a very successful conclusion . . . ."

Despite Mrs. Atwood's opposition, Secretary Fall and the Interior Department worked steadily through the summer

Figure 17.   Francis Wilson. From Twitchell, *Leading Facts of New Mexican History.*

and early fall in behalf of Bursum's bill. In early September, Senator Irvine L. Lenroot, the chairman of the Public Lands subcommittee, which was considering the bill, informed both Fall and Burke that he had received letters opposing the measure and he asked for additional information. Burke replied that at his suggestion Twitchell and Renehan had been brought together to draft a compromise. Twitchell, he said, "dominated" the discussion at which the final draft had been written and it was, in Burke's opinion, "the very best that can be hoped for." In much the same fashion, Fall replied that the bill had been drafted in his office and while it might not be perfect, he could not "suggest an amendment to perfect it." In an apparent reference to criticism that the Indians had not been consulted, Fall baldly lied that "by their own choice" the Pueblos had been represented by A. B. Renehan. As for Mrs. Atwood and some of the Indians who had written to complain, he was "confident they have no particular understanding of the questions and problems involved."

The Protest of Artists and Writers Against the Bursum Indian Bill

"To the American Public:

"When legislation affecting the Pueblo Indians of New Mexico has been introduced in Congress by a senator from that state, with the alleged support of the Indians and apparent approval of the Indian office; when it has been briefly questioned by Senator Borah and then accepted by the Senate unanimously, the American public might suppose the legislation known as the Bursum Indian Bill to be an act dealing justly with the Indians and bringing credit to the state and nation responsibly concerned.

"As it happens, the American public would be deceived. The bill, which has passed a misinformed Senate and is now before the house, is grossly unjust to the Indians, violates every official protestation that the government is their protector, and is, moreover, in such imminence of becoming law that only that vaguely accessible power, the public, can prevent a great wrong.

"The Indians, helpless politically, have issued, with one voice from all the pueblos, a dignified but moving manifesto, asking fair play.

"Adding our voice to theirs in this emergency, we, the undersigned, who have had an opportunity to study conditions among the villages and to understand the faithless provisions of the projected law, and who intend doing our best to expose the facts, call upon the American people to protest immediately against the impending Bursum Indian Bill, whether in its present form or with disingenuous amendments. We ask this for the sake of the Pueblos, who, though probably the most industrious and deserving of all our Indian wards, are now threatened with the loss of their lands and of their community existence. We ask it even more for the sake of Americans themselves, as a test of national honor.

(Signed)

F. G. APPLEGATE	HARRIET MONROE
MARY AUSTIN	WILLARD NASH
JOZEF BAKOS	B. J. O. NORDFELDT
RUTH LAUGHLIN BARKER	ELSIE CLEWS PARSONS
GUSTAVE BAUMANN	SHELDON PARSONS
E. L. BLUMENSCHEIN	B. G. PHILLIPS
WITTER BYNNER	OLIVE RUSH
GERALD CASSIDY	CARL SANDBURG
INA SIZER CASSIDY	LEW SARETT
JOHN COLLIER	ELIZABETH SHEPLEY SERGEANT
ALICE CORBIN	J. H. SHARP
RANDALL DAVEY	WILL SHUSTER
FREMONT ELDER	JOHN SLOAN
CHARLES K. FIELD	MABEL STERNE
LEON GASPARD	WALTER UFER
STEPHEN GRAHAM	CARLOS VIERRA
ZANE GREY	HARRIET WELLES
WM. PENHALLOW HENDERSON	STEWART EDWARD WHITE
ROBERT HENRI	WILLIAM ALLEN WHITE
VICTOR HIGGINS	CHARLES ERSKINE SCOTT WOOD
DANA JOHNSON	VACHEL LINDSAY
C. GRANT LA FARGE	MAXFIELD PARRISH
D. H. LAWRENCE	EDGAR LEE MASTERS
RALPH MEYERS	HENRY HERTON KNIBBS

Figure 18.   Artists and Writers Broadside against the Bursum Bill, October 1922. From the John Collier Papers, Yale University Library.

These replies were apparently enough to satisfy Senator Lenroot. On September 7, Bursum, who declined to return to New Mexico for the Republican convention on the ground that the Pueblo bill required his presence in Washington, was authorized by Lenroot to file a favorable report on the bill. Lenroot, who had earlier stated his intention to "go over the bill at length," then left the capital to take his sick wife "to a better climate." There was no time for a hearing before the session ended, and so, on September 11, Bursum, stating to his colleagues that the Public Lands Committee, the secretary of the interior, the commissioner of Indian Affairs, and all parties to the controversy were united in their support for the bill, requested unanimous consent for its approval. After a few routine questions by Senator William Borah of Idaho, the Senate approved S. 3855 and forwarded it to the House, which took no action before the session expired.

When John Collier arrived in Santa Fe, the Senate had just approved the bill. News of its passage, he wrote to Mabel Dodge, was a "body blow" for he had been assured that it would not come up at this session of Congress. "This will mean the ruin of the Pueblos," he told Mabel. "I am sicker at heart than anything has ever made me; but perhaps the bill will be held up yet." Immediately, he set out to organize an opposition. Because of the "almost incredible camorra" which he found in Santa Fe, he warned her not to "mention my present activity to anyone."[1]

But Collier and Mrs. Atwood were not alone in their indignation and foreboding. H. W. Leech, the new Northern Pueblo agent, was also concerned. In a letter to Commissioner Burke written just two days after the Senate passed the bill, Leech forwarded a petition prepared by some of his charges that denounced the bill and focused particular attention on sections 10, 15, and 16. Instead of the Bursum bill, the Indians demanded a commission composed of persons sympathetic to the Indian cause and "in no wise connected with political affairs in the State of New Mexico," which would earnestly strive for "full justice for the Pueblo

Figure 19.   Herbert Welsh, founder and president of the Indian Rights Association. From the Historical Society of Pennsylvania.

Indians as well as for the trespassing settlers." It was Leech's observation that the Indians "have what appears to be good grounds" for offering the petition.

Some of the Anglo residents of Santa Fe were also aroused. Chief among these were Dolly Sloan, the diminutive former business manager of *The Masses*, and the wife of expatriate New York painter John Sloan; Harvard poet Witter Bynner; Alice Corbin Henderson, a former coeditor with Harriet Monroe of *Poetry* magazine; E. Dana Johnson, the editor of the *Santa Fe New Mexican*; Edgar L. Hewett, founder and director of the Museum of New Mexico; and the painter Gerald Cassidy and his wife, Ina. Under the leadership of Margaret McKittrick and Elizabeth Shepley

Sergeant, an essayist who had important contacts with eastern magazines, the group quickly formed itself into the
New Mexico Association on Indian Affairs. Through Elizabeth Sergeant, Collier was put in contact with the association, although it was never to take him fully into its
confidence.

During September and October 1922, Collier's major goal
was to inform the Pueblos about the Bursum bill and to
organize a publicity campaign that would attract national
attention to their plight. In accomplishing the first task, he
was greatly aided by Antonio Luhan, Mabel Dodge's Taos
Indian companion who had taken the place of the departed
Maurice Sterne. In the latter, the entirely fortuitous publication of his "Red Atlantis" article in the October issue of
the *Survey*, gave him an early edge in the competition with
the Santa Fe group, and clearly established his credentials as
the leading defender of the Indian's rights.

Collier began his program of educating the Indians at
Taos where he had "a great many meetings with the duly
elected council." Taos, in turn, furnished him with letters
of recommendation to the other Pueblos. Accompanied by
Antonio Luhan, he progressed down the Rio Grande to Picuris and then Cochiti. At Cochiti the idea of calling all the
Pueblos together in a demonstration of unity was born.
Whether this idea actually originated spontaneously with
the Indians as Collier claimed, or whether it originated with
Collier, who by this time was familiar with the story of the
famous Pueblo revolt of 1680 when the Indians secretly
banded together to drive the Spaniards from their villages,
is unclear. In any event, it immediately appealed to his
sense of the dramatic and he clearly saw the publicity potential in such a gathering. Months later, in an article for
the *Survey*, he would refer to the Santo Domingo meeting
as "the living, undiminished continuum of a democracy
older than the Saxon folk-mote and probably older than the
Athenian democracy."

While he was organizing the Pueblos, Collier was also in
contact with Francis Wilson, the former Pueblo attorney. In

early October the two men got together in Santa Fe to compose an exhaustive analysis of the Bursum bill. Their "blue book" was published in Santa Fe on October 18 and then distributed widely throughout the nation by Mabel Dodge and the New Mexico Association on Indian Affairs. Shortly after it appeared, Collier traveled to California to raise money in order to employ Wilson as the Pueblos' attorney. According to the account in his memoir, which is not verified by his contemporary correspondence, he also sold his New York home at this time and invested the proceeds, some seven thousand dollars, into the cause.

Collier returned to New Mexico in late October to tour several of the southern Pueblos, which had not yet agreed to attend the Santo Domingo meeting. At Laguna he met Father Fridolin Schuster, a Franciscan, who pledged his support and that of several other Franciscan missionaries among the Pueblos. Before setting out for Zuñi, the last of the holdouts, and one whose presence "must be assured," Collier wrote Mabel Dodge to inform her of the publicity campaign he was preparing. The Santa Fe people, he wrote, were strangely "incommunicado" but his own work was "crushingly successful. It will serve to support the more dramatic propaganda we must wage."

On October 31, Collier concluded his meeting with the Zuñi elders, whom he successfully persuaded to attend the All Pueblo Council meeting. Everything was now prepared for the November 5 meeting. In addition to the Pueblo delegates, there would be in attendance besides himself, Wilson and Hanna, the two former Pueblo attorneys, Father Schuster and two of his fellow Franciscans, several Indian superintendents, Margaret McKittrick and Elizabeth Sergeant, from whom he had finally heard concerning the activities of the Santa Feans. Somehow, he wrote, the Santa Fe group had mistakenly concluded that he "wanted to manage that committee or the organization it might create, or prevent it from functioning." Nothing could be farther from his mind, he advised Miss Sergeant. He was certain that their suspicion would "fade away on a face-to-face conference," and he hoped that one could be arranged before the Santo Domingo meeting. In the meantime, it was important to keep news of the council "quiet, for various reasons, till it is over." He also stressed the necessity to get together so that "a unified publicity plan be worked out . . . because otherwise there would be neglected opportunities, overlappings, and most of all, the premature breaking of phases of publicity in a manner to kill the big new possibilities, etc."[2]

On November 5, 1922, at Santo Domingo Pueblo, 121 Pueblo delegates from twenty Pueblos met to discuss the Bursum bill. For two days and "the greater part of two nights" the Indians listened as Collier and others explained the bill's provisions. According to Collier, the meeting was "exclusively in the Indian's hands" with the whites retiring at times when the Indians wished to discuss matters privately. At the conclusion of the meeting, the delegates adopted a memorial addressed to the American people. In it they protested the loss of their lands. They also complained that they had not been consulted about the Bursum bill and that the Interior Department had refused to explain its provisions to them. They refused to accept the jurisdiction of the federal court, which they said would mean the destruction of their traditional form of government. This memorial was translated and written down "verbatim" by Father Schuster and then typed by Collier for release to the press. Although the memorial was itself a major document, Collier counseled in a letter to Frank Kellogg, the *Survey* editor, the truly important thing to be emphasized was that the Pueblos had banded together once again, had made their decision unanimously, and had agreed to form a "permanent junta" to defend their lands and their way of life.

News of the Santo Domingo meeting was quickly disseminated throughout the nation. The *New York Times* printed the memorial the following day and ran a story by Elizabeth Sergeant in its Sunday feature section later in the month. On November 29, Herbert Croly, at the request of Miss Sergeant, ran an editorial in *The Nation* denouncing the Bursum bill, and that same day an article by Alice Corbin Henderson appeared in the *New Republic*. Simultaneously, editorials defending the Pueblos appeared in the *New York World* and the *New York Tribune*, both the results of appeals by Margaret McKittrick and Elizabeth Sergeant. The appearance of these articles produced a request for copy from other newspapers and magazines, which in turn resulted in even greater news coverage in December and January.[3]

The appearance of this adverse publicity produced consternation in Washington, particularly in the office of Commissioner Burke, who now found himself besieged by a flood of inquiries and letters of protest. The commissioner could not have been taken by surprise, for Mrs. Atwood had written him shortly after the conclusion of the Santo Domingo meeting that "there is to be a campaign of publicity through the leading newspapers of the United States and it has been precipitated by that awful Bursum bill. I have counseled all the people with whom I have come in contact to make the publicity educational and to refrain from any attack upon the Indian Office," she advised, but she could not speak for the "artists and writers" in Santa Fe over whom she had no control.

One of the first inquiries came from George Vaux, the chairman of the Board of Indian Commissioners. Although he refused to align himself "with the interests represented by the extreme agitators . . . such as the Women's Organization of Southern California," Vaux wrote, "I do feel that they are on the right track in endeavoring to have the Bursum bill modified." Vaux's letter was followed by a petition against the Bursum bill from a group of influential anthropologists, led by Alfred Kidder of the Peabody Museum at Harvard and Herbert Spinden of the American Museum of Natural History in New York. Burke also received frequent reports from Ralph Twitchell, who complained petulantly about the way his reputation was being tarnished through his association with the bill. While fulminating against the "well meaning" but ignorant people led by that "paid propagandist," John Collier, and his friend, Francis Wilson, who had "engineered" the Santo Domingo meeting, Twitchell, writing as though he were publicly defending himself, insisted that he had not been hired to represent the Indians or to defend their land, but only to represent the federal government and to obtain justice for both sides. At the same time, he advised Burke, he could not defend section sixteen of the bill, which "I argued before the Secretary and yourself against." That was "Renehan's suggestion," he reminded Burke, and despite the fact that Fall had accepted it, Twitchell had not and he was "still opposed to it." Burke responded to all these letters in the same vein. If there were serious objections to the bill, he urged, the opposing parties should get together in an atmosphere of "mutual understanding and cooperation" and reach some sort of compromise so that the issue could be settled. All the "publicity and excitement" surrounding the bill were not conducive to rational solution of the problem. Indeed, he informed George Vaux and Stella Atwood, there seemed to be some "ulterior motive" behind the adverse publicity. It was as though the opponents of the bill were trying to "create sentiment that the Interior Department and the Bureau of Indian Affairs are not honest and that they are attempting to put over legislation that will be unfair to the Indians. It would seem as if the Secretary of the Interior and the Commissioner are entitled to the credit of at least being honest and that they are simply mistaken in their opinion that the bill is fair to the Indians."[4]

As the opposition began to build following the Santo Domingo meeting, Collier, who from the beginning had advised that "the job is a heap more than beating the Bursum bill," decided to increase the pressure. There would be no compromise with the Bursum bill as Commissioner Burke was urging. Instead, a rival bill would be prepared by the Indians' friends, which would, as the northern Pueblos had petitioned Burke in September, create a special commission to resolve the disputed claims. To dramatize the Indian opposition to the Bursum bill, Collier planned to take a delegation of Pueblos to New York in December and then on to

Washington, where they would appear before the House Indian Affairs Committee. In preparation for this trip, he advised Mabel Dodge, "I am seeing the political folk, writing a
lot, seeing the newspaper folk and trying to raise money."
Dr. Haynes and Mrs. Vosburg had entered the fray, he continued. Haynes would contact Senators Hiram Johnson of
California and William Borah of Idaho to enlist their support against the Bursum bill and Haynes would also ask
Gifford Pinchot to meet with Collier during the eastern
trip. Mrs. Vosburg and Dr. Haynes "separately or together
are prepared to do whatever has to be done" in the matter of
finances, but he hoped "not to call on them excessively as
they are our permanent reliance for the fight which this
eastern trip is only an incident in."

On November 21, the day after the Congress reconvened
from its summer recess, Senator Borah, in an unusual move,
requested that S. 3855 be recalled. It had, he said, been
passed during the hectic last days of the last session "under
a misapprehension as to what its terms were." Borah's surprise move produced jubilation in the Collier camp and
strengthened his determination to escalate the struggle.
Under no circumstances, he wired Mrs. Atwood, must the
Interior Department be permitted to amend the Bursum bill
until after she and the Indians had been given the opportunity to testify against it. He urged her to "use utmost
power to prevent action; . . . action before our arguments
heard means war."[5]

By late November the Indian Rights Association had
abandoned its cautious stance and taken its first, halting
steps against the Bursum bill. S. M. Brosius, the IRA's field
agent who was ordinarily solicitous of the Indian Bureau's
reputation, after reading Alice Henderson's article in the
New Republic, wrote that it was "a stunner. Just what the
department deserved." Although Herbert Welsh was still
unwilling to believe that Commissioner Burke had not adequately defended the Pueblos' rights, Brosius was less cautious: "The Indians and their friends had a right to look to
him for protection of the Indians," he wrote in early De-

cember. "Is it enough for him to say that the Pueblos are in
New Mexico and the Secretary has charge of them????"
Other officials placed in a similar uncomfortable squeeze
between loyalty to a superior and the clear call of duty,
would have resigned, Brosius hinted, but "I have heard of no
resignation."

This new critical attitude, however, failed to mollify Mrs.
Atwood, and the IRA became increasingly concerned about
her relationship to Collier. Collier himself was an enigma
to the IRA, which found his direct method of action distasteful. For a few weeks in early October, the IRA was convinced that Collier had been reluctantly forced upon Mrs.
Atwood by "some of those advancing the funds" for her
work. In the vain hope of driving a wedge between Collier
and Mrs. Atwood, Brosius addressed her to complain that
Collier's activities had made the Pueblos unduly suspicious
of the federal government. Quoting one of the IRA's New
Mexico correspondents, Clara True, who had met Collier,
Brosius archly alluded to her comment that Collier smelled
badly. This aside backfired when Mrs. Atwood replied that
Brosius was probably right in saying that Collier needed "a
bath." After all, she chided, during the hectic weeks before
the Santo Domingo meeting, he had been "staying out in
the Pueblos with the Indians, sleeping on floors, getting one
meal a day, and hardly ever spending two nights in one
place." But, she concluded, "Collier has the goods. If the
Bursum Bill is not absolutely wiped out, I miss my guess,
and if so, it will be Mr. Collier's work."

The rising tide of protest that followed the Santo Domingo meeting also had its effect upon Mabel Dodge. Until
then she had been content in the knowledge that it was she
who had "willed" Collier's entry into the Indian field.
Moreover, she had been preoccupied with her most recent
acquisition, English novelist D. H. Lawrence, who arrived
in Taos on the very day the Bursum bill passed the Senate.

Ever since Collier had left Taos after his initial visit during the winter of 1920–21, Mabel Dodge had been searching
for someone who could help her save the American Indian.

In October 1921, she impulsively wrote Lawrence, inviting him to Taos to write a book on the Indians. Her letter caught Lawrence in the right mood. He was tired of England—"It is a dead dog that died of a love disease like syphilis"—and he was yearning for a change. After some indecision—"I *can't* go to America. Not yet. It is too raw for me, and I am too tender for it"—Lawrence at last decided to take the plunge. Someone, he wrote, "must somehow bring together the two ends of humanity, our own thin end, and the last dark strand from the previous, pre-white era." But he dallied first in Ceylon and Australia, and then, almost a year after Mabel's first letter, he appeared in Taos.

The very day Lawrence arrived, Mabel packed him off for a five-day trip to an "Apache gathering 120 miles away across the desert." Lawrence did not find the Apaches "very *sympatisch*," and he was never to feel comfortable in the vastness of the New Mexico desert, but within a month he was able to write that "Taos, in its way, *is* rather thrilling." His attitude toward Mabel Dodge was similarly ambivalent. The cottage she provided was "very nice" and she herself was "very generous," but the "drawback is, of course, living under the wing of the 'padrona.'" By December he had had enough of both Mabel and the Indians and he fled Mabel's compound to the Hawk ranch, 17 miles north of Taos.

During the months of September and October, however, the Colliers and the Lawrences shared adjoining cottages on Mabel's estate. Each night when Collier was not on the road, the guests gathered around the huge fireplace in the main house where, one of them later recalled, "the evening conversations . . . were divided about equally between Collier and Lawrence. Collier talked about his future plans for the Indians, many of which he later carried out . . . ." In this atmosphere, Lawrence was immediately pressed into the campaign against the Bursum bill until he became "sick of it." An article he wrote for the *New York Times* produced one of the few humorous moments in the struggle:

> But I arrive at a moment of crisis. I suppose every man always does, here. The crisis is a thing called the Bursum

Bill, and it affects the Pueblo Indians. I wouldn't know a
thing about it, if I needn't. But Bursum, Bursum, Bursum!!
the Bill ! the Bill ! the Bill ! Twitchell, Twitchell, Twitchell!! O Mr. Secretary Fall, Fall, Fall! Oh Mr. Secretary
Fall! you bad man, you good man, you Fall, you Rise, you
Fall!!! The Joy Survey, Oh Joy. No Joy, once Joy, now Woe!
Woe! Whoa! Whoa Bursum! Whoa Bill, Whoa-a-a!

Like a Lindsay Boom-Boom bellowing it goes on in my
unwonted ears, till I *have* to take heed. And then I sol-
emnly sit down in a chair and read the Bill, the Bill, the
printed Bursum Bill, Section one-two-three-four-five-six-
seven, whereas and wherefore and heretofore, right to the
damned and distant end. Then I start the Insomuch-as of
Mr. Francis Wilson's brief concerning the Bill. Then I read
Mr. C's [Collier] passionate article against, and Mrs. H's
[Alice Henderson] hatchet-stroke summary against, and
Mr. M's sharp-knife jugglery *for* the bill. After which I feel
I'm getting mixed up, and Bear ye one another's Bursum.[6]

At the time Lawrence decided to flee Mabel's too protective custody, her son, John Evans, was also preparing to
move out. In December he was to marry Alice Corbin Henderson's fifteen-year-old daughter. Feeling somewhat abandoned, Mabel's energies were temporarily channeled back
into the Pueblo fight. As she wrote the poet Robinson Jef-
fers: "I put all my force into another kind of fight, another
effort than the one I felt I had lost, and I effected a kind of
dimension between myself and Lawrence by turning my
sympathy away from him, back to the Indians, by an effort
of my will."

Mabel's return to the Pueblo problem is substantiated by
her contemporary correspondence. On November 21, 1922,
she wrote Collier, who had again returned to California,
that she had enlisted the support of anthropologist Elsie
Clews Parsons. Elsie was "up in arms" about the Bursum
bill, she reported, and had promised to speak to her friends,
including the speaker of the House and to Ogden Mills, the
editor of the *New York Herald Tribune*. She would also secure resolutions against the bill from the American Anthropological Association and the American Indian Museum.

Mary Austin, the novelist who had coined the term "Amerindian" a decade before, also wired that she would arrange for free theater appearances in New York if Collier could get the Indians to dance. At the same time, Mabel counseled against taking the Indians east in December: "They will all want to be here for Xmas. And we must select them ourselves. They always vote that their smart, short-haired Americanized ones shall go: just the wrong ones."

Later that same day, Mabel wrote Collier a second time and she also enclosed a letter that he was to forward to Mrs. Atwood. Although she had "been glad to help, all along—especially in the immediate necessity about the Bursum Bill," she had never been able to become excited about Collier's plans for the future because she had never been able "to see any very definite program ahead." There did not seem to be much to do "except ameliorate and reform," she wrote, "and neither of these *thrilled* me, though they seemed necessary." But that very afternoon she had a long talk with Eshref Shevky, which had made her "clearer in my mind about the possibilities in the work" Collier was doing. Suddenly, she saw "the possibility of a '*new form*'—what Lawrence is forever raving about! And you are absolutely cut out to carry it through . . . ." For her part, Mabel was at last ready to pledge her own "energy, time and money *now* where I didn't feel it before." She had been thinking of selling or renting her Taos estate, which had become "a burden to me to run it without any purpose back of it," but when a friend proposed turning it into "a kind of nut's home," she had instantly recoiled. It now occurred to her that "this place of mine should work in as a kind of headquarters for the future . . . for something onward going . . . and the whole thing a base of operations *really* for a new world plan." She also saw herself "involved in this scheme, quite truly and deeply in some—as yet—undeclared manner." She was certain that she "could not get into anything *outside* of Indian work" for when she had "left the White People's world" to live with Tony, "I *really* left it—it was no mental attitude or superficial sensational gesture." Carried away by her newfound enthusiasm, she concluded: "I can easily marry Tony if that will make it more convenient from the worldly standpoint."

In her third letter of the day, to Mrs. Atwood, Mabel elaborated on her plan. The Pueblos, she wrote, in an effort to earn outside income "in unvital unillumined work under [white] masters," were in danger of losing their "whole culture." They could only be saved by "taking them away from the government and by creating a new school system for them." Only Collier could accomplish such a task, but he would have to be "made independent in a financial way . . . and then be let to go ahead." With the nucleus of opposition that had already gathered against the Bursum bill and under Collier's leadership, she told Mrs. Atwood, a "social experiment" could be undertaken among the Pueblos which would lead to a new Indian policy that could "save the government's face." Everyone's energy at the moment was being dissipated in negative ways, but Collier could transform this force into positive channels. "Talk it over with Collier," she urged, "and *promise* him things and get him to promise things."

Collier did not apparently forward Mabel's letter to Mrs. Atwood, but he did reply immediately:

> I know the danger that this work will achieve merely material results and eventuate in welfare and things static. Certainly I am determined that it shall *not* go to such an end. For twenty years I worked at things meant to be dynamic and creative which mainly worked out into amelioration, welfare, etc., and I hope it won't be that way again! As for the Pueblos, there's reason to hope and plan, now, where a year ago we could only dream and lament.
>
> We shall have to establish the right to dictate Indian policy, and build up a truly national movement, and get ourselves strong "on top" politically, before we can demand for the Pueblos the kind of thing you write of. At this time . . . the public policy is wrong and it is being executed still worse and it involves all the Indians; and it can be changed (policy and administration) only through a national effort . . . . We couldn't swing the needed power simply

through a fight based on the Pueblos. *After* power is established, then we can get the fundamental change needed for the Pueblos. © Mrs. Grace Collier

Collier also reported that his efforts to stimulate interest in the Pueblo cause were being well received in both Los Angeles and San Francisco. He had spent most of one day with the regional editor of the *Los Angeles Daily News* and through him had been placed in contact with Max Sterne, a United Press and Scripps syndicate reporter, whom he was bringing back to New Mexico. "The Scripps folk mean to get up a complete case which they can stand back of and to begin a drive and carry it to a finish." Fremont Older of the *San Francisco Call* "came after me unsought . . . . He will do anything we want. Editorials, introductions, etc." Through Older, Collier expected to get all the Hearst papers lined up: "I am cumulatively astonished at the way people of different sorts take the fight up."

Collier also agreed with Mabel's suggestion that the Indians stay in New Mexico until after Christmas. As for himself, "it is now rather plain that I must go to Washington in early December." There he would make preparations for their trip and arrange for them to appear before the congressional committees.

Soon after this avowal to "dictate Indian policy," Collier left California for the nation's capital, via Santa Fe. In Santa Fe he met with the officers of the New Mexico Association on Indian Affairs. Together they agreed to retain Francis Wilson to represent them during the congressional hearings and to adopt a new bill, which they would attempt to substitute for Bursum's. Even as this step was being taken, however, trouble was brewing in the East.

In early December, a group of wealthy New Yorkers who owned property in the Santa Fe area came together to form the Eastern Association on Indian Affairs. In the words of one of the founders, Roberts Walker, the Eastern Association was "a little group rather hurriedly got together in and around New York City by people many of whom were not previously acquainted but who were interested in the crafts and life and art of these Pueblo people." Led by Amelia Elizabeth White, they favored cooperation with the Indian Bureau and they were instinctively opposed to Collier's confrontation tactics. Through General Hugh L. Scott, Mrs. White early on made contact with the Board of Indian Commissioners, and through Margaret McKittrick, she attempted to coordinate the Eastern Association's activities with those of the New Mexico Association. Soon after forming, the group met to discuss a suggestion by General Scott that they organize "on a nation wide basis," but it was decided to postpone such a venture until after the Bursum bill had been defeated. Apparently not yet aware that Collier was a party to Wilson's efforts to draft a rival bill, and believing that "he knows nothing of our plans as yet," Mrs. White expressed concern that Collier might "do something disastrous to them before he learns what it is we are really trying to do." She implored General Scott to meet with Collier and to keep him from antagonizing Fall and Burke: "I do not know him personally but from what I hear it may be difficult to get him to act tactfully."

At the same time, Albert Fall, who had been stung by the criticism directed against his office for its role in both the Bursum bill and the Teapot Dome lease, now lashed out angrily against his detractors. He let it be known in New Mexico that refusal to compromise would leave him with no recourse but to reinstitute eviction proceedings against the three thousand white settlers which had been suspended in 1921. Fall's apparent intention was to unleash a white backlash against the critics of the Bursum bill and to strengthen the hands of the moderate groups like the Eastern and New Mexico associations, which favored compromise.

Fall also decided to mount his own counterpropaganda campaign. On December 13, a few days after Collier arrived in Washington, Fall addressed a thirty-five-page defense of his role in the Bursum bill to Senator Borah. In it he denounced the "propagandists," by whom he claimed Borah had been misled, and he particularly singled out Francis Wilson, whom he charged had been delinquent, while Pueblo attorney, in adequately protecting the lands of Laguna Pueblo. After a lengthy review of the Pueblo problem, Fall challenged the Congress to "provide for an immediate investigation" of the situation, at which time his department would turn over all its evidence that these propagandists had "engaged in misleading statements, some of them in absolutely false statements." The following day, Chairman Homer Snyder of the House Indian Affairs Committee defended the Bursum bill in remarks inserted into the *Congressional Record* and then, at the request of the Interior Department, introduced a slightly revised edition of the bill, which omitted the controversial section 16 and several other less offensive features. In what appeared to be a smoothly orchestrated assault on the opposition, Commissioner Burke had five thousand copies of Snyder's speech printed at his own expense. These copies, together with an equal number of Fall's letter to Borah were then distributed throughout the nation under Snyder's frank.[7]

The sources of Fall's charges were probably Renehan and Twitchell, but he was also aided by information from the same informant who had earlier complained to the IRA that Collier needed a bath, Clara True. Miss True, a schoolteacher, had once served as superintendent of the Potrero Indian school in California. Some time after 1910 she moved to New Mexico, purchased one of the disputed tracts on the Santa Clara reservation north of Santa Fe, and was now employed by the State of New Mexico in a variety of supervisory positions in the Department of Public Education. A staunch defender of "civilization" against "paganism," she had long backed the "progressive" minority among the Pueblos and for years had been a divisive force in Pueblo life. Contemptuous of all forms of traditional Pueblo life, she was stridently opposed to the "uplifters" in Santa Fe who supported the Pueblos in their efforts to resist assimilation. According to Miss True, Francis Wilson was a "fool," Mrs. Atwood, an "old crow," and Collier, a "freak." As for the women in the GFWC, they were just a "mess of hysterical females . . . who are getting wonderful thrills of philanthropy out of saving the Noble Red Man from extinction." Working closely with A. B. Renehan, she wrote both Fall and Burke in early December 1922 insisting that they get Wilson to testify at the congressional hearings about "the vital things which happened when he was Pueblo Indian Attorney." According to Clara True, Wilson in 1912 had approved the sale of a large tract of Laguna Pueblo land, the Paguate tract, to a Colonel Collier of San Diego, whom Wilson was also representing. Despite her obvious instability, she was soon to be employed by the IRA as its New Mexico representative, a position she would hold until well after she became an embarrassing liability to that organization.

Collier arrived in Washington on the morning of December 11 and immediately plunged into a round of conferences with the other Indian defense groups. First he met with Father Schuster and Father William Hughes of the Catholic Mission Board. Hughes was a good man, Collier reported, "but not aggressive at all" and "very solicitous" that nothing be done to injure Commissioner Burke. That afternoon, Collier met with General Scott and Malcolm McDowell of the Board of Indian Commissioners. From them he learned "of the state of terrorism in the Indian Office which Fall had instilled." That same evening he met with William Hard, the Washington correspondent for *The Nation* and with Robert Yard, who briefed him on the similarities between the Bursum bill and the All Year National Park bill. "There is much . . . sensationally much . . . to be got there," Collier wrote, "it is plain that Fall is wusser'n than we thought even."

At Yard's urging, Collier adopted the theme that would dominate the publicity campaign of the next few months. Fall, whom Yard described as "besotted in his sense of power and determined to get both his objects," would have to be made the target of all the opposition groups. Despite the fact that Yard believed the two bills were already "dead as salt mackerel," the only safe course was to "keep the country stirred up" until Harding was forced to remove Fall. The president, Yard wrote Mrs. Atwood, would "stand by his friend, but there is a greater than President Harding whose name is Political Expediency. Why advertise the dull tool, Bursum? Let it always be plain that the hand is Fall's."

Yard also endeavored to remove Collier's suspicions about the other defense groups, particularly the IRA, with which he had been working closely on the All Year National Park bill. The IRA, he explained, opposed both the All Year Park and the original Bursum bill. It was "simply playing a professional hand" in the present crisis, "leaving the alarm to be sounded by others." The important thing, he impressed upon Collier, was that all the opposition groups should stick together and not permit Fall to take advantage of their minor differences. He gave the same advice to Amelia White when she inquired about the advisability of attempting to form a national organization. The GFWC, Yard informed her, had already beaten her "to the job of organizing already existing organizations." It was best to cooperate with Collier.

Following this round of initial meetings, Collier then met for the first time with S. M. Brosius and Commissioner Burke. Brosius, who had heard so many derogatory comments about Collier, was pleasantly surprised: "He is not so bad as he may have been represented," Brosius advised Matthew Sniffen. Nor was Collier inflexible on the Pueblo issue, he learned. The bill that had been drawn up by Francis Wilson would protect many of the white settler's rights and it appeared to be a reasonable compromise. The result of Collier's visit with Commissioner Burke is not evident from the records, but in light of Burke's subsequent support for the Snyder bill, it is not likely that either man learned anything about the other's intentions.

From Washington Collier traveled north to New York with Father Schuster in tow. His purpose was twofold: first, to raise money for Wilson's expenses and to drum up new publicity, and second, to meet with the Eastern Association on Indian Affairs. His money-raising efforts were not particularly rewarding. He did have a long chat with L. N. E. Paulin of the *New York World*, who promised continuing news coverage: "The *World* will help systematically and radically," he reported to Mabel Dodge. On December 22, Collier and Schuster met with Miss White and her associates in a specially called meeting. They discussed the draft bill that Wilson had prepared as a substitute for the Bursum bill, arrangements for the Indians' journey after the first of the year, and Miss White's proposal for a nationwide organization. As the others had done, Collier counseled her against such a move at this time, urging rather that the activities of the already existing organizations be coordinated "through a clearing house." At this meeting Collier also met Frederick Webb Hodge, an ethnologist with the Museum of the American Indian, Herbert J. Spinden, and Warren K. Moorhead, an archaeologist at Philips Academy who was also a member of the Board of Indian Commissioners. As a final item of business, it was agreed to send Wilson a retainer of a thousand dollars. If more money was required, Collier stated, Mrs. Vosburg could be counted upon for a loan.

The day after Christmas, Collier precipitated a decision in Washington on the proper means of introducing Wilson's draft bill. Nearly everyone had advised permitting Bursum to sponsor the bill, but Bursum had given no indication of willingness, and it was now evident that Fall would press the Snyder bill before Congress. "On behalf of the GFWC," Collier decided to let Senator Andrieus A. Jones of New Mexico, the Democrat who had defeated Bursum for this seat in 1916, introduce the bill. "The others passively consented." Immediately after obtaining Jones's consent, Collier called Bursum and "cancelled the offer." Twitchell, Fall, and Bursum, he gleefully reported to Mabel Dodge, "were furiously trying to arrange something, probably a new bill . . . Fall is in a white rage and all are being dominated by their emotions, not their judgment. We should avoid similar mistakes."

As these final preparations were being made for the showdown in Congress, Mabel Dodge precipitated a minor crisis of her own with the Santa Fe group. Margaret McKittrick and Francis Wilson were vetoing all her suggestions for publicity, she complained to Collier. While both of them were good people, they were too "dilatory and hesitant" to keep the copy flowing. She and Shevky had also decided to dramatize the existence of syphilis at Taos. This time a campaign to administer Wassermann tests was to be undertaken, a task that would require most of the money Mabel had earlier promised Collier. Whether it was Mabel's attempt to publicize the syphilis threat, or her criticism of Miss McKittrick's work, or just her general reputation, when the word got out that she intended to accompany the Pueblos to the East, Margaret McKittrick emphatically protested. "I cannot tell you how strongly I feel about Mrs. Sterne's going on," she wrote Collier on December 29. Mabel's presence would only give the opposition additional ground for its counterattack, she warned. Collier must see to it that Mabel did not accompany the Indians to Washington.

Collier replied immediately in the affirmative. In light of Fall's attack on Wilson, it would be better to avoid a situation whereby he might also attack the Indians through an identification with Mabel. He agreed to advise her not to come to Washington, but he would do nothing to stop her if she wished to accompany the Indians to New York. There was no reason to abandon Mabel completely, he advised Miss McKittrick, for "we have used her cooperation thoroughly throughout the battle . . . she is doing good work, her motives are clear, and significant, and we have no more significant support than hers." The crisis subsided when Mabel informed Collier that in light of Fall's "threatening remarks about special agents reports" in his letter to Borah, she agreed it was best not to come.[8]

By the time Mabel Dodge decided not to accompany the Indians, the strategy for the congressional hearings had been completed. On January 11–12, there would be hearings on the All Year National Park bill. Collier decided not to become involved in this fight, but to leave it to Robert Yard and the National Park Association. On January 15, hearings would begin in the Senate on the Bursum bill and on the rival Jones Bill, which Francis Wilson had prepared. The Indians were to leave New Mexico a week before the hearings began to draw publicity. Collier would join them in Chicago and then accompany them to New York, where he and Mary Austin had scheduled several appearances. Mrs. Atwood was to take Mabel's place, and he would brief her on her testimony during the journey.

During the two weeks before the hearings, Collier's mood was alternately confident and doubt ridden. Albert Fall's oft rumored resignation from the cabinet was announced on January 3, 1923. This unexpected event, plus the introduction of the less controversial Snyder bill, temporarily disrupted Collier's strategy, but, as he wrote Mabel Dodge, the original Bursum bill, "thank goodness, is still *not* dead, but can be exploited as a menace and an evidence of conspiracy."

Through his old friends in New York City he arranged for the Indians to appear at the People's Institute on the evening before the hearings began. This, he was certain, would "create big publicity" for the papers and also prepare the way for later appearances. His efforts to raise money in New York, however, continued to be unsuccessful. On January 3, he spoke to the directors of the International Health Board of the Rockefeller Foundation in an attempt to interest them in the Pueblo health problem and he also spoke to the directors of the Commonwealth Foundation. Both turned him down. Somehow he failed to coordinate his plans with those of Mary Austin, whom Mabel had advised him was "energetic and ready to help—full of cream—churn her—churn her." As a result, Mary Austin became "angry at being left out" and while he was eventually able to assuage her wounded pride and to reenlist her in the campaign, he became increasingly fretful at the timidity of the Eastern Association and the "museum folks." The Board of Indian Commissioners, whose support he had earlier termed critical, now closed ranks behind Commissioner Burke; and Warren K. Moorhead, whom Collier was especially counting on for support, was "sharply hauled into line." Collier was also worried about Francis Wilson. "My present job," he wrote just before leaving Washington for Chicago, "is to make sure that Wilson, etc. handle matters with unceasing aggressiveness."

As he prepared to join the Indians on their eastward trip, Collier at last found someone he could trust to direct the publicity campaign that he and Mabel Dodge had decided must be increased during the hearings. Judson King, the director of the National Popular Government League in Washington, agreed to undertake the task. King, who together with Dr. Haynes and Senator George Norris of Nebraska had launched the fight for publicly owned power when the league was founded in 1913, was a man of bold "imagination, audacity and very sound judgment," Collier wrote. "He works like several machines at one time and knows every newspaperman in Washington." King's employment was the direct result of a $700 check from Mabel Dodge, which, Collier gratefully acknowledged, had arrived just at "the moment of greatest need."

The Pueblo delegates left New Mexico on January 10 under the watchful eye of Agent Leech, who immediately informed Commissioner Burke. They were being financed by Mabel Dodge and Amelia White, he reported. In Chicago the Indians were met by Collier, who, through his sister, Eleanor Stanton, arranged to have them housed at several neighboring homes in Winnetka, including that of Harold and Anna Ickes. As a result of the Ickeses' extensive connections, several public meetings were hurriedly arranged, including an appearance at the exclusive Cliff Dweller's luncheon on January 12. Ickes was particularly moved by the speech Collier delivered. The story of "wrongs wantonly committed, if spread broadcast," he wrote his political mentor, Hiram Johnson, "ought to make every decent American's cheek burn with shame." Very little money was raised in Chicago, but the enlistment of Harold Ickes into the cause was a distinct plum. Ickes could not only be counted upon to influence his progressive Republican friends like Johnson, but he also indicated an interest in forming an Indian defense group in Chicago for the longer struggle.

On January 14, the day before the hearings opened, Collier and the Pueblo delegation appeared at the People's Institute, where Collier delivered an impassioned address entitled "The Impending Destruction of the Pueblos—the Oldest Democracy in the World," to an audience of 700 persons. As expected, the meeting attracted favorable publicity and resulted in invitations for subsequent appearances in the city.

By the time the hearings on the Bursum-Jones bills began in the Senate, the House had just concluded its hearings on the All Year National Park bill. In those hearings Robert Yard and others effectively exposed the irregularities in Fall's bill. In an article in *Outlook* magazine, which appeared during the hearings, Yard also hinted at collusion between Fall and Bursum on this and the Bursum bill. The result was a blistering counterattack by Fall when he testified on January 11. Charging that he had been the victim of unsubstantiated and "unfounded criticism" ever since he took office, Fall complained bitterly that his department had become bogged down in defense of its policies and was being prevented from "doing the public's business" by the continual attacks. He had no publicity medium in the Interior Department with which to fight back, he complained, but "if I were to do it over again I would try to get the money and I would pay it out of my private portion if I could not get it any other way." Goaded by his opponents, he finally threatened in his most menacing manner: "I am a public official. If you do not agree with me about a fundamental principle or an immaterial proposition, it is perfectly right to criticize me; but unless you are confident I am a grafter or thief, do not accuse me of being one or even insinuate it." The adversary tone of these hearings was then carried over into the hearings on the Bursum-Jones bills.[9]

The Senate hearings were to prove inconclusive, but they did serve to make clear the distinction between Bursum's bill and the so-called Jones bill that Francis Wilson had drafted in late December.

On the first day of testimony, Ralph Twitchell and Commissioner Burke appeared to defend the Bursum bill and to describe again the manner in which it had been formulated. Both testified that the bill was clearly a compromise between the claims of the Indians and those of the non-Indian settlers. Burke, whose presentation Collier contemptuously described as a "vain-glorious, emotional, almost feeble minded oration," repeated his often stated belief that any inequities created by Bursum's bill could be easily corrected if only its opponents would cease their adamant opposition and sit down with members of the Interior Department staff to work out a compromise.

The brunt of the defense, however, rested upon Twitchell. Under close examination by Senator Lenroot, who was obviously nettled by the way he had been hoodwinked earlier, Twitchell's defense crumbled and his composure wilted. Time and again, despite frequent pleas that his motives had been good, he was forced to admit that the bill's wording worked exclusively to the advantage of the non-Indians. By the time he completed his presentation, there was little doubt that the original Bursum bill was indeed a dead letter.

Following the interrogation of Twitchell, Mrs. Atwood and Francis Wilson came forth to argue the merits of the rival Jones bill. This bill had two major objectives. The first was the creation of a special Pueblo lands commission, which was to be empowered to arbitrate the conflicting claims and to make awards of title and compensation in those cases where both parties were in agreement. Like Twitchell, Wilson believed that 80 percent of the conflicting claims could be disposed of in this manner, without the expense necessarily entailed in a formal court case. Disputes that could not be resolved by arbitration were to be heard by the U.S. District Court of New Mexico where the Indians, upon the request of fifteen Pueblos, would be permitted to name a counsel of their own choice to defend their interests.

The second objective of the Jones bill was authorization

of an expenditure of $905,000 of federal money for irrigation and drainage projects along the Rio Grande. The purpose of this section was to create approximately 20,000 acres of new agricultural land along the river with which to compensate those claimants, Indian and white alike, whose claims were denied. Most of the money requested for this project was to be eventually reimbursed by the users of the land.

Mrs. Atwood's testimony was brief and mainly confined to explaining how she had become involved in the controversy as the representative of the GFWC. Collier did not testify at the Senate hearings, but when interest was shown in the Santo Domingo meeting and both Burke and Twitchell charged that Collier had formulated the resolutions adopted there, he submitted a letter that was published as an exhibit. In it, he strongly defended the ability of the Indians to understand and to react to the problems with which they were confronted. The great evil all Indians suffered, he charged, was the attitude of the "Indian Office that Indians should be treated as incompetents" and denied the normal avenues of information and expression that the constitution guaranteed to all other Americans.

Wilson, not Collier, however, was the spokesman of the Indians before the Senate subcommittee. While regretting that both Burke and Fall had chosen to interpret the criticism of the various anti-Bursum groups "as a personal matter," Wilson charged that it was this very attitude that made legislation like the Bursum bill possible. The idea that the Indian Office "should be permitted to decide everything, to do everything; and that all outside interference with the Indians is, in effect, lese majeste, and almost high treason," was so deeply entrenched, he charged, that the Indian Office had become incapable of comprehending the inequities contained in legislation like Bursum's bill. It was this very blindness that had provoked the Indians' friends to insist upon an independent commission to decide the issue of the disputed claims.

Wilson's defense of a Pueblo lands commission, however, failed to impress Senator Lenroot any more than had Twitchell's defense of the Bursum bill. Since the Jones bill contained no guidelines for the decisions of the commission, Lenroot queried, what would determine its decisions? After some fumbling, Wilson replied that the commissioners would be guided by "good conscience and justice." Could not an unfriendly commission do more harm to the Indians than the Bursum bill, Lenroot persisted. Wilson replied that since the appointments to the commission would have to be confirmed by the Senate, he was confident that the Indian's friends would prevail to ensure that men of "high character" would be chosen. At this point Commissioner Burke sarcastically interjected that the same could be said for the secretary of the interior and the commissioner of Indian affairs, both of whom had been confirmed by the Senate. Lenroot simply expressed his amazement at Wilson's credulity. In much the same fashion as Twitchell had previously done, Wilson now began to admit that his bill, too, contained weaknesses and that it would have to be revised.

On the final day of hearings, Albert Fall appeared. He repeated his intention to resign on March 4, 1923, but, as he had earlier written Senator Reed Smoot, the chairman of the parent committee, until he did so, his department was unalterably opposed to the Jones bill. Not only would the arbitration provision in the bill deprive the whites of due process, he claimed, but the cost of a special commission and a special Indian attorney would be an unnecessary expense upon the American taxpayer. Fall, however, had not appeared before the subcommittee to speak about either of the bills under consideration but to lash out against his detractors, especially Francis Wilson, whom he again accused of mishandling the Pueblo affairs when he was the Pueblo attorney. Much attention was focused on an article that had just appeared in the *New York Times* accusing Bursum and Fall of being financially involved in the Pueblo lands. This allegation was without foundation, as the *Times* was forced to admit in a later retraction, but it probably resulted from

charges made by Robert Yard and Mary Austin. An article
by Collier containing a veiled hint that personal advantage
was involved had also just appeared in the January edition of
Sunset magazine. In any event, Mrs. Atwood and Collier
were thrown on the defensive by Fall's attack and were
forced to deny any role in the publication of the charge.

The hearings ended on a sour note. Fall refused to submit
to examination by Wilson and reiterated his vow to oppose
the Jones bill so long as he remained in office. When Senator
Lenroot elicited pledges from Twitchell and Wilson to work
together on a substitute bill, Fall announced that he would
refuse "to sit down at a conference table with those of a 'faction' who think we are not worthy of trust," a position he
subsequently affirmed in letters to Commissioner Burke
and Judson King after the hearings concluded.

When the Senate hearings ended on January 25, there was
but a week left to prepare for the House hearings, where the
revised Bursum bill introduced by Congressman Snyder
was to be considered. At the request of Congressman E. O.
Leatherwood of Utah, whose wife was a member of the
GFWC, the Jones bill had been introduced in the House in
early January, and with Snyder's permission, it too was to be
discussed.

During the brief interval between the hearings, Collier
and the Pueblos returned to New York City for public
appearances arranged by Collier's old friend, Robert E. Ely,
the director of the League for Political Education. At the
league's Town Hall, Collier and the Indians received $1,400
in donations from Ely's wealthy associates. At the prestigious Economic Club they received a ringing endorsement
for their stand from the club's thousand members, prompt-
ing another angry letter from Fall, which was sent to every
club member. While these well-publicized expressions of
support were encouraging to Collier, his doubts about the
reliability of Francis Wilson and the other defense groups
grew. The Eastern Association, he wrote Mabel Dodge, "are
scared cats" and he detected "divisive influences at work for
compromise." If it came to a showdown, he feared, only Jud-

son King, Mrs. Atwood, and "perhaps" Father Schuster, could be counted on to stand firm in defense of Pueblo claims.

The "compromise" Collier feared did not surface during the House hearings. While admitting that the Snyder bill was an improvement over the original Bursum bill, Francis Wilson nevertheless opposed it because it granted jurisdiction over the Pueblos and their lands to the federal court and because it would uphold the claims of all the non-Indians who could show possession for twenty years prior to June 10, 1910. The most equitable way to solve the problem, Wilson continued to insist, was through the creation of a special commission with arbitration powers. He also insisted that a provision in the Snyder bill that granted tracts of land from the public domain or money compensation to those whose claims were rejected, was impractical. What the dispossessed claimants, Indians and non-Indians alike, needed was water, and the only bill that made any provision for enlarging the irrigable lands along the Rio Grande was the Jones bill.

The congressmen listened patiently to Wilson's presentation, but when Mrs. Atwood took the floor, it became quickly evident that the committee intended to discredit her role as spokeswoman for the GFWC. They wanted to know in detail how much money she had raised, for what purposes it was intended, from whom it came, and how much Collier was being paid. They inquired whether she had received the formal endorsement of the GFWC in her campaign against the Bursum bill and whether the GFWC had authorized her to use its name to collect money. Not only was she forced to admit that very little of the six thousand dollars raised for the Pueblo aid fund had yet been used for this purpose and that the GFWC had not formally approved her fund raising efforts, but she also confessed that Collier's two highly critical articles on the Pueblos in the January and February issues of *Sunset* magazine had not been approved by her; neither had any of the publicity generated by Judson King in the name of the GFWC. Mrs.

Atwood was visibly shaken by the committee's badgering and by the strictures of Congressman Leatherwood, who concluded that she had obviously exceeded her authority in claiming the support of the two million members of the GFWC.

When Ralph Twitchell next appeared to denounce the special commission provision of the Jones-Leatherwood bill as both expensive and a "soviet proposition," Leatherwood, who frankly admitted that he had not read the Jones bill at the time he introduced it, expressed concern. Such a provision, he thought, created "too many fat jobs."

At this point, Collier, who had deliberately adopted a low profile at the hearings, asked for permission to speak. Accusing the committee members of deliberately "crucifying" Mrs. Atwood, he launched into an impassioned attack on the already discredited Bursum bill and then quickly passed on to a general denunciation of the Indian Office. For years, he charged, the Indian Office had failed to make "an effective appeal" either to Congress or the American people for sufficient funds to provide adequate medical treatment for the Indians. As soon as he completed his harangue, the committee, obviously delighted to have the opportunity to question him directly, immediately zeroed in on his role in the publicity campaign.

A letter was produced from a San Francisco newspaper in which it was alleged that every congressman had been sent a copy of the January *Sunset* article at the expense of the GFWC. Collier denied any involvement on his part or that of Mrs. Atwood. The *Sunset* article referred to "certain land-grabbing interests and for the time being, the executive branch of the government." Did that imply that employees of the federal government would benefit from the passage of the Bursum bill? Leatherwood inquired. Collier denied such an insinuation. He had only sought to "convey the impression" that the Interior Department had framed a bill "inexcusably loose by putting in it phraseology which did not protect the Indians and which would destroy them." Nor, when he charged that empowering the federal court to

exert jurisdiction over the Pueblos would "tear their heart
out," did he mean to imply that this had been the "deliberate intent of the framers of the Bursum bill." Congressman
Snyder also wanted to know how Collier could claim in the
two *Sunset* articles that the Bursum bill had been blocked
in the House by the action of the GFWC when his committee had not even heard about the bill until after it had been
withdrawn by the Senate. Collier replied that the bill had
passed the Senate when it "was asleep" and that "maybe"
the same would have happened in the House had it not been
for all the publicity generated.

Satisfied that it had effectively punched large holes in the
propaganda balloon, the committee dismissed Collier and
turned to Assistant Commissioner Edgar Meritt. Testifying
on the last day of the hearing, Merrit told the congressmen
that a special appropriation to enlarge the Pueblo's irrigable
land was unnecessary. If additional irrigated acres were
desirable, the bureau could finance such a project out of
current appropriations. Meritt also discounted Collier's argument for increased medical attention. The Pueblos, he
said, were receiving the same medical care as other Indians
and it was quite adequate. As the hearings ended, Congressman Leatherwood announced that he could no longer support the idea of a special Pueblo lands commission and he
urged that the appropriation request for irrigation and drain-
age projects be dropped from the Jones bill on technical
grounds. As an appropriation item, it would have to be considered separately from a bill to resolve the Pueblo land
question.[10]

As the hearings on the Bursum bill ended, Collier's mind
was already racing far ahead of the Pueblo problem. His attention now focused on a larger enterprise, the formation of
a national organization dedicated to the total reform of federal Indian policy. Confident that the Pueblos were safe until the next session of Congress and eager to take advantage
of the interest in Indians that the publicity against the Bursum bill had generated, he hastily left Washington on Feb-

ruary 17 for Chicago. There he conferred with Harold Ickes
and others, encouraging them to join with his New York
friends, led by Robert F. Ely, in the formation of what eventually became known as the American Indian Defense
Association.

Despite his later recollections, which lumped the Bursum
bill, the Omnibus bill, and Fall's ruling on the executive-
order reservations together in one evil plan, Collier's contemporary correspondence belies the neatness of this thesis.
Indeed, the evidence reveals that he had no knowledge in
mid-February 1923 of either the Omnibus bill, which was
pending in Congress, or of Fall's revocation of Indian titles
to the executive-order reservations. If he had, he would not
have been so eager to leave Washington without exposing
them. Moreover, he was totally unaware that Francis Wilson and the EAIA were feverishly working to arrange a compromise on the Pueblo problem before Congress adjourned
on March 4. As a result, a bill that would have undermined
the Pueblo claim to large sections of land occupied by non-
Indians almost slipped through Congress while Collier was
preoccupied with new investigations in the Southwest and
with fund-raising activities in California.

On February 16, the day after the House hearings on the
Bursum bill ended and the day before Collier left for Chicago, the Senate Indian Affairs Committee began its deliberations on the so-called Omnibus bill. As the name implies,
this bill contained many provisions dealing with Indians,
most of which were quite harmless. But section one, which
called for the pro rata distribution of tribal estates to competent Indians, was a different matter. This portion of the
bill had originally been introduced into Congress by Congressman Snyder a full year before as a separate measure. It
had been warmly supported by Commissioner Burke, who
took credit for its phraseology.

The object of section one was the elimination of the single most perplexing administrative problem that the Dawes
Act had bequeathed to the Indian Office. While that act had
clearly intended to individualize the American Indian and

force him to become self-supporting, it made no provision for the distribution of Indian tribal estates, many of which had grown with the years as the income from the sale of surplus land, timber, minerals, and other natural resources had accrued to tribal treasuries. Thus, while there were in 1923 many formerly allotted Indians who now held fee-simple title to their land and thus were theoretically no longer wards of the government, their claim to tribal property still bound them to paternal supervision by the Indian Bureau. For persons like Commissioner Burke, Albert Fall, and Congressman Snyder, who believed in the wisdom of assimilation, the only way to cut this last tie between the Indian and the federal government was to appraise the tribal wealth and to award a pro rata share to all Indians who were certified to be competent and who had received a fee-simple patent to their lands. Once an Indian accepted his portion of the tribal wealth, section one read, "thereafter, he is entirely emancipated from government supervision." The Five Civilized Tribes and the Osage Indians, whose tribal wealth was large and growing rapidly because of mineral royalties, were specifically exempted from the act. Section one also provided that pro rata distribution could only be initiated by the Indian, not by the Department of the Interior, and that each Indian would be free to reject the award if he did not believe it equitable.

In the Congress, where assimilation and individual responsibility were accepted as the norm, the only questions raised about section one dealt with the determination of competency and the method for liquidating the tribal estates. To those who were concerned that the Indians might be certified competent before they were really capable of assuming the responsibilities of an independent life, Burke offered the assurance that his administration, unlike those of the past, would carefully scrutinize all competency applications and that no Indian incapable of managing his affairs would be permitted to qualify for a share of tribal wealth.

There was greater difficulty in determining how the tribal estates would be liquidated. If every member of a tribe were considered competent, the only method of assigning each individual a share of the corporate wealth would obviously be to sell all tribal property. Such a method would have some obvious drawbacks in the case of tribes that owned extensive mineral deposits. In other instances, to make cash awards to competent Indians might seriously reduce the incomes of the incompetent Indians partially dependent upon periodic payments from the tribal treasury. On this issue Burke was less clear, but his main argument was that the percentage of Indians who could qualify at this time was so small that the total dissolution of tribal assets was not contemplated in the foreseeable future. What he was mainly concerned with was providing an incentive for competent Indians to divorce themselves completely from government controls, at the same time permitting the Indian Office to concentrate its energies and attention on the noncompetent Indians.

Because they were totally unaware of this plan to complete the work begun by the Dawes Act, neither Collier nor any other member of the anti-Bursum forces was present at the Senate hearings, though all were still in Washington. Only Robert La Follette, whose daughter Fola had assured Mabel Dodge in December that her father would help with the Bursum bill, demonstrated any concern about section one. The difficulty that La Follette expressed, referring to the tragic consequences of former Commissioner Sells's policy of issuing competency certificates, was that the secretary of the interior might be tempted to approve Indians for a pro rata award who were not capable of controlling their new wealth.[11]

Collier did not learn about the Omnibus bill until after he had arrived in Chicago. Anticipating the formation of the American Indian Defense Association (AIDA), which would not actually occur until May 1923, he immediately instructed Robert Ely in New York to engage Judson King to fight the measure. Several days later King prepared a press release that threatened "an attack which may rival in intensity the fight against the Bursum bill." Ely himself dispatched four hundred telegrams opposing the bill and he successfully recruited others to do likewise.

On February 23, 1923, a joint meeting between the officers of the EAIA and ad hoc committee of the proposed AIDA was held in Amelia White's home in New York City. Francis Wilson, who had just become aware of the Omnibus bill, briefed the representatives on its provisions and was authorized to return to Washington as their joint representative until the congressional session ended. The following day, he and Helen H. Greeley, the AIDA's newly employed counsel in Washington, issued a public letter to Commissioner Burke in which they denounced especially the "despotic and autocratic" power that the Omnibus bill would confer on the secretary of the interior in the determination of the pro rata shares. This letter, which was widely circulated, labeled the Indian Office's attempt to end its guardianship over competent Indians "a blunder which the people of the United States are likely soon to discover and unlikely to forget."

Despite this last-minute campaign against the Omnibus bill, the Senate Indian Affairs Committee reported it favorably, with only minor amendments. The House committee quickly followed suit. The bill's passage was only narrowly avoided when La Follette denied it unanimous consent on the Senate floor. In response to the argument of Senator Seldon Spencer, who urged adoption because the bill contained authorization for a number of much needed projects "for the welfare of the Indians," La Follette replied: "It has to do with the 'wrong-fare' of the Indians, I think. I insist upon the objection."

In their opposition to the Omnibus bill, the EAIA and Collier's supporters stood alone. There was unanimous support for the bill from the Board of Indian Commissioners and the IRA, both of which agreed with Commissioner Burke that such legislation was necessary if the Indians were ever to be made independent. Malcolm McDowell, Secretary of the Board of Indian Commissioners, expressed amazement to General Scott that the Collier forces had fought to keep Indians "under the jurisdiction of the Indian Office for many, many years." After discussing the opposition with Wilson in his office, McDowell concluded that Wilson had written his letter without having any knowledge of what the bill intended. While Wilson was "fully conversant with the affairs of the Pueblo Indians," he wrote, "he knows little or nothing about other tribes."[12]

Although Wilson may have known little about the bill's content, and while Collier was incorrect in his charges that the Omnibus bill was a part of Albert Fall's scheme to "pulverize all Indian property and Indian group life," deliberately pushed through Congress "while attention was focused on the Pueblos and the Bursum bill," Collier was quite right when he later wrote in a *Sunset* article that had the bill passed, every Indian who took his share of the tribal wealth would thereby have ensured "the end of his days as an Indian." The desirability of Indians remaining Indian was, of course, just emerging as the central issue between Collier and the forces of the assimilationist majority. Yet, however clear that issue appears in retrospect, it was not so explicit in the spring of 1923, even to most of Collier's supporters. The contemporary records indicate that the New Yorkers who organized the opposition to the Omnibus bill considered it more a demonstration of the propaganda potential of the anti-Bursum forces than a fundamental attack upon assimilationist theory. Their delight at defeating the bill was almost childlike, and for a while they briefly contemplated a more ambitious scheme proposed by Judson King that clearly demonstrated the narrowness of their perspective. If King's proposal had been accepted, a young Sioux from Montana, a veteran of World War I who had come to Washington to testify against another provision in the bill dealing with his reservation, would have been cruelly exploited in a slick publicity venture that had as its only goal the embarrassment of the Indian Office and Commissioner Burke.

According to King, the young veteran, who was not identified by name, had been sent by his tribe as an official representative. Although it was customary in such instances for the Indian Office to reimburse delegates' expenses from tribal funds on deposit with the federal government, Burke had refused the young man's request and since he did not have money for the return trip, he was stranded in Washington. If necessary, he informed King, he would walk back to Montana.

"It occurred to me," King wrote, "that tremendous publicity could be made of this if we could organize a series of meetings from here to Montana for him to address on his way." To make sure that the Indian Office could not suddenly change its mind, King secured a promise from the Sioux to remain "quiet" while plans for publicity were made. If the scheme were approved, King intended to arrange for the Indian "to leave here suddenly without Burke's knowing. . . . I will have him wire or write for his veteran's uniform, and get pictures of his tribe, and carry all his official papers, and you can readily imagine the rest. It will be a fine climax to the Pueblo stunt." What happened to the young Sioux is not indicated, but in the absence of any news coverage or other reference to him in the correspondence, one is left with the distinctly uncomfortable feeling that once his publicity value had been lost, he was forgotten by King and the New Yorkers and left to make his way back to Montana, on foot and alone.[13]

Aside from the distance that separated him from Washington during the brief campaign against the Omnibus bill, Collier was also separated from that controversy by his preoccupation with other considerations. As the next chapter will demonstrate, he was hard at work completing arrangements for the formation of the AIDA and arranging for its financial support. Following his visit to Chicago, he spent a week in Taos where, at Mabel Dodge's insistence, he continued his earlier investigation into the Pueblo health situation, particularly the growing problem of venereal disease. From this there resulted an appeal to a Judge Payne in California for assistance in organizing a comprehensive health-care program for the Pueblos at a cost of $42,750 annually. Collier also learned that trouble was brewing on the Navajo reservation, where the discovery of oil had provoked a deci-

sion by Albert Fall to appoint a special commissioner to the
Navajos to handle the negotiations for oil leases. Word of
Collier's impending visit to the Navajo reservation was immediately transmitted by Colonel Twitchell to Commissioner Burke. "If you hear that Collier has gone to the
Navajo country," Burke replied, "please advise me. I will
not tolerate a campaign among the Navajos such as he has
conducted in the Pueblos."

While he was busy stirring all these irons, Collier was
suddenly dumbfounded to learn in early March that during
his absence from Washington, a compromise version of the
Bursum bill had almost passed Congress, with the approval
of Francis Wilson and the EAIA. Even more alarming, his
own New York supporters who clearly did not understand
Collier's own position on the Pueblo controversy, had mistakenly endorsed the bill.

The first effort at compromise was apparently the work of
Roberts Walker, the New York attorney who was one of the
founding members of the EAIA. On February 10, in the
midst of the House hearings on the Bursum bill, Walker, describing himself as "a Vermont Republican" who was neither "an artist nor a sentimentalist," wrote Fall to suggest
that both sides "forget the chatter and get down to brass
tacks." Fall, however, angrily refused this overture. Replying that he was still "very resentful of the methods used by
the propagandists, both in public meetings and in written
and private defamatory and false statements," Fall ridiculed
Walker's request to "sit down and draft a statement that
would be just all around," on the ground that Walker had
showed "no interest in doing so until after you had introduced the propagandists to the Congressional committees."
Walker, however, persisted. He was not a party to the At-
wood-Collier-King cabal, he wrote. And as for Collier, he
had "formed an intense aversion to him as a sensationalist
and as having no apparent interest in the non-Indian settlers." There is no indication that Fall played any role in
drafting the compromise bill that followed, but Walker's
disavowal of Collier undoubtedly played a role in Fall's de-

cision to permit Commissioner Burke to seek the compromise he had so often urged.

On February 18, 1923, the day after Collier left Washington for Chicago, the Senate subcommittee on Public Lands whose chairman, Irvine Lenroot, had genuinely sought to reconcile the warring factions, met to draft a compromise bill. Francis Wilson was forbidden to attend this executive session of the committee on Fall's order, but he was permitted to submit a draft bill indicating the changes he would accept. Commissioner Burke was permitted to sit with the committee.

The Lenroot substitute bill that emerged, and that was quickly approved by Wilson, Burke, and both congressional committees, was a distinct improvement over the original Bursum bill and it accurately reflected the desires of all parties except Collier. As later exchanges between Collier and Wilson revealed, its only failing was that it recognized a limited number of non-Indian claims without compensation to the Indians. For Wilson and his supporters, the recognition of these claims had been inevitable from the beginning. For Collier, who maintained that the Indian claim was inviolate, Wilson's concessions smacked of collusion with the enemy.

The Lenroot bill provided for the creation of a three-man Pueblo Lands Board, to consist of the representatives of the attorney general of the United States, the secretary of the interior, and the president. This board would have authority to determine all lands to which the Indians legitimately held title and to file a suit in the U.S. District Court of New Mexico to quiet title to these lands. Non-Indian claimants who disagreed with the findings of the board were to be permitted to appeal its findings to the district court. Two classes of claimants who might expect to have their claims upheld were defined in sections four and five. First, there were those who could prove "open, notorious, actual, exclusive, continual possession for more than twenty years prior to the passage" of the act, under "color of title." Second were those claimants who, while unable to prove color of title, could demonstrate "claim of ownership" for more than thirty years prior to passage of the act. Whatever the decision of the district court in these disputed cases, the secretary of the interior was to notify Congress of the court's decision and to make recommendations for compensation to the losing party. No compensation, however, was authorized in the Lenroot bill.

With Wilson's approval, Lenroot's substitute bill was accepted by Senators Borah, La Follette, and Jones of New Mexico. It was immediately forwarded to the House of Representatives, where the Indian Affairs Committee likewise approved it on February 27. The House committee, however, felt obliged to comment on the storm of propaganda that surrounded the Pueblo problem. "Nothing to compare with it has heretofore been seen in connection with Indian legislation," the committee report read. "This propaganda has been insidious, untruthful, and malicious and will result in great harm to the Indians of this country if it is permitted to be continued."

On Feburary 28 the Lenroot substitute passed the Senate under the unanimous-consent rule. Senator Jones, who had unsuccessfully defended the right of the Indians to select an attorney to represent them before the district court, attempted to insert such a provision on the floor of the Senate, but his motion was defeated. Otherwise, there was complete agreement on the bill's provisions.

On March 3, the next-to-last-day of the sixty-seventh Congress, the Lenroot substitute was brought before the House of Representatives. Under the unanimous-consent rule, it was killed by an obscure congressman from Kentucky who gave no reason for his opposition. Thus, without Collier's knowledge that anything was amiss, a bill to resolve the Pueblo dispute along lines totally unacceptable to him was narrowly defeated. His anger at being thus outmaneuvered would prove to be deep and long lasting. His tenuous relationship with Wilson and the EAIA would be totally severed within a few months and his own bright dream of a powerful national organization would be permanently crippled.[14]

The American Indian Defense Association
(1923)

Throughout the spring and summer of 1923, Collier's chief concern was the formation of the national organization through which he hoped to force a total reform of federal Indian policy. At the same time, he continued his investigation into Navajo affairs, challenged the Indian Office's restrictions on Indian dances and religious ceremonials, and wrote several articles for *Sunset* and *Survey* magazines. In all these matters, he was handicapped by the steadily widening gulf between himself and Francis Wilson over the Pueblo situation. Not only was there the problem of what Congress might do when it reconvened in the fall, there was also the larger consideration that a permanent split between the various anti-Bursum forces would play into the hands of the opposition and stalemate the movement for other reforms Collier was determined to realize. For months Collier uncharacteristically hesitated to comment publicly on the deficiencies in the Lenroot substitute bill for fear of alienating Wilson's supporters. Beneath the surface calm, however, he and Wilson carried on an increasingly bitter correspondence. By summer they had become irrevocably estranged, and by fall the always tenuous unity of the anti-Bursum forces had been shattered.

The conflict between Collier and Wilson was a basic one, which, curiously enough, had never been exposed during their many months of cooperation against the Bursum bill. For Collier, the *Sandoval* decision in 1913 meant that all encroachments on Pueblo lands since American occupation of the Southwest were illegal. If the federal government had performed its duties as guardian in the proper manner, the Indians would never have lost any of their land. Thus, whatever legislation was written to resolve the problem would have to be based upon a presumption of Indian ownership. The Bursum and Snyder bills were both unacceptable because each recognized some non-Indian claims at the expense of the Pueblos.

Wilson and his supporters, on the other hand, believed that since the federal courts had condoned the alienation of Pueblo lands from 1876 until the *Sandoval* decision, the non-Indians who, in good faith, had purchased Pueblo lands during this period had rights that were as valid as those of the Indians. These rights, they believed, should be recognized by statute. Their objection to the Bursum bill, apart from its obviously inequitable provisions, was that it had not required the non-Indian claimants to prove anything more than simple possession of their lands. Wilson believed that only those claimants who could prove "color of title" or "claim of ownership" in addition to possession should be recognized as lawful owners, but, unlike Collier, he did accept the primacy of these claims. Perhaps because so much publicity was directed against the more objectionable parts of the bill, this fundamental difference between Collier and Wilson remained obscured.

When Collier first learned about the Lenroot substitute bill, three days after it had been narrowly killed in the House, he immediately wired Wilson demanding an explanation. Expressing "amazement and consternation" that Wilson could have approved a bill that placed the anti-

Bursum forces "in the ridiculous disgraceful position of supporting [a] measure which legislates against [the] Indians and gives them nothing," he angrily insisted that Wilson explain how he could reconcile his opposition to the original Bursum bill "with your reported endorsement of section four (and five) with limitation against the Indians and no compensation." Not yet understanding that Wilson had acted in compliance with his instructions from the EAIA and the New Mexico Association, he sent a similar telegram to Margaret McKittrick, urging her also to demand an explanation.

Francis Wilson was not used to such a peremptory challenge to his integrity. The following day he wired Collier back saying he was "shocked at tone your wire . . . think you had better come here and get facts first before you send such wires which are a real injustice to me." If Collier could not "understand the difference between a true adverse possession statute" and similar provisions in the Bursum and Snyder bills, he had, in Wilson's words, "missed the point of all the hearings in Washington." As for the failure to include compensation for the Indians, he explained, such a clause was impossible to obtain because, as Congressman Leatherwood had explained during the hearings, a compensation appropriation would require a separate bill. His attitude toward compensation remained the same. He still believed that the only acceptable compensation would be additional water to irrigate the remaining Indian lands and he intended to work for such a compensation statute at the next session of Congress. Various congressmen and senators had promised their cooperation at that time.[1]

Wilson's explanation was, of course, unacceptable to Collier, who by now was convinced that Wilson had somehow been compromised by the sinister forces of the Interior Department. While awaiting further clarification of Wilson's position, he immediately circulated a memorandum on the Lenroot bill to his closest supporters. Members of the EAIA and the New Mexico Association were carefully excluded.

"The incident has so upset me and it could be so gravely

upsetting to the whole Indian work," he wrote Mary Austin in early March, that he had decided to go immediately to southern California for a conference with Stella Atwood. After that, he would travel to Santa Fe to confront Wilson. He could not fathom how Wilson had "effected with such a beautiful unconsciousness a transition so revolutionary. . . . He was opposed to a limitations statute stubbornly and consistently and his instructions were to keep on opposing it, and now he appears to be unaware or unwilling to be aware of the fact that he changed at all." There were other important matters that needed to be attended to, he concluded. "The Indian Office has overthrown the Navajo tribal government" and "our admired friend Mr. Burke" was threatening to use force to stop certain Indian dances, but "at the moment my chief preoccupation is that matter of the substitute bill."

In a similar vein, Collier wrote Harold Ickes, with whom he was working closely on a merger of the Chicago and New York groups. Wilson had approved "a revolutionary change of policy" after Collier left Washington, he wrote, and then had bound all the anti-Bursum forces to that policy "either on the basis of hurried and unilluminated conferences, or without having the facts to go on at all." In Collier's case and that of the GFWC, "the contents of the substitute bill were not made known until after Congress adjourned. This question of limitations is, of course, the central one around which everything else hangs effecting [sic] the Pueblos." Come the fall, he warned, "we will find all of the pro-Bursum, pro-Renehan, pro-Indian Office forces lined up behind the bill" and "we are in the embarrassing position of having apparently endorsed the bill which reverses our own policy and makes nought the arguments with which we had really managed to wake up the country in the months previously."

The difficulty of convincing even sympathetic white people that the Indians' claims were superior to those of the whites was made evident by the responses of Collier's correspondents. Neither Mary Austin nor Harold Ickes was able to comprehend the distinction Collier was attempting to make between his position and that of Francis Wilson. "I confess that I think you have done an injustice to Mr. Wilson's motives," Mary Austin replied in April, after a trip to Santa Fe and Taos. Everyone in Santa Fe was puzzled by Collier's attitude toward Wilson and the Lenroot substitute bill. For her own part, she could not decide who was right. "I am quite sure, however, that even if we decide on an organization to stand out for your point of view, we will eventually have to compromise on something like Wilson's." The local point of view, she pointed out, would have to be respected and she reminded Collier that Mrs. Atwood was currently lobbying for a national park to be created on land owned by the Palm Springs band of Indians near Riverside, California. There was little difference, she thought, between Mrs. Atwood's position and that of Fall's toward the Mescalero Apaches. "She seems to think that Riverside ought to have the park because they can make better use of the land than the Indians can, and anyway, the park scheme is being managed by friends of hers in whose motives she has perfect confidence. You will find this attitude coming up all the time."

Collier's suspicion of Wilson's motives was more clearly set forth in a letter to Robert Ely. He realized now the mistake he had made in leaving Washington before Congress adjourned, Collier, apologized, but "about the last thing in the world that I could have feared, would have been the *bouleversement* of Wilson and his endorsement of the limitations clause." Wilson had been given "binding, unequivocal" instructions to oppose a limitations clause, instructions that had been "iterated by me almost *ad nauseam*." Because it was "urgent to prevent a break in our ranks if possible and to avoid hurting Wilson in every possible way *short of hurting the cause*," Collier informed Ely that he was avoiding any reference to the Lenroot bill in the articles he was writing for *Sunset* magazine. He was convinced, however, that Wilson had deceived him so that "I should not interpose to throw the organizations against his own already irrevocable endorsement." This decision may have been "only half conscious," he conceded, but Wilson was "a very stubborn and rather personal mental type" who would have to be carefully watched in the future.[2]

During the face-to-face confrontation in Santa Fe in late March, Collier and Wilson were unable to settle their differences. Following that meeting, Wilson prepared an extensive brief in which he defended his support of the Lenroot bill by setting forth the differences between it and the Bursum bill. The Lenroot bill, he wrote, omitted the potentially dangerous extension of federal court jurisdiction over the internal affairs of the Pueblos that the local agents had long advocated. The jurisdiction of the state courts over Indian lands and water rights had been rejected. The admission of secondary evidence as proof of possession and the clause permitting non-Indian claimants to purchase Indian lands with the approval of the secretary of the interior had also been deleted. As for the limitations clauses, which Collier so vehemently opposed, Wilson argued that "the attempt to make proof of possession . . . confer title upon the non-Indian claimants is wholly destroyed and defeated." Instead, the Lenroot bill contained two "true adverse title" provisions, which required the non-Indian claimants to prove either twenty years of adverse possession under "color of title" or thirty years of adverse possession "with claim of ownership." He personally had advocated twenty-five and thirty-five years, but the Senate committee had not accepted this recommendation. In any event, he concluded, the statute of limitations in the Lenroot bill "bears no resemblance to the pretended statute of limitations in the Bursum and Snyder bills."

When Collier received his copy of Wilson's brief, he concluded that "plainer language must be used" than he had employed during their Santa Fe conference. "At Santa Fe, I did not wish to clash with you, so I left unsaid what I now tell you," he wrote on April 13. At Santa Fe, Wilson had insisted that *"of course you must have informed me in our talks from [February] 8th to the 17th inclusive"* that a "shift to a limitations policy was under way. I replied that you certainly had not informed me and my memory is borne out by the event, for I left Washington feeling confident, and entered no protest against a change of policy, undertaken or contemplated, which I would have resisted to the uttermost had I known of it." Wilson, he now charged, had deliberately kept him in the dark to prevent the opposition that he knew would result: "Your conduct must stand condemned."

Whether Wilson actually deceived Collier or whether Collier imagined Wilson's duplicity to cover his own mistake at leaving Washington early is not clear. Most likely, there was a genuine difference of opinion between the two men that had never been made explicit during their months of cooperation. But Collier was not content just to charge Wilson with deception. He insisted upon indulging himself in a wholly gratuitous analysis of the motives that he believed had impelled Wilson's "defection." It was now clear, he wrote, that Wilson had never conceived the Pueblo's plight as "a matter of fundamental social justice." As a lawyer, Wilson viewed the problem merely as a matter requiring "an adequate technical legal defense." Wilson's adherence "to the real cause," Collier now realized, was never based on principle, but only upon his "appreciation of the legal accidents which happened to work in favor of that cause." For this reason, once Wilson became aware of the impact an assertion of the Indian claim would have on the "white settlers" and upon his own political future, he had taken the easy way out by creating "a new legal synthesis, a new lot of legal sanctions, and a perfect feeling of virtue behind the walls of a new ivory tower of legalism." In retrospect, Collier wrote, he could see how Wilson had viewed his approval of the Lenroot bill as a simple choice between the poor Indians (who had "that curious tendency Indians have of evaporating out of all consciousness or ceasing to appear as persons at all !!!") and their handful of true supporters, on the one hand, and an important political victory over Albert Fall (that "was irresistible in its appeal to your . . . vanity, shall I say?") on the other. As a result of Fall's "vicious attack on yourself," Wilson had sought the help of Senators Lenroot and Jones. When these men later asked for his cooperation in getting the substitute bill through Congress, Wilson found himself unable "to buck their opinion and wishes," and instead embraced the compromise that could be "proclaimed as a Victory" in New Mexico. "I expect that incidents of this kind—on the part of individuals and of groups as well—will be not infrequent as the full sweep of our effort goes ahead. They will mean difficulty but not failure. For yourself . . . the issue is in no matter personal between me and you; yet I must tell you that results for the Indians are going to be paramount—quite ruthlessly so—in any controversy ahead." He was carefully refraining from expressing such thoughts in public, Collier warned, only because they would "hurt the cause and give unholy joy to the Indian Office," but he would not shrink from public controversy if Wilson persisted in his support for the Lenroot bill. "Controversy is better than surrender, and when waged it must be waged effectively . . . . You will find this analysis painful to your self esteem," he concluded, "but I want to show that I have not . . . implied that you are a knave or a fool."

On April 17, 1923, Francis Wilson replied in kind. "I have neither the time nor the inclination to answer the mud slinging orgy that you have indulged in this time," he wrote. "As evidence against you, your [own] letters . . . cannot be improved upon and so far as I am concerned they will pass as proof out of your own mouth of your undisciplined and unprincipled mind and temperament." There was a "fundamental and unavoidable" difference between them that he had not perceived earlier, Wilson wrote. Collier, he had discovered, was "instinctively and apparently fundamentally . . . opposed to any orderly process of the law . . . . No law could be passed that would be satisfactory to you because of your attitude and frame of mind toward law in general . . . Your egotism and supreme belief in your own infallibility . . . , is such as to make open minded discussion with you impossible and that, united with the fundamental defect in your mental and moral makeup suggested above, make any future attempt to clarify your mind a wholly useless effort and a task certain to be fruitless. I shall go no farther in the matter."

As usual, Collier had the last word. On April 22, in the final exchange of correspondence, he agreed with Wilson that the difference in their philosophical positions was indeed fundamental. "You accept the existing synthesis as being final . . . and sancrosant," he wrote. "I mean the existing business system with all its legal apparatus." What he was fighting for, Collier said, was "a *new* synthesis . . . a sociological synthesis . . . a system more life giving and just." To achieve that end, it would be necessary to demonstrate unceasingly that the "present bureaucratic monopoly over the Indians" was both "un-American and, in spirit at least, anti-constitutional." Wilson, he was sure, would not subscribe to this view.

Following this exchange, Collier's New York supporters terminated their affiliation with Wilson, and he ceased to play an official role in the Pueblo claims case. There was a final quarrel when Wilson submitted his bill for $4,984. Whether it was ever paid is not clear. In a report to the AIDA board, Collier wrote that there had never been any understanding as to Wilson's fee, but he considered Wilson's statement "excessive," as did Mrs. Vosburg and Mabel Dodge, who had contributed most of the $1,300 that Wilson had previously been paid. Collier was particularly critical of Wilson's per diem charge of $50 per day, which, he noted, was also assessed for Sundays. He refused to endorse any payment for Wilson's services after February 8, 1923, the day he had earlier determined that Wilson had reversed "his instructions."[3]

All the while his conflict with Wilson was building toward its climax, Collier was hard at work attempting to form the national organization with which to push for other, more funamental reforms of federal policy. By May 1923, despite defections caused by his quarrel with Wilson, the AIDA was officially incorporated in New York, though adequate financial backing was still far from being assured.

Collier wrote in his memoirs that the AIDA was the creation of his old friend Robert Ely. Its formation had been "totally unforseen by me." This recollection is only partially true and, like many of Collier's reminiscences, it is more a reflection of how he wished to remember the unfolding of events than the way they actually occurred.

The idea of the AIDA was born some time in mid-February 1923, about the time Collier left Washington after the conclusion of the hearings on the Bursum bill. While Ely was rounding up a group of his wealthy supporters in New York City, Collier was busy in California. By late February, he had discussed the idea with Mrs. Vosburg, Mrs. Chilberg, and Dr. Haynes. Mrs Vosburg, he reported to Ely, " is all enthusiasm." She had assured him that he must not confine his activities just to the GFWC, but that his energies and talents "must be at the disposal of the new organization." The others agreed that "the new National Organization is the key to the future and will help in any way possible." In order to secure Mrs. Atwood's backing, it was important that Ely and Dorothy Straight, who had agreed to serve as treasurer of the AIDA, write her immediately, describing in detail his earlier work in New York City.

By the time Collier secured the approval of his California supporters, Ely had succeeded in forming the ad hoc committee that mistakenly endorsed Francis Wilson's stand on the Lenroot bill and authorized his retention to fight the Omnibus bill. In this and other early endeavors, Ely worked closely with the EAIA and Amelia White, who agreed to serve as a member of the first executive council. In addition, Ely performed the valuable public relations task of designing a letterhead for the new organization, which contained the names of a large number of well-known philanthropists.

On March 2, 1923, Ely informed Collier that "our committee has decided unanimously that you should be engaged as executive secretary for the year from May 1 next, at a salary of $10,000 and expenses." This handsome retainer, which was double Commissioner Burke's annual salary, and equal to that of the secretary of the interior, was agreed upon by Ely, Dorothy Straight, Fred Stein, and Mary Austin. Of course, if Collier could prevail upon Mrs. Vosburg to continue her payment of $5,000 annually, Ely wrote, that would "simplify our problem during the first year of the society's existence." He also volunteered advice about how Collier might spend the money. "On the basis of our old friendship, I venture to say this personal word to both Lucy and yourself . . . we shall not be pleased if any part of it is used for welfare work. If we had the power and the right, as we have not, to determine the matter, it should be used solely for the Collier family."

"I think looking over the bigness and urgency of the job as it now appears, I am glad you fixed the salary as you did," Collier replied. "All previous undertakings I have been 'up against' look like child's-play compared to this." The salary fixed by the New York group would given him "a freedom of mind that will be very liberating . . . therefore it will be justified from the standpoint of the task." Heeding Ely's advice, he promised not to give the money away; he would take out a new insurance policy and Lucy would quit her health work in June. Mrs. Vosburg was agreeable to continuing her $5,000 payment as part of his salary and "probably she and Dr. Haynes will in addition contribute materially." All in all, things seemed to be going well. In April, Collier planned to visit Harold Ickes in Chicago in an effort to persuade him to merge the Chicago group with the New York committee.[4]

The desirability of forming a national organization was heightened in April when Hubert Work, Fall's successor as secretary of the interior, announced his intention to convene a blue ribbon panel of one hundred persons to advise him on the conduct of Indian affairs. Prompted by the volume of criticism that had surrounded Fall's last months in office, Work originally scheduled the symposium for early summer; later he postponed it until Congress reconvened in December. As two of the Indian Office's chief critics, both

Collier and Mrs. Atwood were issued invitations, but the committee was heavily weighted in favor of the older Indian societies and missionary groups, which favored the continuation of the assimilationist policy. It was therefore most important, Collier believed, that a statement of principles be drafted by the anti-Bursum forces before this meeting, as a platform from which to lobby for major changes in federal policy.

As a step in the direction of formulating such a statement, Collier decided to employ the forum of the League of the Southwest, which was scheduled to meet in Santa Barbara, California, in early June. This meeting would be considerably different from the previous one in San Diego where Albert Fall had been the featured speaker. "The making of an Indian program is in my hands," he informed Mabel Dodge. He wanted her to come and to bring several Pueblos with her. In addition, he planned speeches by Mary Austin, Mrs. Atwood, and himself. Herbert Hagerman, the new Navajo commissioner, and A. B. Renehan would also be invited. He hoped there would be "some lively debate."

By the time Collier concluded these preliminary arrangements, rumors of his quarrel with Francis Wilson were circulating freely in New Mexico. The New Mexico Association, he was convinced, had already given in to Wilson. For that reason it was more important than ever to secure the support of Harold Ickes and the Chicago group. Before he could leave for Chicago, however, the breach occurred. Shortly thereafter, Collier learned that not only had "Miss White's group in New York" decided to back Wilson, but also that "some of the Chicago group . . . especially Mr. and Mrs. Harold Ickes, I believe," were engaged "in a very energetic subterranean work . . . designed to alienate our Eastern friends from the thorough going program we are seeking to realize." At the last minute, the visit to Chicago was postponed, apparently while Collier pondered this latest development.

An interval of indecision followed. In late April, Collier sent Mrs. Vosburg a copy "of the final reverberation of my 'controversy' with Mr. Wilson." The situation was critical, he said. Miss White, the Ickeses, and Mary Austin had all been seduced by "the Tempter," who was "showing them a way which will be far less arduous than our way; which will bring quick applause; whereas our program will require of them a sustained effort, and a ferocity of struggle which most of them hardly bargained for."

The argument of Wilson and Miss White, he summarized, was that the Lenroot bill represented "common sense; criticism of it implies radicalism" and would fatally "split our ranks." Ickes and Mrs. Austin favored accepting the Lenroot bill because "sufficient outside pressure" had already been exerted. The time had come, according to them, "to stop our aggressive campaign and shelve our fundamental contentions such as those calling for a clean-up of the whole Indian Office." Instead, they urged, it was time to consolidate; "let us now get inside and work with the officials!!!" How far are all these arguments or rather temptations and influences going to prevail?" he asked.

The thing to do, Collier told Mrs. Vosburg, was to act boldly, before the defectors could amalgamate. Unless he was soon armed with "tangible proof of support for the things I am contending for, which is *pledges of financial support toward the fundamental, thorough going program*" of reform, the movement begun by the fight against the Bursum bill would collapse. If she, Dr. Haynes, and Mabel Dodge could immediately state "what minimum of gifts through the year from May 1st on can be expected," his hand would be greatly strengthened when he met with the Chicago group.[5]

On May 14, 1923, the AIDA was legally incorporated in New York. Four days later the first official meeting of the board of directors was held in New York City. Robert Ely was named chairman of the board, with George Haven Putnam, the elderly founder of G. P. Putnam's Sons publishing company, named honorary chairman. John Collier, "Research Agent of the Indian Welfare Committee of the General Federation of Women's Clubs," was made executive

secretary. Other officers were Robert Ingersoll Brown, sec-
retary, Mrs. Willard D. (Dorothy) Straight, treasurer, and
Mary Austin, chairman of the publicity council. In addition
to these officers, the initial executive council consisted
of Hamlin Garland, John R. Haynes, Harold Ickes, Mrs.
James L. Laidlaw, Fr. Fridolin Schuster, Fred Stein, Mrs.
Vosburg, Amelia White, and two prominent Chicagoans:
Carter Harrison, former five-term mayor and editor of the
Chicago Times, and Ralph Fletcher Seymour, a designer
and publisher of fine editions of literary classics. Although
Ely had succeeded in his efforts to ensure that "the Chicago
group is well represented," none of them attended the first
board meeting. Neither did the California members. Apart
from Collier, all those present were native New Yorkers.[6]

Immediately after this first board meeting, Collier left for
Chicago. With the AIDA now a reality, he hoped to ensure
the continued participation of Ickes and the others in its deliberations. As a result of his break with Wilson, he was less
sure that he could persuade them to merge completely with
the AIDA. What could be accomplished, he believed, was
the immediate adoption of a comprehensive statement of
goals by the AIDA board through which it could establish
its leadership in the area of Indian affairs. From Chicago he
dispatched a "sixth rewriting" of such a statement. While
he did not expect the board to adopt his draft verbatim, he
did hope it would stimulate them to adopt "a concrete
statement" at once. Such a statement would be of great advantage at the meeting in Santa Barbara and it would also be
"welcomed by the Chicago Association and folks in the far
West," as a means by which a common purpose could be
pursued.

Collier's reception in Chicago was decidedly cool. His
failure to notify the Chicagoans of the meeting until two
days before it was held was in part responsible for the lack
of a quorum. But Carter Harrison declined to attend, send-
ing word that he was "not personally interested in tackling
the Indian problem as a whole." In the absence of a quorum,
no action was taken, but the members present did agree to

share in the Pueblo legal costs during the summer. The discussion then turned to "sharp questioning about the intentions of the New York group."

The central problem was Ickes's suspicion that the New York members of the AIDA intended to dominate "permanently the Defence [sic] Assn. or whatever national organization may arise." Ickes "never said what was in his mind," Collier reported, but it was obvious he believed "that New York leadership kills any national movement." He was also nettled that Ely had placed his name on the AIDA letterhead without obtaining his consent and that he was "only being consulted at a distance."

The Chicago group, Collier learned, was unified in its "insistence that there must be *one inclusive* national organization and this must be secured at once before difference of opinion about policies had time to arise." Attempting to allay their suspicions about the AIDA's dominance of such an organization, he suggested that instead of attempting to form a national organization immediately, they should concentrate on adopting, "if possible, a common statement of principles and of program." If agreement could be reached on common goals, they could then either merge into "one organization forthwith" or they could continue to maintain their separate identities until fall, at which time a "great Convention" of all Indian defense groups would be called. At that time, depending upon the will of the delegates, a decision could be made as to whether each should merge into some new organization or whether one of them would become "the National Organization." When Ickes remained skeptical, Collier adjourned the meeting with the suggestion that the Chicagoans propose "a union of efforts towards getting a powerful nation-wide organization formed before the next Congress."

Less than a week after the Chicago meeting, Collier expressed reservations about the concessions he had made to Ickes. "I have thought a lot more about that Chicago group," he wrote. "I have an impression that I may have leaned over too far in my advice in the direction of submerg-

ing our individuality as an Assn. and seeking to make the
Chicago group feel good." Ickes, he concluded, "is self seeking and avid and will be difficult . . . concession will arouse
a demand for more concessions . . . All in all we shall not be
able to neutralize their sectional prejudices by any concessions which it is in our power to make save the concession
of standing aside, and that we must not do . . . ." Instead, he
had decided, the AIDA must "develop our own personality
as an organization, and get into the position where if need
be, we, with the Federated Women can swing the whole
job . . . ."[7]

Collier's decision to abandon further efforts to merge the
Chicago and New York groups was made easier by two very
recent developments. One was the reinstatement of Stella
Atwood as the chairman of the Indian Welfare Committee
of the GFWC. The second was the adoption of the AIDA's
"Announcement of Purposes" by a host of eastern organizations at a meeting in New York in early June.

After her appearance before the congressional committees in Washington, Stella Atwood found her tenure as
chairman of the Indian Welfare Committee severely challenged. Mrs. E. O. Leatherwood, the Utah congressman's
wife, and a Mrs. Parker, the president of the New Mexico
Federation of Women's Clubs, both demanded her replacement on the ground that she had exceeded her authority and
had embarrassed the GFWC by her unauthorized request
for money in its name. Commissioner Burke joined in the
attack by writing directly to the national president of the
GFWC, Mrs. Thomas G. Winter, urging that Mrs. Atwood
be reprimanded for her part in the publicity assault on the
Indian Bureau.

Instead of removing Mrs. Atwood, however, Mrs. Winter
defended her activities, giving, in Collier's words, "a vigorous and sweeping endorsement of what she has done and
how she has done it." In her reply to Commissioner Burke,
Mrs. Winter brushed aside his criticism with the comment
that it was often difficult to distinguish between a subordinate's "individual and official activities." While she person-

ally deplored the adverse publicity that the controversy had generated and she regretted the criticism that it brought to the GFWC, she had decided to take it all "with a grain of salt." She suggested that Burke do likewise.

Mrs. Winter's endorsement, however, was not enough to prevent a fight for control of the Indian Welfare Committee at the federation's annual meeting in Atlanta in late May 1923. There, Mrs. Atwood, now recovered from what Collier earlier described as "timidity and incipient panic" following her appearance in Washington, demanded that the federation take a "more courageous stand" in behalf of the Indians, endorse the retention of Collier as her research assistant, and authorize her to collect money in its name. In all of these she was strongly opposed by Mrs. Leatherwood, Mrs. Parker, and Nina Otero Warren, the socially prominent sister of former New Mexico Governor Miguel Otero, who had been employed by Commissioner Burke shortly after the defeat of the Bursum bill. Following "a fierce meeting" at which Mrs. Atwood threatened to resign and take her case to the rival League of Women Voters, all her demands were met. Her victory, she reported to Collier ten days after his Chicago meeting, "was not just a generalized walk over," but one in which she received the "various kinds of powers . . . needed . . . to organize the women behind a complete program."[8]

Shortly after receiving this good news, and while he and Mary Austin were conducting an assault upon the Indian Office before the League of the Southwest, Collier received totally unexpected information of cooperation between the AIDA and a number of other organizations, including the EAIA and the New Mexico Association. At the invitation of the EAIA, delegates from several Indian societies met in New York on June 10 to "set forth a Magna Carta for Indians." Although the meeting was dominated by EAIA members, most notably Warren K. Moorhead and Herbert J. Spinden, who also represented the American Anthropological Association and the American Association for the Advancement of Science, both the AIDA and the New Mexico

Association were well represented. At the conclusion of the one-day conference, a series of recommendations proposed by Spinden were adopted. Definitely reformist in tone, these recommendations were identical to those adopted by the AIDA board following its receipt of Collier's "sixth rewriting" of a statement of purpose. Less bombastic than those submitted by Collier, the recommendations nonetheless clearly bore his stamp. In the field of education, they called upon the Indian Office to develop, "instead of suppressing," the Indians' commitment to "group loyalties and communal responsibilities." Not just agriculture and industry, but the development of Indian arts and crafts, were encouraged. More doctors and nurses and an emphasis upon preventive medicine were recommended. Indians should be given "religious and social freedom in all matters not directly contrary to public morals" and all efforts to interfere with their "religious dances or customs should be frowned upon."

The record does not indicate how Ely was capable of effecting this cooperation with the EAIA, but two weeks later, with Collier this time in attendance, the same organizations met again and formally adopted "the Red Man's Magna Carta tentatively drafted" at the previous meeting. This time Ely presided over the meeting, and the IRA, through Matthew Sniffen, also participated. The seven-point "program" adopted was again taken, word-for-word, from the AIDA's published "Announcement of Purpose." With this sort of unity building, it was less necessary than before to worry about Ickes and the Chicago group.[9]

Following the unexpected harmony that prevailed after the New York meetings, Collier turned his attention for the remainder of the summer to preparations for the fall congressional session, to his writing, and to the Navajo situation, which he had earlier described as potentially serious. A number of new people entered the Indian field and some old supporters, notably Robert Ely and Mabel Dodge, withdrew.

Thoughout 1923 and 1924, the most important vehicle for Collier's ideas was *Sunset* magazine, a crusading journal published in San Francisco that continued the muckraking tradition well into the 1920s. Originally a travel magazine founded by the Southern Pacific Railroad in 1898 to advertise the West, *Sunset* was sold to its employees in 1914 and converted into a literary journal. Its editor, Walter Woehlke, was a German immigrant who had established himself as a freewheeling and hard-hitting critic of corporate greed in California in the prewar years. How Collier and *Sunset* came together is undocumented, but Collier and Woehlke were kindred spirits in their zeal for overturning the status quo, and their friendship, fashioned during these early years of the Indian reform movement, became deeper with the passage of time. After 1928, when *Sunset* was sold to its present owner, the L. W. Lane Company, Woehlke became an important force in the AIDA hierarchy and after 1933 accompanied Collier to Washington.

The two articles that Collier published in *Sunset* during the Bursum bill debate were followed by a third in March and a fourth in May. The March article, "Our Indian Policy," was an indictment of the Indian Office's "autocratic" control over the Indians, based primarily on Collier's experience among the Pueblos. The May article, "No Trespassing," set forth the thesis that the Bursum and the Omnibus bills were related and that Fall had attempted to sneak through the latter while attention was focused on the Pueblos. Collier attributed the defeat of both bills to the role of the GFWC. True to his promises made during the spring, Collier refrained in both articles from any comment upon the Lenroot bill or the role of Francis Wilson in its drafting.

During the summer Collier completed two more articles. Both stressed the need for a thorough overhaul of federal policy. In "America's Treatment of Her Indians," he set forth the reform program that had been adopted by the AIDA board and the New York groups in their "Magna Carta" statement, without mentioning either of these actions. The second article, "American Congo," was less sensational than its title implied. It predicted that before the next Congress, "the struggle toward a new Indian policy

and a new administrative spirit," which had begun with the
Bursum bill fight, would spread "to include the red race as a
whole." The "Indian's day has begun," it trumpeted; "an
All-American and All Indian movement is under way."

Perhaps in an effort to offset Collier's publicity, Commissioner Burke, who had refused earlier requests, now submitted to an interview by a reporter from *Colliers* magazine.
Published in May under the title "He Carries the White
Man's Burden," the article depicted Burke as a product of
the old frontier and a politician of "old style, unshakable,
regularity." Burke's support for the Bursum bill was dictated
by loyalty to his chief, Albert Fall, the article stated: "Burke
is regular all the way. It did not occur to him to desert his
party chief. It could not occur to him. He has no machinery
in which to register such a thought." Although not designed
to be critical, this portrait of Burke did little to enhance his
public image, and when Bruno Lasker of the *Survey* sent
him an advance copy of Collier's "American Congo" article
for comment, he refused to engage in a debate. The one
thousand words that Lasker offered him were not enough in
which to reply adequately to all of Collier's distortions, he
replied. To Congressman Homer Snyder he confided his real
reason for refusing: "the more he [Collier] is recognized by
those in official position, the more prominent he becomes
and the more demand there will be for his writings." Although Burke was undoubtedly correct in this assessment,
his assumption that the controversy would subside if he ignored it clearly demonstrated his inability to comprehend
either Collier's vision or his tenacity.[10]

Had Burke been aware of the friction within the anti-
Bursum camp, he might not have been so defensive. In June,
just after his successful cooperation with the EAIA, Robert
Ely resigned as chairman of the AIDA. No reason for his resignation survives, but it is evident that he had never intended to do more than get the organization started and
enlist some of his wealthy friends in its support. His resignation did not come as a surprise to Collier, who had a replacement ready: Irving A. Bacheller, a former editor of the

New York World. Though Bacheller's fame was short-lived, he was a popular novelist who had written fourteen books, the most recent of which, a biography of Abraham Lincoln, was on the best seller list in 1920. Bacheller wanted "to study Indians," Collier informed Mabel Dodge, and both he and his wife were capable "of helping the cause materially—including money help." Bacheller was to serve as president of the AIDA for little more than a year, during which time he did nothing to further its aims and only acted when prompted by Collier. Throughout these early years particularly, the AIDA was an organization that existed only on paper and whose sole function was to provide Collier with a calling card and some degree of financial help.

At the same time that Ely quit, Mabel Dodge also gave notice of her impending retirement from the Indian field. For some time she had been worried about rumors that government investigators intended to expose her unorthodox living arrangement with Tony Luhan, both to discredit the Pueblos and perhaps to separate her from Tony. Ralph Twitchell, who despised Mabel's "bohemian" conduct and her influence at Taos, was apparently the source of these rumors. When Mary Austin visited Santa Fe in April, she learned that Twitchell had attempted to intimidate all of Mabel's friends there "by stories of what the Justice Department would do to [Collier], me, and Mabel." These threats so frightened Alice Henderson that she went to Taos to warn Mabel. Though Mary Austin refused to take the threat seriously, she did agree that there was a definite possibility of a "newspaper scandal." The result was that Mabel, who had given some thought earlier to leaving Taos, now decided to obtain a divorce from Maurice Sterne and marry Tony. They would "go away quietly and be married," Mary Austin reported, "and remain away until the fact of their marriage would cease to be news." Collier refused to become involved in Mabel's decision. He had no advice for her "problem," he wrote. "The idea of your being rushed either into or out of marriage is profoundly unwelcome."

There was no problem with Tony's wife, Candelaria.

Since at least 1920 there had been a formal contract, drawn up by Candelaria's lawyer and approved by the Taos council, whereby Mabel agreed to pay Candelaria thirty-five dollars per month for life, in return for her peaceful acquiescence in Tony's liaison with Mabel. But Mabel had never bothered to divorce Maurice Sterne, although they had been separated since shortly after her arrival in New Mexico. Sterne, however, had requested a divorce in the spring of 1922 when he wrote to say that he had fallen in love with a student at Elizabeth Duncan's school. In April, at the suggestion of Francis Wilson, Tony moved to Santo Domingo and divorce proceedings were begun.

On May 14, 1923, Mabel wrote to her friend, Carl Van Vechten: "I want to be the first to tell you that Tony and I were married a short time ago. That's-that." She did not, however, leave Taos immediately. Instead, she and Tony stayed on until October, when they accepted an invitation from the Colliers to winter in Mill Valley. By that time her financial support to the AIDA had dwindled away to almost nothing. Despite several appeals from Collier for money, she replied that she was unable to pledge further support because her mother, upon whose largess she was still partially dependent, had been "ominously" silent for some time. Besides, she wrote some time in the early fall, she had come to the conclusion that Collier's tactics were self-defeating: an "atrocious fight will defeat its own ends, our ends." She was particularly critical of the "fierce Sunset articles," which she though were doing more harm than good. Although they remained good personal friends, Collier informed the AIDA board in early 1924 that "Mrs. Dodge has retired from politics and no longer contributes."[11]

While Mabel Dodge and Robert Ely were withdrawing from the Indian scene, there were others who were just entering, four of whom were to figure prominently in events later that year: Herbert Hagerman, the special commissioner to the Navajos, Nina Otero Warren, Dorothy Straight, and Adolph Augustus Berle, Jr., the attorney chosen to replace Francis Wilson.

In early January 1923, Albert Fall, in one of his last actions as secretary of the interior, appointed Herbert J. Hagerman, formerly territorial governor of New Mexico and a prominent rancher in southeastern New Mexico, as special commissioner to the Navajos. The purpose of this appointment, according to Fall's correspondence, was to ensure that anticipated "oil development on the Navajo Reservation" would be conducted efficiently and quickly. Experience in negotiating oil leases through specially called tribal council meetings on the San Juan portion of the reservation had proven cumbersome and unsatisfactory to the oil companies. Moreover, both Fall and Commissioner Burke had come to have reservations both about the abilities of the local agents to handle these leases and the wisdom of permitting each Navajo jurisdiction to act independently of the others. New Mexico politics may also have entered into the decision, though there is no evidence to support this view. As Senator Bursum's old nemesis, Hagerman may have been chosen by Fall as a means of limiting Bursum's growing influence in New Mexico politics. There is no doubt, however, that Hagerman was chosen by Secretary Fall, not Commissioner Burke, and that Burke was instructed by Fall to make out the necessary appointment papers without prior consultation.

Hagerman, who had been living in semiretirement from politics since his ouster by Roosevelt in 1907, responded eagerly to Fall's invitation. About the time the Bursum bill hearings were being conducted, he journeyed to Washington, where he not only conferred with Fall and Burke, but also conducted a thorough survey of Navajo records in the Indian office. When Fall subsequently promulgated regulations creating a Navajo tribal council in which all the Navajo jurisdictions were to be represented, thus inaugurating the first steps ever toward Navajo nationhood, Hagerman, on the basis of a conference with each of the local agents, recommended a number of major modifications in the document, which not only enlarged the number of Navajo representatives on the council, but also increased their power.

These recommendations were approved by Fall's successor, Hubert Work, and by Commissioner Burke before the convening of the first tribal council in the spring of 1923. Despite these modifications, the new tribal council was clearly to be controlled by the special commissioner, who would negotiate all oil leases in its name and without whose presence the council was forbidden to meet.

The announcement of Hagerman's appointment and the promulgation of Fall's regulations for the formation of a Navajo tribal council were the events that first drew Collier's attention to the Navajos. Shortly afterward, he became aware of Fall's ruling on the executive-order reservations, prompted by the discovery of oil on the Navajo reservation. Convinced that the Navajo situation was in some way connected with Fall's other nefarious schemes, he wrote on March 1923 that the "Indian Office has instituted a coup d'etat, overthrowing the Navajo form of self-government." He was not sure why, "but of course they have a reason." In his assumption that the Navajos possessed some kind of prior tribal government like the Pueblos', Collier was totally wrong. But his theory of a coup fit in well with his belief that Fall was engaged in a conspiracy against the Indians and, despite later evidence to the contrary, he continued to persist in this interpretation. In the early 1930s, when Hagerman and Collier became deadlocked over Pueblo matters, Collier resurrected this theory of the Navajo tribal council's origin in a successful effort to drive Hagerman from office.

Collier's suspicion of Hagerman and the Navajo situation was, however, quieted in the summer of 1923 when Collier made his first tour of the vast reservation and conferred directly with Hagerman. By this time, the revised regulations were in effect, and Collier found Hagerman to be a thoroughly charming and dedicated man. Hagerman, he wrote to Paul Kellogg, "is the most reassuring official I have met in the Indian Service." In the two articles he wrote on the Navajos that summer, Collier was generous in his praise of Hagerman and optimistic in his prediction for their betterment under his supervision.[12]

Unlike his knowledge of the Hagerman appointment, Collier's knowledge of Nina Otero Warren's new role did not come until some months after she had been made an inspector in the Indian service. As the sister of former territorial Governor Miguel Otero, Mrs. Warren was a Republican with political ambitions of her own. In the 1922 state convention, at which Bursum was renominated for Fall's seat, she successfully won her party's nomination to oppose Senator A. A. Jones by a decisive vote of 446 to 99 over Congressman Nestor Montoya. When she was defeated in the fall election, she immediately sought a federal appointment in the Interior Department from Fall. Because she was also chairman of the Public Welfare Committee of the New Mexico GFWC and was sympathetic to the Mexican American settlers on the Pueblo lands, Burke envisioned her as the ideal replacement for the incompetent Colonel Dorrington, whom he fired shortly after Fall resigned. Assigned to the territory of southern California, Arizona, and New Mexico, Mrs. Warren's primary responsibility was to keep an eye on Collier and to report his every contact with the Indians immediately to Commissioner Burke.[13]

Much less is known about the role of Dorothy Whitney Straight, the wealthy (Standard Oil) heiress who became the treasurer of the AIDA upon its formation in May 1923. When Dorothy Whitney was still a child, her mother died. Before her death she extracted a promise from a good friend, Beatrice Bend, that young Dorothy be reared "to the good and useful life." Under Miss Bend's guidance, Dorothy was thoroughly schooled in settlement-house work in New York City. She also became affiliated with the Consumer League, founded in 1916 by Collier's close friends Dr. James Peter Warbasse and his wife, Agnes. In 1911 during a trip to the Far East, she met and soon afterward married Willard Straight. Under the influence of her husband, who urged her to "use your wealth to put ideas into circulation," and Herbert Croly, whose *Promise of American Life* stimulated her desire to participate in the creation of a better America, she provided the financial backing that made possible the launching of the liberal *New Republic* in 1914. For the next

thirty-nine years, Dorothy Straight provided an annual subsidy, which averaged $95,000, to keep the *New Republic*
afloat. In 1921 when the *Survey* decided to embark upon an
illustrated version, *Survey Graphic*, she became one of its
earliest and most generous benefactors. Her role in the
AIDA, however, is a shadowy and somewhat mysterious
one. Although she is frequently mentioned in the correspondence of the early years, none of her own letters, if
there were any, survive. The AIDA financial records, always
incomplete and spotty at best, reveal only that she was a
frequent contributor during the years 1923–25, usually giving $500 at a time, perhaps monthly. These contributions
were apparently contingent upon the AIDA's ability to
match them with other donations, but the critical nature of
her support is attested by Collier's comment in 1923 that
"the only person of wealth whom we have always been able
to call on at a time of need is Mrs. Straight."[14]

The choice of Adolph A. Berle, Jr., as the AIDA's legal
counsel took place shortly after Collier's break with Francis
Wilson. Berle's recollection was that Collier came to the
New York firm where Berle was a junior partner, seeking
advice on the Pueblo problem. "Nobody in the firm had
much interest in it," he recalled, except himself, "so I took a
vacation." Collier's contemporary correspondence, however, indicates that he was personally "unacquainted with
Berle," and had nothing to do with the choice. That decision
was made by Robert Ely, who had been steered to the firm
because of its recent work in protecting the lands of the Papago Indians of southern Arizona against a claim by a group
of Los Angeles speculators.

Berle was eminently qualified for the task. A child prod-
igy who entered Harvard at age fourteen, he received his
bachelor's degree with honors three years later; he went on
to become the youngest graduate of the Harvard Law School
at age twenty-one. Immediately after completing his legal
studies, he entered the law office of Supreme Court Justice
Louis Brandeis. When World War I broke out, he joined the
army. During the war he served in the military intelligence

branch, Caribbean section, and afterward was one of the experts chosen to accompany President Woodrow Wilson to the Versailles peace negotiations. Quickly disillusioned by Wilson's many compromises, he resigned in 1919, entered the prestigious New York firm of Rounds, Hatch, Dillingham and Debevoise, and began to teach at the Harvard Law School. As a result of his wartime work in the Dominican Republic, Berle had become "quite familiar with old Spanish colonial law," a prerequisite for anyone who hoped to draft legislation resolving the Pueblo crisis, and through his mother, who before her marriage had been a missionary to the Sioux, he could even claim a degree of empathy with the Indians. Hired by Ely in May 1923, he spent the summer researching the problem and in August joined Collier in New Mexico to get a close-up view of the situation.[15]

It was the appearance of Collier, Berle, and Mrs. Atwood in New Mexico in early August 1923 that finally broke the fragile bond of cooperation with the EAIA and the New Mexico Association that Robert Ely had so carefully negotiated in June.

Berle arrived in Santa Fe on August 3 and was immediately taken in tow by Collier. Two days later he went to Taos to meet Mary Austin and Mabel Dodge, whose celebrity status he acknowledged in his diary by placing an exclamation point after her name. For two hours they poured over a draft bill that Berle had prepared as a substitute for the Lenroot bill, then agreed that an All Pueblo Council should be convened at Santo Domingo on August 25. In the meanwhile, Berle, Collier, and Tony Luhan were to visit several of the northern Pueblos, where they would confer with the local councils. Berle was also taken on a tour of some of the disputed tracts. "It is no joke to evict the Mexicans," he noted in his diary; "it goes against my grain to throw out a family whose land is tilled and whose house is surrounded by hollyhocks and larkspur. No help for it though. We must get them some compensation."

If Berle was aware of the tension that Collier's presence

generated in Santa Fe, he gave no trace of it in his journal entries. On August 6 he "ran into" Francis Wilson at the Santa Fe courthouse, where the two men reviewed the situation. On August 8 he met with several members of the New Mexico Association. At their suggestion, he eliminated "certain sections' of the draft bill he was preparing, and agreed to brief them about the final proposals that he would put before the All Pueblo Council on the evening of August 24. Then, according to Alice Henderson, he "left town," and was not seen again until the day before the council convened.

The members of the New Mexico Association were angered by Collier's convening of the All Pueblo Council without consulting them, and they were not appeased when Berle unveiled the details of his bill on August 24. Essentially it called for the relinquishment of Indian title to certain areas that had long been occupied by non-Indians, but only if compensation was made for these losses. Other agricultural lands might also be relinquished, with compensation, but Berle's draft clearly stated that no lands should be taken from the Pueblos without their consent. The bill also called for compensation to the non-Indian claimants who would be evicted from their lands.

Immediately, the New Mexico Association members protested. Berle's bill, they argued, was not only "incomplete," but it was also "unsound," for it promised the Pueblos more than they could legitimately expect to get and would leave them dissatisfied and angry. Neither Collier nor Berle, however, indicated a willingness to modify the draft further. As a result, when the council met the following day, the two opposing white groups were both present, as was the Indian Office in the person of Nina Otero Warren.

At the August 25 meeting, ninety-eight Pueblo delegates representing all the Pueblos assembled. Berle, Collier, Mrs. Atwood, Tony Luhan, and Mary Austin were there for the AIDA: Margaret McKittrick, Witter Bynner, and Alice Henderson represented the New Mexico Association. The meeting opened with an explanation of Berle's bill. As soon as

Berle finished, Mrs. McKittrick, spearheading what Berle termed a "raid by the New Mexico Association," attempted to break up the meeting. Pleading that Berle's bill did not "represent all the associations interested in Indian Welfare" and that Collier had "sprung" this meeting without consulting the other groups, she asked the Pueblos not to take any action until a program on which all could unite had been formulated. The delegates, however, permitted Collier to speak and, at the end of his defense, they adopted a set of resolutions that he had prepared. With this, the New Mexico Association members stalked out of the assembly and, in Alice Henderson's words, "the break that we tried to avert all summer, occurred."

The resolutions the Pueblos adopted were then forwarded by Collier to the directors of the AIDA. They were both lengthy and explicit. No land should be taken from the Pueblos without their consent, and if then taken, only with compensation. The Pueblos would agree to recognize the non-Indians' rights to several townsites, church sites, cemeteries, and "public service corporations," and would agree to exclude them from litigation if compensation, equal to their agricultural value, were paid. The federal government was to blame for the necessity of evicting other claimants and should recognize its obligation to compensate them. The "peculiarly flagrant land seizures" that had taken place since the Joy survey should be "dealt with drastically and at once." A law should be passed making it a federal crime to encroach on Pueblo lands; the title to Pueblo lands must be affirmed by a law that would deny the right of non-Indians to claim them through the "adverse possession" statutes of New Mexico Territory. Where Spanish land grants overlapped the Pueblo claims, the Indian claim should be restored or compensation made. Finally, the delegates authorized the AIDA and the Indian Welfare committee of the GFWC to take the necessary legal steps to protect their claims. According to Collier, all the delegates approved these resolutions, except those from Laguna, who were not authorized to bind their people.

Five days later the break with the New Mexico Association was made final at a meeting of the association's directors in Santa Fe. There Francis Wilson denounced Collier's high-handed tactics, particularly the resolutions that he had put before the delegates, saying that unless they were challenged, their adoption would mean that only the AIDA and the GFWC would be recognized as the Indian's benefactors. Such an event, he protested, was "not fair to the Indians nor to us." By this time, however, the die had been cast. Collier and Mrs. Atwood, refusing to meet with the New Mexico Association, left Santa Fe on September 5 for the "West via the Southern Pueblos."[16]

Collier's decision to break with the New Mexico Association, a conscious one with which he had been wrestling since May, ended the months of indecision that had followed his clash with Francis Wilson. Although his hopes for a single national organization were now in shambles, the confrontation at the Santo Domingo meeting strengthened his determination and zeal to forge ahead, no matter what the cost. From California, where he was writing a scathing attack on Wilson and the other associations for *Sunset*, he urged the New York board members in September to cut the organization's losses by ceasing all effort to pacify Amelia White and Roberts Walker, who "are playing into the opposition's hands." Father Schuster was also lost, he advised. The Franciscan order had pushed him "into a passive and shameful allegiance with the Wilson-Renehan group."

To gird themselves for the coming battle in Congress, Collier urged that the AIDA hire a Santa Barbara newspaperman recommended by Judson King, Cash E. Asher, as its "field man in the Southwest." Berle, "who has done such a good job in preparing a bill to defend the Pueblos," should be permanently retained "on a part-time basis" to handle all the association's legal work. Mary Austin, he urged, should be named the AIDA's "local representative" in New Mexico now that the "New Mexico Association has defected."

Holding the Pueblos in line and convincing his New York

supporters that they should go it alone, however, was not an easy matter. While he was awaiting a reply from New York, Collier found it necessary to address all the "Governors and councils of the Pueblos" in a lengthy letter in which he exhorted them to stand firm in defense of the resolutions they had just adopted. The New Mexico Association, he warned, had abandoned the goal of returning all the land that was rightfully theirs, and Francis Wilson had "gone over to the opposition." There would be an effort, he predicted, on the part of Margaret McKittrick and Witter Bynner to persuade the Pueblos to change their statement and to support the Lenroot bill, which "would deprive the Pueblos of their land titles." Until he could return to New Mexico, he cautioned them to trust no one but Mary Austin, Mabel Dodge, or Ina Cassidy.

Collier's fear of the New Mexico Association was justified. Witter Bynner, who had just returned from Mexico with D. H. Lawrence, and thus found himself the object of Mabel's attention, was at least partially responsible for her growing coolness toward Collier's work. He had been present at the Santo Domingo meeting, he wrote Mabel, and "could swear that it was Collier and Berle and not the Indians who did the 'instructing.'" While he admired both Collier and Wilson, "at the present juncture Collier seems to me almost as mad as Mrs. Austin, and Wilson at least as sane as myself . . . ." Collier's conduct at the Santo Domingo meeting, he charged, was "immoral" in that he had not only encouraged the Indians to demand more than they could "possibly or rightfully get," but he had also "most grievously . . . persuaded [the Indians] to think us delinquent." The New Mexico Association and representatives of the EAIA, meeting in Santa Fe shortly after the Pueblo council, had concluded that they could no longer "contribute money to Collier's cause" and that they must hasten to consolidate "all reasonable spirits in this movement lest Mr. Collier, Mrs. Atwood, and Mrs. Austin should commit . . . it to extravagances which might preclude the possibility of any congressional action at all." It "saddens me," he concluded, to see Mabel "committed to a faction of mischief and futility."

The news from New York was no more encouraging. Berle and Bacheller both attempted to dissuade Collier from antagonizing the other groups, and Berle in particular urged caution in pressing the attack upon the Lenroot bill. An open controversy with the other organizations, he advised, "should be avoided." Otherwise, any legislation resolving the problem might be blocked. Bacheller was concerned primarily with the tone of Collier's letter to the Pueblo governors. Not only would it alienate the other associations whose support was desirable, but it might also confuse the Indians.

Collier's replies to both men indicated clearly how little his activities were governed by the national board. A major mistake had been made in April, he replied, when the AIDA "sat by silently" while Wilson and the others "engineered the Lenroot compromise." There was no point in compounding that error now when it was a certainty that none of the other groups could "be brought into line." The only course left was to take the offensive and mount an exposé of Wilson and the New Mexico Association for their role in the drafting of the Lenroot bill. To that end, he was already at work preparing publicity, which "should begin breaking in November."

Collier's interpretation of what happened at the Santo Domingo meeting is also instructive. Everything possible had been done since April "to avoid hurting Wilson and the New Mexico Association," he told Bacheller, because there had been a general agreement to hold all propaganda in abeyance until August when the All Pueblo Council was to be reconvened. At that meeting, he charged, it was the representatives of the New Mexico Association who destroyed the Indians' confidence in their white friends when they informed the delegates that "their white supporters were not in agreement." Having failed to defeat Berle's proposals, they then walked out of the council and immediately "began a campaign to destroy the Indian's confidence" in him-

self, Mrs. Atwood, and the AIDA. "Thereupon," he was
forced to give the Pueblos and the GFWC "information
which would enable them to protect themselves from untrue propaganda."[17]

It was Collier, of course, who prevailed. In the November
issue of *Sunset*, the article Mabel Dodge labeled as too
"fierce" appeared. In it Collier branded Francis Wilson as
the Indian's erstwhile friend who defected in the closing
hours of the previous Congress. Wilson and the other Indian
societies, he charged, had persisted in their betrayal at the
August 25 council meeting. Only the AIDA and the GFWC
now stood between the Pueblos and the forces determined
to take their land. The article ended on a plea, "Will you
help?," and instructed readers to send their checks to the
New York office.

During the fall of 1923 defections from the board of the
AIDA increased. Amelia White withdrew her support, saying that she could not countenance Collier's attack on the
New Mexico Association nor could she any longer tolerate
his disposition to denigrate "others who do not share his
opinions." The names of Harold Ickes and Carter Harrison
were ordered stricken from the AIDA's letterhead following their resignations in November, and Father Schuster's
name was removed somewhat later. Though Collier believed throughout his life that Schuster had been forced to
withdraw his support, this was not the case. In a letter to
Malcolm McDowell, written in December 1923, Schuster
explained that he had had nothing to do with Collier since
their joint appearance before Congress during the Bursum
bill hearings. Although "at first everyone welcomed him
as a representative of the General Federation of Womens
Clubs," Schuster wrote, Collier had proven himself "too
radical and self centered and conceited." When Wilson
"would not lend himself to Collier's infamous schemes," he
reported, Collier became "very bitter" and as a result had
"slandered Wilson most shamefully. I am of the opinion
that the American Indian Defense Association is a one-man
affair, and that one man is Collier."

By the end of 1923, although the AIDA remained solvent, its treasury was almost bare. That portion of Collier's salary assumed by the AIDA in May was not paid after August, and only sizable gifts from Dr. Haynes and Dorothy Straight, and a final $300 check from Mabel Dodge in November, made it possible to end the year in the black. Several important studies that Collier had hoped to initiate in the fall—one of the Indian medical service, a second on the Indian Office's administrative methods, and a third on Indian laws—had all been scrapped for lack of funds. Collier himself became so bogged down in fund-raising activities, from which he wrote Mabel Dodge "I must be freed," that he sent Cash Asher to New York to launch a major financial drive in January 1924. As the year ended, the reality of the AIDA's situation contrasted sharply with the bright vision of a single, unified, national organization with which it had begun.[18]

More significant for the future, however, was the developing image of the AIDA as a "one-man affair," as Father Schuster had characterized it. Despite its panoply of directors, officers, and prominent advisors, the AIDA would never be able to broaden its appeal much beyond a handful of wealthy supporters whose allegiance was more to John Collier than to the Indians. New supporters would be recruited as old ones dropped away, but the history of the AIDA would continue to be marked by clashes between Collier and his benefactors until, of the original founders, only Dr. Haynes and Stella Atwood remained.

Collier's last major activity in 1923 was his attendance at the meeting of the Council of One Hundred on December 12–13. The resolutions adopted by the delegates there showed clearly how much attitudes toward the Indians had changed during the past year. They also foreshadowed the difficulties to be encountered in any effort to obtain additional reforms in the years ahead.

When the council convened in the auditorium of the Interior Department to hear opening addresses by Secretary Work and Commissioner Burke, sixty of the one hundred

invited guests were in attendance. In addition to the repre-
sentatives of the various Indian defense societies like Collier, Mrs. Atwood, Margaret McKittrick, Matthew Sniffen,
Herbert Welsh, and Amelia White, there were the "museum
people," whom Collier had come to distrust during the
course of the debate over the Bursum bill: Frederick Hodge,
Herbert Spinden, and Clark Wissler, the curator of the
American Museum of Natural History. The Board of Indian
Commissioners was represented by George Vaux, General
Hugh Scott, Warren K. Moorehead, and Flora Warren Seymour, an attorney and author who would soon emerge as
one of Collier's most articulate critics. There was also in
attendance a distinguished group of assimilated Indians,
which included the past presidents and officers of the defunct Society of American Indians: Arthur C. Parker, the
Reverend Sherman Coolidge, Charles Alexander (Ohiyesa)
Eastman, Thomas L. Sloan, the Reverend Henry Roe Cloud,
Dennison Wheelock, and Father Philip Gordon, a supporter
of the recently deceased Carlos Montezuma. The press was
represented by Will Irwin and Oswald Garrison Villard. The
churches had spokesmen from all the major religious denominations: Bishop Hugh L. Burleson, secretary of the
Board of Missions of the Protestant Episcopal Church; Fa-
ther William Hughes of the Catholic Mission Society and
Bishop Thomas J. Shahan, rector of the Catholic University; Rabbi Stephen S. Wise, founder of the Free Synagogue
of New York and the Federation of American Zionists; and
Gustavus E. E. Lindquist, a Lutheran missionary affiliated
with the YMCA and the Inter-Church World Movement.
Representing the public-at-large were Bernard M. Baruch,
William Jennings Bryan, C. Hart Merriam, and novelist
Mary Roberts Rinehart. The purpose of the meeting, Work
announced, was to assemble in one place "100 intelligent
men and women to give me the benefit of their knowledge,
judgment and advice . . . ." Their advice was necessary, he
continued, because upon taking office he had discovered
that "those interested in these aboriginal Americans . . . and
those responsible to the Government for official acts were

at variance on many details and . . . the public mind was in
a state of chaos on this subject."

Following the secretary's opening remarks, the delegates
elected Arthur C. Parker as chairman and General Hugh
Scott as vice-chairman of the session. At the suggestion of
Herbert Spinden, an agenda dealing with six broad topics
was adopted: health and sanitation, education, land policy
and economic welfare, legal status and citizenship, problems of tribal life, and the decentralization of the Indian Office. One hour of general discussion was to be allotted to
each topic; all resolutions were to be referred to a resolutions committee, which would recommend action at the
closing session on December 13. Despite attempts to keep
the discussion focused on general topics, the issues that
commanded the most attention were precisely those that
had brought about the crisis in Indian Affairs under Albert
Fall: the Pueblo land problem and the status of the executive-
order reservations. There was also spirited debate on the
topics of Indian citizenship and the government's policy toward Indian religious ceremonies and dances.

The issue of the executive-order reservations was introduced by Commissioner Burke himself in his introductory
speech. Ever since Fall's ruling in the Harrison case, he explained, the Indian Office had been searching for a way to
prevent its application. A bill calling for the payment of all
royalty and lease monies to the Indians had just been introduced into Congress and Burke asked the council to support
its passage. The response of the delegates was swift and
unanimous. Not only did they vote to request Congress "to
vest the title of said reservations in the Indians occupying
them," they also called upon Secretary Work to suspend all
departmental proceedings related to the sale or lease of
minerals in these lands until Congress had acted on the title
question.

The Pueblo issue was not so easily resolved. Collier
wanted the council to create a committee to investigate the
problem and to submit a recommendation directly to Congress. When that was rejected as being beyond the council's

jurisdiction, Margaret McKittrick rose to oppose discussion of the topic entirely, on the ground that it was too complex for intelligent discussion in the limited time available. In the debate that followed, two points were clearly established. The delegates were sympathetic to a resolution calling for compensation by the federal government to both Indians and whites for any losses they might incur. They were also in agreement that the court cases suspended by Fall and Twitchell should be vigorously pursued to determine the issue of ownership. The debate also clarified the differences between Collier and the supporters of the Lenroot bill. Collier was certain that if the courts were allowed to rule, they would find the federal government negligent in its guardianship responsibilities to the Pueblos and would also uphold the Pueblo title to all lands in their possession in 1848. Margaret McKittrick was just as certain that the courts would find that the New Mexico territorial statutes of limitation would be upheld and that settlers who had obtained their lands before 1912 would have their titles upheld. Malcolm McDowell of the Board of Indian Commissioners referred to this clash as "a little duel" that "did not develop the fireworks some people had expected. In justice to John [Collier], I must tell you that he did not make what I would call a serious effort."

The issue of Indian citizenship, one that Collier by his own admission never considered important, provoked considerable emotion and rhetoric, but it was finally defeated in a close vote at the closing session. In 1924, as a result of the application of the Dawes allotment policy, more than two-thirds of all Indians were already citizens, and many delegates, led by the Omaha Indian attorney Thomas J. Sloan, believed it shameful that the remaining one-third were denied the rights of citizenship. But General Scott and the missionary leaders who argued that citizenship offered few tangible benefits to older full-blooded Indians and might instead subject them to victimization by unscrupulous local and state governments, carried the majority in a close vote at the final session. Despite the council's refusal to support blanket citizenship for all Indians, a bill to this effect passed Congress the following year.

But the issue that, surprisingly, occasioned the most heated exchanges dealt with Indian religious freedom. On the first day of the meeting, William Jennings Bryan, then at the height of his antievolution crusade, introduced a resolution commending the federal government for its encouragement of the activities of all religious denominations on Indian reservation. Only Herbert Spinden and Collier, who unsuccessfully inquired if it were true that Indian children in government boarding schools were being forcibly indoctrinated into Christianity, raised objections, and Bryan's resolution passed easily. But later, when a resolution in support of a recent directive from Commissioner Burke threatening to suppress "immoral" Indian dances was introduced, Collier was joined by Professor Lew Sarett of Northwestern University, Warren K. Moorehead, and C. Hart Merriam, with the result that the controversial resolution was initially tabled. At the final council session, however, the missionaries, led by Bishop Burleson and Gustavus E. E. Lindquist, succeeded in removing the resolution from the table by attaching to it a statement upholding the "cultivation of all lawful ancient ceremonies, rites, and customs of the Indian race . . . ." This time it passed, but the importance of the religious freedom issue was not lost on Collier, who left the meeting determined to press it more fully in the year ahead.

Both Collier and Elizabeth Shepley Sergeant criticized the council meeting in articles published the following spring in the *New Republic* and *Sunset*. Each emphasized an event that took place on the afternoon of the last day, thereby reducing the time allotted for debate of the resolutions presented by the predominantly assimilationist resolutions committee. Collier believed this event especially symbolic of the ineffectual nature of the conference.

At the invitation of President Calvin Coolidge, the delegates assembled at the White House in the early afternoon of December 13. No spokesman for the delegation had been named nor did the president have any words of wisdom for the group. Instead, much to the surprise of Collier and others, Ruth Muskrat, a Cherokee "princess" clad in "skins, her head bound with a bead fillet," stepped forward to present the "Great White Father" with a copy of Gustavus E. E. Lindquist's recently published *The Red Man in The United States*, bound in a beaded cover especially prepared "with loving and painstaking care" by "Indian women on the Cheyenne Reservation in Oklahoma." Making no attempt to veil his disgust at the incident, Collier reported in the March issue of *Sunset* that "not one fundamental proposition [was] put across" during the conference and "the only exchange of ideas" during the potentially fruitful meeting with the president was the "presentation of a copy of missionary Lindquist's survey of the Indians, a book crowded with defects and biased in favor of the missionary standpoint."

The Council of One Hundred proved to be the last stand of the assimilationist forces that had significantly influenced government policy since the late nineteenth century. In the years that followed, the forces of reform increasingly followed the path Collier and the AIDA were blazing. In December 1924, when Secretary Work was asked if another meeting of the council would be held, he responded in the negative, citing a poll he had taken of the 1923 delegates, who, he said, "were almost unanimous that there is no necessity for a meeting of the Council in the near future." The constant drumfire of opposition to government policy continued, however, and in 1926 Work turned to the Brookings Institution for a thorough, objective evaluation of the Indian Office. The resultant report was an almost total victory for Collier and the antiassimilation forces.[19]

9

The Religious Freedom Issue (1924–25)

Following the recess of the Council of One Hundred, Collier returned to New Mexico to organize support for the Pueblo bill prepared by A. A. Berle the previous summer and to mobilize opposition to a revised Lenroot bill, which Bursum introduced in December 1923. On January 17, 1924, the All Pueblo Council was convened a second time at Santo Domingo. The delegates were briefed by Collier on the legislative situation, and a small band of dancers was chosen to accompany him to the East. Shortly thereafter, the group journeyed to New York for a series of publicity and money-raising appearances and then went to Washington, where they were received by President Coolidge.[1]

Collier's role in the final drama of the Pueblo land legislation, however, was limited. During the Washington visit, he became ill and returned to California where he underwent surgery for an unspecified illness in late March.[2] By the time he had recovered sufficiently to travel again, the Pueblo Lands Act had been hammered out in Washington.

The primary responsibility for negotiating a satisfactory settlement of the problem thus fell to A. A. Berle, who, as a result of his earlier work, was retained by the AIDA on a full-time basis from December 1923 to June 1924.

In Mid-January 1924, Senator Charles Curtis was persuaded to introduce Berle's bill into the Senate. It stated clearly the position of the AIDA: all lands owned by the Pueblos at the time American sovereignty was established in the Southwest still belonged to them and could not be relinquished without their permission and payment of adequate compensation. Berle's argument was that the Pueblos, as wards of the federal government, had been unfairly and illegally despoiled of their lands by the failure of their guardian, the United States, to protect their rights adequately. The questions of title and compensation were thereby squarely joined in the rival Lenroot and Curtis bills. This time, however, the public acrimony that had accompanied the debate over the Bursum bill was to be avoided. A subcommittee composed of the two New Mexico senators, Bursum and Jones, with Alva Adams of Colorado as chairman, was created to meet with the opposing attorneys and charged with responsibility for effecting a compromise. In the absence of formal hearings, our understanding of what transpired in these confrontations is necessarily limited, but correspondence among Collier, Berle, and Adams during March and April 1924, the period of the most intense negotiations, provides a glimpse of the most important concessions and the arguments advanced for their acceptance.

The major debate centered on the applicability of the New Mexico territorial statutes of limitation to the disputed Pueblo lands. In November 1923, Francis Wilson, now on the side of the anti-Collier forces, drafted a statutes-of-limitation clause, which was inserted in the revised Lenroot bill introduced by Bursum in December. This clause ultimately became sections 4a and 4b of the Pueblo Lands Act of 1924. According to its provisions, all non-Indian claimants who could prove "open, notorious, actual, exclusive, continuous, adverse possession" under color of title from January 6, 1902, to the date of passage of the act, or similar possession "with claim of ownership but without color of title" from March 16, 1889, to the date of passage of the act, were to be given title to their claims and the Indian title voided. The dates chosen by Wilson were those specified in the New Mexico territorial statutes of limitation, and their acceptance, he argued, would legitimize and protect the truly valid non-Indian settlers' claims.

Berle's response to the revised Lenroot bill was that its statutes-of-limitation clause was unconstitutional on two counts: one, because the New Mexico statutes of limitation could never have run against the federal government in its capacity as guardian to the Pueblos, and, two, because the inclusion of the statutes in the Pueblo bill would create a retroactive right in the non-Indians. Berle's argument impressed the senators enough that they notified Commissioner Burke of the problem, thereby precipitating an investigation "to see if there is any merit in the contention that [Berle] is advocating." Apparently there was.

The result of the debate on the statutes of limitation was that they were incorporated into the Pueblo Lands Act exactly as drafted by Wilson, but with the addition of two important qualifications. One of these was that the non-Indian claimants would also have to demonstrate continuous payment of taxes on their lands from the dates specified in sections 4a and 4b to the date of passage of the act. The second was that the Pueblos, at any time before the actual patenting of land to the non-Indians, could assert an independent claim in federal court based on "any existing right" they might have had prior to passage of the act. In effect, this second qualification removed the objection to the "retroactive" nature of the statutes of limitation.

Having provided the non-Indians with the possibility of establishing a valid claim to their lands, the subcommittee then agreed that both the Pueblos and the "good faith" non-Indians who lost lands were entitled to compensation from the federal government. The decisions on title and the determination of compensation values would be made by a three-man Pueblo Lands Board. The non-Indians could dispute the findings of the Pueblo Lands Board in title matters in the federal district court, and the Pueblos could contest the compensation awards in the same court.

Despite their absolute stance in defense of the Pueblos' claim to all the disputed land the year before, Collier and Berle now agreed to support the amended bill. At least four reasons for their change of mind emerge from the correspondence. One was their acceptance of the facts of political life. The non-Indians and their political representatives would accept no legislative solution to the vexing land problem that did not guarantee, as a minimum, the protection of the territorial statutes of limitation. The only alternative to acceptance of the statutes would be a lengthy and costly court case, which the Pueblos, despite Collier's confidence in the federal courts, might lose. The second reason was the assurance of compensation, which had earlier been denied. A third reason was the strong belief in the Collier camp that few, if any, of the non-Indians would be able to show continuous payment of taxes on lands they claimed. Because of this belief, they did not expect the losses of the Pueblos to be serious. Fourth, it was believed that the threat of an independent Pueblo suit would exert sufficient pressure upon the Pueblo Lands Board to decide any doubtful cases in favor of the Indians.

Once a bargain had been struck on the terms of the amended bill, Bursum was permitted to take credit for its introduction and the Lenroot and Curtis bills were dropped. A hitch developed at the last moment when the committee deleted the provision making the Pueblo compensation awards binding on the federal government and instead substituted a provision making them merely a "recommendation" to the Congress. Berle, in consultation with the hospitalized Collier, adamantly refused to accept the change. Advised by Senator Adams that Congress would not accept "a measure which provides that the decision of any administrative board shall be the equivalent of a conclusive judgment against the United States," and that unless they dropped their opposition, "it is highly unlikely that any bill affecting this subject will be passed," Collier and Berle accepted defeat. "The denouement in the Pueblo land situation is a bitter disappointment," Berle wrote Collier, but "I have replied [to Senator Adams] that as between a bill which does not provide a binding award of compensation and no legislation at all, we prefer nothing."

Then, through a direct appeal to the chairman of the parent Public Land Committee, E. F. Ladd, Berle saved the bill and the compensation provision. With Ladd's approval, he hastily drafted an amendment subjecting the compensation awards to review by the federal district court, but making the court's action binding on the federal government. This proved acceptable, and the bill then sailed through both houses of Congress and was signed into law on June 7, 1924 (43 Stat., 636).[3]

In Collier's writings, attention is focused on the defeat of the first Bursum bill and relatively little is said about the Pueblo Lands Act or its implementation. Perhaps this is because most of the assumptions upon which he based his acceptance of the act proved false in the years that followed. Collier had hoped to influence appointments to the board to ensure its sympathy to the Pueblo position, but instead it was Francis Wilson and his supporters who secured the appointment of Roberts Walker as chairman. Collier took credit for the appointment of Herbert Hagerman, but Hagerman was the Indian Office's choice, and in time the two men grew to hate each other. Most of the board's decisions favored the settlers and its compensation awards were far less than those that had been expected. Many of its awards to the Pueblos were later overturned in the district court, which interpreted the continuous tax payment requirement for the non-Indians in such a way as to make it virtually inapplicable. By 1931, when the board completed its work, the Pueblos had lost many acres of irrigated land for which they had been awarded very little compensation. The only defenses left were prosecution of the independent suits or new legislation. At that time, Collier mounted a furious campaign in both the court and the Congress, which succeeded only when he became Indian commissioner in 1933.

But all of this lay in the future. In May 1924, as the Pueblo Lands Act was making its way through Congress, Collier left his hospital bed to seek financial support for the necessary legal defense before the Pueblo Lands Board and he went to New Mexico to launch his second assault against the "system."

Collier's decision to raise the cry of Indian Office interference with the religious freedom of American Indians was prompted by concrete problems at Zuñi and Taos, but it was launched within the context of a much broader attack on the all-pervasive concept of Indian assimilation. Almost from the beginning of federal Indian policy, the government had welcomed the activities of the churches and their missionaries in its efforts to educate and "americanize" the Indians. So prevalent was the idea that Indian culture and Indian religion were retarding influences that no one questioned the close alliance between church and state until late in the nineteenth century when the use of federal funds to support sectarian schools was challenged and the practice ended. Nevertheless, the mission schools continued to play an important role in Indian education; and in the government's own boarding schools attendance at Christian religious services and religious education classes was required.

In his struggle to win recognition for the right of Indians to practice their native religions, John Collier made Commissioner Charles Burke the symbol of evil in much the same way he had used Albert Fall in the fight against the Bursum bill. Burke's concept of religious liberty certainly did not rise above that of the conventional wisdom, but in many respects he was a victim of the past and of various missionary groups, which, enraged by Collier's effrontery, chose to make the issue of religion a test of their continued support of federal Indian policy. Burke was often caught between the two extremes, with the result that he satisfied neither.

The religious issue was both heightened and obscured in the 1920s by a parallel issue close to Burke's heart, the education of Indian children. Despite forty years of increasing federal appropriations for Indian education, there were an estimated 21,000 Indian children who did not attend school at the beginning of his administration. For 18,000 of these, no schools existed. The problem was most acute in the Southwest, particularly among the Navajos, who were just beginning to come into close contact with whites. To rectify this situation, Congress in 1920 ordered the compulsory attendance of all Indian children subject to federal jurisdiction (41 Stat., 408), but did not significantly increase appropriations for Indian education. To comply with the law, Burke issued orders bringing the Indian country under the provisions of state compulsory-school laws, and he encouraged Indian agents to place as many students as possible in local public schools. Government day schools and boarding schools were expanded, but the latter failed to accommodate the burgeoning enrollment. Former military posts in Arizona and New Mexico were hastily converted to boarding schools, and thousands of Indian children were forcibly transported to schools miles from their homes. The implementation of the compulsory-education law resulted in many abuses and hardships throughout the 1920s, and because religious worship and instruction in government boarding schools were also compulsory, the controversy over religious freedom was exacerbated. Where Collier saw a problem of religious freedom in the schools, Burke saw interference with the compulsory-education requirement. It was inevitable that they would clash.[4]

Burke, however, was more vulnerable on another count. Early in his administration he was prevailed upon by Indian agents, missionaries, the Board of Indian Commissioners, and the Indian Rights Association of Philadelphia to institute a ban on Indian dances, some of which were alleged to be immoral, others merely nuisances that interfered with the planting and harvesting of crops. In defense of their appeals, the lobbyists presented Burke with charges of degrading practices that accompanied or were integral parts of the native dances. Two of the most sensational reports were submitted by Leo Crane, the Southern Pueblo superintendent, and by officials of the Indian Rights Association. Because of the secretive nature of the reports, neither was submitted to impartial observers for corroboration, and Burke, who knew nothing about the Indians described or their ceremonies, apparently accepted them at face value.

The Indian Rights Association charges dealt with the Hopi Snake dance and went back to the year 1913 when S. M. Brosius and Matthew K. Sniffen, in the company of Theodore Roosevelt, witnessed the dance. "The barbarism of the whole celebration exceeded everything that we thought possible on this continent," the two IRA investigators reported, demanding that the Indian Office conduct an investigation. In 1920–21 an inspector was sent to Hopi, where he took "volumnious testimony under oath," which purported to show that the dance was accompanied by the "utter abandon of moral and legal restraints imposed by marital obligations" and by the "most depraved and immoral practices." Crane's report referred to "affidavits" on file in his office that had been collected by former Superintendent Lonergan in 1915. Crane said they documented "obscenities connected with the religious rites of the more backward pueblos and their barbaric cruelties when inflicting punishment." Whether Crane sent a copy of Lonergan's "affidavits" to Burke or whether Lonergan's original report and supporting documents were unearthed from the Indian Office files is not clear, but by 1923 a file of documents had been loaned to the Indian Rights Association by Burke, and duplicate copies began to be circulated surreptitiously around the country under the title of the "Secret Dance File."[5]

The Lonergan report on secret dances in the northern Pueblos was a compilation of affidavits taken from Anglos, Spanish Americans, and some Christian Pueblo Indians. Most of them were crudely worded descriptions of sexual acts, which the parties claimed to have witnessed at various Pueblos. A series of documents on Santo Domingo complained that the Indians there imitated animals mating and that the clowns exposed themselves to women who responded by fondling the clowns' genitals. At Cochiti there were reports of men fondling women's breasts; at Zia one informant claimed to have seen young girls naked, simulating intercourse with the clowns; and at Jemez there were charges of sodomy. At the time Lonergan compiled the folder, his superiors in Washington did not know what to do with it. After persistent inquiries, Lonergan was told that an inspector was being sent to investigate the situation and also to investigate charges that had been directed against him by the Indians. Inspector H. S. Traylor's report in April 1916 gave Lonergan a clean bill of health. Lonergan was the victim of charges that were either "forgeries or the work of ignorant people who did not know what they had signed," Traylor wrote; the agent had been unfairly attacked because he was "waging a war with every weapon our uncertain jurisdiction gives him" against the pagan "caciques, governors, and principalities." At the same time, Traylor, who professed himself "a believer in religion, education, and civilization," confirmed the excesses of Lonergan's original report, adding some new charges of his own. Young girls, he claimed "are forced to surrender their bodies to the bestial passions of Governors," and "the spews of hell, the cacique with his imps, the Captains of War, the Governors and his Principalities, lead the wild orgeries [sic] and force all . . . old and young, ignorant and educated, the willing and the outraged, the unclean and clean, to take their place and part in these awful scenes and practices."[6]

Because of his uncritical acceptance of reports like those from Lonergan and the IRA, Burke was easily persuaded in April 1921 to issue "Circular No. 1665" in which he advised all Indian superintendents that while the Indian Office did not intend to "denounce all forms of Indian dancing," it nevertheless recognized that "under the most primitive and pagan conditions" dances were "apt to be harmful." If necessary, superintendents should be prepared to repress a dance "by punitive measures when its degrading tendencies persist." In addition to the Sun Dance, which had been banned for years, Burke ordered restrictions on dances involving "self-torture, immoral relations between the sexes, the sacrificial destruction of clothing or other useful articles of protection, the reckless giving away of property, the use of injurious drugs or intoxicants" (*read* peyote), and any dance that lasted for prolonged periods of time, thereby causing neglect of "crops, livestock, and home interests."

The following year Burke was invited to a conference of missionaries in his home state to discuss problems among the Sioux. There he was persuaded to draft a supplement to Circular No. 1665, which urged that Indian dances be limited to one a month "in the daylight hours of one day in the midweek," and abolished them completely in April, June, July, and August. The supplement also urged that no one under the age of fifty be permitted to participate in the dances, that "a careful propaganda be undertaken to educate public opinion against the dance," and that there be "close cooperation between the Government employees and the missionaries in those matters which affect the moral welfare of the Indians." Accompanying the supplement was "A Message to All Indians," which contained a veiled threat of repression against "giveaway" dances, dances involving torture or the handling of "poisonous snakes," and those that conflicted with the limitations set forth in the dance supplement. He could issue "an order against these useless and harmful performances," Burke told the Indians, but he preferred that they "give them up of your own free will." At the end of one year he would ask all superintendents to report on compliance with his recommendations. If their reports should "show that you reject this plea, then some other course will have to be taken."[7]

Burke's original directive, Circular No. 1665, appears not to have received any public attention, but release of the supplement and the public "Message to All Indians" in February 1923 during the uproar over the Bursum bill, produced a torrent of adverse mail. Surprisingly, Collier was not involved in this controversy. Instead, following an Associated Press bulletin from Santa Fe on March 8, 1923, which stated that "ceremonial dances by the New Mexico Pueblo Indians

Figure 20.   Cartoon on the Indian dance prohibition. *New York Tribune*, June 1, 1926. From the John Collier Papers, Yale University Library.

which annually bring thousands of visitors from the entire country have been forbidden except in the wintertime by Charles H. Burke," it was individuals like Roberts Walker, Nina Otero Warren, and Amelia White who voiced their opposition. In most of his replies, Burke played the innocent, protesting that no "order" had been issued against the dances, only an appeal, and that the message had been primarily intended for the Plains Indians. To many of his critics he wrote that "the Pueblo or Hopi Indians never entered my mind," but to others he confided that he regarded the Snake dance to be "indecent, disgusting," and that it would be banned. He told Miss White that he intended to suppress "celebrations like those described in the Lonergan report" and he did not approve of permitting Indian children to perform their native dances in the Indian schools. It was better, he thought, that they be instructed in other dances such as the "Maypole Dance."[8]

Although Burke pulled back from further public statements on the dance subject during the remainder of 1923, he released the secret dance file to S. M. Brosius of the Indian Rights Association of Philadelphia, who began to circulate copies among sympathetic parties. One of these apparently found its way to Gustavus E. E. Lindquist, who referred to it in his *The Red Man in the United States*. Lindquist claimed the file documented "obscenities and barbarisms in Indian religious rites," and Burke, who wrote the introduction to the book, praised the missionary influence that sought to lead the Indians away from their "benighted and sometimes degrading" traditions. Because of Burke's support for their position, the missionaries at the Council of One Hundred meeting had successfully forced the vote on the controversial resolution commending Burke for his issuance of Circular No. 1665. This, coupled with Burke's personal intervention into a controversy at Taos and a publicity campaign against the dances in the national press, brought Collier into the fray in the late spring of 1924.

At the time of the Committee of One Hundred meeting, there had been a series of "letters to the editor" in the *New*

York Times on the topic of Indian dances. One of them, by Edith Dabb, an associate of Lindquist, defended Burke's efforts to abolish the dances, thereby provoking independent replies from Collier and Frederick W. Hodge. Hodge wrote that he had recently noted "with amazement" a number of editorials in local newspapers characterizing the Pueblo dances as "demoralizing" or "indecent." These editorials, he charged, were based on the "grossest misinformation" and had been apparently designed to bias members of the Council of One Hundred who had no personal knowledge of the Pueblos or their ceremonials. During thirty years of observation at Zuñi, the pueblo that "most adheres to its primitive customs," Hodge claimed he had never once observed any "indecency." Collier wrote that the recent propaganda failed to distinguish between the sometimes earthy behavior of the "delight makers, the secret society of sacred clowns," and the religious ceremonies. It had the virtue, however, of bringing to a head the issue of "cultural toleration." "Do we or do we not believe in religious liberty?" he asked.

In February, emboldened by the council's support for the dance ban, the Indian Rights Association of Philadelphia began issuance of a new publication, *Indian Truth*, which was directed to the assimilationist-missionary group. The April 1924 issue was devoted almost entirely to the dance question and was filled with references to the secret dance file. That same month Mary Austin and Flora Warren Seymour, a member of the Board of Indian Commissioners, squared off in an exchange in the *Forum*. Emphasizing that the recent controversy over Pueblo lands was but a part of the larger Indian problem, Mrs. Seymour argued in favor of a hard-line assimilationist solution that called upon the government to abandon its role of guardian and instead advocated that Indians be turned loose to stand on their own feet. The Indian, she wrote, had become the "favored child of the nation," enjoying "cradle-to-grave security" denied to poor whites. She charged that the "sentimentalists," typified by Collier and his supporters, would encourage the Indians to "go back to the old picturesque dances and worships" instead of embarking on the road of hard work and civilization. In reply, Mary Austin wrote that Mrs. Seymour had revealed herself "only shallowly acquainted with the Indian himself" and, like the Indian Office, she was "sloppily inaccurate on all points touching the history, the psychology, the racial capacity, and the cultural conditions of the tribes. . . ." Instead of forcing Indians to become poor imitations of white men, she argued, the time had come to recognize "the rapidly growing appreciation of such Indian culture as remains to us, as a National Asset, having something of the same value as the big trees of California and the geysers and buffalos of Yellowstone," and she called upon the Indian Office to abandon its "subservience to the Missionaries" and to abandon its "unreal educational system" whose "whole tendency . . . is to destroy the essential quality of the Indian . . . ."[10]

During his enforced invalidism, Collier had time to contemplate the publicity value of the growing debate over Indian dances and their relation to the larger religious-liberty issue. For some time he had been receiving reports from Zuñi that indicated that the Indian agent there had become embroiled in a struggle with the priests who chose the tribal governor. Then, in April, he was informed that Commissioner Burke and Secretary Work had personally gone to Taos to deliver an ultimatum that two boys withdrawn from school for religious training would have to be returned. By insisting upon the "sacredness of his authority," Collier wrote Cash Asher, "the damfool Burke" had played into their hands. "The Pueblos, aside from the land question, are going to be a storm center . . . over the cultural and religious question," he predicted on the basis of initial reports from Taos. "I believe a renewed attack on this cultural and religious liberty issue, with positive statements of the value of the ethical etc. system of the tribes, will lead us to a new public and into the whole Indian question in the wholesomest way."[11]

Upon his arrival in New Mexico, Collier conferred with the Taos Indians and learned the details of the meeting they had had with Commissioner Burke and Secretary Work on

April 18. Earlier in the year, at the suggestion of his supervisor of education, Burke had ordered a ban on the performance of native dances at the commencement exercises of the Santa Fe Indian school. Shortly afterward, he received a request from the Taos authorities to withdraw two boys from the government school for eighteen months of religious instruction. Failing to find a record of similar requests in the past, Burke called upon Northern Pueblo Superintendent C. J. Crandall for explanation and advice. Crandall's reply was that a government school had just been constructed at Taos and for the first time an effort was being made to enroll all the children. To grant the Indians' request would "almost mean a surrender of our attempt to educate these Pueblos in our Christian civilization," Crandall replied, but to deny it completely would only arouse the Indians. A compromise permitting the absence of the students for two weeks each year was suggested and Burke concurred. The Taos Indians, however, refused to accept it, and on April 18 Burke and Secretary Work appeared in New Mexico to confer with the Taos authorities.

What transpired at the April 18 meeting became thereafter a matter of dispute. Collier, writing for the pueblo, claimed that Burke "denounced the old customs and religions," calling those who practiced them "half-animal," and that Crandall, in the presence of Burke and Work, had ordered the Taos council to return the boys to school and had done so "unquestionably with sharp rudeness." Both Burke and Work denied that an order "barring religious instruction" had been given or that Burke had called the Indians "half-animal." In fact, Burke later wrote Antonio Romero, the governor at Taos, a delegation from Taos had called on him at his hotel in Santa Fe after the meeting, "extending a cordial good-bye and presenting me with a turquoise ring." He had left New Mexico with no idea that his "request" that the pueblo comply with the compulsory-education requirement had "upset" them. Shortly afterward, however, Walter Ufer and other artists began securing affidavits from various Indians as to what had been said by the government officials, and a few days later Tony Luhan, according to a report from Crandall to Burke, "was in Santo Domingo spreading stories as to speeches made by you and Work . . . ." From there he went to Cochiti and "like Paul Revere, on to San Felipe, Sandia, Isleta, and possibly Jemez." The result was a convocation of the All Pueblo Council at Santo Domingo on May 5.[12]

The purpose of the All Pueblo Council meeting was to tie together recent events at Taos and Zuñi with the religious-liberty issue raised by Burke's Circular No. 1665 and subsequent pronouncements. After a morning session at which Collier reported on the progress of the Pueblo Lands Act and then explained Burke's dance regulations, the meeting was recessed. During the break, Collier and two AIDA members from newly formed chapters in California drafted a "declaration" of religious freedom. Beginning with a recitation of the recent directives against Indian dances, the declaration denounced as "shamefully untrue and without any basis of fact or appearance" allegations that the Pueblo's secret dances were "a ribald system of debauchery," proclaimed their belief that "if the right to withdraw the children of Taos for religious instruction be withdrawn, then the Indian religion will die," and drew attention to the Indian Office's policy of compelling children "to receive the teachings of the Christian religion no matter what the parents or the clans may desire." Nothing was said publicly about the Zuñi situation because of the failure of Zuñi to send delegates to the meeting.

Immediately following the All Pueblo Council, Collier and his friends went to Taos, where they spent two more days in council meetings. At these sessions a letter was drafted stating the refusal of Taos to abandon the religious instruction of boys. Collier's activities were closely monitored by Superintendent Crandall and Inspector Warren, both of whom warned Burke that Collier and "the artists" were very active and that Collier was "evidently seizing upon the opportunity to start another campaign, the cry of which shall be 'religious liberty.'" Burke's response was to get in touch with Ralph Twitchell, asking him to consider an injunction against Collier should it be demonstrated that he was "visiting the different pueblos and exciting insurrection as he has done on other occasions." Burke sent a similar request to Secretary Work, but the department solicitor advised against it. At that point, perhaps because the school year was approaching its end, Burke adopted a position of public silence on the topic.[13]

Ironically, in his decision to raise the religious-liberty issue, Collier was not alone. Three days before the meeting of the All Pueblo Council, a band of Christian Indians had been called into session at Santa Ana to form the Council of Progressive Christian Indians. Its purpose was to demand that the Indian Office protect Christian Indians from the baneful influences of the pagan "caciques and governors" and to force the election of governors in place of their selection by the priests. Collier knew nothing of this rival organization until its white proponents, Matthew K. Sniffen, Clara True, and Nina Otero Warren appeared at the All Pueblo Council meeting to observe and take notes.

Although Collier believed that the Council of Progressive Christian Indians was the handiwork of the Indian Office, the records indicate otherwise. It was Clara True and Nina Otero Warren who, believing that Christian Indians at Santa Clara, San Juan, Cochiti, and Santa Ana were being harassed and persecuted for their unwillingness to participate in "pagan ceremonials," planned the convocation. Their concern was primarily with two families, the Hunts of Santa Ana and the Melchors of Cochiti, and with factional differences at Santa Clara, where Clara True lived.

In the Pueblo communities, work on irrigation ditches is a communal affair and assignments of land are made by the tribal officers. In the spring of 1924, Edward Hunt, a Christian Acoma Indian adopted by Santa Ana Pueblo, refused to perform work on the community ditch. At almost the same time, Joseph Melchor, an educated Cochiti Indian whose parents had refused for years to participate in pueblo ceremonies, also refused to work on that pueblo's community ditch. Melchor's case was unique in that after returning from school he had spent years clearing thirty acres of unclaimed and untilled land within the pueblo, which he then irrigated from a ditch owned by Spanish Americans, not by the pueblo. Melchor claimed to have negotiated an agreement with former Superintendent Lonergan in 1921 whereby, since he did not receive water from the pueblo ditch, he was excused from work upon it. Ordered to perform community work by the governor of Cochiti, he refused and appealed to Superintendent Crandall, who sided with the governor. On March 18, Crandall ordered Melchor and his father to perform the work as ordered by the governor, warning that if they did not, the land would probably be reclaimed by the tribe and given to others. When Melchor again refused, his fences were torn down and the land was given to other members of the pueblo. The Spanish Americans, however, refused the new possessors access to their ditch, with the result that nothing was grown on the land that year.

At the Council of Progressive Christian Indians on May 2, the delegates, who numbered fewer than twenty, adopted resolutions demanding that the Melchors be given back their land and that the controversy between Hunt and the officers of Santa Ana be resolved. The delegates also demanded that the government protect their right to practice Christianity and support their refusal "to conform to outgrown customs"; that the selection of tribal officers be democratized through abolition of the power of the caciques and implementation of the ballot; and that the amount of community work be determined by the amount of land occupied, with no work for those who made their living away from the pueblo. Superintendent Crandall attended the meeting and was infuriated at Mrs. Warren's usurpation of his authority. He was also totally opposed to the idea of interference with the traditional method of allocating land and the requirement of community labor on the ditches. Commissioner Burke was dismayed at the prospect of attacks from Collier on the left and the IRA on the right.[14]

Both Collier and the IRA viewed the religious-freedom is-

sue as a vehicle for enhancing the stature of their organizations, but it was the IRA that initially reaped the most
benefit from the issue. In the fall of 1923, in conjunction
with the GFWC and the AIDA, the IRA had conducted an
investigation of the scandalous probate system in eastern
Oklahoma, where corrupt county judges, in cooperation
with unscrupulous attorneys, were involved in plundering
the estates of Indians of the Five Civilized Tribes. The report, *Oklahoma's Poor Rich Indians*, was supposed to appear before the meeting of the Council of One Hundred, but
it was not finished in time. As a result, in January 1924,
Sniffin wrote to John D. Rockefeller, Jr., requesting funds
for printing 10,000 copies. With the support of the National
Council of Churches, Sniffen promised that the report
would be widely circulated and would result "in a storm of
righteous indignation" that would force Congress "to enact
the legislation needed to correct this intolerable situation."
In April the Rockefeller Foundation reported that its Committee on Benevolence was prepared to contribute $5,000 in
1924 and to pledge an additional $3,000 in 1925 and $1,000
in 1926, provided that matching funds could be raised in the
last two years. This was welcome news indeed for the IRA,
whose income had declined precipitously in recent years. In
May 1924, following a recommendation from Sniffen, the
IRA made the momentous decision to hire Clara True as its
"associate secretary" and to make the defense of the Council of Progressive Christian Indians and the abolition of the
secret dances its chief causes in the future. Armed with the
Rockefeller grant and Miss True's services, the IRA's first
step was to divorce Collier and Stella Atwood from the
GFWC at the convention to be held in Los Angeles in June.[15]

Unaware of the IRA's militance and its new funding, Collier too planned to use the GFWC convention for advancing
his position on religious freedom. But he found no support
for a campaign on this issue in the AIDA hierarchy in New
York. Instead, following receipt of an ambitious proposal
from Collier for the coming year, Berle notified him that
the executive committee had voted not to undertake any
new campaigns until the liabilities it had incurred for the

Pueblo defense had been paid. Those liabilities consisted of Collier's salary, which had been unpaid since December 1923, and Berle's fee, which was also unpaid. In addition, Berle wrote, "while sympathizing fully with your point of view," there were additional reasons for avoiding a clash with the Indian Office on the religious issue. For one, Berle did not think "that there is even a sporting chance of securing favorable action in the courts preventing compulsory attendance of the Indian children, or permitting them to be withdrawn from school for as long a period as one year. No other religion in the country can exact this, and none does."

More important, however, was the danger of upsetting the passage of the Pueblo Lands Act, which was coming up for a vote in the House. Surely, Berle cautioned, "with a Washington situation which is hair-trigger in the extreme . . . you would be the last to endanger the results of two years' work now about to become effective . . . ." On the same day that Berle wrote to warn Collier against endangering the passage of the Pueblo Lands Act, Collier wrote the AIDA board that he had discussed the matter with Mrs. Atwood, and since there was no assurance that the Pueblo Lands Act would pass anyway, they had decided "that this concern should not dissuade us from standing up and striking out in the religious issue which is, if possible, more fundamental *and practical* than the land issue."[16]

Despite the opposition of the New York office, Collier plunged ahead with the religious-freedom issue. Following his meetings at Santo Domingo and Taos, he visited other Pueblos on his way to Zuñi. There he found the newly organized coalition of Clara True, Nina Otero Warren, and Matthew Sniffen waiting for him, strengthened by the addition of Father Schuster and a Father Woods from the national office of the Bureau of Catholic Indian Missions. They had been meeting with tribal officials and the local superintendent, C. J. Bauman, for two days, during which period, Collier reported, they had "blackguarded Mrs. Atwood, myself, and the AIDA." The result was that Collier's meeting with tribal officials turned into "sort of a fencing match in which

Mrs. Warren tried to deflect the Indians from stating the facts . . . ." A full report on the Zuñi situation, Collier wrote, would take 10,000 words. Stymied in his efforts to arouse the Zuñis to action, Collier returned to California to write an exposé on Zuñi (it appeared in *Sunset* in July) and to mobilize the California branches of the AIDA behind the Pueblo legal defense and the religious-liberty issue.[17]

The Zuñi situation was a complex one, only imperfectly understood by both sides. It involved primarily a breakdown in the traditional method of appointing the tribal governor and his assistants. Before the early years of the twentieth century, the civil officers of Zuñi were appointed by a council of senior priests, whose choices were installed through the intermediary of a lesser group of priests, the Bow Priests. This system had evolved in order to free the religious leaders from contamination by the problems and quarrels associated with civil rule. But the status of the Bow Priests waned significantly in the late nineteenth century as their function, warfare or the protection of the village, became less necessary. It was destroyed in the early 1900s when the Bow Chiefs' authority was successfully challenged by an accused witch, Nick Tumaka, who succeeded in having federal troops enter the village and arrest the Bow Chiefs for torturing witches. Thereafter the religious leaders were forced to become more intimately associated with civil affairs, and factions developed.

Factionalism at Zuñi was further intensified after 1917 by the activities of an archaeological field party, headed by Frederick W. Hodge of the Heye Foundation's Museum of the American Indian, and by the establishment of a Catholic mission at the village in 1921, at the insistence of the Catholic agent, C. J. Bauman. Although there were few converts to Catholicism, opposition to the agent and the church became crystallized into an anti-Catholic faction, while the agent's supporters became known as the pro-Catholic faction. The religious chiefs were similarly divided, with two of them, Ciaotawa and Hustitio, favoring the pro-Catholic position and the other four opposing. In 1924, as the result of a series of incidents, the two minority chiefs appointed Nick

Tumaka governor and the pueblo was soon in an uproar.

Shortly after Hodge began his excavations at the ruins of Hawikuh, he apparently uncovered some ancient Spanish canes, which once had symbolized civil authority at Zuñi. For years the symbol of civil authority at Zuñi had been a cane given them by Abraham Lincoln. Now, like the other pueblos, they had both the Lincoln and the Spanish canes to pass from governor to governor. Hodge gave the canes to the incumbent governor, a member of the anti-Catholic faction, and this new symbol of the governor's prestige apparently angered Superintendent Bauman.

In late 1923 the rumor began to circulate from the pro-Catholic faction that Hodge's excavation work was desecrating the graves of Zuñi ancestors. Shortly thereafter, Owen Cattell, a cameraman with the Hodge expedition, requested permission to film Zuñi ceremonial dances. The governor and his lieutenants, whom Bauman later charged were "determined to dominate the people contrary to the will of the majority," gave their permission. When some of the Zuñis protested, the "officers talked down the opposition." But later in December, during the annual Shalako dance, Cattell appeared and began filming. At this, "many of the Indians got so wrought up that conditions at one time were bordering on a riot," according to Bauman's report. The agent intervened at this point and ordered Cattell out of the pueblo. Following the Shalako, the religious priests relieved the civil officers who had given permission to the movie crew of their duties and left the offices vacant until late December, when they appealed to Bauman to have Washington prevent further excavation and moviemaking. Shortly thereafter, Bauman intercepted a letter from Hodge in which Hodge claimed that the Indian Office was delighted by recent events because it wished to put a stop to all "Zuñi ceremonies and dances" and to turn control of such events over to the Catholic church.

Cattell's version of what happened was different. He claimed in a letter to Commissioner Burke that Bauman had opposed his filming of the Zuñi ceremonies, but had relented when Cattell secured permission from a council composed of all the important priests and officials except the two members of the pro-Catholic faction. His authority thus questioned, Bauman stirred up the "rowdiest elements in the pueblo" to prevent further filming and then announced publicly that he feared the "riot" had placed the governing authorities in serious trouble, intimating that it was likely they would be removed from office. Cattell left the village as ordered, but, he told Burke, he learned after his departure that government police had seized the Spanish and Lincoln canes and ousted the governor and his assistants.

In March 1924, largely as a result of demands from Collier that the situation be investigated, an Indian Office inspector was sent to Zuñi. His report stated that the Zuñi officials had indeed given Cattell permission to film, but only because Hodge had told them that Commissioner Burke was attempting to do away with all Indian dances. Hodge had argued that if the dances could be filmed and shown to the American public, people would see that they were not evil. Permission to film was then given, but the Shalako was not included. Following the "riot," the governor offered to resign, but was advised to stay on until new officers were appointed. In February a new governor, Nick, was selected by the minority, pro-Catholic priests and, although this was not a popular choice, inspector C. V. Safford reported, it was "permissible under Zuñi custom." Safford then lectured the religious chiefs against the blandishments of "Collier and Mrs. Atwood in rather strong language," and left. Shortly afterward, at the request of Agent Bauman, new canes and badges were sent from Washington and distributed to Nick and his aides. The old canes and Lincoln badges that had previously been the symbols of office were retired from service. There the situation rested until the following year when Collier resurrected it again, this time representing it more accurately as government intrusion into the internal affairs of the pueblo.[18]

Following Collier's departure for California, Clara True and Mrs. Warren quickly mobilized a group of progressive Pueblos, whom they took to Los Angeles to represent the

cause of the Christian Indians at the GFWC's annual meeting. For some time Mrs. Warren had been in communication with Mrs. E. O. Leatherwood, the congressman's wife
who was also president of the Utah Federation of the GFWC.
During the uproar over the Bursum bill, Mrs. Leatherwood
had invited Mrs. Warren to the Utah state convention to
speak on the "immorality of Indian dances," and while her
prediction at that time, that the "views of the artists and
writers will be repudiated," had not yet been justified, she
was eager to try again. Since then she and Mrs. Leatherwood had been searching for some means to topple "our
dear old friend" (Stella Atwood) from her chairmanship of
the National Committee on Indian Welfare. The formation
of the Council of Progressive Christian Indians offered a
means to that end.

In late May, Mrs. Warren and Clara True, accompanied
by a band from the Santa Fe Indian school, met delegates to
the GFWC convention at the railroad depot and persuaded
"thirty seven car loads" of them to attend a presentation by
the "Christian Pueblos" in the patio of the state museum.
There they were treated to a demonstration of "two historical dances," performed by progressives dressed in "perfectly
beautiful old ceremonial heirlooms," and to an appeal by
Desiderio Naranjo of Santa Clara for protection from persecution by the "pagan Pueblos." So successful was this
venture that, at the suggestion of Matthew Sniffen, it was
decided to take a delegation of progressives to Los Angeles
to counter the Collier-Atwood propaganda. "A hearing at
Los Angeles is now inevitable," Mrs. Warren wrote Sniffen
on the eve of the convention.[19]

Although the decision to take the progressive Pueblos to
Los Angeles was a last-minute affair, it was remarkably successful. Warned of the strategy, Collier pressed Charles Lummis into preparing a pamphlet denouncing the progressives
as "paid propagandists of the Indian Bureau" who were being
manipulated by forces opposed to the Pueblo Lands Act.
Distributed to the delegates as they entered the convention
center for the session on Indian welfare, Lummis's attack

exacerbated the situation. Collier and Mrs. Atwood spoke on the Pueblo problem, but a resolution that they had prepared calling for constitutional protection of the Indians' right to religious liberty was sidetracked by the resolutions committee. Collier's presentation, Clara True reported, was so smooth "one could hardly put a finger on where he had advocated paganism." Nevertheless, she was sure that his speech was full of "half lies. I could hardly tell where the lies were myself, yet the whole thing was wrong."

Following Collier's speech, the cause of the progressive Pueblos was presented by Nina Otero Warren and Ida May Adams, a Los Angeles attorney who was one of the authors of the Indian Citizenship Act, which had just become law. Miss Adams "ripped" the Collier-Atwood position and concluded her presentation by presenting "old Melchor," whom she charged had "lost his home because he worshipped the Christian God." At the end of the session, an innocuous resolution calling for reorganization of the Indian Office to the end that all Indians might receive "justice" was adopted. But the real strength of the True-Warren-progressive faction was revealed when it was announced that the appointment of a chairman for the Indian Welfare Committee would be delayed until fall when new officers of the GFWC would meet in executive session in Washington.[20]

The decision to postpone the reappointment of Mrs. Atwood touched off a furious behind-the-scenes battle for the remainder of the summer. Sensing victory, the True-Warren faction lobbied strenuously against her reappointment and enlisted the support of Mrs. Grace Thorpe Baer, the president of the New Mexico Federation of Women's Clubs. At the invitation of Nina Otero Warren, whose efforts were encouraged by the Indian Office, Mrs. Baer was brought from Roswell to Santa Fe in late July; there she was briefed by Mrs. Warren, Clara True, A. B. Renehan, and Edgar L. Hewett, the director of the School of American Archaeology in Santa Fe. She was informed, especially by Hewett, that Collier, in the name of the GFWC, had been "inciting [the Pueblos] to an alarming extent to distrust the government . . . ."

As a result of this visit, Mrs. Baer immediately wrote the new president of the GFWC, Mrs. John W. Sherman, opposing Mrs. Atwood's reappointment and recommending that the position of "research agent" be abolished.

Upon receipt of Mrs. Baer's letter, Mrs. Sherman wrote Stella Atwood to suggest that representatives of both sides of the controversy attend the executive board meeting in Washington in September. Mrs. Atwood wired in reply that she had no money for the trip, would not attend, and that if there were any charges against her or Collier, they should be made in writing. Collier, in a more conciliatory tone, informed Mrs. Sherman that he thought her suggestion a good one and that he would attend such a meeting if requested. In the end, no representatives from either faction were invited and a compromise of sorts was adopted. Stella Atwood was reappointed to the chairmanship of the Indian Welfare Committee, but she was instructed by the executive committee that "research specialists" were unnecessary. In this way Collier's official affiliation with the GFWC was severed.[21]

Collier's ouster from the GFWC should have produced joy in the camp of his opponents, but any tendency to celebrate was tempered by the revelation that they had lost the greater fight in the Pueblo country. During the summer, Commissioner Burke decided not to force compulsory attendance of the boys at Taos and he ruled in favor of the Pueblos' right to demand community work from their members.

At Taos the decision to permit the boys to leave school for religious training was reached through a series of compromises. Superintendent Crandall first advised Burke that the best course was to insist upon enforcement of the compulsory-schooling requirement, but to make no attempt to force the boys' return. If the demands of the Taos council were to be publicly accepted, he warned, "we virtually surrender to the Indian government and they become dictators . . . ." In June, Burke notified Crandall that the government would acknowledge the right to remove children from school if the number was small and the Taos council would agree that all children should attend school until they completed the sixth grade. Calling the whole incident "a tempest in a teapot which could have been amicably settled without Collier," he notified Crandall that in this way "we can arrange to comply without losing our argument." Although not entirely pleased with the decision, Crandall met quietly with the Taos council in mid-August and informed them of the commissioner's decision. He warned, however, that the boys must be returned to school to complete their education once they had finished the course of religious instruction and he also informed them that religious liberty worked both ways: no one was to be forced to participate in ceremonials against his wishes. To emphasize his authority, Crandall issued orders that all schoolboys at Taos must have their hair cut short and adopt "citizen clothes while in school." This prompted a petition for his removal, but for the most part Taos remained quiescent for the next year.[22]

More alarming to the IRA was Burke's decision in July that community work would be required of all Pueblo residents. Community work was a form of taxation, Burke wrote, and was necessary for the economic good of the community. At the same time, he advised pueblo officials to consider a money payment or the hiring of a substitute in lieu of work, and he instructed them not to schedule work on Sundays or holidays except in emergencies. He also stated his opinion that the Melchors should be given back their land and have their fences restored if they would agree to conform in the future.

Immediately, the IRA protested the decision through Matthew Sniffen, who wrote Burke that his directive not only was harmful to the Melchors, but that it endangered the freedom of all the Christian Indians because it did not make clear that participation in community work "does not include participation in dances and ceremonies." Burke, he charged, had "ignored the BIG issue of the Pueblo controversy, which is real religious liberty." Burke replied that the issue of religious liberty had been given careful consideration and he had concluded "purposely" to omit any reference to religious liberty in his instructions "because we

were not satisfied that there is any serious interference with
the religious beliefs of any considerable number of Pueblos,
and furthermore, we are refusing to recognize that in any of
the propaganda being circulated by a certain agitator there
is involved any question of religious liberty . . . ."

Burke's decision to unhold the Pueblo governors and their
councils brought S. M. Brosius to New Mexico in early August. Burke's order, he reported, had created a deplorable situation among the progressive Pueblos, who were now being
subordinated to the "commands of the ignorant, pagan Indians." Unless they were supported by their "outside friends,"
the progressives would soon be ruined financially and be
forced to "abandon entirely what has been taught to them
in the Government schools on their upward road to civilized habits of living." The Melchors had refused to accept
Burke's ruling and, with the help of Clara True, had retained
A. B. Renehan to protect their interests, he reported. On behalf of the IRA, Brosius guaranteed Renehan's fee. He also
encountered Mrs. Grace Thorpe Baer, whom he briefed on
Collier, "the propagandist against the progressive element
and the upholder of the immoral practices of the Pueblos."
As a result of this meeting, Brosius predicted that "Collier-
ism is doomed in New Mexico."[23]

The opposition of the IRA placed Commissioner Burke in
a difficult position, which was made more unbearable by an
article appearing in the *New York Times* on July 13. Drafted
originally by Collier, the article was rewritten by Cash Asher
and appeared almost simultaneously with Collier's defense
of religious freedom, "Persecuting the Pueblos," in the July
issue of *Sunset*. Having just survived Collier's onslaught
against the Bursum bill, Burke now found himself pilloried
on the religious-liberty issue, despite the fact that he was
moving to uphold the Pueblo authorities at Taos and Cochiti.
He was further frustrated when his own efforts to reply to
Collier's "false" charges were ignored by the *Times*. No order denying Indians the right to instruct their children in
"ancient tribal rituals," or affecting their right to perpetuate
"any of their so-called religious rites or any of their tradi-

tional and ancient customs," had been issued, Bruke wrote
to the managing editor. "The real point at issue is that of
compulsory education . . . . It seems to me that [Collier's]
claim that compulsory education is an unwarranted interference with religious liberty is very far-fetched." Convinced
that the *Times* was "desirous of discrediting the Government's administration of Indian Affairs," and hoping to re-
gain the favor of the IRA, Burke blundered again when he
agreed to support the IRA's distribution of a letter by the
former head of Indian Office's liquor enforcement division,
W. E. ("Pussyfoot") Johnson.

On August 1, Johnson, now the director of the World
League Against Alcoholism, temporarily visiting in the
United States, penned a lengthy diatribe against Pueblo
dances, which he charged were based upon phallic worship
and were "hideous, obscene, and revolting." Stating that he
had been requested to tell the truth about the dances by
some of his former Pueblo friends and that he had had access
to "file after file of inspector's reports in the Indian Bureau"
and the IRA offices (when in reality he had been recruited
by Clara True and had access only to the IRA copy of the
secret dance file), Johnson painted a lurid picture of sexual
excess, and ended with the wholly fictitious charge that the
boys at Taos had been withdrawn "for a two year course in
sodomy." So extreme were Johnson's charges that it was little wonder the *New York Times* refused to publish them,
but by this time Burke and the IRA had become so paranoid
that Burke volunteered to mimeograph the letter in the Indian Office for distribution by the IRA to members of the
Council of One Hundred and others "who have been poi-
soned with Collier's propaganda."[24]

Burke's offer coincided with the entrance into the fray of
Herbert Welsh, the aging founder of the IRA. Content thus
far to let Sniffen and Brosius do the society's work, Welsh
was horrified by the contents of the secret dance file, which
confirmed everything he had ever believed about the American Indian. Independently wealthy, the son of a "solid Philadelphia businessman and practical philanthropist," Welsh

believed that as a young man of thirty he had abandoned a promising career as a painter in order "to give our Indians . . . a fair chance to live and support themselves honestly," and to be saved from "rum drinking and sexual licentiousness." In 1882 he founded the IRA and dedicated it to the extension of Christianity and the private ownership of property among the Indians. Although he himself had often been critical of the Indian Office, Welsh had never questioned the general direction of the assimilationist philosophy, and he found Collier's brand of criticism distasteful in method and destructive in aim.

In mid-August 1924, Welsh, upset because Commissioner Burke had refused to uphold the Melchor family's resistance to tribal officers, notified the IRA membership of the Rockefeller grant and informed them that with this new source of income, the IRA had launched a "critical and tremendous struggle" to protect the Christian Indians from persecution "by their reactionary, heathen breathren." Commissioner Burke and Secretary Work, "who once nobly protected these people," had now "weakened from their original excellent position" as a direct result of the unfortunate but "great propagandist power of Mr. John Collier," he wrote. To counteract the baneful influence of Collier, Welsh instructed IRA members to write directly to President Coolidge and to insist that he countermand these two officials, whose actions had abandoned the Christian Pueblos to those who were attempting to force them to "support the loathsome, degrading, obscene rites which lurk hidden in the heart of the old religion." A "magnificent letter" by W. E. Johnson, "full, powerful in expression and overwhelming in indictment," was available from the IRA office for those who requested it.

The mass distribution of "Pussyfoot" Johnson's letter, coupled with a letter from Welsh in the *New York Times* in October, in which he urged the Indian Office to curb "pagan ceremonies," produced another storm of public indignation, but it was not all favorable to the IRA. Frederick W. Hodge was again compelled to deny the charges and to deny the

Figure 21.   John Collier (second from right) and Pearl Chase (second from left) at the Santa Barbara Mission, circa 1924. Courtesy of the University Library, University of California at Santa Barbara.

"fanatical outburst" of Johnson; and Alfred Kroeber, whom Collier had been unsuccessfully urging to become involved, was at last aroused. Kroeber wrote Welsh requesting a copy of the "sheaf of affidavits" in the secret dance file. "Frankly, I suspect exaggeration somewhere," he wrote, but if the documents should reveal some "important element that I and other anthropologists have failed to discover in studying Pueblo religion," he was willing to study the matter. Welsh replied that the dance file was so objectionable that it could not be transmitted through the U.S. mail, but that Kroeber was welcome to view it at the Philadelphia office.

The only humorous moment in this otherwise dreary

controversy came in September when Welsh distributed copies of an article on "The Quaker Saint, John Woolman," and Collier, hearing of it, requested one for himself. "I have hope even for that brilliant, but as we think, misguided man, Mr. John Collier," Welsh wrote in a letter chiding Secretary Work for his timidity. "If John Collier should become converted by the Grace of God to the religion of John Woolman . . . our contention will have been gained and this unhappy, ridiculous, and at the same time tragic controversy, will have come to an end." Welsh was shortly disabused of his optimism when Collier wrote him to protest the IRA's constant references to the secret dance file, whose "affidavits simply do not prove what they say and are difficult to deal with because they are unprintable." Although expressing "great respect" for what Welsh had done in the past, Collier informed him bluntly that he was "misinformed" on the dance issue and in a second letter accused him of being manipulated by Clara True and A. B. Renehan because he considered "the annihilation of the Indian culture system to be desirable" and "the Pueblo social institutions of no worth." Nor were Kroeber, Hodge, and Collier the only ones to be offended by Welsh's vehemence. Amelia White complained that Welsh's diatribes were "doing more harm than good to the Indian Rights Association," and Charles Burke wrote that "it is apparent that he is becoming more erratic and that age is affecting him. . . ."[25]

If Herbert Welsh and Charles Burke had known the desperate financial condition of the AIDA in late 1924, they might not have been in such a panic. The truth was that with the passage of the Pueblo Lands Act most of the AIDA's eastern financial support evaporated. For the next year Collier was forced to devote most of his time to fund-raising activities in California, which left him little time to attack the system.

The first warning of financial problems came in the spring of 1924 when A. A. Berle completed his work on the Pueblo bill and submitted his resignation. Berle had been paid only

$450 for his services since the previous December and was understandably anxious to settle his account before leaving. Collier, however, was characteristically unconcerned. He was, moreover, peeved at Berle's failure to dedicate himself to the cause and he was particularly upset that Berle had not supported him in pushing the religious-freedom issue. Collier himself had not been paid a salary from the AIDA from the time Berle was hired (although he continued to receive $5,000 a year from Mrs. Vosburg) and he had paid most of his expenses since that time out of his remaining inheritance. The cause was so important, he wrote the AIDA board, that "whatever happens to the budget, I shall somehow manage to keep on with the work." Only ill health could stop him. Berle's dunning letters continued on through the summer, but at the end of the year he still had not been paid.[26]

Nor had the work of Cash Asher in New York been successful. His major effort to raise money, an "Old Frontier and Indian Ball" in the spring of 1924, was a "grand financial failure" in which many guests were admitted without paying and the bartender "made good his escape with four or five hundred dollars of our money." Following a board decision in May not to authorize any new expenses until old liabilities were paid, Asher could not even assemble a quorum of the board until the fall, despite frequent pleas from Collier for help with the Pueblo legal defense work. The board, Asher informed Collier, "has become rather detached." In the meanwhile, most of the available money was vanishing "in the scramble after more" and it was impossible for him to do anything, "flat broke as we are." In February 1925, he made one last effort in the form of the "Aztec Ball" at the Ambassador Hotel. Not only did the project lose money, but its "unseemly and ribald features . . . so fully contravening a wholesome respect for law and the amenities of life," resulted in the resignations of Rodman Wanamaker and Joseph Kossuth Dixon, the president and secretary, respectively, of the National American Indian Memorial Association, from the AIDA national advisory board. Following this second disaster, Asher submitted his resignation, which was accepted in May 1925.[27]

To stave off the collapse of the AIDA, Collier turned to his California friends. During the summer of 1924, he succeeded in organizing branches of the AIDA in San Francisco and Los Angeles and in restructuring a branch in Santa Barbara, which had been formed in 1923 shortly after incorporation of the national office. Although these AIDA chapters had the appearance of substance, with officers and boards of directors, they were essentially fronts for several wealthy Californians who were devoted to Collier. The Santa Barbara chapter, for instance, was really Pearl Chase, a wealthy, civic-minded dynamo whose contributions to city planning, conservation, national parks, and a bewildering number of other causes, are still little known outside California. From 1923 to 1933 she was the conduit for sizable periodic contributions from a reclusive, neurasthenic philanthropist, William Bingham, II. The southern California chapter in Los Angeles was Collier's old friend, Dr. John Haynes. The northern and central California chapter in San Francisco was more broadly based and active. Initially it was directed by Jay B. Nash, director of parks, recreation, and physical education in Oakland and an old friend of Collier's from his People's Institute days, and by Walter Woehlke. But the real strength of the San Francisco chapter derived from three wealthy benefactors: Charles de Y. Elkus, Max L. Rosenberg, and Chauncey Goodrich. Rosenberg was a director of the firm of Rosenberg Brothers. Goodrich was a member of the Shafter family, an attorney who retired from active practice when he was forty to devote himself to "public work" and the "management of a group of family estates." He was also a student of the American Indian, and, according to Collier, had "published the authoritative treatise on Indian law as affecting California Indians." By 1925 Rosenberg and Goodrich were jointly underwriting $500 per month for Collier's salary. Charles de Y. Elkus, son of a wealthy Sacramento drygoods merchant whose wife was the sister of Michael and Charles de Young, founders of the *San Francisco*

Figure 22.   James W. Young (extreme left) and John Collier (third from left) on the trail to Blue Lake, summer 1926. The Taos Indian (second from left) has been identified by Donald Collier as Antonio Mirabal. An account of this trip, which resulted in Collier and Young being turned away from the religious ceremonies at Blue Lake, was published by Young in the Field Museum of Natural History *Bulletin,* 37 (November 1966), pp. 6–7. Courtesy of Field Museum of Natural History and Donald Collier.

Chronicle, was a graduate of Stanford University and Harvard Law School. A close personal friend of Collier, he had purchased property within one of the Pueblo grants near Santa Fe in the early 1920s. Although he may also have made financial contributions to the AIDA, his primary contribution was supervision of the Pueblo legal defense, which was largely underwritten by Dr. Haynes. All of the Californians were dedicated to the Pueblos, but they were also insistent that Collier become involved in the protection

of California Indians, particularly the Mission and Palm
Springs Indians. For this reason, and to effect the reorganization of the AIDA, Collier was forced to spend most of
his time in California until the fall of 1925.[28]

The organization of the California chapters came just in
time. During the fight to oust Mrs. Atwood from her post in
the GFWC, Matthew Sniffen had discovered a weak link in
the chain of Collier's supporters in the person of Kate Vosburg. Even before the uproar at the GFWC convention in
Los Angeles, Mrs. Vosburg had expressed reservations about
Collier's activities. Her concerns were not ideological, although she did feel the agitation over religious freedom was
interfering with more important things, but personal. As
early as March 1924, she had voiced concern about Collier's
frenetic activities, expressing the belief that if he continued the pace he would kill himself and "she said she simply
would not be a party to it." Her agreement to finance Collier
for two years would expire in the fall of 1924 and while she
indicated "she was more than willing to help him personally . . . she would not agree to do it if he kept on the way
he had been doing." Mrs. Vosburg had also broken with
Stella Atwood, whose reappointment she "bitterly opposed."
Collier found it "impossible for me to pretend to agree with
her" and at a meeting in mid-September Mrs. Vosburg informed Collier that her "contribution to my salary will
cease after November." Sniffen, who had learned of the potential break in August and who received a personal visit in
Los Angeles from Mrs. Vosburg several days after her confrontation with Collier, took partial credit for the victory,
predicting that with his financial support weakened and his
repudiation by the GFWC imminent, "Collier's work will
soon cease."

Sniffen, however, failed to reckon with Collier's determination and his uncanny ability to survive. Notified by
Dr. Haynes that he had heard "very disquieting rumors"
that the GFWC had severed its connections with Collier,
and that he was having second thoughts about underwriting
the Pueblo defense in light of this development, Collier as-

sured Haynes that recent events would have no influence on his work. "The opposition has believed that if I were killed off, or the mass-support [of the GFWC] separated from me, the indictment [of federal Indian policy] would simply lapse," he wrote Haynes, but they were wrong. Adequate financial support could be obtained simply by finding "the proper methods" to dramatize the plight of the Indians, he was convinced. "It is the role of our group to continue developing our indictment of the 'System' and to force on Congress the task of uprooting that which is a system of virtual peonage, of exploitation, and special privilege of the meanest sort." In a letter to another friend, Collier expressed the current difficulties in terms of an analogy from his camping days: "It is as though a 200 pound camp-pack has been increased to 400 pounds; the marching is painful and slower but we will make camp all right."[29]

The IRA, however, was not yet through in its efforts to undermine Collier. In September, Harvey M. Watts, a newspaperman from Philadelphia and a friend of Herbert Welsh, was recruited to take the offensive directly to the AIDA president, Irving Bacheller. Assembling a sheaf of AIDA newsletters on the religious-freedom issue that had been mailed out over Bacheller's signature, Watts sent them directly to Bacheller, with a covering letter calling attention to the "absurd position" in which he was being placed "by the violence of the propaganda carried on by your paid Secretary Collier and by Mrs. Austin . . . ." When he received no reply to his first letter, Watts wrote again the following month, this time insisting that Bacheller take a stand on the religious-liberty issue, either by repudiating Collier or by defending his "perfectly stupid and amazing insistence that the Indian shall be forced back into a degrading barbarism, resistant to the Christian religion . . . ." Two weeks later Bacheller notified Welsh that he had accepted the AIDA presidency "only at the earnest solicitation of my friend. John Collier," that he would not enter the controversy because he had been too busy to keep up with it, and that because he was so busy and could devote "little attention to the affairs of that Association," he had submitted his resignation. Although he was embarrassed by Bacheller's defection, Collier wrote that "his resignation is just as well. He never was able to apply himself as he thought at the start he might do." Bacheller's resignation was not formally accepted until six months later, while Collier toyed with the idea of interesting Hamlin Garland in the post. In the end, Haven Emerson, a distinguished physician, professor of public health administration at Columbia University, and a friend of Collier from his People's Institute days, was named to the post.[30]

The defection of Bacheller, the paralysis of the New York office (which maintained its existence only through the continued contributions of Dorothy Straight), and the loss of Mrs. Vosburg's subsidy made reorganization of the AIDA the major priority for 1925. In December 1924, Collier finally broke away long enough to confront the New York board. Before the meeting he confided to Fred Stein that his personal finances had been reduced to less than zero. "Since the Indian work began we have used up almost exactly $6,000.00 which was inherited money stored away against the boy's schooling," he wrote. In July, Lucy had been forced to quit working to attend to John, Jr., who had severely injured his arm in an accident that had produced "a good deal of bone destruction at the joints"; his own hospital bills from the operation were unpaid; and since Mrs. Vosburg's decision, he had had "no salary from any source." Only the "unexpected offer" of assistance from his brother-in-law, Henry Stanton, a partner in the Chicago office of the J. Walter Thompson advertising company, had saved him from having to choose between diverting money from the "Pueblo legal costs . . . or else quitting the Indian work . . . ." Facing the inevitable, the New York board voted to "invite" the California branches to "assume leadership," with the request that this be done in such a way "as not to diminish the responsibility of the New York Division." To reduce pressure upon the New York board's indebtedness, Collier moved that his salary be removed from its budget after January 15, 1925, and the motion was adopted.

In early 1925 there was a series of board meetings in California, the result of which was the preparation of a "minimum subsistence budget" providing for the Pueblo legal defense, a $6,000 annual salary for Collier and some limited travel funds. No funds for operation of the branch offices were included. The budget was underwritten by Dr. Haynes, William Bingham, Dorothy Straight, Rosenberg, and Goodrich. To the list of major donors was now added the name of James W. Young, the partner of Collier's brother-in-law in the Chicago office of J. Walter Thompson. Like Charles de Y. Elkus, Young had come to New Mexico in the early 1920s, vacationed yearly thereafter in Santa Fe, and had become captivated by the Pueblos. He first met Collier in 1923 when the Pueblo delegation passed through Chicago on its way to the Bursum bill hearings. A specialist in magazine advertising, Young was persuaded by Collier and Henry Stanton to attend a meeting of the San Francisco board in February 1925, at which time he put forth a proposal for "some kind of publication" to educate the public and to increase AIDA membership. When he offered the facilities of the J. Walter Thompson firm to produce the magazine, his personal "supervision of the publication," and a contribution of $1,000 to get it launched, the proposal was accepted. In June 1925, the first issue of *American Indian Life* appeared. While it never rivaled the *National Geographic* as Young originally envisioned, it did provide a powerful voice for Collier's reform program and a counter to the IRA's *Indian Truth*. In time, Young was prevailed upon to donate annual sums up to $3,000, until the 1929 stock market crash caused him to retrench.[31]

By the spring of 1925, for the first time in its existence, the AIDA was experiencing a degree of financial stability. After considerable thought, it was decided not to close the New York office, but to maintain it as the symbolic national headquarters. Consideration was given to making the national office responsive to the California chapters through the appointment of Californians to its board, but this too was dropped. Instead, following the remarriage of Dorothy Straight in the summer of 1925 and her resignation as trea-

surer, most of the Bingham gift was thereafter funneled from
Santa Barbara to New York to pay the headquarters' expenses. At the insistence of Dr. Haynes and Max Rosenberg,
Collier was kept busy hustling contributions and member-
ships in California and lobbying before the state legislature
for "an investigation of California Indians.." These efforts
culminated in November 1925 in a performance of Pueblo
dances at the Fairmont Hotel in San Francisco. Highlighted
by presentations of "The Taos Pueblo Singers" and "The
Taos and Tesuque Dancers," the program also consisted
of speeches by Collier on the "Significance of the Pueblo
Dances" and a talk by Sotero Ortiz, chairman of the All
Pueblo Council, entitled "What the Indian's Religion Means
to Him." According to Collier's report, some $11,000 was
raised by the performance and an earlier one in Salt Lake
City, which, after expanses, netted between $6,000 and
$8,000. More importantly, he wrote, "were the hundreds,
even thousands, of new friends enlisted . . . and the large
political help which was ensured through the meetings held
by the delegates."[32]

By the time Collier was again able to assume the offensive against the Indian Office in the early fall of 1925, the
controversy over the Indian dances had largely subsided.
This was due in no small part to excesses by Herbert Welsh,
which completely alienated the IRA from the Indian Office.
    In the fall of 1924, when Collier and the AIDA were expe-
riencing their most serious difficulties, Welsh launched an
attack on Commissioner Burke for his alleged retreat "from
the safe, conservative view" he had previously held "regarding the defense of the progressive Christian Indians of the
Pueblos. . . ." In the annual report of the IRA, Welsh charged
that only Brosius, Sniffen, and "our new representative, Miss
Clara D. True," were holding the line against the tremendous
assault made upon [the Christian Pueblos] by those who
wished to sweep the old government policy into chaos. . . ."
With copies of the annual report, Welsh sent form letters
to all the Episcopal bishops of the United States in which

he made charges against the pagan Indians at Cochiti, Santo Domingo, and Taos exceeding anything yet reported: whippings, beatings and even "unreported deaths." The result, Burke reported, was that he was "deluged by letters from Episcopal Bishops . . . prompted by Welsh." In February 1925, Burke wrote Welsh demanding that he produce his evidence for the "cruel beatings and deaths" that he had alleged. That same day he notified Matthew Sniffen that the secret dance file would no longer be made available to the IRA: "We doubt very much the wisdom of circulating the contents of what you term the Secret Dance File, as we do not believe it would serve any good purpose."

Burke's coolness toward the IRA only intensified Welsh's ire. In March, he again circularized the bishops to complain that Burke, who "joined our Church under the influence of Bishop Hare," was unwilling to rise above his commitment to "the interests of the Republican Party," and was being intimidated by the "writer-artist-scientist" group led by John Collier. This outburst prompted a response from the Episcopal bishop of the missionary district of New Mexico, Fred B. Howden, who conducted an investigation of the southern Pueblos and reported that the charges of beatings and death were "exaggerated" and that sexual immorality among the Pueblos was, "on the basis of comparison with whites, . . . not at all abnormal." When Burke had Bishop Howden's letter copied and mailed to his detractors, Welsh angrily wrote the bishop that he did not understand the situation, enclosed a copy of the dance file, and informed him that since Burke had not corrected the immoral conditions in the "ample time" allotted him, the IRA "must now make our appeal to the public conscience of this country." Nothing apparently was done to make good this threat. In June, Sniffen appealed to former President William Howard Taft in behalf of the progressive Pueblos, and Taft dutifully wrote Coolidge. But his letter did not urge the IRA position. Instead, voicing a weariness that was probably shared by many others, Taft sympathized with the government's plight. During his own administration, he told Coolidge, the "situation which was

least within my grasp and least satisfactory for investigating purposes was the dealing with the Indians." Often caught
between "the cupidity and rapacity of their neighbors," and
"the transcendental but impractical views of the extremists," he had found it "very difficult" ever to reach a "satisfactory conclusion to Indian matters."[33]

In addition to the mounting evidence that the IRA campaign against the Pueblos was poorly grounded in the facts,
there were other problems within the IRA that were not
made public. In early 1925, Clara True was fired from her
post as associate secretary. Because of the success that she
and Mrs. Warren had enjoyed at the GFWC convention and
their partial victory in separating Collier from the GFWC,
she had been permitted, at the request of the Indian Office,
to remain in New Mexico with Mrs. Warren during the fall
and early winter of 1924 to participate in yet another investigation of the Pueblo situation. During this time, True informed her superiors, she had also made contact with several
wealthy philanthropists who were contemplating the creation of a $300,000 trust fund for the IRA. This arrangement,
Sniffen later explained, seemed justified at the time because
the Pueblo situation "had been so grossly misrepresented in
the public press . . . that it was having a very injurious effect
on our financial constituency."

The difficulty was that the money was never pledged and
repeated efforts to have Miss True come east for fund-raising
work were ignored. At last, in early January 1925, she was
ordered to Philadelphia. Once there, she argued repeatedly
with Welsh and others about the nature of her assignment.
IRA officials insisted that she become involved in "developing our financial constituency," especially since the time
was approaching for the renewal of the Rockefeller grant,
which was contingent upon matching contributions. Miss
True, however, insisted that her "duty as a Christian" was
to remain in New Mexico and there win the struggle for the
progressive Pueblos. On February 14, at a specially called
board meeting, Welsh gave her written instructions, which
stated that she was to remain in Philadelphia to raise money

and to increase the IRA membership. Miss True accused Welsh of "using some harsh epithet to her, burst into tears," and fled the meeting. Later that day she announced that she was returning to New Mexico. "To avoid the appearance of dissention," she wired Sniffen that she was taking leave without pay.

Clara True's abrupt departure created grave problems for Herbert Welsh. On February 20, he was forced to explain the situation to the IRA board. Blaming the Indian Office for "extraordinary tactics of stupid obstruction," which had prevented the "great reforms which we, Miss True, and other had designed . . . from being successful," Welsh informed the board that Clara True was undoubtedly suffering from knowledge that the Christian Indians were still being unjustly persecuted. At the same time, her erratic behavior over the past five months had caused him to become increasingly "uneasy about her." On three different occasions, he reported, she had promised documents of the "highest importance" and each time she had failed to produce them. Furthermore, during the eight months of her employment, he "never could tell . . . what she was doing." Other board members agreed that she was "not a desirable person to represent the association" and that she was unqualified to raise money. At the close of the meeting it was agreed to accept her resignation, and a telegram to that effect was dispatched to New Mexico.

Clara True, however, refused to admit that she had resigned. She insisted that she had been "dismissed" and that the IRA had abandoned the Christian Pueblos. There would be no public admission on her part that her affiliation with the IRA had been severed. Indeed, upon her return to New Mexico, she assisted the progressives to regroup and she reported in February, they had soon forced the enemy "to run up a white flag." All this had been done with full credit to the IRA. If her dismissal were to be made public, the announcement "will have to come from Philadelphia."

By the summer of 1925, backlash from the dance controversy and embarrassment over the Clara True affair made

Herbert Welsh increasingly snippy and discontented. In July he learned that an investigation of the Pueblos that he had ordered Matthew Sniffen to conduct ("rape on women, beatings, and even murder etc.,") was to be conducted instead by Brosius, whom he considered "unequal to the task." Comparing his authority to that of the "President of the United States," Welsh insisted that he alone had the authority to designate agents for such tasks, and he demanded, "Who made that arrangement and why was I not consulted in regard to it?" He then petulantly announced that he was willing "to have all my suggestions brushed aside and disregarded and even my executive rights invaded, for the time is very near at hand when the Society will have to get along without me, and I am enthusiastically sure that in this new era the work will be done better than if one so thoroughly identified with the ancien regime were around to muddle and complicate the acts and designs of the new one." Six months later, on the forty-third anniversary of the founding of the IRA, Welsh submitted his resignation "before I more completely distress my associates . . . with the inevitable weaknesses and puerilities of old age." The resignation was not accepted until 1927, but the IRA had been seriously damaged by the dance controversy. It had lost its influence over the Indian Office and seen its premier position among Indian defense societies diminished.[34]

The ouster of Clara True was paralleled by the firing of Nina Otero Warren. In December 1924 the Interior Department reorganized its inspection division, making all inspectors responsible to the secretary rather than to the individual bureaus. Mrs. Warren was the first to be discharged. Privately, Commissioner Burke confided that she had been let go because she had been involved in her brother's political campaign for governor the preceding fall, but under the circumstances, it seems probable that Burke was relieved to have an excuse to detach himself from someone who had become so clearly attached to the IRA position.

With the removal of Clara True and Nina Otero Warren, the Melchor and Hunt problems were soon cleared up. In a series of meetings coordinated by Superintendent Crandall, the Cochiti governing council agreed in May 1925 to restore Melchor's land and to exempt him from community work "except his legitimate share of road upkeep" and ditch work if he took water from a community ditch. In June, Santa Ana Pueblo bought the property of Edward Hunt for $3,375, using reimbursable funds from the Indian Office. By fall, the cause of the progressive Pueblos was dead. One of them had "run amuck," Clara True reported. Another at Santa Clara had died of cancer. Indian Inspector Safford had died, as had Emil Bibo, the Bernalillo trader who had provided several affidavits alleging obscenities, and the young governor of Santa Clara Pueblo was in the process of dying. Matthew Sniffen reported in September that Miss True had "few friends" left in Santa Fe, where she was regarded as "brilliant but unbalanced, a dangerous woman and a double-crosser."[35]

The decline of the IRA and the dance issue coincided with the reorganization of the AIDA and Collier's return to New Mexico. It was not long before he found new ammunition for his cause.

In early 1925 the Zuñi priests appointed a new governor from the anti-Catholic faction. When Agent Bauman presented him with the canes and badges, which had been requested from Washington the previous year, the governor refused to accept them, saying that only the Spanish canes donated by the Hodge expedition were acceptable as symbols of his office. Bauman, who had collected the old canes and badges at the request of the previous governor, Nick, now insisted that he knew "nothing of their whereabouts" and refused to make the Spanish canes available. When the Zuñis petitioned Commissioner Burke for the restoration of the ancient canes, nothing was done, and resentment against Bauman mounted at the pueblo.

Then, in May, two members of the peyote cult at Taos appeared at a ceremony dressed in nonceremonial attire. Warned to leave, they refused and were later brought before the Taos council, which assigned them a fine of $2 or a single lash with a leather whip, applied "on the back through the blanket and clothes." The two men chose to receive the lash and one of them stated publicly that he had done so in order to seek the intervention of the Indian Office. Throughout the summer, Agent Crandall conferred with Commissioner Burke, and in late July Burke authorized the arrest of the Taos council. On the eve of the annual Taos pilgrimage to their sacred Blue Lake, Crandall arrested all but one member of the Taos council, transported them to Santa Fe where they were jailed under $500 bond, and the following day took them before the federal judge, Colin Neblett. Immediately, the AIDA attorney assigned to the Pueblo land defense, Richard Hanna, stepped into the case. Judge Neblett, in a ruling similar to the one he had delivered years earlier in the case of northern Pueblo Superintendent Lonergan, ordered the Indians released, saying the federal courts had no jurisdiction in the matter. Shortly thereafter, Collier arrived on the scene and a meeting of the All Pueblo Council was called for August 31, 1925.

The focus of the council was upon the Taos and Zuñi situations and the problem of government interference in the governance of the pueblos. But Collier also revived interest in the religious-liberty issue by informing the Indians of the contents of the secret dance file; he also interjected the issue of "personal liberty" by denouncing a plan formulated during the summer by Edgar Hewett and Superintendent Crandall that would have forbidden the northern Pueblos to attend the annual Gallup fair and the southern Pueblos to attend the Santa Fe fiesta. In July, Crandall had warned Cochiti officials that if their people attended the Gallup fair, they would be "put under arrest and returned or sent to jail." Following his arrest of the Taos officials, the threat seemed to portend a new wave of Indian Office interference in Pueblo affairs.

At the conclusion of the one-day meeting, the delegates signed a "Declaration to the President of the United States, the Congress, and Our Friends the American People." The

Figure 23.   Lucy Wood Collier, circa 1926. Courtesy of John Collier, Jr.

declaration appealed "against the effort to destroy our self-government"; for "fair play in the treatment of our religions," including a denunciation of "shameful statements [which] have been secretly circulated among important people" and which were "false in every part and are slanderous and libelous"; and it asked why the Indian Office was attempting to take away "human liberties and our personal dignity" guaranteed by the laws of Spain, Mexico, and the United States. The declaration closed with a reminder that three years earlier the Pueblos had appealed against the confiscation of their lands and they had been heard. "Now we meet to appeal for things more sacred to us and more necessary to our life even than our lands."

In attendance at the Santo Domingo meeting as the representative of the Indian Office was Herbert Hagerman, the special representative to the Navajos and a member of the

Pueblo Lands Board. Immediately following the meeting, he sent Commissioner Burke a lengthy report, which faithfully reproduced the arguments Collier had made. Although he was not sympathetic to Collier, whom he accused of staging the meeting "as a vehicle to get publicity for the Taos incident," Hagerman cautioned Burke that the Pueblos were "apparently very much interested in Collier's references to interferences with their religious rights," and that they also regarded the seizure of the Zuñi canes as a very serious matter. He did not think they were very much interested in the personal-liberty issue, except at Cochiti.

During his presentation to the council, Collier had informed the delegates that the AIDA was prepared to file suit to get the Zuñi canes restored. Perhaps at Hagerman's initiative, however, a decision was reached after the meeting that all references to Zuñi would be omitted from the published version of the declaration, which Collier intended to broadcast, until after Hagerman had had an opportunity to investigate the Zuñi imbroglio. True to his promise, Hagerman went to Gallup in mid-September and conferred with Agent Bauman. There he told Bauman that he should return the Spanish canes to the Zuñi officers and, then, thinking that the matter was settled, he returned to Santa Fe without conferring with the Zuñi officials. Shortly thereafter, Collier published a version of the declaration in which "all references to the Zuñi canes were omitted." Hagerman was nevertheless "incensed" that any publicity had been accorded the Santo Domingo meeting. Collier, he informed Burke, was truly a "nuisance," but he did not think he should be taken "too seriously." The important thing was that the three Pueblo agents "should strive to give him no real cause for his propaganda."

Hagerman's order, however, was not obeyed. Although Bauman "collected four old canes" from the previous governor and his lieutenants, he insisted that the present incumbents were satisfied with the recently acquired "Washington canes." In October, Hagerman came to Zuñi, where he and Bauman sat down with the governor and the priests. The four canes Bauman had collected from "Zuñi Nick" were thereupon delivered to the "caciques," as was the Lincoln cane, which Nick had previously relinquished. During the conference, three other canes were brought in from various parts of the pueblo; two were still missing. Having turned over all the available canes to the governing officials, Hagerman informed them that in the future the government would recognize only the Lincoln cane as the symbol of authority at Zuñi and that it was their responsibility to safeguard it. This "they seemed to accept." As for the canes and badges that Bauman had ordered in 1924, Hagerman reported, they had not "apparently been used at all." Having received the old Spanish and Lincoln canes, the governor of Zuñi returned these "Washington canes" to Hagerman with the request that he take them with him. "Not to do so would only have caused more trouble," Hagerman informed Burke. Although he did not specifically reprimand Bauman for his role in the Zuñi controversy, Hagerman did report that he believed Zuñi would now be quiet "if the Superintendent will refrain in spirit as well as in practice from taking sides in the religious controversy" and if outside agitators "will let them alone."[36]

Although the Zuñi situation did become quiescent for several years thereafter, Collier was able to keep the issues of Pueblo self-government and religious freedom alive through the continued blunders of Superintendent Crandall. Shortly after Collier left New Mexico in the fall with the dancers and singers for the Fairmont Hotel gala, Crandall released a statement to the *New Mexico State Tribune* charging that the dancers were being "financed by Soviet money from Moscow," which was also being used "to create disturbance and revolution." Although he later denied any role in the *Tribune* story, Crandall had made a similar charge against Collier just before the All Pueblo Council. The basis of his accusation was that Collier was traveling among the Pueblos in the company of "a so-called lawyer . . . from San Francisco by the name of Leo Rabinowitz which smacks very much of Russian Communism." Collier, who was still sensitive to the charge of being a "Red" from his California experience, immediately protested to Burke, who denied his office's involvement.

But Commissioner Burke had apparently tired of the continuing controversy with Collier over the Pueblos. In October he wrote that it was his opinion that Collier "is going to hang himself in time and it is only a question of giving him plenty of rope." His office in the future would adopt a policy of "refraining from noticing his activities more than is actually necessary."

In the early months of 1926, Burke's new attitude received its first test. At Jemez, the governor requested permission to exempt some of the children from attendance at the Catholic day school there "three times a year for four days each time." Backed by Fr. Fridolin Schuster, who had vowed to "do all I can to break [Collier's] hold on the Pueblos," the nun in charge of the school refused and appealed to Southern Pueblo Agent S. A. M. Young, who in turn requested instructions from Burke. Young's inclination was to order the arrest of the Jemez governor on the ground of obstructing the compulsory-education law, but he recognized that "the question of freedom in religious matters would be brought up by the professional up-lifters or sentimentalists" and he was not certain that "the office would sanction bringing about the storm which might arise . . . ." Such action, he was certain, "would cure the difficulty . . . but I am not so sure whether it would be wise to pay the price," especially since the Indian Office had been unable to "sustain Crandall in forcing attendance at Taos."

While the Washington office was deciding what to do at Jemez, Crandall reported that the Taos council had approved the removal of yet another student over the protests of the principal. Crandall also requested permission to prosecute under the compulsory-education law. Coinciding with his request, Burke received a lengthy letter from Haven Emerson demanding the ouster of Crandall because of his "increasing disposition toward tyrannical acts which verge on persecution." The letter, which was drafted by Collier, went

Figure 24.   John Collier and two young boys in New Mexico, circa 1926. Courtesy of Pearl Chase.

on to list a series of charges against Crandall that it alleged
were resulting in "accumulated bitterness, insecurity and
destruction to morals and health" at Taos. Emerson's letter
was quickly followed by one from Collier, who expressed
"astonishment" that "religious persecution of the Pueblos was being resumed" by Superintendents Crandall and
Young. Burke's response to the new controversy came on
March 10 when he sent telegrams to both Crandall and
Young instructing them not to take legal action, but to submit reports and "await further action." To this "change
of front" Crandall protested. Burke's failure to back the
Pueblo superintendents, he wrote, meant that the government might as well "pull down the American flag at Taos
and allow the Indians to dictate and to remove their children from the day school . . . ."

Crandall was right. In his response to Haven Emerson and
several congressmen, Burke denied that the issue of religious freedom was "involved in any of these cases," and he
insisted that if the Indian Office's critics would just "give
the office the opportunity to explain its position, or ascer-
tain the basis of our action . . . much of the ground for misunderstanding or criticism would be eliminated." His office
was striving to be "reasonable and fair with the Indians," he
protested, but the Pueblos were not abiding by agreements
they had made about the number of children to be released.
The best way to resolve the problem was to "have a definite
understanding with each Pueblo as to its exact number to
be excused for religious instruction," and this he proposed
to do before the schools opened again in the fall. To Crandall he wrote that his repeated threats to put Indians behind
bars were being "seized by our critics . . . to bring about an
embarrassing situation. The time has arrived when the Indians must be dealt with in a manner different from that of
twenty years ago." Since "outside sources seem to have no
trouble in obtaining copies of your correspondence . . . it
becomes necessary that you be more tactful and discreet
in your letters and instructions." The point was driven
home the following fall when one of the two Taos boys who

had precipitated the problem two years earlier returned to school. Ordered to cut his hair before entering school, he refused. Crandall backed the school principal and informed the boy's father that if his son's hair was not cut, the boy would be denied entrance to the day school and sent away to a government boarding school. Before the crisis subsided (with the father's decision to have his son's hair cut), Burke wrote Crandall warning him not to precipitate another controversy. If the Taos Indians decided to take more students out of school for religious training, they were not to be opposed, he directed.[37]

The right of Indians to practice their native religions and to exercise control over their internal affairs was obscured many times in the 1920s by the vehemence of the propaganda war, which drowned out rational discussion of these issues. It was also complicated by the Indian Office's legitimate attempts to enforce the new compulsory-education law and its less defensible effort to maintain an often repressive authority over its Indian wards. One might wish that the battle had ben fought over something more substantial than the secret dance file or the Zuñi canes or Herbert Welsh's fantasies, but the truth is that similar battles over equally distorted issues were commonplace in the 1920s as the forces of secularism eroded the values of the nineteenth century and forced the bewildered defenders of the old order into often absurd positions. However squalid or petty the fight may seem in retrospect, Collier had successfully demonstrated by 1926 that attempts to coerce Indians into an abandonment of their religious heritage would be vigorously opposed and he had raised the question of whether the federal government should seek to inculcate Christian values through its administration of Indian affairs. Nothing more could be done until he himself became Indian commissioner.

By the time the religious-freedom issue died down, Collier was already pushing ahead on a less controversial but politically more difficult issue, that of Indian ownership of the executive-order reservations. This was an issue that

took him out of the Pueblos and into the realm of the Navajos. It would lead to his first significant legislative victory,
the Indian Oil Act of 1927, and to the formation of a sympathetic coalition of progressive Republicans in the United
States Senate.

Defending the Title to Indian Reservations
(1922–27)

Albert Fall's decision to apply the General Leasing Act to Indian reservations created by presidential executive order was based on his belief that "lands withdrawn from the public domain by Executive order for the use of the Indians are lands 'owned by the United States' within the purview of that term as used in the act of February 29, 1920, and may be included within an oil and gas prospecting permit under section 13 thereof." Fall was not alone in this belief, and there was ample evidence in the history of the executive-order reservations that public-domain lands, once withdrawn from entry for the creation of Indian reservations, had later been restored and claimed by westward-moving whites. The legal status of executive-order reservations was not, therefore, well defined. They were instead the products of administrative expediency, created by presidents to protect western Indians after Congress abolished the treaty system in 1871, and, as such, they inhabited a legal limbo whose dimensions had been little explored before Fall's ruling in the Harrison case.[1]

Although Fall was intent only upon breaking the impasse over the development of oil and gas on the executive-order reservations and in securing a portion of the royalties for the states, his decision had obvious detrimental side effects on the Indians involved. Under it, for instance, Indians would receive none of the royalties from oil or gas production; instead, the monies would be divided among the state, the general reclamation fund, and the federal government. For another, they would have no control over the development of these lands, which could be exploited at the will of the prospectors. And, if the argument Fall employed were pushed far enough, even their ownership of the surface rights of these lands could eventually be challenged.

At the time Fall made his ruling in June 1922, no oil had yet been discovered on the Navajo reservation. But three months after he issued his decision, oil was discovered southeast of Shiprock, New Mexico, within the boundaries of that portion of the reservation created by treaty in 1868. This strike, on what was known as the Hogback, brought oilmen and speculators flooding into the area. Within a few weeks the local superintendent, Evan Estep, reported that the executive-order reservation just a few miles to the east of the Hogback was being overrun "by all kinds of classes of speculators, fly-by-nights, bootleggers, and other forms of criminals." Estep also complained that he had been threatened and offered bribes. "Conditions on this part of the reservation have assumed the status of a scandal."[2]

The discovery of oil on the Hogback precipitated a number of decisions in the Indian Office indirectly related to the problem occasioned by Fall's ruling. Since 1891 the law had been clear on the leasing of treaty reservations: leases were to be approved by "the authority of the council speaking for such Indians . . . in such quantities and upon such terms as the agent in charge may recommend, subject to the approval of the Secretary of the Interior" (26 Stat., 795). The difficulty was that the Navajos had no tribal council. The lease of the Hogback had been approved by a hastily called council of Navajos living in the San Juan jurisdiction of the

Navajo reservation, but the Indians then balked at further leases, thereby angering the oil companies. The Indian Office also became increasingly doubtful about the validity of this arrangement and about the ability of Agent Estep to supervise the leases. It was for this reason that Albert Fall appointed Herbert Hagerman as special commissioner to the Navajos in early 1923. Hagerman was charged with supervising the creation of a Navajo council, which would represent all sections of the vast reservation and negotiate all future leases. In July he convened the first meeting of the new Navajo tribal council, which gave him authority to act in its behalf in negotiating future leases, and in October he presided over the first of three auctions at which leases on the treaty portion of the reservation were sold. Hagerman's appointment by Fall and the creation of the Navajo tribal council in turn aroused Collier's suspicion, but, after meeting with Hagerman in the late summer of 1923, Collier gave him his approval and warm endorsement. In the meanwhile, Albert Fall had resigned, and his successor, Hubert Work, inherited the problem of his ruling on the executive-order reservations.[3]

Secretary Work was understandably confused about the recent ruling on the executive-order reservations and he received conflicting advice from his subordinates. Commissioner Burke, who opposed the Harrison decision, but who would not confront Fall, wrote Work three weeks after Fall's resignation to protest the ruling and to request that the department solicitor be asked for an opinion. Work agreed and although he issued three prospecting permits during his first months in office, he refused to sign any more after July. At that point, hard pressed by oilmen and some congressmen, Holm O. Bursum for one, and by his own first secretary, E. C. Finney, whom Burke accused of having helped to write the Harrison decision, Work began to waver. In November he notified Burke that he no longer felt justified "in overruling my predecessor" and that he was instructing Finney to resume issuing prospecting permits in order to hasten the determination of oil's existence on the executive-order reservation. At the same time, he promised to introduce legislation the following month that would give the Indians all the royalties from any discoveries on the executive-order reservations. Alarmed because he thought he had "an understanding that pending an inquiry . . . there would be nothing done further with reference to recognizing permittees," Burke demanded an audience with the secretary. There he was told that the authorization for the permits had gotten by Work "through a misunderstanding" and that nothing would be done to authorize new permits.[4]

In December, Work did introduce a bill that would have struck a compromise between Commissioner Burke and the proponents of the Fall decision. Under its terms, leases on executive-order reservations would be administered under the terms of the General Leasing Act as Fall had decreed, but all royalties derived would be "deposited to the credit of the tribe for whose benefit the reservation was created." Although the bill was reported favorably by the Senate committee, no action was taken during the first session of the sixty-eighth Congress.[5]

The failure of the administration bill was probably related to the opinion of the Interior Department solicitor, John H. Edwards, which was given to Secretary Work in February 1924. In reply to Work's inquiry about the nature of Indian title to the executive-order reservations, Edwards was guarded. In the absence of a positive grant (something few tribes received, even under a treaty), "fee to lands set apart for the benefit of Indians, whether by treaty, Act of Congress, or executive order, remain in the United States subject to further disposal by Congress," he wrote. Their rights, however, were not to be treated lightly where "executive order reservations have been undisturbed for years . . . ." To the question of whether the executive-order reservations were subject to the General Leasing Act, Edwards was more emphatic. The answer was no. It was incongruous, he wrote, that Congress should have passed an act in 1919 (41 Stat., 31) expressly providing for the opening of executive-order reservations to the mining of metalliferous minerals and granting all royalties to the Indians, "yet under the Harrison decision they would get nothing." On the day that he received the solicitor's opinion, Work forwarded it to the attorney general with the request that he, too, rule on the issues involved, and he simultaneously notified the commissioner of the General Land Office that no leases or permits were to be issued or approved, pending the attorney general's decision. In reply to a request from Senator Charles Curtis as to how many permits and leases had been issued under Fall's ruling, Work wrote that no leases had been issued. Approximately twenty prospecting permits had been granted, all of them on the Navajo reservation, and all but three during Fall's tenure. Approximately 425 applications for permits had been received.

Three months later, Attorney General Harlan Stone rendered his decision. The General Leasing Act of 1920 was not applicable to executive-order Indian reservations, he wrote, citing many legal decisions and earlier legislation that indicated that the Congress and the courts had consistently regarded treaty and executive-order reservations as one. "The important matter here," he wrote, "is that neither the courts nor Congress have made any distinction as to the character or extent of the Indian rights as between executive order reservations and reservations established by treaty or act of Congress. So, if the General Leasing Act applies to one class, there seems to be no ground for holding that it does not apply to the other." In reply to a question from Work about what he should do in the case of those individuals and companies that had been issued prospecting permits, Stone informed him that he should immediately cancel all permits where the permit holders had failed to show "diligence"; but in the case of those who had complied with the terms of their permits, the Interior Department would have to obtain a court order to cancel their permits. Stone suggested that they first take Harrison and the companies to whom he had transferred his permit, the Midwest Oil Company and the Southwest Oil Company, to court because they had indicated an intention to contest his interpretation. In July a suit was filed in the U.S. District Court, Utah, to cancel Harrison's permit.[6]

Despite the fact that both the department solicitor and the attorney general had ruled against the application of the General Leasing Act to executive-order Indian reservations, Secretary Work's bill was reintroduced into Congress in December 1924 without change. This time it received attention in both houses, each of which accepted its underlying premise, that the General Leasing Act would govern the administration of oil development on executive-order reservations. There was disagreement, however, over the amount of royalties the Indians should receive. In the previous Congress, the Indian Oil Leasing Act of 1924 had been passed, permitting the states to levy a production tax on Indian treaty lands equal to that levied on non-Indian lands (43 Stat., 244). The House now amended Work's bill to extend this production tax to executive-order reservations. The Senate, however, insisted that 37.5 percent of Indian royalties be paid to the state in which the executive-order reservation was located, "in lieu of taxes," the same amount these states would have received under the General Leasing Act. When the Senate insisted on its position, the House conferees gave in, but at this point Commissioner Burke intervened through Republican Representative Frederick W. Dallinger (Massachusetts), who had the bill defeated on a point of order.[7]

The month following Burke's defeat of a legislative solution to the executive-order snarl, the U.S. District Court in Utah handed down a decision in the Harrison case, finding in favor of the defendants. According to Judge Tillman D. Johnson, "the equities are all in favor of the defendant" because the government's claim failed to allege any "substantial rights with respect to the government or anyone else." What the government's case had been, one can only wonder, for the judge went on to write that no claim had been asserted "that these lands have been occupied by Indians or can possibly be occupied by Indians in any practical way. It is a desert unfit for occupancy by any human being." The case was appealed by the government, but the Eighth Circuit Court refused to rule on the lower court's decision and instead certified to the Supreme Court two questions: (1) Was there authority in the secretary of the interior to issue Harrison's permit under the General Leasing Act? (2) If the answer to the first question was no, could the government's suit to cancel the permit be maintained in light of the fact that the defendant had acted in good faith and had expended a considerable amount of money? By 1926 there existed the curious situation in which the federal court had ruled in favor of Fall's decision, while the Interior Department solicitor and the attorney general had ruled against it. Congress could still resolve the issue through legislation, and, consequently, a flurry of bills was introduced in 1926.[8]

It was against this background of judicial and legislative maneuvering that Collier entered the controversy in early 1926. Buoyed by his successes against the Bursum bill and the dance regulations, and with adequate financial support from his California backers, he moved to Washington in January 1926, took a desk in the offices of his friend Judson King, and began to lobby for a bill that would give the Indians all the proceeds from oil and gas development on executive-order reservations and remove the cloud to their title that Fall had raised. In this endeavor, he was greatly aided by Representative James A. Frear (Wisconsin), who had bolted the Republican party in 1924 to follow Robert La Follette, Sr., and Burton K. Wheeler in their formation of the Progressive party. As a result of his defection, Frear was stripped of his seat on the powerful House Ways and Means Committee and demoted to the Indian Affairs Committee. How and when the two men made contact is uncertain, but the AIDA records do indicate that a short-lived Wisconsin chapter of the AIDA was formed in 1925 as a result of efforts by Cash Asher and Collier.[9]

Attention first centered upon a bill introduced by Democratic Representative Carl Hayden (Arizona), a member of the House Indian Affairs Committee. It was clearly in the nature of a compromise and, as such, was favored by Commissioner Burke. Under Hayden's bill, the leasing of executive-order Indian reservations would be administered according to the provisions of the Indian Oil Leasing Act of 1924, not the General Leasing Act of 1920, as Fall had directed. To this extent, the treaty and executive-order reservations would be recognized as equal. To pacify those who insisted that the states were entitled to the same share of oil royalties they would have received under the General Leasing Act, however, Hayden's bill provided that the states would receive 37.5 percent of the Indian royalties, as long as such monies were used "for the construction and maintenance of public roads within the respective reservations" or "for the support of public schools attended by Indian children." Just why Hayden thought the states would be satisfied with this curious, complicated arrangement is not clear. More important, in recognition of the district court decision, his bill also provided that all permit holders under Fall's ruling would, if they discovered oil, be dealt with according to the terms of the General Leasing Act. This meant that the successful discoverer of oil would be permitted to pay the Indians a royalty of only 5 percent on one-fourth of his permit instead of the 12.5 percent royalty mandated by the Indian Oil Leasing Act of 1924. A powerful issue, that of equities under the Fall ruling, was thereby injected into the already complicated situation.

Commissioner Burke testified in favor of the Hayden bill. In his testimony he explained that his primary interest was in securing legislation that would permit development of executive-order reservations under the Indian Oil Leasing Act of 1924 rather than the General Leasing Act. Although he had opposed the granting of 37.5 percent of the Indian royalty to the states in the previous Congress, so long as the states were compelled to expend this money on projects useful to the Indians, as proposed in Hayden's bill, Burke said he would not oppose this provision. He was opposed in principle to recognizing any rights of the permit holders under Fall's ruling, but he realized that this concession was probably necessary to secure passage of the bill.

The only opposition to the Hayden bill at the hearings came from Collier and Frear. Both of them favored the clause placing the executive-order reservations under the Indian Oil Leasing Act of 1924 and both accepted the necessity of recognizing the rights of the permit holders. They objected, however, to giving the states 37.5 percent of the Indian royalties, stating that they believed the Indians would be better served by a production tax on their lands as provided for in the Indian Oil Leasing Act of 1924.[10]

Shortly after the House concluded its hearing on the Hayden bill, the Senate began hearings on two far more threatening bills introduced by the senators from New Mexico, Andrieus A. Jones and Sam G. Bratton, who had defeated Bursum in 1924. The Jones bill was especially onerous in that it sought to legitimize the Fall ruling. Under its terms, the General Leasing Act would be applied to all executive-order reservations, the states would receive 37.5 percent of oil royalties (with no requirement that any of the money be spent for Indian benefit), and, in addition to recognizing the rights of permit holders under Fall's ruling, all 425 applicants for permits would be reinstated. Bratton's bill, which was similar to Hayden's, but less favorable to the Indians, would place the development of the executive-order reservations under the Indian Oil Leasing Act of 1924, give the states 37.5 percent of the oil royalties (provided that a portion, "as determined by the legislature," be spent on schools and roads within the reservation), and restore some, but not all, of the applicants for permits.

There was little discussion of the reactionary Jones bill, and when Commissioner Burke testified, he stood firm in behalf of the Hayden bill as the best compromise for the Indians. He had not changed his mind "one bit" on the right of the Indians to the executive-order reservations, he told the senators, but he had acquiesced in the compromise contained in Hayden's bill in order to placate other members of the Interior Department, including Secretary Work, and the opposition in the Congress. He was adamantly opposed to those clauses in the Bratton and Jones bills reinstating some or all of the applicants for prospecting permits. Since they had not received permission from the department to prospect, they had not lost anything, and were not, therefore, entitled to consideration.

By the time of the Senate hearing, however, Collier and Frear had decided to launch an all-out attack on the Indian Office and Commissioner Burke. On March 4, Frear took to the floor of the House "to speak on the misgovernment of the American Indians by the Bureau of Indian Affairs." His remarks referred to many instances of "gross mismanagement" by Burke, but he was particularly harsh in his examination of Burke's attitude toward the Navajos. The Hayden bill, he charged erroneously, would restore the rights of 400 "speculators" rejected by the attorney general and force the Indians to pay all state taxes levied on oil production, thereby permitting the oil companies to avoid any tax payments. Not content with these reckless charges, Frear quoted Collier as his authority for the charge that the various oil bills were the work of the Indian Office, not of the congressmen who had introduced them. Displaying his ignorance of Collier's criticism of the allotment system and of conditions on the Navajo reservation, he charged that if Burke were truly interested in protecting the Indian's title to the executive-order reservations, he could allot "millions of Executive Order acres" immediately and thus vest title in the Indians.

Following Frear's outburst, Collier appeared before the Senate committee examining the Jones and Bratton bills. There he repeated his opposition to those sections in all the pending bills that would give the states 37.5 percent of the Indian royalties in lieu of other taxes. Such a provision, he maintained, implied that title to these lands still remained in the federal government. If, instead, the executive-order reservations were brought completely under the Indian Oil Leasing Act of 1924 and taxed in the same manner as non-Indian lands, the implication would be that the Indians owned these lands in the same way that they did the treaty reservations. He then confronted the senators with the issue that everyone had been attempting to avoid: "Apparently it is going to be difficult, perhaps impossible, to pass a law authorizing the development of these reservations without adopting a theory as to the nature of this title. It will be desirable to waive this question, but it apparently cannot be waived. Therefore it has to be argued." He himself was willing to leave "the question exactly where it is, pending a court decision," but if legislation were to be passed, "the matter must be decided one way or the other." Then, in line with Frear's statements on the House floor, he charged that it was the Indian Office that was behind the attempt to avoid a determination of Indian title to the executive-order reservations. So long as the executive-order reservations remained the creatures of the executive branch of government, he charged, "it places in the hands of the Indian Bureau a power that is almost inestimable, one that can be used in the control of commercial opinion, public opinion in politics, a power to give or to withdraw."

Also appearing before the Senate committee was Herbert Hagerman, the special commissioner to the Navajos. Shortly after his appointment in 1923, Hagerman had made a study of the executive-order reservation problem and had concluded that Fall's decision was correct. It would be impossible to get Congress to approve legislation that would deny the states what they believed to be theirs, he wrote Burke in September 1923, and in 1924 he advised the commissioner that "strategically the Department would be in a better position with Congress if it would assent in principle to a division of possible royalties on non-treaty lands" on a three-way basis among the Indians, the states, and the reclamation fund. Although he had not approached the Navajos on this subject, he was certain he could obtain their consent without "much trouble." Commissioner Burke, however, would not accept Hagerman's compromise suggestions. "We can never stand for only giving the Indians 33.3% of any royalties that may come from oil leases on lands within the Executive order reservations," he replied to Hagerman. "If we should favor the Fall proposition . . . we would come in for some very severe criticism and, in the face of precedents, which are uniform, we must stand against any legislation that fails to recognize the principle that the Indians should be protected in their rights to Executive Order reservations, the same as others." Although he agreed to follow Burke's course, Hagerman refused to accept his argument, saying that he believed that someday the commissioner would have to compromise with the western states.

In March 1926, Hagerman was in Washington to confer with Interior Department officials about an approaching auction for oil leases on the treaty portion of the Navajo reservation. At the invitation of his friend Senator Sam Bratton, he was asked to testify before the Senate committee. During his brief appearance, he told the senators that he believed the Navajos would accept the royalty division contained in the Bratton and Jones bills, which would give them 62.5 percent and the state 37.5 percent. In fact, he thought they would be satisfied with 50 percent. Immediately, Collier challenged Hagerman's statement and advised the Senate committee "to obtain the context, the title record, of the discussion in the course of which [the Navajos] said that they were willing to take 50% and let the rest go . . . ." Upon close questioning by Senator La Follette, Hagerman admitted that the Navajo tribal council had expressed a belief in 1925 that the executive-order and treaty reservations were identical and that the Navajos should receive all the royalties from both but, he added, "I do not think there would be any trouble . . . to get from the council a formal declaration" accepting 50 percent of the royalties on the executive-order reservation. Following Hagerman's testimony, Senator La Follette expressed his belief that the executive-order reservations should be treated in exactly the same way as the treaty reservations, and a month later a bill to this effect was introduced into the Senate.[11]

Before the new Senate bill was introduced, the House committee, at Hayden's request, abandoned the provision in its bill granting the states 37.5 percent of the royalties from executive-order reservations. Calling this procedure "unnecessary and of no advantage to the states," the committee recommended that all royalties from oil and gas production on executive-order reservations be deposited in the U.S. Treasury "for the use and benefit of the Indians." It also provided that the states could levy a production tax on these lands, just as they could under the Indian Oil Leasing Act of 1924. The bill was, however, also amended to recognize the rights of the 425 applicants to whom Secretary Work had denied prospecting permits. Except for his latter change, Hayden's bill now conformed to the specifications Collier had set forth in his testimony before the congressional committees.

The House committee report provoked a minority report by Frear, but the nature of his protest was most peculiar. Rather than denouncing the inclusion of the 425 applicants, a provision he had earlier erroneously attributed to Commissioner Burke, Frear's report said nothing about this aspect of the amended House bill. Instead, he based his opposition on the highly speculative proposition that the House committee had eliminated the royalty payment to the states in an effort to create "a parliamentary smokescreen." When the amended House bill went to the Senate, Frear charged, the section granting the states 37.5 percent of the oil royalties would be put back in the bill and when it was then returned to the House, the debate would be conducted under the pressure of a conference report in which the time would be "entirely controlled by the proponents of the 37.5 percent tax proposal." His report also alleged that the production-tax clause was open to the interpretation that the Indian royalties would be taxed by the states, but that the revenues of oil producers would not. No evidence was ever presented to substantiate these almost paranoid accusations.[12]

On April 10 Commissioner Burke, who had been seething at the charges Frear had made against him on the House floor, took advantage of a House hearing to denounce his critics. For three hours he defended his record against the many charges Frear had leveled at him and he denounced the congressman in blistering language for having "blindly" accepted Collier's "propaganda." With regard to the executive-order reservations, Burke carefully retraced his stand, pointing out that before Collier and Frear had ever become interested in the issue, it was he who had blocked the first undesirable bills in 1925. There had never been any change in his insistence that Indians owned the executive-order reservations just as they owned the treaty reservations, he stated. In backing the Hayden bill, he had agreed that the states could take 37.5 percent of the royalties from oil production "in lieu of taxes," but only if the money was expended for their benefit, and there had been no intimation that this should in any way permit the oil producers to go untaxed. And he had agreed to recognize the rights of the permit holders only because he had been told that without this concession, no legislation would be passed. Following Burke's testimony, Collier was denied the right to reply, with the result that Frear took to the House floor again to deliver another indictment of the Burke administration. This time, he charged that Burke had blocked a bill that he, Frear, had introduced to vest title of the executive-order reservations in the Indians and to restrict the ability of the executive branch to diminish the boundaries of executive-order reservations. He also insisted that Burke had been remiss in not opposing the inclusion of the applicants in the amended House bill.[13]

Whether as a result of the Collier-Frear attack, or simply because they opposed the Fall ruling, in April three members of the Senate committee came out in favor of a new bill, which placed the executive-order reservations on exactly the same footing as the treaty reservations in the matter of oil and gas production. Drafted by Republican Senator Ralph H. Cameron (Arizona) and backed by La Follette and Wheeler, the new bill provided for leasing the executive-order reservations under the Indian Oil Leasing Act of 1924; gave the Indians all royalties from production and specified that these funds could not be expended without consultation with "said Indians or their tribal council"; provided for a state production tax that could also be levied on the oil producers; and forbade any changes in the boundaries of executive-order reservations without the express approval of Congress. The Cameron bill, however, also recognized the rights of those same applicants under the Fall ruling who had been approved in Bratton's original bill. The only opposition to the new bill came from Senator Bratton. Arguing that New Mexico was a poor state in which 43 percent of the land was owned by the federal government and thus not subject to taxation, and that if oil were discovered, roads and bridges would have to be built, Bratton attempted to place the 37.5-percent royalty provision for the states back in the bill. This effort was defeated in committee when his colleagues told him that raising money for these expenses was the purpose of the production tax.

Bratton then offered an amendment providing that until the states should levy a production tax upon Indian lands, they should be paid a sum equivalent to the tax on non-Indian lands. When his colleagues questioned this curious arrangement, Bratton was evasive. Then Collier explained that under the New Mexico constitution, "Indians not taxed" were not permitted to vote; a production tax on Indian lands might result in the enfranchisement of the Indians. Despite this revelation, the committee accepted Bratton's amendment. Emboldened by this success, Bratton then attempted to reinstate all the applicants under the Fall ruling and to insert a disclaimer that "nothing in this act" should be construed as fixing the title to these lands in the Indians. In both instances he was rebuffed. When the Cameron bill went before the full Senate, Bratton again attempted to have all the applicants restored, and he was again defeated. Arguing against Bratton, La Follette stated that all the other members of the Senate committee believed that title to the executive-order reservations was in the Indians.

When the Cameron bill went to the House, it was substituted for the Hayden bill, with one change: Bratton's peculiar provision allowing the states to obtain revenue from Indian lands without imposing a production tax was deleted, and the states were left with the option of passing a production tax or foregoing this source of revenue. The bill then went to President Coolidge, who vetoed it on July 2, 1926. According to his veto message, Coolidge had two objections. First, the bill unfairly discriminated between the permit holders and the applicants, all of whom he believed should be recognized on an equal basis. Second, the bill was of "doubtful propriety" in that it attempted to legislate a solution to a problem that was pending in the courts. Coolidge's second objection was apparently not serious, for at the next session of Congress, the Cameron bill, amended to include all applicants and permit holders, was reintroduced. After brief and perfunctory hearings, at which Collier and Frear made no opposition to the inclusion of the applicants, the amended bill was then approved by both houses of Congress and signed by Coolidge on March 3, 1927 (44 Stat., 1347).

The Indian Oil Act of 1927 was the most important single piece of Indian legislation passed in the 1920s. Although the question of Indian title to the executive-order reservations was not explicitly resolved, it had been aired, and the debates revealed that it was the intent, at least of the Senate, that Indian title to the treaty and executive-order reservations be equated as nearly as possible without making a formal declaration to that effect. Once the bill was signed, the government entered into an agreement with Harrison's attorneys whereby the judgment of the Utah district court was set aside in return for dismissal of the appeal to the Supreme Court. In this way, a judicial resolution of the question was avoided.[14]

Credit for this important victory must be attributed to Collier, who alone had insisted that a theory of title would have to be adopted if legislation satisfactory to the Indians were to be passed. It was unfortunate that his success was marred by the reckless and inaccurate charges that his spokesman, Congressman Frear, hurled against Commissioner Burke because Burke was, after all, essentially correct in his assessment of the power of the oil lobby. In the

Indian Oil Act of 1927, the oilmen, with the tacit approval of Collier and Frear, got exactly what they wanted: the right to explore the executive-order reservation and to exploit any discoveries they might make under the favorable terms of the General Leasing Act. All of Frear's grossly unfair charges against Burke could not erase this fact. In the end, Collier and Frear quietly conceded not only the claims of the permit holders but also those of the 425 applicants, something they had earlier vociferously and erroneously blamed Burke for doing.[15]

The reason for the vehemence of the Collier-Frear attack on Commissioner Burke in the spring of 1926 is better understood in the context of two other bills that Burke supported in this same session of Congress, one of which, the Lees Ferry bridge bill, was closely tied to the Indian Oil Act.

For many years Congress had financed improvements on Indian lands through the mechanism known as "reimbursable debts." To construct roads, bridges, irrigation projects, and other public works on Indian reservations, Congress routinely passed appropriation bills authorizing the use of federal funds, but making these funds subject to recovery or reimbursement from Indian tribal funds on deposit in the federal treasury. Since many tribes had no tribal funds, this device served to satisfy the congressional appetite for the pork barrel. By means of this fiction, support could often be obtained for measures of an otherwise dubious nature, particularly if the projects were advantageous to whites who lived near the reservations. The customary method of justifying such projects was to obtain a statement from the secretary of the interior that a certain bridge or highway would be useful to the Indians. Little opposition to this practice was evidenced before 1920 when Congress, by law, directed that the Interior Department begin to collect some of the outstanding Indian debts.

In 1925, Congress authorized the expenditure of $100,000, reimbursable "from any funds now or hereafter placed in the treasury of the Navajo Reservation Indians," for the con-

struction of a bridge across the Colorado River 6 miles below Lees Ferry, Arizona. The following year, despite the fact
that Arizona had refused to appropriate its matching share
of the bridge's cost, an attempt was made to appropriate the
Indian portion. Ten years earlier there probably would have
been no opposition, but now that the discovery of oil on
the treaty portion of the reservation had produced about
$116,000 of revenue, the situation was quite different. The
bridge was a particularly vulnerable target because its critics easily revealed that while there were few Navajos living
in its immediate vicinity, it was conveniently located along
the route of a proposed arterial highway to the northern rim
of the Grand Canyon National Park.

There were other problems. In 1923 the five Navajo superintendents had raised the question of repaying reimbursable
debts from the Navajo oil revenues in their first meeting
with Herbert Hagerman. Hagerman, who was unfamiliar
with the practice, in turn wrote Commissioner Burke for instructions, stating his opinion that the Navajo oil royalties
should be placed in a special fund separate from both gratuity and reimbursable funds, and only be used for purposes
approved by the tribal council. After some delay, Burke replied, telling Hagerman that the Indian Office had already
drawn up a list of priorities for expending the oil revenues
and that it would "only be good business to expend some of
the oil money for improving roads and bridges." When the
Navajo delegates to the third tribal council meeting assembled at Ft. Wingate in July 1925, however, they drew up
their own list of priorities and made formal objection to the
use of tribal funds "for such purposes as the bridge at the
ferry across the Colorado" River and another proposed bridge
on the San Juan River in New Mexico.

By 1926 the Lees Ferry bridge had also become a pawn in
the fight for the U.S. Senate seat held by Ralph H. Cameron,
the Republican incumbent who was being challenged by
Carl Hayden, the Democratic congressman. Hayden, who
had also introduced the oil-leasing bill that Collier and
Frear opposed, was insisting upon the construction of the

bridge with Indian money as part of his campaign, and in this endeavor he was strongly backed by Henry F. Ashurst, the Democratic senior senator. Cameron, who had sponsored authorization of the bridge in 1925 on the basis of a letter from Secretary Work stating that it was for the benefit of the Indians and would "facilitate their communication with whites," now reversed his position after learning that the Navajo tribal council was opposed to the project. Teaming with Sam Bratton of New Mexico, Cameron now insisted that the bridge was primarily for the benefit of tourists and the Fred Harvey interests who controlled concessions at the Grand Canyon National Park. Together, the two men were successful initially in striking funds for the bridge from the appropriation bill. They were unwittingly aided in this endeavor by Hagerman, whose private correspondence to Republican Senator George H. Williams (Missouri) opposing the bridge and the use of Navajo tribal funds for this purpose was published in the *Congressional Record* in early 1926.

Despite the opposition of Cameron, Bratton, Collier, and Frear, the Lees Ferry bridge appropriation, with its reimbursable feature restored in conference committee, passed Congress on March 2, 1926, and went to the president for signature. Two days later, Frear unleashed his assault on Burke on the floor of the House. Calling for a ten-man, joint congressional committee "to investigate any charges of neglect, dissipation of funds, improper treatment, or mismanagement of the American Indians," Frear specifically charged that Burke and the Indian Office had "approved and supported bills that have looted the treasury of the Navajo Indians" and that "the only justification of this looting is found in a plea that a reimbursable charge to be paid by the Indians will not be paid immediately." Although Frear's proposal for a congressional investigation was not adopted, the passage of the Lees Ferry bridge bill and the publicity that Collier and Frear subsequently gave to it were undoubtedly factors in creating the favorable climate in the Senate which resulted in the passage of the Indian Oil Act of 1927.

In attacking Burke for his support of the Lees Ferry bridge, the Collier-Frear forces were able to hammer home two essential criticisms of his administration. The Navajos were opposed to this use of their money, and Burke, as he had in the case of the Pueblos, not only refused to listen to their protests, but did his best to suppress them from coming before Congress. He was not a champion of the Indians whose welfare was entrusted to his office by law. Second, Burke as a former congressman and member of the House Indian Affairs Committee, was confortable with the compromises and the trade-offs that were traditionally a part of Indian legislation. He was probably sincere in his belief, expressed on a number of occasions, that the Navajos would never be asked to repay the cost of the bridge, that this was just a means of getting a bridge built, which Congressman Hayden needed to impress his constituents. What had happened with the advent of Collier, however, was that the old ways were now being questioned. Issues of principle and of fairness, including the right of Indians to be heard when matters relating to their welfare were under discussion, were being introduced in 1926 and these were not issues for which Burke's experience had prepared him. In his willingness to temporize and to make concessions, something to which his long years of service in the House had inured him, Burke clearly demonstrated that he was not prepared to assert the rights of Indians when they clashed with those of whites, and, indeed, that he did not even understand that in most cases the Indians had any rights. Although they had unfairly characterized Burke's position on the issue of the executive-order reservations, Collier and Frear were absolutely correct in their criticisms of his stand on the Lees Ferry bridge.[16]

The other bill that Collier and Frear criticized was one that would have authorized courts of Indian offenses on Indian reservations. What was unique about this bill was its attempt to provide legislative authority for courts that had already been functioning for more than forty years. In the 1880s the assumed power of the federal government to enforce "law and order" on Indian reservations was severely undermined in the Supreme Court decision, *Ex parte Crow Dog*, in which the court ruled that a reservation Indian could not be tried for the murder of another Indian because no federal law had been passed curtailing the exclusive jurisdiction of a tribe over its members. Crow Dog could be punished under the laws of the Sioux, but he could not be hanged, even though he had been convicted and sentenced to death in a federal court. In 1885, to correct this anomalous situation, Congress passed the Major Crimes Act (23 Stat., 385), which provided for federal jurisdiction over seven crimes: murder, manslaughter, rape, assault with intent to kill, arson, burglary, and larceny. In 1909 assault with a deadly weapon was added (35 Stat., 1088). Apart from these eight major crimes, however, there was no federal or state jurisdiction over other crimes and misdemeanors committed by Indians against other Indians on reservations.

Because of the void between the limited jurisdiction of the federal courts and the unwritten tribal codes, and to "americanize" the Indians, Secretary of the Interior Henry M. Teller authorized the creation of "courts of Indian offenses" in 1883. Although these courts were supplied with an abbreviated criminal and civil code drawn up by the commissioner of Indian affairs, their jurisdiction was really far more sweeping. In practice, the native judges appointed by the local Indian agent were expected to rule upon any matter brought before them by the agent. By 1900 the number of these extralegal courts was dwindling as many Indians came under the jurisdiction of the states following their compliance with the requirements of the Dawes Severalty Act, but they were still in existence on the unallotted reservations and in those areas where Indians remained in trust status.[17]

The passage of the Indian Citizenship Act in 1924 brought with it an expectation that Indians would be brought in line with other Americans in the areas of civil and criminal law. At the same time, the states were reluctant to bring Indians into their courts because their jurisdiction was unclear and because they had no police powers on the reservations. To resolve the problem, the Indian Office in 1926 introduced a bill to apply the civil and criminal laws of the United States to Indians on reservations and to grant the federal district and circuit courts jurisdiction over "crimes and misdemeanors or other violations of federal statutes on Indian reservations." For those offenses "for which there is no punishment provided for in federal law," the bill proposed that the courts of Indian offenses be given jurisdiction, "under regulations prescribed by the Secretary of the Interior." These courts, otherwise unchanged from those created in the 1880s, were now to be authorized to fix punishments of up to six months' imprisonment or labor, or fines up to $100, or both. In addition, because of the difficulty the Indian Office was experiencing in tracing the heirs to Indian lands, custom marriage and divorce were to be abolished. Henceforth, in these two areas, Indians would be forced to comply with the laws of the state in which they lived.

However necessary or desirable the clarification of legal jurisdiction over reservation Indians was, the 1926 Indian Office bill was not the answer. It was an easy target for civil libertarians like Collier and Frear, who pointed out that the existing courts of Indian offenses were clearly in violation of constitutional guarantees of personal freedom because they did not provide for trial by jury or appeal. Labeling it "A Bill Authorizing Tyranny," Collier appeared before the House Indian Affairs Committee together with a host of Indian representatives including S. M. Brosius, the IRA representative, who also opposed its passage. In his testimony, Collier insisted that the existing courts of Indian offenses be abolished and in their place the federal courts be given jurisdiction. A "definite code of laws" that would incorporate tribal customs in those areas where tribal cohesion and authority still existed should be written, he argued. Where the authority of the tribe had disintegrated, he favored a code based on state law, but administered by the federal courts. Although his suggestions were considered impractical, the fact that so many different groups opposed the bill for one reason or another resulted in its defeat in committee. The only defense came from Assistant Commissioner E. B. Meritt, who spent much of his time denouncing Collier as a "paid propagandist" seeking financial donations for his cause. In view of the seriousness of the issues involved, Meritt's diatribe did little to enhance the Indian Office's already tarnished reputation.[18]

In addition to their attacks upon the Indian Office for its role in the executive-order reservation battle, the Lees Ferry bridge, and the courts of Indian offenses, Collier and Frear also used the 1926 congressional session to raise other troubling questions about Commissioner Burke's administration of Indian affairs. One of these involved his handling of Indian trust estates, and the other was concerned with the adequacy of Indian health care.

Following the publication of the joint AIDA-IRA study, *Oklahoma's Poor Rich Indians*, in 1924, the House Indian Affairs Committee began an investigation of the Oklahoma probate system. Because Burke backed the investigation, his detractors also brought charges against him, one of which was that he had approved a questionable trust arrangement involving a wealthy, elderly Creek Indian by the name of Jackson Barnett. Burke was exonerated by the committee in 1925, but the wisdom of the agreement continued to be questioned.

Jackson Barnett was one of those fabled Oklahoma Indians on whose allotment oil was discovered in great quantities. By 1920, when he was literally abducted by a white prostitute who drove him to Kansas and Missouri and married him in both states, he was a millionaire. Fearful that Barnett would be victimized by his new wife and bogus heirs, Burke approved an agreement in 1922 whereby $1.1 million of Barnett's money on deposit in the Interior Department would be placed in two equal trust accounts, one in the name of the American Baptist Home Mission Society as an endowment for Bacone College, and one in the name of Mrs. Barnett. Each of the trusts was to provide Barnett with an annual income for life. Burke's motive was clearly

to protect Barnett, but his action was challenged both by
Barnett's legal guardian, who filed suit to have the trusts declared invalid on the ground that neither he nor the Oklahoma probate court had been consulted in the matter, and
by Frear and Collier, who charged that in creating the trusts
Burke exceeded his authority by giving away money he was
legally charged with preserving. The suit dragged on until
1927, when a federal district judge ruled that Barnett was incompetent to enter the trust agreement, and ordered the
trusts dissolved.

Collier and Frear were not interested in the jurisdictional
battle between the Interior Department and the Oklahoma
probate courts that motivated Commissioner Burke. Their
concern was with the mismanagement of Indian property,
which they believed Burke's creation of the trust involved,
and with the cozy relationship implied in the commissioner's award of Barnett's estate to a religious body. Collier's
dogged pursuit of the Barnett trust would continue into the
late 1920s and would ultimately be a factor in driving Burke
from office.[19]

The other issue that Frear and Collier alluded to during
the 1926 congressional session was the deplorable condition
of Indian health care. This had been a major concern of Collier's ever since he first visited Taos in 1921, but it was not
until 1926 that he obtained information upon which to make
a case.

In 1924, Commissioner Burke received a report on health
conditions on Indian reservations that he had commissioned
the American Red Cross to undertake the year before. The
study was made by Florence Patterson, a public-health nurse
who was known to Haven Emerson, the president of the
AIDA. Health conditions in the Indian country, she reported,
"are serious." There was an alarming prevalence of trachoma
and tuberculosis in the Southwest, she said, and there were
severe defects in the health-care system in nearly all of the
boarding schools she visited. Burke's medical supervisor
was skeptical of Patterson's report and, at his request, it was
not made public. Emerson, however, who had access to

the report, blasted the government's lack of attention to the problem, and Collier and Frear accused Burke of suppressing the report. In the years to follow, they would successfully demonstrate that the medical and health services of the Indian Office were woefully inadequate, that the problem was in part occasioned by Burke's unwillingness to acknowledge it because of political and fiscal considerations, and that the Indian Office lacked any concept of a preventive health-care program.[20]

The full impact of Collier and Frear's attack on the Indian Office during the 1926 congressional session was not immediately apparent, however, and it produced some consternation among Collier's California supporters. In March, James Young was approached by Chauncey Goodrich, who expressed the opinion that "John is attempting entirely too many things, with the possible result of dissipating his time, energy, and money." Young agreed with this assessment, replying that if Goodrich had "received as many bulletins from Washington as have snowed down upon my desk from day to day," he must have felt that "keeping up with what John was doing was like trying to follow a football game when you know nothing about football." As a result of the concern among Collier's financial supporters, Young went to Washington in March to get at "first hand an understanding of what it was all about."

"For argumentative purposes," Young told Collier and his friend Judson King that what they were doing in attacking so many different aspects of the Indian problem "was all wrong and not getting at the real job that we had to do," namely, publicity and education "aimed at the destruction of the Indian Bureau," which Young called "an antiquated, stupid, and possibly corrupt administrative machine . . . ." Once he began to listen to Collier and King, however, Young was pleasantly surprised to learn that they agreed with him and he came away from the meeting convinced that "all that had been done so far was to the good and made important contributions towards the end I held in mind." While there was little hope that the Indian Office could be re-

formed by "a single piece of legislation," Young was made to
see that Collier's strategy for the moment was simply to
block bills the Indian Office was backing; not to block the
Indian oil-leasing bill sponsored by Burke "would have been
a crime," he wrote. The chief value of Collier's work, he reported, was in "the education of Congress itself and in the
education of ourselves as to what we have to do and how to
do it. I am quite convinced that John's efforts . . . have added
immeasurably to our strength and prestige and power to
make ourselves felt in the situation and have won some valuable allies in Congress."[21]

Young's tentative assessment of Collier's success was vin-
dicated later in the summer of 1926 when Secretary Work,
once again responding to growing criticism of the Indian
Office, turned to the Brookings Institution with the request
that it conduct a thorough and nonpolitical investigation of
Indian affairs. Obliquely referring to the congressional investigation that Frear and Collier had demanded, Work announced that he was requesting the investigation because
of "the circulation of published propaganda," which was
"having the effect of discrediting the Government" in the
eyes of Indians and "disturbing the public mind on this
question of human interest." Appearing before the House
Appropriations Committee later in the year, Commissioner
Burke was more blunt. The Brookings investigation had
been requested, he said, to prevent "a partisan investigation" by the Indian Office's critics.[22]

Commissioner Burke's fading credibility was further evidenced in the summer of 1926 when he once again sought
to unseat Stella Atwood from her position as chairman of
the Indian Welfare Committee of the GFWC. For the previous two years Mrs. Atwood had found it difficult to work
with her superior, a Mrs. Miller, who headed the welfare department of the GFWC and who apparently had made careful plans to oust Mrs. Atwood from her position. Just before
the vote that would determine the chairmanship for another two years, a special delivery letter from Commissioner Burke arrived, in which he charged that Mrs. Atwood

had exceeded her responsibilities by furnishing inaccurate information to Senator Burton K. Wheeler. Wheeler in turn had used this information to attack the Indian Office in a speech during the vote on the Indian Oil Leasing Act. Burke's intervention, however, backfired. Mrs. Atwood was reelected, and to strengthen her position, the Indian welfare committee was removed from Mrs. Miller's jurisdiction and transferred to the more hospitable department of American citizenship.[23]

In retrospect, it is possible to see that the years 1926–27 marked the turning point in the history of federal Indian policy. The methods of the assimilation policy, if not the policy itself, had been severely criticized by Collier and his supporters, with the result that they could no longer be used without challenge. In the fight over the Bursum bill and the executive-order reservations, Collier served notice that Indian land titles could no longer be subverted just because they interfered with the ambitions of white Americans. In his defense of Pueblo ceremonials and dances, he asserted not only a legitimate claim to religious freedom, but he also hinted that the preservation of Indian cultural and religious values was necessary to their survival as a people. In his efforts to defeat the bill that would have given statutory authority to the courts of Indian offenses, Collier reminded Americans that Indians, too, had civil rights that must be respected. And in the conflict over the Lees Ferry bridge and the Zuñi canes, he successfully asserted the right of Indians to a limited degree of self-determination. While it would be an exaggeration to say that he had succeeded in defeating the forces of assimilation, he had clearly challenged their supremacy and forced them into a stalemate.

While successfully backing the Indian Office into a position of defense, Collier had yet to articulate his own reform program positively. It is probable that he had not yet formulated such a program, although the "Announcement of Purposes" promulgated by the AIDA in 1923 can be interpreted as an embryonic formulation of his later Indian New Deal.

The "general principles" stated in that document were still vague enough to be compatible with assimilationist theory, as indicated by their adoption by the Eastern Association on Indian Affairs and the Indian Rights Association at the harmony meeting in New York in June 1923. The emphasis in the "Announcement of Purpose" was upon reform in the areas of education, health care, credit and marketing, legal protection, religious freedom, and government observance of its "fiduciary obligations" to its wards, all of which were acceptable to enlightened assimilationists. It is also probable that in 1927 few persons outside his own small group of supporters were aware of Collier's earlier work in New York and California, which so clearly marked him as an exponent of the then novel philosophy of cultural pluralism. Indeed, during the years under discussion in this volume, so much of Collier's time and effort had been devoted to the kind of fire-fighting activities that James Young and Chauncey Goodrich had criticized in 1926, that he was generally viewed by his opponents as simply an opportunist, an activist, or, as the Indian Office often phrased it, a "paid propagandist." The truly revolutionary nature of his ideas and his goals was hidden from all but a few of his closest associates.

But the march of events was on Collier's side. Faith in the virtues of agriculture, which had been a major factor in the drive to break up Indian reservations earlier in the century, was on the wane in the 1920s as farmers experienced economic depression a full decade before the industrial sectors of the economy. Once the depression spread after 1929, the equally strong faith in rugged individualism would be shaken, and communal and cooperative schemes would become popular. Protestant Christianity no longer commanded the attention that it had enjoyed in an earlier era, when bringing the gospel and the church to primitive peoples was confidently assumed to be a part of America's mission. Even the strong bias of Anglo-Saxon racial superiority was beginning to wane after a decade of nativist intolerance. By the late 1920s, America was on the verge of social and political upheaval that would pave the way for the emergence of minorities who had previously been restrained from advancement.

Even before the onset of the Great Depression, however, events were already moving in Collier's direction. In 1927 the Brookings Institution released the report that Secretary Wilbur had commissioned after the meeting of the Council of One Hundred. While it stopped short of endorsing a policy of cultural pluralism, it was devastating in its criticism of the failures of assimilation. That same year Collier persuaded his newly found supporters in the U.S. Senate to create a subcommittee to conduct its own investigation of Indian affairs and he then proceeded to direct the subcommittee's work. During the next five years, the subcommittee traveled to nearly every Indian reservation in the country, further exposing the failures of the assimilation policy and generating pressure for reform. In 1929, the subcommittee forced the resignation of Commissioner Burke, and his successor in that office, Charles J. Rhoads, a Quaker investment banker, pledged himself to implement the reforms suggested by the Brookings Institution report. When Rhoads proved incapable of keeping his pledge, Collier seized the initiative, and as the winds of reform gusted across the nation in 1932, opening the doors of government to new and sometimes radical ideas, Collier became an obvious candidate for the post of Indian commissioner. His rise to power and the reforms he implemented during the New Deal will be the subject of volume two.

Appendix

An Appeal by the Pueblo Indians of New Mexico
To the People of the United States

We, the undersigned representatives of the 20 pueblos of New Mexico, assembled in council at Santo Domingo on November the 5th, 1922, make this appeal to the American people for fair play and justice and the preservation of our pueblo life.

We, the Pueblo Indians, have always been self-supporting and have not been a burden on the government. We have lived in peace with our fellow-Americans even while we have watched the gradual taking away of our lands and waters. Today, many of our pueblos have the use of less than an acre per person of irrigated land, whereas in New Mexico 10 acres of irrigated land are considered necessary for a white man to live on. We have reached a point where we must either live or die.

Now we discover that the senate has passed a bill, called the Bursum bill, which will complete our destruction, and that congress and the American people have been told that we, the Indians, have asked for this legislation. This, we say, is not true. We have never asked for this legislation. We were never given the chance of having anything to say or do about this bill. We have studied the bill over and found that this bill will deprive us of our happy life by taking away our lands and water and will destroy our pueblo government and our customs which we have enjoyed for hundreds of years, and through which we have been able to be self-supporting and happy down to this day.

The bill will take away our self-respect and make us dependent on the government and force us into court to fight over and to settle things which we have always settled among ourselves without any cost to the government.

Before this bill passed the senate we had trusted the government, and now we find that unless this bill is beaten, the government will betray our trust. We cannot understand why the Indian

379

office and the lawyers who are paid by the government to defend our interests, and the secretary of the interior, have deserted us and failed to protect us this time. The Pueblo officials have tried many times to obtain an explanation of this bill from officials of the Indian office and the attorneys of the government and have always been put off and even insulted, and on one occasion when a Pueblo Indian talked with that government attorney who drew this Bursum bill, about the bill, he was told that he was "ungrateful" and "no good." Knowing that the bill was being framed, a delegation from Laguna, the largest pueblo, waited 11 hours for a chance to discuss it with the Commissioner of Indian Affairs at Albuquerque. At the end of this time, the commissioner granted 10 minutes, in which he answered no question that the Pueblos had come to ask.

After we failed to get an explanation from government officials who are supposed to help us, we have ourselves studied what this bill will do to our life and our land, and have come together today to make a move by which we can appeal to the American people.

The Pueblos, as is well known, existed in a civilized condition before the white man came to America. We have kept our old customs and lived in harmony with each other and with our fellow-Americans.

This bill will destroy our common life and will rob us of everything which we hold dear—our lands, our customs, our traditions.

Are the American people willing to see this happen? (SIGNED) **Pueblo of Taos:** John D. Archuleta, Governor; Tomas Romero, Antonio Romero, Antonio Lujan. **Pueblo of San Juan:** Santana Archuleta, Governor; Jose Ramos Archuleta, Sotero Ortiz, Jose Madrid Cruz. **Pueblo of Santa Clara:** Manuel Tafoya, Governor; Juan Jose Gutierrez, Santiago Naranjo. **Pueblo of San Ildefonso:** Juan B. Gonzales, Governor; Julian Martinez, Santiago Martinez, Romando Vigil. **Pueblo of Nambe:** Juan Vigil Galunuelar, Agustin Vigil, Loreto Vigil, Gabriel Trujillo. **Pueblo of Tesuque:** Elias Suazo, Governor; Martin Vigil. **Pueblo of Cochiti:** Marcial Quintana, Governor; Lorenzo Herrera, Alcario Montoya, Elutrio Suina, Juan Jose Trujillo. **Pueblo of Santo Domingo:** Santiago Perin, Governor; Julian Lotrob, Lieutenant Governor; Juan Cattu, Jose A. Calabasa, Jose Ortiz, Francisco Tenorio, Francisco Renio, Julian Tenorio, Pedro Lopez, Ambrosio Coriz, Victoriano Mechen, Jose Telesfor Aguilar, Francisco Renio, Trinidad Coriz, Roque Garcia, Francisco Abeyta, Leandro Madler, Diego Benavides, Juan Garcia,

Valentin Crispin, Tomascito Tenorio, Juan Calabaza, Pedro Pajarito, Ventura Garcia, Jose Coriz, Jose Tenorio, Santiago Abeyta, Jose Leandro Coriz. **Pueblo of San Felipe:** Jose Domingo Valencia, Governor, represented by Santiago Chavarria; Domacio Gallegos, Donaciano Sanchez, Juan Ignacio Mantano, Santiago Esquibel. **Pueblo of Santa Ana:** Jose Emilio, Rafael Armijo, Edward Hunt, Hinio Garcia, M. Romero, Isidro Antonio, Henio Tenorio, Rafael Antonio. **Pueblo of Zia:** Lorenzo Medina, Lieutenant Governor; Isidro Shije, Jose Reyes Shije, Andres Pino. **Pueblo of Jemez:** Felipe Yeppa, Governor, represented by Jose Romero; Jesus M. Baca, Jose Manuel Yepa, Pauline Toya, Pablo Toya, Jose Reiz Loreta. **Pueblo of Pecos:** Jose Romero, Pablo Toya. **Pueblo of Sandia:** Lorenzo Lucero, Governor; Juan Abilo, Nasorio Giron, Juan Antonio Trujillo. **Pueblo of Isleta:** Remigio Lucero, Governor; Juan T. Abeyta, Cresencio Ancey, Antonio Abeyta, Secretary of the Meeting. **Pueblo of Laguna:** Frank Pisano, Governor; Bert Wetmore, Lieutenant Governor; Lorenzo Ribera, James Hiowa, Walter S. Sarracino, Pablo Johnson, Marcelino Abeyta, Ulysses G. Pisano, Pablo Abeyta, Charles Kie, Chairman of Meeting. **Pueblo of Acoma:** Juan Pablo Garcia, Governor; Juan S. Garcia, James H. Miller, Frank Ortiz. **Pueblo of Picuris:** Juan D. Archuleta. **Pueblo of Pojoaque:** Agustin Vigil, Gabriel Trujillo. **Pueblo of Zuni:** Eleuterio Luna, Governor; Adelesa Juan Perea, Lieutenant Governor; Abelicio Palawati, Ernest Seciwa, Lorenzo Chavez, Eulalio Bautisto, Leopoldo Eriacho, Norman Napetcha.

Abbreviations Used in the Notes

ABF-HL: Albert B. Fall Papers, Huntington Library.

ABF-UNM: Albert B. Fall Papers, University of New Mexico Library (microfilm).

CdeYE: Charles de Young Elkus Papers, private collection.

CLAI: California League of American Indians Papers, Bancroft Library, University of California, Berkeley.

CSHIC: Records of the California State Housing and Immigration Commission, Department of Industrial Relations, Division of Housing, San Francisco.

HLS-LC: Hugh L. Scott Papers, Manuscript Division, Library of Congress.

HOB-UNM: Holm O. Bursum Papers, University of New Mexico Library.

IRA-HSP: Indian Rights Association Papers, Historical Society of Pennsylvania.

JC-Yale: John Collier Papers, Yale University Library.

JRH-UCLA: John Randolph Haynes Papers, Department of Special Collections, University Research Library, University of California, Los Angeles.

MD-Yale: Mabel Dodge Luhan Papers, Collection of American Literature, Beinecke Rare Book and Manuscript Library, Yale University.

PC-UCSB: Pearl Chase Papers, The Community Development and Conservation Collection, Department of Special Collections, University Library, University of California, Santa Barbara.

PI-CU: People's Institute Papers, Cooper-Hewitt Collection of Manuscripts and Archives, Cooper Union Library.

PI-NYPL: People's Institute Records, Manuscripts and Archives Division, New York Public Library, Astor, Lenox and Tilden Foundations.

NA,RG 48: National Archives of the United States, Records of the Office of the Secretary of the Interior.

NA, RG 75: National Archives of the United States, Records of the Office of Indian Affairs.

WGH-OHS: Warren G. Harding Papers, Ohio Historical Society.

Notes

Chapter 1: Childhood and Adolescence (1884–1906)

1. Much of the information in this chapter is based upon Collier's memoir, *From Every Zenith* (Denver: Sage Press, 1963); *see* especially pp. 15–26 for the account of his first seventeen years. Quotations attributed to Julia Collier Harris are taken from a typescript family history made available to me through the courtesy of Mrs. Eleanor Collier Keenan. The family history was written in the early 1930s and covers events to 1897, the year of Susie Collier's death and Julia Collier's marriage. For the quotation about the undemonstrative nature of his family, *see* Collier to Mabel Dodge (Luhan), 21 May (no year), Collier correspondence, Mabel Dodge Luhan Papers, Collection of American Literature, Beinecke Rare Book and Manuscript Library, Yale University, (hereinafter MDL-Yale), New Haven, Conn. For the death of Susie Collier, see *Atlanta Constitution*, 20, 23, 24, 26 March 1897. In his study of Collier, Kenneth Philp stated that Susie Collier died of addiction to laudanum and he attributed this interpretation to Grace Collier, Collier's third wife. *See* Kenneth R. Philp, *John Collier's Crusade for Indian Reform, 1920–1954* (Tucson: University of Arizona Press, 1977), pp. 5, 253.

2. For the public career of Charles A. Collier, *see*: *The National Cyclopaedia of American Biography*, s.v. "Charles A. Collier,"; Thomas H. Martin, *Atlanta and Its Builders*, 2 vols. (n.p.: Century Memorial Publishing Co., 1902), 2: 645; Franklin M. Garrett, *Atlanta and Its Environs*, 3 vols. (New York: Lewis Historical Publishing Co., 1954), 2: 149–52, 313–15; Wallace P. Reed, *History of Atlanta, Georgia* (Syracuse, N.Y.: D. Mason and Co., 1889), pt. 2, pp. 20–22; Walter G. Cooper, *Cotton States and International Exposition* (Atlanta: Illustrator Co., 1896), pt. 2, p. 143; *Atlanta Journal*, 22 July 1955; "Cotton States and International Exposition," *Harper's Weekly*, 19 January 1895, pp. 59–60; and City of Atlanta, *Annual Report, 1897* and *1898* (Atlanta Public Library).

3. The shooting incident and Charles Collier's death were both reported in the *Atlanta Constitution*, 28, 29, 30 September 1900. *See* Collier, *From Every Zenith*, pp. 25, 31, for the interpretation that his father committed suicide. Kenneth Philp has accepted this interpretation, adding that Charles Collier killed himself as a result of becoming involved in a "financial scandal" and because of grief "over his wife's death and the family's tarnished honor" (Philp, *John Collier's Crusade for Indian Reform*, p. 5). I have uncovered no evidence that Charles Collier was involved in any financial scandal, although Julia Harris's family history does suggest that he had greatly depleted his wife's inheritance. Moreover, Collier's brother, Charles A. Collier, Jr., and his two sisters, Mrs. Louise Collier Whiteley and Mrs. Eleanor Collier Keenan, all strenuously objected to the interpretation of their parents' deaths when *From Every Zenith* was published in 1963. Charles Collier filled his copy of *From Every Zenith* with marginal corrections, and his two sisters have attributed many of Collier's statements in the book to his "exaggerated sense of imagination." Correspondence with Mrs. Charles A. Collier, 18 September 1970; Mrs. Louise Whiteley, 7 February 1970; interview with Mrs. Eleanor Keenan, 11 October 1970.

4. Collier, *From Every Zenith*, pp. 34–48. The statement that "he was wild, naive, and ignorant" is found in Biographical Account, John Collier Papers, Yale University Library (hereinafter JC-Yale), New Haven, Conn.

5. Collier, *From Every Zenith*, pp. 59–65. Lucy Wood's father served in the Civil War and was the owner of a shoe factory in Philadelphia. Her mother was a descendant of Huguenot French who came to America via Switzerland. Interview with John Collier, Jr., 21 March 1980.

6. Hutchins Hapgood, *A Victorian in the Modern World* (New York: Harcourt, Brace, and Co., 1939), p. 413. John Collier, Jr., has confirmed Hapgood's assessment of his mother's personality. His mother, he recalled, was "very much involved in the here and now . . . with the human essence of whatever was in front of her," while his father was preoccupied with abstractions and ideals. Both John Collier, Jr., and Donald Collier have confirmed that Lucy Collier suffered from manic depression. Although her illness is hinted at in letters from the early 1930s, and becomes more evident in correspondence of the early 1940s, John Collier, Jr., has stated that his mother experienced emotional problems

from her youth, dating from an incident "when a spirit lamp blew up in her face." Early in her married life, she underwent depth psychoanalysis, probably with Dr. A. A. Brill, the first Freudian practitioner in the United States, but according to John Collier, Jr., "it was of no particular value." Interview with Donald Collier, 28 December 1974; interview with John Collier, Jr., 21 March 1980.

7. Collier, *From Every Zenith*, pp. 62–66.

Chapter 2: The People's Institute (1906–14)

1. Collier, *From Every Zenith*, p. 68.

2. Eric Goldman, *Rendezvous With Destiny* (New York: Vintage Books, 1956), p. 60.

3. *Who Was Who in America*, s.v. "Robert E. Ely"; Collier, *From Every Zenith*, p. 69.

4. *The National Cyclopaedia of American Biography*, s.v. "Charles Sprague-Smith"; Moses Rischin, *The Promised City* (Cambridge, Mass.: Harvard University Press, 1962), pp. 212–14; Charles Sprague Smith, *Working With the People* (New York: A. Wessels Co., 1904); Collier, *From Every Zenith*, p. 69; Collier, "Charles Sprague-Smith," *Survey*, 9 April 1910, p. 8.

5. Jacob Riis, "The People's Institute of New York," *Century Magazine*, April 1910, pp. 850–63; *New York Times*, 22 April 1906.

6. Riis, "The People's Institute of New York," pp. 850–63; *New York Times*, 22 April 1906; Rischin, *The Promised City*, p. 213; Minutes of the Board of Trustees, 20 February 1908, People's Institute Records, Manuscripts and Archives Division, New York Public Library, Astor, Lenox and Tilden Foundations (hereinafter, PI-NYPL), New York, N.Y.; Collier, "The People's Institute," *Independent*, 30 May 1912, pp. 1144–48; Collier, "The People's Institute," *World Today*, February 1909, pp. 170–75.

7. Collier, *From Every Zenith*, pp. 70–72.

8. *Ibid.*, pp. 70–71; Collier, "The Lantern Bearers," *Survey*, 3 July 1915, pp. 315–17.

9. Collier, "The Lantern Bearers," *Survey*, 7 August 1915, pp. 423–47; People's Institute, *Fourteenth Annual Report*, People's Institute Papers, Cooper-Hewitt Collection of Manuscripts and Archives, Cooper Union Library (hereinafter PI-CU) New York, N.Y.; Collier, *From Every Zenith*, p. 72.

10. Collier, *From Every Zenith*, pp. 71–72; Collier, "The Lantern Bearers," *Survey*, 7 August 1915, pp. 423–27; Collier, "The Lantern Bearers," *Survey*, 2 October 1915, pp. 9–14.

11. Wilton A. Barrett to Collier, 16 January 1934, JC-Yale.

12. Allan Nevins and John A. Krout, *The Greater City* (New York: Columbia University Press, 1948), pp. 72–77; Collier, *From Every Zenith*, pp. 73–76.

13. Eleanor Glueck, *The Community Use of the Schools* (Baltimore: Williams and Wilkins Co., 1927), p. 16–17; Allen F. Davis, *Spearheads for Reform* (New York: Oxford University Press, 1967), pp. 75–83; Mary P. Follette, *The New State* (New York: Longmans, Green and Co., 1920), pp. 206–16, 363–73.

14. C. A. Perry, *Wider Use of the School Plant* (New York: Survey Associates, 1913), pp. 271–73; Glueck, *The Community Use of the Schools*, pp. 18–36; Sidney Dillick, *Community Organization for Neighborhood Schools* (New York: William Morrow and Co., 1953), pp. 59–62.

15. Glueck, *The Community Use of the Schools*, pp. 18–36; Dillick, *Community Organization for Neighborhood Schools*, pp. 59–62; "Madison Meeting on Social Service," *Survey*, 11 November 1911, p. 1169; George B. Ford, "Madison Conference on Social Centers," *Survey*, 18 November 1911, pp. 1229–31.

16. *New York Times*, 1 July 1917; "Edward J. Ward, "Civic and Social Center Development," *National Education Association Proceedings, 1912*, (Ann Arbor: National Education Association, 1912); Collier, "The Keystone of the Arch," *Survey*, 18 November 1911, p. 1200.

17. Collier, *From Every Zenith*, pp. 79–81; *New York Times*, 15 February 1914.

18. *New York Times*, 22 April 1916; Collier, "City Planning and the Problem of Recreation," *Annals of the American Academy of Political and Social Science*, 51 (January 1914), pp. 208–15; Collier, "The Keystone of the Arch," p. 1200; *New York Times*, 1 July 1917, 27 April 1913; Collier, "Leisure Time, the Last Problem of Conservation," *The Playground*, June 1912, pp. 14–16.

19. *New York Times*, 11 April 1913, 25 May 1913, 21 April 1913; Collier, "City Planning and the Problem of Recreation," pp. 208–15.

20. Mabel Dodge Luhan, *Background* (New York: Harcourt, Brace and Co., 1933); idem, *European Experiences* (New York: Harcourt, Brace and Co., 1935). The quotation describing America as "ugly" is found in *European Experiences*, p. 453.

21. Mabel Dodge Luhan, *Movers and Shakers* (New York: Harcourt, Brace and Co., 1936), pp. 4–6 for description of her apartment; p. 12 for her estrangement from Edwin Dodge; pp. 14–17 for her friendship with Van Vechten and Hapgood; pp. 74–95 for the salon.

22. Max Eastman, *The Enjoyment of Living* (New York: Harper and Brothers, 1948), p. 523. *See also*, Allen Churchill, *The Improper Bohemians* (New York: E. P. Dutton and Co., 1959), and Emily Hahn, *Romantic Rebels* (New York: Houghton Mifflin Co., 1967).

23. Luhan, *Movers and Shakers*, pp. 25–38.

24. *Ibid.*, pp. 186–212; *New York Times*, 7 June 1913.

25. Collier to Mrs. Dodge, undated letter in Collier correspondence, 1913, MDL-Yale; Collier, *From Every Zenith*, p. 80 (Stein), p. 105 (Hapgood); Hapgood, *A Victorian in the Modern World*, p. 336.

26. Collier, "The Lantern Bearers," *Survey*, 1 July 1916, pp. 343–50.

27. *New York Times*, 7 June 1913.

28. Collier, "The Lantern Bearers," pp. 343–50; *New York Times*, 24 May, 6 June 1914.

29. Davis, *Spearheads for Reform*, pp. 208–13; John R. Commons et al, *A History of Trade Unionism in the United States*, 4 vols. (New York: Macmillan Co., 1935), 4, p. 164; *New York Times*, 27 September 1913. In January 1914, Walsh and Margaret Wilson appeared at a luncheon in New York City sponsored by the League for Political Education, at which Walsh advocated increased usage of the schools for political and social purposes: *New York Times*, 25 January 1914.

30. Collier to Mabel Dodge, 31 December 1913, MDL-Yale. The letter is printed without date and with Mabel's explanation of her role in the scheme in *Movers and Shakers*, pp. 144–50.

31. Luhan, *Movers and Shakers*, p. 323.

32. John Collier and Edward M. Barrows, *The City Where Crime is Play* (New York: People's Institute, 1914); a copy of this report is preserved in PI-CU. *See also* Collier, *From Every Zenith*, pp. 79–80; *New York Times*, 15 February 1914.

33. Luhan, *Movers and Shakers*, pp. 159–63; Frederick J. Hoffman et al., *The Little Magazines* (Princeton: Princeton University Press, 1946), p. 239.

34. Luhan, *Movers and Shakers*, pp. 265–79. The affair with Reed is also described in Robert A. Rosenstone, *Romantic Revo-*

lutionary, A Biography of John Reed (New York: Alfred Knopf, 1975), pp. 134–79, 192–93, 202–4, 212–13, 238–40.

35. Collier to Hutchins Hapgood, 19 March, 18 April, 22 April, 26 April 1914; Collier to Mabel Dodge, 26 April, 9 May 1914; all in Collier correspondence, MDL-Yale. *See also* Luhan, *Movers and Shakers*, p. 312; Collier, *From Every Zenith*, p. 82.

36. In a contemporary account of his vicissitudes written to Mabel Dodge on 11 October 1914 (MDL-Yale), Collier mentioned all the ills listed above except the deaths of Lucy Collier's parents. In his memoirs, he listed the deaths, but omitted Lucy's operation; Collier, *From Every Zenith*, p. 82.

37. Ibid.

Chapter 3: The Community-Center Movement (1914–19)

1. Some indication of the importance of Collier's work at the People's Institute is revealed in People's Institute, Budget of Fiscal Year 1913–14, file 3341, PI-CU. In October 1913, Frederick Howe's salary as director was set at $5,000; Collier's salary as civic secretary was $4,000.

2. Collier correspondence, MDL-Yale: Collier to Mabel Dodge (undated), and Lucy Collier, "A Prospectus for the Home School" (undated), both located among the 1915 correspondence; Collier, *From Every Zenith*, pp. 66–67. Charles Collier believes that the school was created because of a poliomyelitis epidemic in New York City. He recalls attending the school for only one year. Interview with Charles Collier, 6 May 1980.

3. Mabel Dodge and John Collier have recorded somewhat different recollections of Isadora's meeting with Mayor Mitchell. *See* Collier, *From Every Zenith*, pp. 107–9; Luhan, *Movers and Shakers*, pp. 319–31.

4. Collier, "The Lantern Bearers," *Survey*, 3 June 1916, p. 251; Collier, *From Every Zenith*, p. 109; Luhan, *Movers and Shakers*, pp. 332–44; Collier correspondence, MDL-Yale: Collier to Mabel Dodge, 6 February 1915; Collier to Mabel Dodge, 3 March 1915; and "A Perspective of the Elizabeth Duncan School," no date.

5. Collier, *From Every Zenith*, pp. 84–87; General Announcements for the years 1915–19, New York Training School for Community Center Workers, PI-CU; *New York Times*, 27 July and 11 August 1915.

6. *New York Times*, 16 April, 21 April, 22 April 1916; "How

Grown-ups Act in School," *Survey*, 6 May 1916, pp. 169–71; John Collier, "Definitions and Debates of the Community Center Conference," *American City*, June 1916, pp. 542–74; Howard S. Braucher, "Community Center Conference," *The Playground*, June 1916, pp. 79–96; Collier, "Self Determination In Community Enterprise," *Survey*, 20 September 1919, pp. 860–72; John Collier to the Trustees of the Training School for Community Workers and of the People's Institute, 14 November 1918, PI-NYPL. In his memoirs, Collier has incorrectly given 1915 as the date of the first National Conference on Community Center Problems.

7. Collier, *From Every Zenith*, pp. 83–84; "For Nationalizing the Neighborhood," *Survey*, 5 May 1917, pp. 131–32; *Chicago Daily Tribune*, 18 April 1917. The *Tribune* reported only that the conference had opened and that Collier addressed the delegates at the first session.

8. Collier to Mabel Dodge, no date (circa 1916), Collier correspondence, MDL-Yale; Luhan, *Movers and Shakers*, p. 484; Mary Heaton Vorse, *A Footnote to Folly* (New York: Farrar and Rinehart, Inc., 1935), p. 130; Churchill, *The Improper Bohemians*, p. 193; Collier, "The Mystery of Lester Ward," August-September 1916, PI-NYPL.

9. Collier, "Criticisms of the Training School as reported by Mrs. C., Mrs. McB., etc.," PI-NYPL.

10. Collier to Dr. Sanderson, 8 August [1917,] PI-NYPL. For the Community Clearing House experiment, *see* Collier, *From Every Zenith*, p. 89; and Edward L. Burchard to Collier, 24 February 1936, JC-Yale.

11. *New York Times*, 1 July, 1 October 1917; Collier, "The Organized Laity and the Social Expert: The Meaning of Public Community Centers," *National Conference of Social Work Proceedings, 1917*, pp. 464–69; Collier, "Home Economics and the Community Center," *The Journal of Home Economics*, July 1917, pp. 319–21; Collier, "School Buildings as Coordinating Places for the Civil Energies of the War," *American City*, June 1917, pp. 588–90.

12. *New York Times*, 24 January, 8 October, 3 December 1917; Collier, *From Every Zenith*, pp. 90–91; People's Institute Correspondence, 1917–1922 folder, PI-CU.

13. Collier, *From Every Zenith*, p. 90; Dillick, *Community Organization for Neighborhood Development*, p. 71; John Higham, *Strangers in the Land* (New York: Atheneum Press, 1967), p. 246;

Collier to the Trustees of the Training School, 14 November 1918, PI-NYPL: undated memorandum (1918) by Collier, PI-NYPL; *New York Times*, 7 March, 19 March 1917.

14. Collier to Edward F. Sanderson, 13 June 1918, PI-NYPL.

15. John Collier, "Democracy Every Day," *National Education Association Addresses and Proceedings, 1918*, pp. 53–54; Carol Aronovici, "Organized Leisure As A Factor in Conservation," and E. L. Burchard, "Community Councils of Defense," *National Conference of Social Work Proceedings, 1918*, pp. 464–73; *New York Times*, 3 July 1918; Collier, "Community Councils—Democracy Every Day," *Survey*, 31 August 1918, pp. 604–6, 21 September 1918, pp. 689–91, 28 September 1918, pp. 709–11.

16. L. Emmett Holt, "Child Health Organization," *Child Labor Bulletin*, 1918, pp. 28–31; Lucy Wood Collier, "The Work of the Child Health Organization," *The American Child*, August 1919, pp. 141–44; Sally Lucas Jean, "Comment," *National Conference of Social Work Proceedings, 1918*, pp. 468–69; Lucy Wood Collier, "Domestic Miracles," *Sunset*, April 1923, pp. 15–17; Lucy Oppen, "Health Game, A Contest in Which Government Plays," *Survey*, 5 April 1919, p. 27, 15 June 1918, p. 322; "The American Child Hygiene Association and the Child Health Organization of America," *School and Society*, 21 October 1922, p. 464; Collier, *From Every Zenith*, p. 89. John Collier, Jr., believes that Lucy Collier's acquaintance with Emmett Holt went back to her first years in New York City. According to him, Lucy Collier "spent a great deal of time" with Holt, went with him on his house calls, and became "fascinated with his practice." Holt was a "brilliant slum doctor," through whose influence Lucy Collier became involved in "a great deal of therapeutic work which she later transferred to public health work." It was also at this time, before the children were born, that Collier left his wife temporarily for another woman. Interview with John Collier, Jr., 21 March 1980.

17. *New York Times*, 13 October, 10 November, 17 November 1918, 12 January, 24 January, 22 May 1919; People's Institute, Minutes of the Meeting of the Board of Trustees, 13 October 1918, PI-NYPL; Collier, *From Every Zenith*, p. 92.

18. Collier to the Trustees of the Training School for Community Workers and of the People's Institute, 14 November 1918, PI-NYPL.

19. Collier to Edward F. Sanderson, 1 February 1919, PI-NYPL. For a recent history of the People's Institute see Robert Fisher,

"The People's Institute of New York City, 1897–1934," (Ph.D. dissertation, New York University, 1974); and also Robert Fisher, "Community Organization and Citizen Participation: The Efforts of the People's Institute in New York City, 1910–1940," *Social Science Review*, September 1977, 474–90.

20. I have pieced together this description of the league from its publicity releases found in the Holm O. Bursum Papers, University of New Mexico Library (hereinafter HOB-UNM), Albuquerque, N.M., and the T. Percival Gerson Papers, box 3, folder 4, Department of Special Collections, University Research Library, University of California at Los Angeles. *See also* Higham, *Strangers in the Land*, pp. 302–3.

21. Dillick, *Community Organization and Neighborhood Development*, p. 80; *New York Times*, 19 July, 11 August, 15 August, 14 October, 8 December, 24 December 1919; John Collier, "Community Councils—What Have They Done and What is the Future?", *National Conference of Social Work Proceedings, 1919*, pp. 473–80; Collier, "Self Determination in Community Enterprise," *Survey*, 20 September 1919, pp. 870–72; Collier, "Urban Community Organization," *The American Child*, November 1919, pp. 252–57.

22. Collier, *From Every Zenith*, p. 93.

23. Since this section of the book was written in the early 1970s, four critical accounts of the Indian New Deal have appeared, each of which has added significantly to the much needed reappraisal of the era: Donald L. Parman, *The Navajos and the New Deal* (New Haven: Yale University Press, 1976); Kenneth R. Philp, *John Collier's Crusade for Indian Reform, 1920–1954* (Tucson: University of Arizona Press, 1977); Graham D. Taylor, *The New Deal and American Indian Tribalism* (Lincoln: University of Nebraska Press, 1980); and Laurence M. Hauptman, *The Iroquois and The New Deal* (Syracuse: Syracuse University Press, 1981).

Chapter 4: Discovering the American Indian (1919–21)

1. Collier, *From Every Zenith*, p. 126.

2. *The National Cyclopaedia of American Biography*, s.v. "Simon J. Lubin"; Higham, *Strangers in the Land*, pp. 121, 241; State of California, Department of Industrial Relations, Division of Housing Administration, *Manual* (20 April 1962), section 0050; State of California, Commission of Immigration and Housing,

Annual Report, 1919 in *Appendix* to the *Journals of the Senate and Assembly of California*, 43d sess., 1919, V.

3. Minutes of the California State Housing and Immigration Commission, in the files of the California State Department of Industrial Relations, Division of Housing Administration, San Francisco (hereafter *Minutes*, CSHIC): 27 June, 29 August 1917; 17 January, 20 April, 6 May 1918; 4 January, 25 July, 24 October, 12 December 1919; 28 January, 11 March 1920. *See also* General Federation of Women's Clubs, *A Suggested Program for Americanization* (1919), copy in the California State Library, Sacramento; CSHIC, *Americanization: California's Answer* (Sacramento: State Printing Office, 1920); Commission of Immigration and Housing, State of California, *Annual Report, 1921*, in *Appendix* to the *Journals of the Senate and Assembly of California*, 44th sess., 1921, V; California State Board of Education, *Fourth Biennial Report*, 1921, in *Appendix* to the *Journals of the Senate and Assembly of California*, 44th sess., 1921, II; Collier, *From Every Zenith*, pp. 115–18.

4. *Minutes*, CSHIC: 4 February, 24 March, 18 May, 24 May, 3 July, 19 July 1920. *See also* State of California, Commission of Immigration and Housing, *Ninth Annual Report, 1923* in *Appendix* to the *Journals of the Senate and Assembly of California*, 45th sess., 1923, IV.

5. For the activities of the Better America Foundation, *see* John Randolph Haynes Papers, Department of Special Collections, University Research Library, University of California, Los Angeles (hereinafter JRH-UCLA). For Collier's resignation and the activity of the CSHIC, *see Minutes*, CSHIC: 18 October, 22 October, 5 November 1920; and Simon J. Lubin to R. Justin Miller, 27 October 1920, CSHIC.

6. George E. Mowry, *California Progressives* (Berkeley: University of California Press, 1952), pp. 16, 39, 80, 140, 291; Collier, *From Every Zenith*, p. 116; Collier eulogy on Haynes, 11 November 1937, JC-Yale; Collier memo on Haynes, December 1927, Winifred Pomeroy Papers, courtesy of Miss Pomeroy.

7. Collier, *From Every Zenith*, pp. 117–18; Van Deren Coke, *Taos and Santa Fe: The Artist's Environment* (Albuquerque: University of New Mexico Press, 1963); Hahn, *Romantic Rebels*, pp. 205–9; Mabel Dodge Luhan, *Taos and Its Artists* (New York: Duell, Sloan, and Pierce, 1947), p. 11; E. Peixotto, "American Painters Give Serious Study to the American Indian," *Scribner's Magazine*, August 1916, pp. 257–70. The quotations are from

Erna Ferguson, *Our Southwest* (New York: Alfred A. Knopf, 1940), p. 276, and Erna Ferguson, *New Mexico, A Pageant of Three People* (New York: Alfred A. Knopf, 1951), p. 374.

8. For her boredom with her New York friends, *see* Mabel Luhan, *Edge of the Taos Desert* (New York: Harcourt, Brace, and Co., 1937), p. 273; for Sterne's letter, *see* MDL-Yale, Sterne correspondence, and *Movers and Shakers*, p. 534. Emilie Hapgood was the former wife of Norman Hapgood, the editor of *Collier's* magazine.

9. Collier to Mabel Dodge, Sunday, 11th (no date) and Collier to Mabel Dodge (no date), both in MDL-Yale.

10. For Collier's arrival in Taos, *see* Mabel Dodge to Carl Van Vechten, 11 December 1920, MDL-Yale, Van Vechten correspondence. For his recollection of the Taos experience, *see* Collier, *From Every Zenith*, pp. 123–27. For the role of Collier and the Gulicks in the formation of the Camp Fire Girls, *see* Collier, *From Every Zenith*, pp. 97–98; Helen Buckler et al., *Wo-He-Lo, The Story of the Camp Fire Girls, 1910–1960* (New York: Holt, Rinehart and Winston, 1961), pp. 5–11, 43–44, 153; and William D. Murray, *The History of the Boy Scouts of America* (New York: Boy Scouts of America, 1937), p. 11.

11. Collier to Haynes, 12 January 1921 and Collier to Dr. Lucas, 30 March 1921, both in JRH-UCLA. Dr. Lucas is not identified in the correspondence, but John Collier, Jr., has identified him as William P. Lucas, a prominent pediatrician in San Francisco with whom Lucy Collier worked closely in her continuing interest in child health care. John Collier, Jr., believes that his mother and Lucas may have been in love, but that because of his respect for Collier, Lucas refused to pursue the matter. Interview with John Collier, Jr., 21 March 1980. *See also* Collier to Commissioner of Indian Affairs, 30 July 1921, National Archives, Record Group 75 (hereinafter NA, RG 75), Northern Pueblo Agency files.

12. Collier to Mabel Dodge, 17 May 1921, MDL-Yale.

13. San Francisco State Teachers College, *Announcement of Courses, 1922* and *Preliminary Announcement of Summer Session, June 26–August 4, 1922*. Collier's name does not appear in the 1921 announcement, apparently because he was hired after it had already gone to press. I have, therefore, based my account of Collier's teaching career on the course descriptions he wrote for the summer session, 1922, and the academic year, 1922–23, although he resigned in September 1922. *See also* Collier to Haynes, 1 July 1922, JRH-UCLA.

14. Most of my information about Mrs. Atwood is taken from a

typescript biography made available to me by Mrs. Grace King, Mrs. Atwood's cousin. *See also* Stella Atwood, "The Case for the Indian," *Survey Graphic,* October 1922, pp. 7–11; Mrs. Atwood's testimony in U.S., Congress, House, Indian Affairs Committee, *Pueblo Indian Land Titles, Hearings on H. R. 13452 and H. R. 13674,* 67th Cong., 4th sess., 1–15 February 1923, pp. 178 ff; U.S., Congress, House, Indian Affairs Committee, *Indians of the United States, Hearings,* 66th Cong., 1–3d sess., 1919–20, 3:1091; NA, RG 75, Board of Indian Commissioners, tray 63: Mrs. Charles C. Arnold file.

15. For the Burke-Atwood correspondence, *see* NA, RG 75, Office of the Commissioner of Indian Affairs (Burke), Personal and Semi-Official file: Mrs. Stella Atwood, 1921–32.

16. For the Coggeshall removal, *see* Warren G. Harding Papers, Ohio Historical Society (hereinafter WGH-OHS), Secretary of the Interior (Indian Affairs), box 24, file 11353. For Mrs. Atwood's association with the Indian Rights Association, *see* Indian Rights Association Papers, Historical Society of Pennsylvania (hereinafter IRA-HSP), 1921 correspondence: Brosius to Welsh, 4 September 1921; Sniffen to Welsh, 14 September 1921.

17. NA, RG 75, Office of the Commissioner of Indian Affairs (Burke), Personal and Semi-Official file: Atwood to Burke, 21 September 1921.

18. Ibid.: Burke to Atwood, 11 October 1921; Atwood to Burke, 6 December 1921; Atwood to Burke, 15 December 1921; Burke to Atwood, 7 January 1922. For Twitchell's correspondence, *see* Albert B. Fall Papers, University of New Mexico Library (hereinafter ABF-UNM): Atwood to Charles Safford, 9 January 1922; Twitchell to Atwood, 17 November 1921; Twitchell to Atwood, 21 January 1922.

19. NA, RG 75, Office of the Commissioner of Indian Affairs (Burke), Personal and Semi-Official file: Atwood to Stephen Mather, 19 December 1921; Atwood to Burke, 24 March 1922. *Also,* Collier to Mabel Dodge, 18 March (no year), MDL-Yale.

20. For Collier's description of the Azusa meeting, *see* Collier to Dr. Haynes, 12 May 1922, JC-Yale. Collier told Haynes that he saw Mrs. Vosburg's proffer of aid not as a "choice, but only a duty." It was clear, he thought, that Mrs. Atwood was incapable of carrying the effort alone. In later years he played down his own role even more, as when he told members of the House Indian Affairs Committee that "the thing was pressed on me by Mrs. Vos-

burg out of blue sky . . . I was seeking to help get money for Mrs. Atwood to pay her expenses and to get her a helper, not dreaming I would do the work. . . ." U.S., Congress, House, Indian Affairs Committee, *Pueblo Indian Land Titles, Hearings on H.R. 13452 and H.R. 13674,* 67th Cong., 4th sess., 1923, 182.

21. The incident of the letter and check from Frank Wills is found in the Atwood mss. in the possession of Mrs. Grace King. Mrs. Atwood's itinerary during the summer of 1922 can be traced in the following: Collier to Mabel Dodge, 9 May 1922, MDL-Yale; Atwood to Charles Lummis, 12 June 1922, Lummis Papers, Southwest Museum, Los Angeles; U.S., Congress, House, Indian Affairs Committee, *Pueblo Indian Land Titles, Hearings on H.R. 13452 and 13674, 1923,* 67th Cong., 4th sess., 79, 180–81. For her anger over the second Bursum bill, *see* NA, RG 75, Office of the Commissioner (Burke), Personal and Semi-official file: Atwood to Burke, 1 August and 18 August 1922.

22. NA, RG 75, Office of the Commissioner (Burke), Personal and Semi-official file: Atwood to Burke, 1 August, 18 August, 31 August 1922; and Burke to Atwood, 9 August, 24 August 1922.

23. For the *Survey Graphic* article, *see* the several letters from Collier to Mabel Dodge and Mabel Dodge to the *Survey* editor, no date, in Collier correspondence, MDL-Yale; and *Survey Graphic,* October 1922, pp. 7–20. For Collier's letter to Dr. Haynes, *see* Collier to Haynes, 1 July 1922, JRH-UCLA.

Chapter 5: Federal Indian Policy to 1922

1. F. P. Prucha, "Andrew Jackson's Indian Policy: A Reassessment," *Journal of American History,* 56 (December 1969): 531–32.

2. Angie Debo, *A History of the Indians of the United States* (Norman: University of Oklahoma Press, 1970), p. 115.

3. Commissioner of Indian Affairs, *Annual Report to the Secretary of the Interior, 1917* (Washington, G.P.O., 1918) (hereinafter CIA, *Annual Report*), 21; Lawrence C. Kelly, *The Navajo Indians and Federal Indian Policy, 1900–1935* (Tucson: University of Arizona Press, 1968), pp. 132–34. For a recent treatment of the Sells's competency commissions see Janet McDonnell, "Competency Commissions and Indian Land Policy," *South Dakota History,"* (Winter 1980), pp. 21–34.

4. David H. Stratton, "Albert B. Fall and the Teapot Dome Affair" (Ph.D. diss., University of Colorado, 1955), pp. 15–28; Wil-

liam A. Keleher, *The Fabulous Frontier: Twelve New Mexico Items* (Albuquerque: University of New Mexico Press, 1962), pp. 209–16; David H. Stratton, ed., *The Memoirs of Albert B. Fall* (El Paso: Texas Western Press, 1966), p. 58.

5. U.S., Congress, Senate, *Congressional Record*, 62d Cong., 2d sess., 1912, 48, pt. 7: 6491; *ibid.*, 63d Cong., 2d sess., 1914, 51, pt. 4: 3318. For Fall's statement of New Mexico lands in federal control, *see* Albert B. Fall Papers, Huntington Library, San Marino, California (hereinafter ABF-HL), box 53, Fall to Secretary of the Interior, 6 May 1913.

6. Fall to B. C. Hernández, 13 April 1912, ABF-UNM; Kelly, *The Navajo Indians and Federal Indian Policy*, pp. 28–34. The petition of the New Mexico legislature is in NA, RG 75, Navajo files.

7. Fall to W. C. Reid, 29 May 1918, ABF-UNM.

8. Fall to Governor E. C. Mechem, 16 June 1920, and C. V. Safford to W. O. Hall, 28 June 1920, ibid.; Charles W. Eliot to Herbert Welsh, 27 January 1921, IRA-HSP; Welsh to Henry C. Lodge, 9 February 1921, and Lodge to Welsh, 16 February 1921, (copies) in Hugh L. Scott Papers, Library of Congress, Manuscript Division (hereinafter HLS-LC); correspondence in Presidential Personal Correspondence, box 650, file 300646, WGH-OHS; Belle C. and Fola La Follette, *Robert M. LaFollette*, 2 vols. (New York: Macmillan Co., 1953), 2: 1024; Burl Noggle, *Teapot Dome: Oil and Politics in the 1920s* (Baton Rouge: Louisiana State University Press, 1962), pp. 20–25.

9. J. Leonard Bates, *The Origins of Teapot Dome* (Urbana: University of Illinois Press, 1963); Morris R. Werner and John Starr, *Teapot Dome* (New York: Viking Press, 1959); Stratton, "Albert B. Fall and the Teapot Dome Affair"; Noggle, *Teapot Dome*.

10. John Collier, *Indians of the Americas* (New York: W. W. Norton Co., 1947), pp. 246–47; Collier, *From Every Zenith*, pp. 133–35.

Chapter 6: Albert B. Fall and the Genesis of Reform

1. For a detailed description of the Mescalero Apache reservation, *see* Mescalero Apache reservation, *Annual Narrative Report, 1920*, NA, RG 75; and Fall to Senator Selden P. Spencer, 21 June 1922, ABF-UNM. For Fall's land and cattle enterprises, *see* the following: Keleher, *The Fabulous Frontier*, pp. 219–20; Stratton, "Albert B. Fall and the Teapot Dome Affair," p. 111; C. L. Sonnich-

sen, *Tularosa: Last of the Frontier West* (New York: Devin-Adair Co., 1961), pp. 247–72.

2. Although he was apparently unaware of Fall's interest in supplying the railroad with water from the Mescalero reservation, William A. Keleher provided a detailed statement of the El Paso and Northeastern's water problems in *The Fabulous Frontier*, pp. 299–313. For Fall's contracts with the Interior Department and the railroad, *see* Mescalero Apache reservation, *Annual Narrative Report, 1914*, NA, RG 75; Fall to Ernest Stecker, 28 February 1920, and memorandum of W. M. Reed to Cato Sells, 3 June 1921, including attachments of correspondence with Fall dating back to 1910, ABF-UNM. For the Three Rivers townsite project, *see* Fall to Clarence C. Chase, 7 September 1917, ABF-UNM.

3. ABF-UNM: Fall to W. A. Hawkins, 20 May 1917; Fall to Mahlon T. Everhart, 23 May 1917; Fall to C. C. Chase, 7 September 1917. *See also* Dorothy Jensen Neal, *Captive Mountain Waters* (El Paso: Texas Western Press, 1961), pp. 65–74, for additional information on Fall's dealings with the railroad.

4. For agent Jeffries's plan, *see* Fall to Father William H. Ketcham, 14 February 1914, ABF-UNM. For Stecker's revival of the idea, *see* Stecker to Commissioner of Indian Affairs, 14 May 1920; Stecker to Fall, 15 May 1920; and Fall to Stecker, 9 June 1920, ABF-UNM. For Fall's continued difficulties with Shanta Boy over the use of the water, *see* Fall to Stecker, 28 February 1920, and Stecker to Fall, 14 January 1921, ABF-UNM.

5. For Senator Curtis's action on the Mescalero timber bill, *see* C. Safford to Fall, 10 January 1921, ABF-UNM. For Stecker's attempts to smooth over Fall's quarrel with Shanta Boy and his ouster by Fall, *see* Stecker to Fall, 14 January 1921, ABF-UNM; and Stecker to H. L. Scott, 19 February 1922, and Burke to Stecker, 4 February 1924, HLS-LC. Engineer William H. Reed's report is in Reed to Commissioner of Indian Affairs, 3 June 1921, ABF-UNM. The use of Doheny's money to purchase the Harris-Brownfield Ranch is described in Stratton, "Albert B. Fall and the Teapot Dome Affair," p. 124.

6. For the early history of these park bills, *see* the correspondence in Mescalero Apache files, NA, RG 75 and National Parks Service files, NA, RG 48. For Fall's role in the park bills, *see* ABF-UNM: Fall to Mark Thompson, 10 May 1912; Fall to James A. Baird, 12 July 1912; Fall to W. D. Murray, 22 July 1912; Fall to M. K. Wylder, 2 November 1921; and U.S., Congress, Senate, *Con-*

gressional Record, 62d Cong., 2d sess., 1912, 48, pt. 6: pp. 5729, 5995.

7. Fall's activities in behalf of the Mescalero Park bill and the opposition that he aroused between 1914 and 1916 are based upon the following: Mescalero Apache files, NA, RG 75; Board of Indian Commissioners files, NA, RG 75; National Parks Service files, NA, RG 48; U.S., Congress, Senate Congressional Record, 63d Cong., 2d sess., 1914, 51, pt. 3: 2290; ibid., 64 Cong., 1st sess., 1916, 53: pt. 1: 314, 493; Matthew Sniffen, "Conditions Among the Indians of the Southwest," Quarterly Journal of the Society of the American Indians, 1914, pp. 51–53, and 1915, pp. 270–72, in Sonnichsen, Tularosa, pp. 245–72. For the IRA opposition to Fall, see Herbert Welsh to the New York World, 12 February 1921, and Brosius to Sniffen, 8 November 1922, IRA-HSP. A report on the mining leases, setting forth the names of the leaseholders, is contained in Mescalero Apache reservation files, NA, RG 75. It is, however, impossible to confirm or deny the IRA charges from this correspondence.

8. For the roles of Burgess and Hawkins, see their 1921 correspondence in ABF-UNM. For the meeting with Welsh, see Welsh to S. K. Humphrey, 1 November 1921, IRA-HSP.

9. Fall's proposals to have the federal government return a portion of the public domain to the states and to construct a road between the Mescalero reservation and the Elephant Butte reservoir are outlined in ABF-UNM: Fall to Dear Senator, 22 June 1921; Fall to Charles Springer, 22 June 1921; and Fall to M. K. Wylder, 2 November 1921.

10. Commissioner Burke's letter of opposition and other correspondence relating to the park bill are located in Mescalero Apache reservation files, NA, RG 75. Mather's opposition is recorded in Robert Shankland, Steve Mather of the National Parks (New York: Alfred A. Knopf, 1951), pp. 217–22. The opinions of Agent Morgan and the minister are in ABF-UNM: Burgess to Fall, 13 March 1922 and Fall to Morgan, 27 March 1922. Fall's decision not to support the Burgess-Bursum bill is described in a series of letters written in May-June 1922, found in ABF-UNM.

11. Fall's decision to oppose the Burgess-Hawkins-Bursum bill and to submit his own substitute is described in ABF-UNM: Mark Thompson to Fall, 18 May 1922; C. V. Safford to Mark Thompson, 29 May 1922; Fall to Fred Morgan, 14 June 1922; and in correspondence contained in NA, RG 48, Legislative Files.

Fall's substitute bill appears in U.S. Congress, Senate, Indian Affairs Committee, *Defining the Rights of the Mescalero Apache Indians . . . and Creating the All-Year National Park*, 67th Cong., 2d sess., 1922, Rept. 805. For the conversion of Agent Morgan, IRA attorney S. M. Brosius, and Commissioner Burke, *see* Malcolm McDowell to Hugh L. Scott, 2 June 1922, HLS-LC.

12. For Fall's opposition to the Mescalero timber bill, *see* Fall to Senator Spencer, 21 June 1922, ABF-UNM. His duplicity in handling the Mescalero council is based on extensive correspondence in ABF-UNM and Mescalero Apache reservation files, NA, RG 75.

13. U.S., Congress, Senate, *Congressional Record*, 67th Cong., 2d sess., 1922, 62, pt. 6: 6041, and pt. 10: 10063–65.

14. Yard's opposition to the All Year Park is based on correspondence in the following: WGH-OHS, National Parks file, box 153, file 73968–69; Fall to Burgess, 11 August 1922, ABF-UNM; and Bursum to P. T. Jackson, 12 May 1924, HOB-UNM.

15. ABF-UNM: Edward L. Medler to Senator Thomas B. Catron, 26 April 1914, and Fall to Medler, 4 May 1914; Kelly, *The Navajo Indians and Federal Indian Policy*, p. 39.

16. Kelly, *The Navajo Indians and Federal Indian Policy*, pp. 48–58.

17. ABF-UNM: Solicitor Edwin Booth to Holm O. Bursum, 10 January 1922, and Fall to Burke, 9 March 1922.

18. Fall's decision to open the Navajo reservation can be traced in the following: Navajo files and General Services files, NA, RG 75; U.S., Congress, House, Indian Affairs Committee, *To Authorize the Leasing of Unallotted Lands on the Navajo Indian Reservation, Hearings on H.R. 11687*, 67th Cong., 2d sess., June 5, 1922; U.S., Congress, House, *Congressional Record*, 67th Cong., 2d sess., 1922, 62, pt. 7: 7156; and Daniel M. Green, ed., *Decisions of the Department of the Interior in Cases Relating to the Public Domain* (Washington, D.C.: G.P.O., 1923), 49: 139–46.

19. U.S., *Statutes at Large*, 41, pt. 1, pp. 31–34; U.S., Congress, House, Indian Affairs Committee, *Indians of the United States*, 66th Cong., 3d sess., 1920, Rept. 1133; U.S., Congress, House, *Congressional Record*, 67th Cong., 1st sess., 1921, 61, pt. 5: 4664; U.S., Congress, House, Indian Affairs Committee, *Reorganize the Indian Service*, 66th Cong., 3d sess., 1921, Repts. 1189 and 1228; General Services files, NA, RG 75.

20. U.S., Congress, House, Indian Affairs Committee, *Appraisal of Indian Property, Hearings on H.R. 9852*, 67th Cong., 2d sess.,

23 February 1922; U.S., Congress, House, Indian Affairs Committee, *Appraisal of Tribal Property of Indians*, 67th Cong., 2d sess., 1922, Rept. 755.

21. Herbert O. Brayer, *Pueblo Land Grants of the "Rio Abajo"* (Albuquerque: University of New Mexico Press, 1939), pp. 1–26; Sophie D. Aberle, "The Pueblo Indians of New Mexico, Their Land, Economy, and Civil Organization," *American Anthropologist* Memoir No. 70, (October 1948) pp. 7–9; *U.S.* v. *Joseph*, 94 U.S. 618; U.S., Congress, Senate, Indian Affairs Committee, *Pueblo Indians of New Mexico, Hearings on S. 6085*, 62d Cong., 3d sess., 13 February 1913; U.S., Congress, Senate, Public Lands and Surveys Committee, *Pueblo Indian Lands, Hearings on S. 3865 and S. 4223*, 67th Cong., 4th sess., 15–25 January 1923, pp. 55–57; General Services files, NA, RG 75.

22. Leo Crane, *Desert Drums* (Boston: Little, Brown and Co., 1928), pp. 278–94; *U.S.* v. *Sandoval*, 231 U.S. 28; Brayer, *Pueblo Grants of the "Rio Abajo,"* pp. 26–30. For Wilson's ouster, *see* ABF-HL, box 54, folder 3. For the Joy survey, *see* General Services files, NA, RG 75. For Agent Lonergan's problems, *see* ABF-UNM: M. C. de Baca to Commissioner of Indian Affairs, 23 January 1916; Lonergan to Commissioner of Indian Affairs, 2 March 1916; unsigned to Fall, 1 March 1917; *also*, ABF-HL box 55, folder 13; Northern Pueblos Day School, *Annual Narrative Report, 1920*, NA, RG 75; U.S., Congress, Senate, *Congressional Record*, 64th Cong., 2d sess., 1917, 54, pt. 3: 2115.

23. Crane, *Desert Drums*, pp. 278–305; Northern Pueblos Day School, *Annual Narrative Report, 1920*, NA, RG 75; Southern Pueblos Day School, *Annual Narrative Report, 1920*, NA, RG 75. For the plank in the 1920 Republican platform, *see* New Mexico Republican Party Platform, 9 September 1920, ABF-UNM. For opposition to the Indian citizenship bills, *see* U.S., Congress, House, Indian Affairs Committee, *Indians of the United States, Hearings*, 66th Cong., 1–3d sess., 1919–20, 3: 595–604, and Southern Pueblo files, NA, RG 75. For Agent Crane's criticism of Pueblo self-government, *see* NA, RG 75: General Services files; Northern Pueblos Day School, *Annual Narrative Report, 1920*; and Southern Pueblos Day School, *Annual Narrative Report, 1920*. For the Pueblo and the white claimants' protests, *see* Southern Pueblos Day School, *Annual Narrative Report, 1920*, NA, RG 75, and Juan Abila to Fall, 9 March 1920, ABF-UNM.

24. For Payne's draft, *see* Payne to Senator Charles Curtis, 6

January 1921, NA, RG 48, Legislative files; and C. Safford to Fall, 10 January 1921, ABF-UNM. Hernández's bill and Sells's reply to Hernández are in General Services files, NA, RG 75.

25. For Bursum's political career and the origin of his feud with Fall, *see* Donald R. Moorman, "A Political Biography of Holm O. Bursum, 1899–1924" (Ph.D. diss., University of New Mexico, 1962), pp. 161, 182, 211–27, 237–45; H. B. Hening, ed., *George Curry, An Autobiography* (Albuquerque: University of New Mexico Press, 1958), pp. 195–96, 287–94; Stratton, "Albert B. Fall and the Teapot Dome Affair," p. 75; and HOB-UNM, 1921 correspondence. For Fall's growing bitterness toward Bursum after the 1920 national convention, *see* his 1921 correspondence in ABF-UNM.

26. Moorman, "A Political Biography of Holm O. Bursum," pp. 261–63; Merritt C. Mechem Papers, New Mexico State Records Center and Archives, Santa Fe, N. M., Bursum correspondence, 1922.

27. For S. 1938 and S. 2274, *see* the following: General Services files; Southern Pueblo files; Northern Pueblo files, all in NA, RG 75; and Brosius to Sniffen, 27 June 1921, IRA-HSP. For Twitchell's appointment, *see* Fall-Twitchell correspondence, December 1920–July 1921, ABF-UNM. For the controversy between Crane and the Pueblo governors and for Dorrington's appointment, *see* Southern Pueblo files and General Services files both in NA, RG 75; and Fall to Father Fridolin Schuster, 31 May 1921, ABF-UNM. For Twitchell's request for a conference with Fall and a delay in the ejectment suits, *see* Twitchell to Fall, 31 October 1921, ABF-UNM; and Judge Colin Neblett to firm of Rodey and Rodey, 24 August 1922, JC-Yale. For Twitchell's report, *see* General Services files, NA, RG 75, and U.S., Congress, Senate, Public Lands and Surveys Committee, *Pueblo Indian Lands, Hearings on S. 3865 and S. 4223*, 1923, pp. 49–52.

28. For the removal of Johnson and Crane, *see* Merritt C. Mechem Papers, Tesuque Pueblo file, 1922, New Mexico State Records Center and Archives, Santa Fe, N. M.; ABF-HL, box 69, folder 5, and box 70, folder 18; ABF-UNM: Fall to Burke, 4 March 1922, Burke to Safford, 23 January 1922, and Fall to Herbert Welsh, 25 March 1922; NA, RG 75, Office of the Commissioner, Personal and Semi-Official file, 1921–23 (Burke): Burke to Stella Atwood, March 11, 1922; HLS-LC, box 49, January–May 1922; and Crane, *Desert Drums*, pp. 266–72.

29. The evolution of the Bursum bill is traced in Kenneth Philp,

"Albert B. Fall and the Protest from the Pueblos, 1921–1923," *Arizona and the West* 12 (Autumn 1970): 237–54. While Philp's account is generally reliable, it is based solely upon government documents and thus fails to comprehend the paramount role of Renehan and Bursum in designing the final bill. For Twitchell's draft of the Pueblo bill and the Renehan-Bursum amendments, *see* General Services files, NA, RG 75. In this latter source there is a single sheet on which the signatures of Fall, Renehan, and Twitchell appear in an endorsement of the amendments.

Chapter 7: The Bursum Bill (1922–23)

1. For Mrs. Atwood's exchange with Herbert Welsh, *see* IRA-HSP: Atwood to Welsh, 26 August, 10 November, 2 December 1922; and Welsh to Atwood, 23 November 1922. For the Senate passage of S. 3855, *see* General Services files, NA, RG 75; Fall to Lenroot, 9 September 1922, ABF-UNM; 1922 miscellaneous correspondence, HOB-UNM; and U.S., Congress, Senate, *Congressional Record*, 67th Cong., 2d sess., 1922 62, pt. 12: 12323–24. Collier's letter is in MDL-Yale, no date, 1922 correspondence.

2. Agent Leech's opposition to the Bursum bill and the petition of the Northern Pueblos are in General Services files, NA, RG 75. Several versions of Collier's activity in the formulation of the All Pueblo Council are related in the following: U.S., Congress, House, Indian Affairs Committee, *Pueblo Indian Land Titles, Hearings on H.R. 13452 and H.R. 13674*, 1923, pp. 185, 245; U.S., Congress, Senate, Public Lands and Surveys Committee, *Pueblo Indian Lands, Hearings on S. 3855 and S. 4223*, 1923, pp. 120–21, 178–79; John Collier, "American Congo," *Survey*, August 1, 1923, pp. 467–76. Collier's relations with the Santa Fe group are related in Collier to Mabel Dodge, 25 October 1922, MDL-Yale, and Collier to Miss Sergeant, 31 October, 1922, JC-Yale.

Soon after she arrived in New Mexico, Mabel met Tony Luhan, whom Sterne instinctively disliked. As a matter of fact, Sterne was repelled by all the Pueblos, whom he termed "dirty, smelly Indians." In his memoir, Sterne accused Mabel and Tony of adultery shortly after their first meeting. To accommodate their trysts, Mabel "set up a teepee on the lawn of the Manby home" in Taos and each night "a solitary horse and rider" would arrive and depart. When Sterne finally confronted Mabel with his displeasure, she ordered him to leave, which he did. Sterne's verdict: "In Tony, Mabel at last found the perfect rainbow, resplendent with all the nuances of the spectrum . . . . What psychoanalysts, artists, and writers could not accomplish, the Indian medicine man did." Maurice Sterne, *Shadow and Light,* ed. Charlotte Leon Mayerson (New York: Harcourt, Brace, and World, Inc., 1965), pp. xxiv–xxvi, 111–47.

3. For the Santo Domingo meeting, *see,* in addition to testimony before the House and Senate committees listed in n. 2 *supra: New York Times,* 7 November, and 26 November 1922; Collier to Frank Kellogg, 5 November and 10 November 1922, JC-Yale; John Collier, "The Pueblos' Last Stand," *Sunset,* February 1923, p. 19–20. For the campaign to enlist New York magazines and newspapers, *see* numerous letters by Elizabeth S. Sergeant, October–November 1922, and Margaret McKittrick to Collier, 18 November 1922, JC-Yale; Elizabeth S. Sergeant, "Last First Americans," *The Nation,* 29 November 1922, p. 570; Alice Corbin Henderson, "Death of the Pueblos," *New Republic,* 29 November 1922, pp. 11–13; *New York World,* 29 November 1922; *New York Tribune,* 28 November 1922; Erna Fergusson, "Crusade from Santa Fe," *North American Review,* Winter 1936, pp. 378–79.

4. NA, RG 75, Office of the Commissioner, Personal and Semi-Official, 1921–32 (Burke): Atwood to Burke, 10 November 1922, and Burke to Atwood, 14 November 1922. The correspondence between Burke and Twitchell, Burke and George Vaux, and the petition from Kidder and Spinden are in General Services files, NA, RG 75.

5. The origins of the New York trip and the entrance of Dr. Haynes and Mrs. Vosburg into the controversy can be traced in Collier to Mabel Dodge, 16 and 25 November 1922, MDL-Yale; *also,* Haynes to Johnson, 22 November 1922, and Haynes to Pinchot, 1 December 1922, JRH-UCLA. Borah's recall is in U.S., Congress, Senate, *Congressional Record,* 67th Cong., 3d sess., 1922, 63, pt. 1: 11. A copy of Collier's telegram to Mrs. Atwood threatening "war" is in MDL-Yale, no date, Collier correspondence, 1922.

6. For the IRA's changing attitude, *see* IRA-HSP: Brosius to Sniffen, 4 November, 1922; Atwood to Brosius, 15 November 1922; and Brosius to Sniffen, 1 December 1922. For the role of D. H. Lawrence, *see* Harry T. Moore, ed., *The Collected Letters of D. H. Lawrence,* 2 vols. (New York: The Viking Press, 1962), 2: 671–728; Edward Nehls, ed., *D. H. Lawrence: A Composite Biography,* 3 vols. (Madison: University of Wisconsin Press, 1957–59), 2: 197–98, 487. Lawrence's essay on the Bursum bill appeared in

the *New York Times*, 24 December 1922, and was partially re-
printed in Mabel Dodge Luhan, *Lorenzo in Taos* (New York: Alfred A. Knopf, 1932), p. 54.

In a letter to his mother-in-law, 5 December 1922, Lawrence
gave this unflattering portrait of Mabel Dodge: "You have asked
about Mabel Dodge: American, rich, only child, from Buffalo on
Lake Erie, bankers, forty two years old, has had three husbands—
one Evans (dead), one Dodge (divorced), and one Maurice Sterne (a
Jew, Russian, painter, young, also divorced). Now she has an Indian, Tony, a stout chap. She had lived much in Europe—Paris,
Nice, Florence—is a little famous in New York and little loved,
very intelligent as a woman, another 'culture carrier' who likes to
play the patroness, hates the white world and loves the Indians
out of hate, is very 'generous,' wanted to be 'good,' and is very
wicked, has a terrible will-to-power, you know—she wants to be
a witch and at the same time a Mary of Bethany at Jesus' feet—a
big, white crow, a cooing raven of ill-omen, a little buffalo."
Moore, ed., *Collected Letters of D. H. Lawrence*, 2: 730.

Lawrence was also critical of Collier. In a letter to Mabel
Dodge, 8 November 1923, he wrote: "Don't trouble about the Indians. You can't 'save' them; and politics, no matter *what* politics, will only destroy them. I have said many times that you
would destroy the Indians. In your lust for even a Saviour's power,
you would just destroy them. The same with Collier. He will destroy them. It is his saviour's will to set the claws of his own
White egotistic *benevolent* volition into them. Somewhere, the
Indians know that you and Collier would, with your salvationist
but poisonous white consciousness, destroy them. Remember,
Jesus, and the Good, in our sense, in our mystic sense, not just the
practical; Jesus, and the Good as you see it, are poison for the Indians. Moore, ed., *Collected Letters of D. H. Lawrence*, 2: 760–61;
also in Luhan, *Lorenzo in Taos*, p. 120.

7. For Mabel Dodge's revived interest in the Indians and Col-
lier's reply, *see* Luhan, *Lorenzo in Taos*, p. 107; and JC-Yale:
Mabel Dodge to Collier, 21 November 1922, two letters; Mabel
Dodge to Mrs. Atwood, 21 November 1922; and Collier to Mabel
Dodge, 26 November 1922. For the organization of the Eastern
Association on Indian Affairs, *see* General Services files, NA, RG
75; Amelia White to Scott, 2 and 12 December 1922, HLS-LC; and
testimony of Roberts Walker in U.S., Congress, Senate, Public
Lands and Surveys Committee, *Pueblo Indian Lands, Hearings*

on S. 3855 and S. 4223, 1923, p. 109. For Fall's counterattack, *see* Borah correspondence and Pueblo Indian Question files, ABF-UNM; U.S., Congress, Senate, *Congressional Record*, 67th Cong., 4th sess., 1922, 64, pt. 1: 806–810; and telegrams from Mrs. Atwood to Fall in U.S., Congress, Senate, Public Lands and Surveys Committee, *Pueblo Indians Lands, Hearings on S. 3865 and R. 4223*, 1923, p. 275.

8. Clara True's correspondence is in ABF-HL, box 54, folder 11. Collier's account of his meetings in Washington is in Collier to Mabel Dodge, Monday midnight [11 December 1922], MDL-Yale. Robert Yard's account of his meeting with Collier is in Papers of the California League of American Indian, Bancroft Library (hereinafter CLAI) Berkeley, Ca.: Yard to Atwood, 13 December 1922, and Yard to Amelia White, 13 December 1922. Brosius's meeting with Collier is described in Brosius to Sniffen, 15 December 1922, IRA-HSP. The meeting with the Eastern Association on Eastern Affairs is described in HLS-LC, various letters, June-December 1922, and in Collier to Mabel Dodge, 25 December 1922, MDL-Yale. The decision to bypass Bursum and the opposition of Miss McKittrick to Mabel's trip east are in Collier to Mabel Dodge, 26 December 1922, MDL-Yale; Margaret McKittrick to Collier, 29 December 1922, Collier to McKittrick, 2 January 1923, Mabel Dodge to Collier, 29 December 1922, Collier to Mabel Dodge, 2 January 1923, and Mabel Dodge to Collier, 4 January 1923, all in JC-Yale.

9. Collier's activities and his moods during the two weeks before the hearings can be traced in his January 1923 correspondence with various persons, in JC-Yale, and his January 1923 correspondence with Mabel Dodge, in MDL-Yale. The employment of Judson King is also included in the above correspondence. For evidence of King's activities, *see* press releases in JC-Yale and Judson King Papers, Library of Congress, Washington, D.C., box 70. The activities and intelligence operations of the Indian Office are in General Services files, NA, RG 75. Harold Ickes's involvement in the crusade is based on a letter from Ickes to Hiram Johnson, 12 January 1923, in the Hiram Johnson Papers, Bancroft Library, University of California, Berkeley, and on correspondence between the author and Louise Stanton Whitely. The appearance at the People's Institute is recorded in the *New York Times*, 15 January 1923, and in the attendance folder, 1916–25, PI-CU. The hearings on the Mescalero National Park are in U.S.,

Congress, House, Committee on Indian Affairs, *Mescalero National Park Project, Hearings*, 67th Cong., 4th sess., 1922–23. Additional information on the role of Robert S. Yard is contained in his article "New Mexico Aflame Against Two Bills," *Outlook*, 17 January 1923, p. 124; Yard to James A. Carroll, 2 September 1922, ABF-UNM; and Yard's correspondence with various officials in WLH-OHS, box 153, files 74012-15, 74020. *See also* John Collier, "Plundering the Pueblos," *Sunset*, January 1923, pp. 21–25.

10. The major sources for this discussion of the House and Senate hearings are U.S., Congress, Senate, Committee on Public Lands and Surveys, *Pueblo Indian Lands, Hearings on S. 3855 and S. 4223*, 1923; U.S., Congress, House, Committee on Indian Affairs, *Pueblo Indian Land Titles, Hearings on H.R. 13452 and H.R. 13674*, 1923; and General Services files, NA, RG 75. Collier's activities between the hearings, Fall's resignation, the controversy over the *New York Times* article, and the appearance before the Economic Club are in *New York Times*: 3 January, 21 January, 25 January, 9 February 1923; Fall to Reed Smoot, 15 January 1923, and Fall to Members of the Economic Club, 3 February 1923, ABF-UNM; Fall to Burke, 24 January 1923, and Fall to Judson King, 27 January 1923, General Services files, NA, RG 75. Collier's characterization of Burke's appearance before the Senate committee is in a letter to Mabel Dodge, 15 January 1923, MDL-Yale. His magazine articles that appeared during the hearings were "Plundering the Pueblos," *Sunset*, January 1923, pp. 21–25, and "The Pueblos Last Stand," *Sunset*, February 1923, pp. 19–22.

11. Collier's visit to Ickes and his ignorance of the Omnibus Bill are documented in the correspondence of Harold Ickes to Hiram Johnson, 1 February and 20 February 1923, Hiram Johnson Papers, Bancroft Library; Robert E. Ely to Collier, 2 March 1923, and Robert I. Brown to Collier, 7 March 1923, CLAI. The Omnibus Bill is described in U.S., Congress, Senate, Indian Affairs Committee, *Appraisal of Indian Property, Hearings on H.R. 13835*, 67th Cong., 4th sess., 16 February 1923; U.S., Congress, House, *Authorize Secretary of the Interior to Appraise Tribal Property of Indians*, 67th Cong., 4th sess., House Report 1429; and General Services files, NA, RG 75. Mabel Dodge's successful effort to enlist Robert La Follette through his daughter is described in Mabel Dodge to Collier, 29 December 1922, JC-Yale.

12. King's press release is in the papers of Charles de Young Elkus, no date (hereinafter cited as CdeYE). The joint meeting be-

tween the founders of the American Indian Defense Association and the directors of the EAIA at which the Omnibus Bill strategy was discussed are in Robert I. Brown to Collier, 7 March 1923, CLAI. Wilson's open letter to Burke is in General Services files, NA, RG 75. Support for the Omnibus Bill by the Board of Indian Commissioners and the IRA are in Welsh to Helen H. Greeley, 5 March 1923, IRA-HSP; and McDowell to Scott, 1 March 1923, Board of Indian Commissioners, NA, RG 75. La Follette's statement is in U.S., Congress, Senate, *Congressional Record*, 67th Cong., 4th sess., 1923, pt. 6: 5389.

13. Collier's denunciations of the Omnibus Bill are contained in *From Every Zenith*, pp. 134–35; *Indians of the Americas* (Mentor, rev. ed.), pp. 246–47; and his contemporary article, "No Trespassing," *Sunset*, May 1923, pp. 14–15. King's proposal to exploit the young Sioux is in Robert I. Brown to Collier, 7 March 1923, CLAI.

14. The health proposal for the Pueblos is in Collier to Judge Payne, 27 February 1923, JC-Yale. Fall's appointment of the Navajo special commissioner is in Kelly, *The Navajo Indians and Federal Indian Policy*, pp. 61–62. Collier's first intimation of knowledge of the Navajo problem is in Collier to Robert Ely, 11 March 1923, CLAI. The Burke-Twitchell exchange is in General Services files, NA, RG 75. The Walker-Fall correspondence is in ABF-UNM: Walker to Fall, 10 February 1923; Fall to Walker, 20 February 1923; and Walker to Fall, 24 February 1923. The history of the Lenroot substitute bill can be traced in U.S., Congress, House, Committee on Indian Affairs, *Titles to Lands Within Pueblo Indian Land Grants*, 67th Cong., 4th sess., House Report 1728, and U.S., Congress, Senate, *Congressional Record*, 67th Cong., 4th sess., 1923, 64, pt. 5: 4876–79, and pt. 6: 5544. Collier did not become aware of the Lenroot bill until at least March 6: Collier to Wilson, 7 March 1923, CLAI.

Chapter 8: The American Indian Defense Association (1923)

1. Collier to Wilson (telegram), 7 March 1923; Collier to Margaret McKittrick (telegram), 7 March 1923; Wilson to Collier (telegram), 8 March 1923; all in CLAI.

2. Collier to Mary Austin, 14 March 1923; Austin to Collier, 13 April 1923; Collier to Ickes, 14 March 1923; Collier to Ely, 11 March 1923; all in CLAI.

3. Francis Wilson, "Report on Outcome of the Opposition to

the Bursum Bill and the Snyder bill," no date, CdeYE. Collier to
Wilson, 13 April 1923; Wilson to Collier, 17 April 1923; Collier's
report on Wilson's statement of services, no date; all in CLAI.
Collier to Wilson, 22 April 1923, JRH-UCLA.

4. Collier, *From Every Zenith*, pp. 69, 157; and Collier to Ely, 1
March 1923, Ely to Collier, 2 March 1923, Robert I. Brown to Collier, 7 March 1923, Collier to Ely, 11 March 1923; all in CLAI.

5. Collier's plans for the Council of One Hundred meeting and
for the League of the Southwest meeting are in Collier to A. A.
Berle, 29 May 1923, CLAI; and Collier to Mabel Dodge, 9 April
1923, MDL-Yale. His belief that the New Mexico Association had
decided to back Wilson is in Collier to Mr. Johnson, no date,
CLAI. The defection of Amelia White and the Ickeses is discussed
in Collier to Mrs. Vosburg, 22 April 1923, JRH-UCLA.

6. Papers on the formation, legal incorporation, and minutes
of the first meeting of the board of directors of the AIDA are in
JC-Yale, and Robert Ely to Commissioner Burke, 4 May 1923,
General Services files, NA, RG 75.

7. Collier's report on the Chicago meeting and his draft of a pro-
posed statement of principles are in "Report on Conference with
Chicago Indian Rights Society," 22 May 1923, CLAI; and Collier
to Members of the Executive Committee, 21 May 1923, JC-Yale.
His later reservations about concessions to Ickes are expressed in
Collier to A. A. Berle, 29 May 1923, CLAI.

8. The fight for Mrs. Atwood's reinstatement is described in the
Burke-Winter correspondence, February 1923, in General Services
files, NA, RG 75; Atwood to Sergeant, 21 July 1923, JC-Yale; copy
of telegram from Atwood to Collier, no date, MDL-Yale; several
loose pieces of correspondence describing the Atlanta convention, and Collier to A. A. Berle, 29 May 1923, all in CLAI.

9. The meetings resulting in the adoption of the "Magna Carta"
statement are described in the *New York Times*, 10 June and
24 June 1923. The AIDA's "Announcement of Purposes" is in JC-
Yale. There is very little information on the League of the Southwest meeting; see *New York Times*, 10 June 1923, and Alois B.
Renehan, *The Pueblo Indians and Their Land Grants* (Albuquerque: privately published, 1923).

10. For the *Sunset* and Woehlke, *see* Theodore Peterson, *Magazines in the Twentieth Century* (Urbana: University of Illinois
Press, 1958), p. 343; Bates, *The Origins of Teapot Dome*, pp. 29,
50; and personal correspondence with Paul C. Johnson, author of

The Early Sunset Magazine (San Francisco: California Historical Society, 1974). Collier's articles during this period were: "Our Indian Policy," *Sunset*, March 1923, pp. 13–15; "No Trespassing," *Sunset*, May 1923, pp. 14–15; "America's Treatment of Her Indians," *Current History*, August 1923, pp. 771–78; "American Congo," *Survey*, 1 August 1923, pp. 467–76. For Commissioner Burke, *see* Herbert Corey, "He Carries the White Man's Burden," *Colliers*, 12 May 1923, p. 13; Burke to Bruno Lasker, 28 June 1923, and Burke to Snyder, 13 August 1923, both in General Services files, NA, RG 75. *Sunset's* attack on the Indian Office was not confined to articles by Collier. In the June 1923 issue, an article by General Hugh L. Scott was converted into an editorial attack upon Burke for his alleged neglect of a band of Paiute Indians. Scott was mortified at being thus used. Not only had the editors twisted his meaning, he apologized to Burke, but they had also called attention to his membership on the Board of Indian Commissioners, something which he had "carefully refrained from doing myself"; *see* Malcolm McDowell to Burke, 22 May 1923, in General Services files, NA, RG 75.

11. For Ely's resignation and Collier's choice of Bacheller, *see* Collier to Mabel Dodge, 24 May 1923, MDL-Yale. For Mabel's divorce and her decision to retire from Indian work, *see* the following: Collier to Mabel Dodge, 9 April 1923, and an undated letter (circa 1920) describing her arrangement with Candelaria, in MDL-Yale; Mary Austin to Collier, 13 April 1923, CLAI; Twitchell to Burke, 19 November 1923, Leech to Burke, 11 January 1923, with clipping from *The Maverick* dated 25 August 1920, and letters of A. R. Manby to Burke, especially 19 January 1923, and 31 October 1923, in General Services files, NA, RG 75; Sterne to Mabel Dodge, 7 May 1922, MDL-Yale, Sterne correspondence; Mabel Dodge to Carl Van Vechten, 14 May 1923, Carl Van Vechten Papers, Collection of American Literature, Beinecke Rare Book and Manuscript Library, Yale University, New Haven, Conn.; Luhan, *Lorenzo in Taos*, pp. 114–16; Mabel Dodge to Collier, no date (circa 1923), and Collier to Executive Committee of the AIDA, 30 April 1924, CLAI. Mabel was surprisingly apprehensive about the way her eastern friends would react to the news of her marriage to Tony. When Collier was in New York in May 1923, he raised the subject during an evening with Dorothy Straight and several other members of the AIDA board. "Each was interested and hospitable to the event," he reported. "No hint of any feeling of queer-

ness at your marriage to an Indian"; Collier to Mabel Dodge, no date, MDL-Yale. For Sterne's account of the divorce and his infatuation with the fifteen-year-old Vera, whom he met at the Elizabeth Duncan School, *see* Sterne, *Shadow and Light*, pp. 160–74.

12. For Hagerman's appointment, *see* Fall-Burke-Hagerman correspondence in ABF-HL, box 51, folders 5 and 19; Kelly, *The Navajo Indians and Federal Indian Policy*, pp. 61–64; Collier to Ely, 11 March 1923, and Collier to Mary Austin, 14 March 1923, both in CLAI; Collier to Kellogg, 6 October 1923, JC-Yale. In the Navajo article subsequently published in the *Survey*, Collier wrote of Hagerman: "All over the reservation I had met golden opinions of him, and I had become convinced that his handling of the difficult problem of leasing the Navajo oil lands had been disinterested and efficient. In brief, Commissioner Hagerman is the Navajos' best present hope." In the *Sunset* article, he wrote: Hagerman is "a hard-working, frank, amused, inofficious and transparently honest official . . . . He has studied the Navajo problem broadly and in practical detail and he bids fair to provide that leadership and initiative which during years past have not been provided by those at the top of the Indian Bureau or permitted to those at the bottom." Collier, "Navajos," *Survey*, 1 January 1924, p. 334; "The Fate of the Navajos," *Sunset*, January 1924, pp. 11–13, 62.

13. Stella Atwood to Nina O. Warren, 14 September 1922, JC-Yale; Warren-Fall correspondence, 1922, in ABF-HL, box 8, Patronage and Favors folder; Bursum to Mrs. Warren (telegram), 8 September 1922, HOB-UNM; Twitchell to Burke, 21 March 1923, and Twitchell to Burke, 23 January 1925, in General Services files, NA, RG 75.

14. Goldman, *Rendezvous With Destiny*, pp. 178–79; Charles Forcey, *The Crossroads of Liberalism* (New York: Oxford University Press, 1961), pp. 172–74; "Tenth Anniversary of Survey Associates," *Survey*, 15 November 1922, pp. 273–75; Collier, *From Every Zenith*, p. 102; Collier to Haynes, 24 October 1923, JRH-UCLA. W. A. Swanberg, *Whitney Father, Whitney Heiress* (New York: Charles Scribner's Sons, 1980), is the most recent and the most complete treatment of Dorothy Straight, but it does not mention her connection with the AIDA.

15. For Berle's career, *see* Maxine Block, ed., "A. A. Berle," *Current Biography, 1940* (New York: H. Wilson Co., 1941), pp. 78–79; J. F. Carter, *The New Dealers* (New York: Simon and Schuster, 1934), pp. 330–32; Beatrice B. Berle and Francis B. Jacobs, eds.,

Navigating the Rapids (New York: Harcourt, Brace, Jovanovich, 1973), pp. 15–19. For Collier's comment on Berle's employment, *see* Collier to Stella Atwood, 2 May 1923, CLAI. The work of Rounds, Hatch, Dillingham, and Debevoise in the Papago case is documented in Records Concerning the Papago Land Case, 1918–20, NA, RG 75, and CIA, *Annual Report, 1919*, pp. 64–65.

16. Berle and Jacobs, eds. *Navigating the Rapids*, pp. 15–19; Collier to Board of Directors of the AIDA, 25 August 1923, JRH-UCLA; Alice Corbin Henderson to Elsie [Elizabeth Shepley Sergeant], 1 October 1923, JC-Yale; Nina Otero Warren, Report on the Santo Domingo Council, General Services Files, NA, RG 75.

17. Collier to L. R. E. Paulin, 9 September 1923; Collier to the Governors and Councils of the Pueblos, 11 September 1923; Collier to Certain Members of the Board of Directors of the AIDA, 19 September 1923; Collier to Irving Batcheller, 16 October 1923, all in JC-Yale; Witter Bynner to Mabel Dodge, 21 and 25 September 1923, CLAI.

18. Collier, "The Pueblos' Land Problem," *Sunset*, November 1923, p. 15; Amelia White to Herbert Welsh, 4 December 1923, IRA-HSP; Collier to Cash Asher, 9 April 1924, CLAI; Fridolin Schuster to Malcolm McDowell, 20 December 1923, Board of Indian Commissioners, NA, RG 75. For the financial plight of the AIDA, *see* financial statements in CLAI, JC-Yale, JRH-UCLA, and several undated letters from Collier to Mabel Dodge, MDL-Yale. Although I have made repeated attempts to identify Cash E. Asher, all my efforts have proved unsuccessful. I have a strong hunch, however, that Collier's Cash Asher is the same man who perpetrated the Chief Red Fox hoax of the early 1970s. See *The Memoirs of Chief Red Fox*, ed. and intro. by Cash E. Asher (New York: McGraw-Hill, 1971).

19. This account of the Council of One Hundred is based mainly on the transcript of the meeting, the official *Minutes* published in mimeograph form, and the correspondence of Secretary Work on the proposed second meeting, all of which are filed in Board of Indian Commissioners, NA, RG 75. *See also* Collier, "The Red Slaves of Oklahoma," *Sunset*, March 1924, pp. 9–11; Elizabeth Shepley Sergeant, "The Red Man's Burden," *New Republic*, January 16, 1924, pp. 199–201; Hazel W. Hertzberg, *The Search for an American Indian Identity* (Syracuse: Syracuse University Press, 1971); and Kenneth R. Philp, *John Collier's Crusade for Indian Reform*, pp. 49–52.

In his private correspondence, Collier wrote that the Council meeting had been "exciting" and that it had served the purpose of educating a great many people. But, he complained, the "Indian Bureau, Board of Indian Commissioners and Protestant Missionary elements, plus the New Mexico Assn. and the Eastern Assn. elements" had constituted a bloc against discussion of the "Pueblo matter." He was also incensed at the choice of Arthur Parker as chairman: "Parker took the chair and proved so unacquainted with parliamentary law, and so stupid generally, that it was necessary for his managers to visibly manage him throughout the meeting; so the atmosphere of wire-pulling and frame-up was evident throughout." Clark Wissler, he reported, was so angry at the choice of Parker that he "departed the meeting promptly," as he had told Collier "he would do in case that deal was effected." Collier was also perturbed by the role of Charles Eastman, whom he called "the Sioux who had taken a job under Burke." Eastman, he reported, "proved absolutely renegade to his race."

His major criticism, however, was reserved for the incident of the meeting with President Coolidge. "We went in a body to see President Coolidge at the White House; and when we had assembled around him, lo! There marched up a ravishingly beautiful Indian girl and presented to Coolidge—What? A copy of Lindquist's absurd religious survey of the Indians, the book that advocates dance suppression, etc. The Y.M.C.A. and the Presbyterian Mission Board had slid one over and the President himself thought, as the reporters did, that we, C. of 100, were presenting the Lindquist book through our charming (tho to us unknown) spokeswoman. The Catholics foamed gently at the mouth, the rest of us were amused or outraged according to our temperaments. It was a cheap trick, and typical of the conduct of the meeting as a whole, but the girl was lovely! Coolidge promptly invited her into his dining room for lunch and departed from us others . . . . This is not for publication, of course." Collier to Mr. Hoffman, 14 December 1923, Pearl Chase Papers, Community Development and Conservation Collection, University of California at Santa Barbara Library (hereinafter PCP-UCSB).

Chapter 9: Religious-Freedom Issue (1924–25)

1. Minutes of the All Pueblo Council are located in JC-Yale and General Services files, NA, RG 75. A report on the meeting by inspector Nina Otero Warren and descriptions of the eastern trip are also contained in the General Services files, NA, RG 75. See also Father Fridolin Schuster to Malcolm McDowell, 24 January 1924,

Board of Indian Commissioners, NA, RG 75; and *New York Times* 31 January, 3 February, and 9 February 1924.

2. Correspondence describing Collier's operation and subsequent inactivity during the final negotiations on the Pueblo Lands Act is located in CLAI. In a letter to Cash Asher dated 28 April [1924], Collier reported that he was "well of the operation" but in its aftermath was experiencing "a debility such as I never before knew, accompanied with the most stubborn insomnia." The insomnia, a lifelong ailment, which led to his dependence upon alcohol for relief in later years, "has been 'coming to me' from the fact that I've worked over-intensely for two years without let-up on the Indian matter . . . . ." His doctor had ordered him to take a vacation, to the "sea, trip, or woods," and he promised he would take "a few days to break the contact with work sharply." Instead, he plunged directly into the religious-freedom issue and the organization of the Pueblo legal defense fund in early May.

3. This account of the passage of the Pueblo Lands Act is based on extensive correspondence from August 1923 to June 1924 in the following collections: General Services files, NA, RG 75; CLAI; and JC-Yale. The topic of the Pueblo Lands Board will form a separate book.

4. See General Services files, NA, RG 75, for the regulations on compulsory education and for the regulations on religious worship in government schools.

5. Indian Rights Association, *Thirty First Annual Report* (Philadelphia: Indian Rights Association, 1913) p. 15, and *Forty First Annual Report* (Philadelphia: Indian Rights Association, 1923), p. 20. *See also* Southern Pueblo Agency, *Annual Narrative Report, 1921*, NA, RG 75.

6. Lonergan's report is in Pueblo Day School, NA, RG 75. H. S. Traylor's report is in Southern Pueblos Day School, NA, RG 75. Eight documents from a copy of the secret dance file found in the National Anthropological Archives, Smithsonian Institution, have recently been published. *See* Martin B. Duberman et al., "Documents in Hopi Indian Sexuality: Imperialism, Culture, and Resistance," *The Radical History Review*, 20 (1979): 99–130. Fred Eggan brought this item to my attention.

7. Copies of Circular No. 1665 (26 April 1921), the supplement to Circular 1665 (14 February 1923), and the Message to All Indians (24 February 1923), are in CLAI and NA, RG 48, 5–1, and 5–6. Minutes of Burke's meeting with the Sioux missionaries at Pierre, South Dakota, on 24 October 1922, and correspondence protest-

ing the issuance of the dance circulars are located in General Services files, NA, RG 75.

8. See the correspondence in General Services files, NA, RG 75; and correspondence in NA, RG 48, 5–6.

9. Brosius to Welsh, 8 August 1923, IRA-HSP; Gustavus E. E. Lindquist, *The Red Man in the United States* (New York: George H. Doran Co., 1923), introduction, and pp. 268 and 392. Brosius took a copy of the secret dance file with him to New Mexico where, he reported, "a golden opportunity opened for publicity" in the person of Nina Otero Warren. Mrs. Warren copied "the voluminous file" describing "the vile performances attending the dances of the Hopis and Pueblos," and would use it to alert members of the Utah GFWC at their annual meeting the following month. "The leaven is working," he boasted; the radical "Artists and Writers who are attacking the Bureau" would soon be discredited. In Santa Fe, Brosius also encountered Collier, whom he described as "slightly saner than he was last winter, but his conversation, and manner, indicate to me that he is not normal." Brosius to Welsh, 11 August 1923, IRA-HSP; also in General Services files, NA, RG 75.

10. *New York Times*, 2 December, 16 December, 20 December 1923; *Indian Truth*, April 1924; Flora W. Seymour, "The Delusion of the Sentimentalists," and Mary Austin, "The Folly of the Officials," *Forum*, March 1924, pp. 273–88. Mrs. Seymour was particularly critical of Collier, whose activity against the Bursum bill she likened to the plot of a grade B "movie thriller": "Finally, in the last reel appears the handsome hero, in the guise of a well-paid publicity agent of a committee of well-meaning but ill-advised ladies. With a commanding gesture he turns back the pursuers, clasps the maiden to his manly bosom, and all is well. The enraptured audience breaks into applause and again is celebrated the triumph of sentimentality over intelligence."

11. Collier to Cash Asher, 28 April 1924, CLAI.

12. The major source for this account of the trouble at Taos is in Northern Pueblo files, NA, RG 75, but *see also* General Services files, NA, RG 75.

13. General Services files, NA, RG 75. *See also* Collier to Burke, 7 May 1924; "Declaration of the All Pueblo Council"; and "Brief Report Concerning Religious Liberty etc. in New Mexico," 15 May 1924; all in JC-Yale.

14. The formation of the Council of Progressive Christian Indians, as viewed from the government's point of view, may be

traced in NA, RG 75: Northern Pueblos files (which contain a copy of the minutes of the meeting) and General Services files. The IRA position is related in IRA-HSP, and *Forty Second Annual Report* (Philadelphia: Indian Rights Association, 1924), pp. 42–44.

15. IRA-HSP: Sniffen to John D. Rockefeller, Jr., 30 January 1924; W. S. Richardson (Rockefeller Foundation) to Sniffen, 25 April 1924; and Sniffen undated memo (circa January 1925), "In Re Agreement with Miss True." Correspondence concerning the report, *Oklahoma's Poor Rich Indians*, and the original typescript may be found also in IRA-HSP. Actually, Collier benefited most from the report in his article, "Red Slaves of Oklahoma," *Sunset*, March 1924, pp. 9–11.

16. Berle to Collier, 9 May, 14 May, and 22 May 1924, CLAI; and Collier to Members of the Board of Directors, 22 May 1924, JC-Yale.

17. Collier, "Report Concerning Religious Liberty issue in New Mexico," 15 May 1924, JC-Yale; correspondence in Northern Pueblos files, NA, RG 75; and Sniffen to Welsh, 6 May 1924, IRA-HSP. Acknowledging that the situation at Zuñi was a "bad" one, Sniffen informed Welsh that he intended to go to Zuñi to block Collier's expected visit. Collier, he warned, "proposes to make a nationwide fight for religious liberty (or tyranny) and the churches (of all denominations) ought to take aggressive measures to combat his propaganda." Sniffen also reported that he had recently taken new testimony from Emil Bibo, a trader at Bernalillo, and some of the progressive Indians relating to the secret dances, which were so vile that he had become "nauseated to hear Collier's smooth words about the purity of the Pagan Pueblo party."

18. This account of the Zuñi situation is based primarily on correspondence in Zuñi files, NA, RG 75. But *see also* Collier, "Persecuting the Pueblos," *Sunset*, July 1924, p. 50; John Adair and Dorothea C. Leighton, *People of the Middle Place* (New Haven: Human Relations Area Files Press, 1966), pp. 48–58; and Fred Eggan and T. N. Panday, "Zuñi History, 1850–1970," in *Handbook of North American Indians*, vol. 9: *Southwest*, ed. Alfonso Ortiz (Washington, D.C.: Smithsonian Institution Press, 1979), pp. 474–81.

19. For Mrs. Warren's relation to Mrs. Leatherwood, *see* Brosius to Welsh, 11 August 1923, IRA-HSP; and E. O. Leatherwood to Burke, 5 December 1923, General Services files, NA, RG 75. For the decision to take the Progressives to Los Angeles, *see* Mrs. Warren to Sniffen, 1 June 1924, IRA-HSP.

20. Clara True to Sniffen, 23 June and 1 July 1924, IRA-HSP;
American Indian Life Bulletin, October 1928, and Collier to Officials of the Pueblos, 25 June 1924, JC-Yale; *The Indian and Religious Freedom* (pamphlet of the AIDA), 2 July 1924, JC-Yale.

21. Burke-Otero Warren correspondence on Mrs. Baer, August
1924, and Mrs. Baer to Mrs. John W. Sherman, 6 August 1924, all
in General Services files, NA, RG 75; Collier-Atwood correspondence, August-September 1924, CLAI.

In later years Collier became confused about events at this convention, charging that Mrs. Atwood was "driven" from her chairmanship in 1924 at Los Angeles, and Kenneth Philp, following
Collier, has repeated the error. Mrs. Atwood remained as chairman of the Indian Welfare Committee until 1928, though her stature was much diminished after 1924. *See* Collier, *From Every
Zenith,* p. 141; Collier, *Indians of the Americas,* p. 254; Philp,
John Collier's Crusade for Indian Reform, p. 62.

22. *See* correspondence in Northern Pueblos files and General
Services files, NA, RG 75.

23. For Burke's decision upholding community labor, *see* General Services files, NA, RG 75. For the IRA response, *see* correspondence in the July-August 1924 correspondence file, IRA-
HSP.

24. *New York Times,* 13 July 1924. Burke's correspondence with
the *New York Times* is in General Services files, and Northern
Pueblos files, NA, RG 75. "Pussyfoot" Johnson's letter is in General Services files, NA, RG 75.

25. See Welsh's autobiographical statement (1925) and his correspondence for August-November 1924, in IRA-HSP; his correspondence with the Indian Office in General Services files, NA,
RG 75; *New York Times:* 19 October and 26 October 1924; Collier's correspondence with Welsh, November 1924, in CLAI; and
Burke's correspondence with Amelia White in General Services
files, NA, RG, 75.

26. Berle-Collier correspondence, April-June 1924, CLAI. The financial records of the AIDA do not indicate if Berle was ever paid,
and in the last exchange between the two men that I could find,
Collier accused Berle of "a lack of attachment to the A.I.D.A. Inc.
and to its larger purposes" and of a "willingness to swing the destiny of an organization and a cause around the fact of a postponed
payment to yourself of $1,900.00." Collier to Berle, 10 December
1924, CLAI.

27. Collier-Asher correspondence, May 1924–May 1925, CLAI.

28. The organization of the California chapters and the demise of the New York office is described in voluminous correspondence in CLAI. The best description of Pearl Chase is in *Soundings, Collections of the University Library*, 4 (December 1972), University Library, University of California at Santa Barbara. William Bingham, II, was the son of a wealthy Cleveland merchant and financier. In 1917 he inherited from his bachelor uncle, Oliver Hazard Payne, a considerable fortune, made from investments in oil, tobacco, steel, coal, rails, and tractions. Unable to complete college preparatory school because of his affliction, Bingham traveled widely and devoted his time to philanthropy, particularly medical and neurological research. At the time of the formation of the Santa Barbara chapter, he was a neighbor to Miss Chase. Following the Santa Barbara earthquake of 1925, he left the city and spent the remainder of his life in Bethel, Maine, where he endowed a clinic for "nervously exhausted patients," and in Miami Beach, Florida. It is possible that Bingham's support was also solicited through his cousin, Dorothy Payne Whitney Straight. *National Cyclopedia of American Biography*, s.v. "William Bingham, III." Rosenberg and Goodrich remain shadowy figures, but their financial contributions are detailed in CLAI. The information on Charles de Y. Elkus is taken from a family memorial issued in 1963, from his diary of a trip to New Mexico in 1924, both in CdeYE, and from correspondence with his son, Charles, who made the family papers available to me.

29. For Sniffen's efforts to undermine Mrs. Atwood and his visit with Mrs. Vosburg, *see* his correspondence, August–September 1924, in IRA-HSP. For Collier's response, *see* Collier correspondence, August–September 1924, in CLAI, and Collier-Haynes correspondence, September–October 1924, JRH-UCLA.

30. Watts-Bacheller correspondence, September–November 1924, IRA-HSP; Collier to Asher, 13 October 1924, CLAI. Haven Emerson was the subject of a Columbia University Oral History interview, but despite his continuance as national president of the AIDA until the early 1930s, there is no mention of this aspect of his career in the interview.

31. The reorganization of the AIDA and the shift of financial control to the California chapters is described in extensive correspondence and board minutes in CLAI, JC-Yale, and PCP-UCSB. The personal information on James W. Young is contained in correspondence from Young and Mrs. Louise Collier Stanton Whitley to the author.

32. January–July 1925 correspondence in CLAI and JRH-UCLA. For the Pueblo performance in San Francisco, *see* PCP-UCSB.

33. Indian Rights Association, *Forty Second Annual Report* (Philadelphia: Indian Rights Association, 1924), pp. 4, 16; November 1924–June 1925 correspondence, IRA-HSP; General Services files, NA, RG 75. At the same time that Welsh launched his offensive, Edgar L. Hewett, the director of the Museum of New Mexico and the School of American Research in Santa Fe, also attacked Collier in the pages of *El Palacio* and *Art and Archaeology*, JRH-UCLA.

34. December–February 1925 correspondence, IRA-HSP, especially Welsh to the Board of Directors, 16 February 1925, and Minutes of Special Meeting of the Board of Directors, 20 February 1925. Mabel Dodge Luhan obtained a copy of Welsh's letter to the Episcopal bishops and attempted to interest H. L. Mencken in the controversy. When he declined, she asked Elsie Clews Parsons to write an article about "the incompatibility between those emasculated religions and the virile religion of the Indian," which had "symbolically, a sexual basis." See Luhan to Mencken, 21 May 1925, and Luhan to Dear Elsie, 10 June [1925], JC-Yale.

35. For the firing of Nina Otero Warren, *see* Brosius to Sniffen, 4 December 1924, IRA-HSP. The solution to the Melchor-Hunt problem is described in True to Fr. Schuster, 4 May 1925, IRA-HSP, and correspondence in General Services file, NA, RG 75. The decline of Clara True's influence is detailed in June–September 1925 correspondence, IRA-HSP.

36. The declaration of the Santo Domingo council is in CLAI; a copy of Crandall's letter threatening to confine the northern Pueblos to the Santa Fe fiesta and Cochiti officials with arrest is in JC-Yale. The Zuñi cane controversy is in Zuñi files, NA, RG 75.

37. The primary source for the continuing difficulty over the religious-freedom versus compulsory-schooling issue is correspondence in Northern Pueblos files, but *see also* General Services files, NA, RG 75. Crandall remained unrepentant. In December 1926 he told the *New Mexico State Tribune* that his thirty-five years of experience in the Indian Service had convinced him that "law and order can never be enforced under the old tribal customs." Collier's efforts to "assist the pueblos in retaining self-government under their old tribal laws and customs" should not be taken seriously, he advised. The following year Crandall was

transferred or retired, and thereafter the recurrent crises in the pueblos subsided. Zuñi Agent Bauman was also transferred in 1926, but the Zuñi problem continued on into the 1940s.

Chapter 10: Defending the Title to Indian Reservations

1. See chapter 6, n. 17 and the discussion of the executive-order reservations in *Felix Cohen's Handbook of Federal Indian Law* (Albuquerque: University of New Mexico Press, 1971), pp. 299–302.

2. Estep to Burke, 19 October 1922, San Juan Navajo files, NA, RG 75.

3. Kelly, *Navajo Indians and Federal Indian Policy*, pp. 48–58, 61–72.

4. The major file on the resolution of the Harrison decision is NA, RG 48, 5–18. But *see also* Bursum to Work, 19 December 1923, San Juan Navajo files, NA, RG 75; Commissioner Burke's testimony in U.S., Congress, Senate, Committee on Indian Affairs, *Development of Oil and Gas Mining Leases on Indian Reservations, Hearings on S. 1722 and S. 3159*, 69th Cong., 1st sess., 1926, pp. 53–55; and U.S., Congress, House, Committee on Indian Affairs, *Leasing of Allotted Indian Lands, Hearings on H.R. 8823*, 69th Cong., 1st sess., 1926, pp. 70–71.

5. U.S., Congress, Senate, *To Provide for the Disposition of Bonuses, Rentals, and Royalties from Unallotted Lands in Executive Order Indian Reservations*, S. Rept. 669 to accompany S. 876, 68th Cong., 1st sess., 1924.

6. Correspondence in NA, RG 75, and U.S. Department of Justice, *Official Opinions of the Attorneys-General of the United States* (Washington: G.P.O., 1926), 34: 171–92.

7. U.S., Congress, House, Committee on Indian Affairs, *Leasing of Allotted Indian Lands, Hearings on H.R. 8823*, 69th Cong., 1st sess., 1926, pp. 70–71; U.S., Congress, House, *Congressional Record*, 68th Cong., 2d sess., 1925, 66, pt. 5: 5433.

8. The decision of Judge Johnson and the action of the circuit court are printed in U.S., Congress, House, Committee on Indian Affairs, *Leasing of Executive Order Reservations, Hearings on H.R. 9133*, 69th Cong., 1st sess., 1926, pp. 82–87.

9. Correspondence in CLAI. Frear's papers in the Wisconsin Historical Society collections make no mention of his brief affiliation with Collier.

10. U.S., Congress, House, Committee on Indian Affairs, *Leas-

ing of Executive Order Reservations, Hearings on H.R. 9133, 69th Cong., 1st sess., 1926: provisions of the bill, pp. 1–2; Burke's defense of the compromise, pp. 23–24; Collier's testimony, pp. 41–42.

11. U.S., Congress, Senate, Committee on Indian Affairs, *Development of Oil and Gas Mining Leases on Indian Reservations, Hearings on S. 1722 and S. 3159,* 69th Cong., 1st sess., 1926: provisions of the bills, pp. 1–5; Burke's testimony, pp. 53–61; Collier's testimony, pp. 70–75, 90–91; Hagerman's testimony, p. 108. *See also* Congressman Frear's remarks in U.S., Congress, House, *Congressional Record,* 69th Cong., 1st sess., 1926, 67, pt. 5: 5032–5050; and Kelly, *Navajo Indians and Federal Indian Policy,* pp. 73–74.

12. U.S., Congress, House, Committee on Indian Affairs, *Oil and Gas Mining Leases Upon Unallotted Indian Lands,* H. Rept. 763 on H.R. 9133, 69th Cong., 1st sess., 1926.

13. Burke's defense is in U.S., Congress, House, Committee on Indian Affairs, *Leasing of Allotted Indian Lands, Hearings on H.R. 8823,* 69th Cong., 1st sess., 1926. Frear's remarks are in U.S., Congress, House, *Congressional Record,* 69th Cong., 1st sess., 1926, 67, pt. 7: 8065–8081. Although there was substance to many of the other charges Frear made in the House (to be discussed later in this chapter), it is my conclusion that on the issue of the executive-order reservations, Frear was always incorrect. Furthermore, I regard the charge that both he and Collier made, that the Indians needed congressional protection to keep the executive branch from reducing the boundaries of the executive-order reservations, as specious. In the twentieth century, the executive order was used only to expand the boundaries of Indian reservations and, for that reason, specifically in the case of the Navajos, Congress forbade further use of the executive order in 1918. At no time did anyone ever suggest that the executive-order reservations be reduced or abolished. The image of Congress as protector of the Indians against a rapacious Indian Office was a product of Collier's imagination and one that served him well during the 1920s, but it was also one that would haunt him in the 1930s when he became Indian commissioner. See Kelly, *Navajo Indians and Federal Indian Policy,* pp. 30–36, 92–96, 128–131, and Lawrence C. Kelly, "John Collier and the Indian New Deal: An Assessment," in Jane F. Smith and Robert M. Kvasnicka, eds., *Indian-White Relations: A Persistent Paradox* (Washington: Howard University Press, 1976),

pp. 230–40. Since Frear had been in a much better position to denounce the inclusion of the 425 applicants in the amended House
bill and had not, his charge against Burke in this case was thoroughly irresponsible.

14. U.S., Congress, Senate, Committee on Indian Affairs, *Oil
and Gas Mining Leases on Indian Reservations, Hearings on S.
3159 and S. 4152*, 69th Cong., 1st sess., 1926, pp. 24–84; U.S., Congress, Senate, *Congressional Record*, 69th Cong., 1st sess., 1926,
67, pt. 10: 10914–10925; U.S., Congress, House, *Congressional
Record*, 69th Cong., 1st sess., 1926, 67, pt. 10: 11381–11397; Coolidge's veto message is in U.S., Congress, Senate, *Message from the
President of the United States Returning Without Approval the
Bill (S. 4152) to Authorize Oil and Gas Mining Leases Upon Unallotted Lands Within Executive Order Indian Reservations, and
for Other Purposes, S. Doc. 156*, 69th Cong., 1st sess., 1926; dismissal of the Harrison suit is described in NA, RG 48, 5–18.

15. In his discussion of the Indian Oil Act of 1927, Kenneth Philp
failed to comprehend this aspect of the bill because of the difficulty
he encountered in distinguishing among the permit holders, the
applicants, and the "prospectors." His account, heavily dependent
upon the Collier papers, tends to view this event as well as many
others, only from Collier's viewpoint. Philp, *John Collier's
Crusade for Indian Reform*, pp. 75–78.

16. Kelly, *Navajo Indians and Federal Indian Policy*, pp. 83–87,
96–99. In Burke's defense, it should be pointed out that the Lees
Ferry bridge had originally been approved in the Indian Office as a
gratuity appropriation. Burke believed that Frear's attack upon him
was motivated by "malice" and a total "lack of regard for the truth"
because he had given this information to Frear before the March 4
speech. Both he and Secretary Work were correct in referring to the
reimbursable provision as a "gesture" and as a "policy of Congress
so firmly established that it is not believed . . . that it can be reversed at this time." The trouble was that Collier was forcing these
kinds of political "deals" out into the open, and he would soon have
the Senate on his side.

17. William T. Hagan, *Indian Police and Judges* (New Haven:
Yale University Press, 1966), pp. 108–20; William A. Brophy and
Sophie D. Aberle, *The Indian: America's Unfinished Business*
(Norman: University of Oklahoma Press, 1966), pp. 45–60.

18. U.S., Congress, House, Committee on Indian Affairs, *Reservation Courts of Indian Offenses, Hearings on H.R. 7826*, 69th

Cong., 1st sess., 1926: the bill, pp. 1–2; Collier's testimony, pp. 18–23; Meritt's testimony, pp. 85–90.

19. Angie Debo, *And Still the Waters Run* (Princeton: Princeton University Press, 1940), pp. 324–50; Philp, *John Collier's Crusade for Indian Reform*, pp. 84–85; Kelly, *Navajo Indians and Federal Indian Policy*, pp. 137–38.

20. Kelly, *Navajo Indians and Federal Indian Policy*, pp. 181–84; U.S., Congress, House, *Congressional Record*, 69th Cong., 1st sess., 1926, 67, pt. 7:8068, 8075–76; the Patterson report was finally released in 1928 and was published in U.S., Congress, Senate, Committee on Indian Affairs, *Survey of Conditions of the Indians in the United States, Hearings . . . Pursuant to Senate Resolution 79*, 70th Cong., 2d sess., 1929, pt. 3, pp. 955–1017.

21. Young to Chauncey Goodrich, 13 March 1926, CLAI.

22. Secretary Work's news release on the investigation is contained in an article by E. B. Meritt in Board of Indian Commissioners, NA, RG 75. Burke's testimony is in U.S., Congress, House, Committee on Appropriations, *Interior Department Appropriation Bill, Fiscal 1928, Hearings before a Subcommittee*, 69th Cong., 2d sess., 1926, p. 418.

23. Collier-Atwood correspondence, June 1926, in JC-Yale, and Collier, "Confidential Report on the General Federation Struggle at Atlantic City," 15 June 1926, PCP-UCSB.

Note on Sources

This study of John Collier and federal Indian policy is based mainly upon archival and government document sources. The archival sources containing Collier's correspondence proved surprisingly numerous, but they were discovered only over a period of many years.

When I talked with John Collier in 1960, I asked him if he had any personal papers and he told me that he had retained only a few fragmentary items. Not until 1968, when I visited Talpa again shortly after he died, did I learn that he was simply trying to protect his privacy while he wrote his memoir, *From Every Zenith*, which appeared in 1963. Actually, the Collier papers that were given to Yale shortly before his death are quite extensive. They deal mainly with his career after 1922 when he entered the Indian field. At the time I used these papers, they were still in the large boxes in which they had been shipped. The collection has now been cataloged and an extensive index with cross-references compiled. Anyone wishing to consult the documents I have cited should have no difficulty in locating them in the Yale index. Also at the time I used the papers, the literary rights were tightly controlled by Grace Collier, Collier's third wife. Since then the papers have been microfilmed and are now available commercially; how that affects Mrs. Collier's copyright restrictions is not clear to me.

As a result of Collier's statement that he had not preserved his papers, I was forced to seek other collections, papers of persons with whom he might have corresponded. Despite the statement in *From Every Zenith* that a search had been made for the papers of the People's Institute and the conclusion that they no longer existed, I found some of the papers at the Cooper Union in 1964 and, through the diligence of William Eppes of the Cooper Union Library, the other important and larger collection of People's Institute papers was eventually found in a warehouse under the custody of the New York Public Library. At the times that I viewed these papers, those at the Cooper Union had been cataloged, but those at the New York Public Library were still in large storage boxes.

Apart from Collier's *From Every Zenith* and his *Indians of the Americas*, both of which recount the influence of Mabel Dodge Luhan on Collier's career, the only published sources dealing with Collier when I began my work (except the newspaper and journal sources listed in the notes to chapters 1–3), were the four volumes of *Intimate Memories* published by Mabel Dodge Luhan in the 1930s. The frequent allusions to Collier in these volumes led me to inquire of Yale if the unpublished volumes in this series were available. They were not because of restrictions that had been placed upon them, but I was told of the existence of some one hundred letters from John and Lucy Collier among Mabel Dodge Luhan's papers. After several years of negotiation, these letters were finally made available to me through the courtesy of Grace Collier and John Evans. They proved invaluable in reconstructing Collier's activities and his thoughts during the years 1907–20.

My account of Collier's California career is based almost entirely on the records of the California State Housing and Immigration Commission, which are in the custody of the Department of Industrial Relations, Division of Housing, State of California, in San Francisco, and the papers of John Randolph Haynes at UCLA. The Haynes papers, surprisingly, appear to have been little used by students of twentieth-century history although they contain a wealth of information on Haynes's involvement in numerous enterprises besides those of the American Indian. The Haynes papers are exceptionally well organized and indexed, and they were most helpful in tracing the organization of the AIDA and Collier's political activities in the 1920s.

For Collier's activities in the 1920s the single most important source is the papers of the California League of American Indians at the Bancroft Library. To my knowledge, these papers have not been previously used. The reason for this is apparently the title of the collection, which fails to indicate the true significance of the papers. They are actually the files of the Northern California branch of the AIDA during the years when the California branches directed the AIDA. (The records of the New York branch of the AIDA appear to be in the Collier papers at Yale.) The initial drafts of this book covering the 1920s had to be completely revised after

I became acquainted with the CLAI papers. The CLAI was apparently a successor organization to the AIDA when it collapsed after Collier became commissioner of Indian affairs. These papers were not cataloged when I used them, and like the papers of the People's Institute, were stored in a satellite depository of the Bancroft Library.

Two other sources that I found useful for reconstructing the period of the 1920s were the papers of Charles de Y. Elkus, which were in the possession of his son when I used them in the early 1970s, and the papers of Pearl Chase, which were in Miss Chase's home in Santa Barbara, California. I do not know what disposition may have been made of the Elkus papers, but the Chase papers have subsequently been donated to the University of California Library at Santa Barbara. They are excellently cataloged and indexed and constitute a very large collection.

My account of Albert Fall's Indian activities in chapters 6 and 7 is heavily dependent upon the Fall papers at the University of New Mexico Library and the Huntington Library. When the Fall papers were purchased by the Huntington, permission was given to the University of New Mexico to microfilm the collection. Because it was easier for me to use the New Mexico collection, most of my citations are to the microfilm edition, but I later found documents at the Huntington that I either overlooked in the microfilm edition or that, perhaps, failed to be included in the microfilm edition. The original documents at the Huntington have been superbly cataloged and indexed, while the index to the microfilm edition appears to be only a listing of the various files as they were received from the Fall family. Permission to use the Fall papers, including the microfilm edition, must be obtained from the Huntington Library.

Lesser collections that proved useful on specific topics were the Holm O. Bursum papers at the University of New Mexico, a small, well-arranged, collection, and the Warren G. Harding papers at the Ohio Historical Society. The Harding papers are meticulously indexed and therefore easy to use, but there is disappointingly little on Albert Fall and Indian affairs.

My discussion of the religious-freedom issue in chapter 9 is heavily dependent upon the papers of the Indian Rights Association in the Historical Society of Pennsylvania. These papers, like those of Collier at Yale, have been microfilmed since I used them and are now available commercially. The portion of this extensive collection (dating back to the 1880s) that I used was organized mainly by chronology.

The government's position on the Indian issues discussed in this volume is extensively recorded in two record groups in the National Archives. Record Group 75, the records of the Office of Indian Affairs, is a huge collection in which I have been working periodically for twenty years. It is impossible to describe the many separate divisions of this record group employed in this volume. Each Indian jurisdiction has its own set of records, assembled under a filing system ranging from 001 to 999. Those records most frequently used in this volume are the various Pueblo records, the various Navajo records, and the General Services files, which embrace topics pertaining to many or all Indian groups. I have omitted the individual file citations to documents listed in the footnotes to this volume, but they are available in my unpublished notes. Record Group 48, the papers of the Office of the Secretary of Interior, are similarly voluminous, but the most frequently useful items are usually contained in the 5–1 category. A guide to Record Group 75 is available in two volumes from the National Archives, and a guide to Record Group 48 is expected soon.

Index of Names

Abbot, F. B., 172
Abbott, Lyman, 26, 44
Adams, Alva, 296–99
Adams, Ida May, 319
Addams, Jane, 20, 44
Adler, Felix, 25
Andrews, W. H., 171
Arnold, Mrs. Charles C., 126
Aronovici, Carol, 61, 80, 106
Asher, Cash E., 284, 288, 308, 322, 327–28, 355, 413n
Ashurst, Henry F., 154, 367
Atwood, Stella: and American Indian Defense Association, 264–65; biographical sketch, xxviii, 125–27; and Charles Burke, 127–30, 133–35, 211–13, 221–22, 270–71, 374–75; on Bursum bill, 129, 133–35, 211–14; and Collier, 124–36, 214, 223, 257, 264–66, 281–84; and Albert B. Fall, 129–30, 159, 211–14; and General Federation of Women's Clubs, 125–27, 133, 270, 318–20, 374–75; on Indian agents, 127–28; on Indian policy reform, 128–29; on Indian religious freedom, 318–20; and Indian Rights Association, 127–28, 211, 213, 224, 322–26, 334–35; and national park proposal, 259; *Survey Graphic* article, 136; Taos national monument project, 130; testifies before congressional committees, 239–40, 243–44
Austin, Mary: in American Indian Defense Association, 268; and Bursum bill, 227, 236, 242; and

Collier, 40, 227, 236, 257–58, 266–67, 271, 275, 282, 284; on Indian dances, 307–8

Bacheller, Irving A.: and American Indian Defense Association, 274–75, 286, 331–32; editor of *New York World*, 275
Baer, Grace Thorpe, 319–20, 322
Baker, Newton D., 77, 109
Baldwin, Henry de Forrest, 31, 60
Ballinger, Richard, 157, 181
Barnett, Jackson, 371–72
Barrows, Edward J., 35, 46
Baruch, Bernard M., 289
Bates, Mattie, 52
Bauman, C. J., 314–16, 339, 342–43
Beard, Charles, 60–63
Beard, Mrs. Charles, 82
Beard, Daniel, 119
Bend, Beatrice, 279
Berkman, Alexander, 40
Berle, Adolph A., Jr.: and American Indian Defense Association, 281, 296, 326–27, 419n; biographical sketch, 280–81; and Collier, 280–81, 286, 419n; on Lenroot bill, 281, 286; and Pueblo Lands Act, 282–84, 295–99; and religious freedom issue, 314, 327
Berninghaus, Oscar, 115
Bibo, Emil, 339
Bingham, William, II, 328, 333–34, 419n
Blumenschein, Ernest, 115
Boas, Franz, 61
Bonnin, Gertrude, 126

Index of Subjects